PERSEPHONE'S
REVOLUTION

PERSEPHONE'S REVOLUTION

Pluto's Path to the End of Empire

by

Rosie Finn

REVELORE PRESS | OLYMPIA WA | 2024

First edition published in 2024 by
Revelore Press

Book and cover design by Jenn Zahrt.
Cover art by Arrington de Dionyso.
Technical diagrams by Alberto Forero.

Publisher's Cataloging-in-Publication
(Provided by Cassidy Cataloguing Services, Inc.)
Names: Finn, Rosie, author.
Title: Persephone's revolution : Pluto's path to the end of empire / by Rosie Finn.
Description: First edition. | Olympia WA : Revelore Press, 2024. | Includes bibliographical
                references and index.
Identifiers: ISBN: 9781947544543 (paperback)
Subjects: LCSH: Astronomy--Social aspects. | Pluto (Dwarf planet) | Declination (Astronomy)--Social
              aspects. | Persephone (Greek deity) | World history. | Social problems. | Social change. |
              Self-actualization (Psychology) | Paradigms (Social sciences)
Classification: LCC: QB703.S6 F56 2024 | DDC: 523.49/22--dc23

ISBN: 9781947544543

Printed worldwide through Ingram.

Revelore Press
1910 4th AVE E PMB141
Olympia WA 98506
United States
www.revelore.press

For Fiorin

Table of Contents

PART IV: THE FUTURE 163

APPENDICES 277

Acknowledgements

After working on this project for almost twenty years, there are many people who assisted, encouraged, read parts of it, and supported me, but none more consistently than Marie Poland, who from the start has never waivered in her enthusiasm for this work. Shari Trnka, the original upcycling re"love"ution activist, also supported me from the beginning, offering unique insights, especially in setting me straight about Persephone. My brother, Ray Finn, the brilliant historian, read and reread, edited, and offered copious notes as a navigator through the winding roads of history. Dreamy Sea, always available to read my stuff, has helped steer me in the right direction many times. My first official editor, Cameron Steele, helped me take a massive unorganized research project and make it into a book. It was her suggestion to weave the Persephone myth into the book, for which I am most grateful. My second editor, Ariel Birks, with deep respect for the work, finessed a mountain of words into a presentable work and assisted me through a difficult part in the journey. My final editor, publisher, and midwife of this book, Jenn Zahrt, has made it all happen.

There have been many companions along the way whose insight and support have mattered to me. Dan Dial taught me about how astrology works. A deep bow of gratitude to my friends, Jessica Rose, for our writing retreats, Tammy Putvin, for our late night talks, Teri Tellevik, for the practical life hacks, Lisi Raskin, for inspiring me with your courage to change the world, Kristin Rubis, for helping me get the word out and for being such a brave kick-ass Leo, and Larry Smith, for introducing me to Walter Russell and for being excited about the work. You all have heard me talk about "the book" for years with patience and enthusiasm.

Lani Vento, my fairy godmother, and benefactor provided the exact perfect support that made it so that I could write, and work, and parent. Many clients and students who took my classes and have heard me talk about this project for years, helped me see more clearly and understand more truly what I was writing about and why. My community in Olympia, Jodi and the workers at Traditions Fair Trade, the folks at Radiance in all its iterations, especially Karin and Andrea, Brian at the tea shop, the Soup and Sacred Geometry Group, and the Sherwood community, especially David Greiner, Susie Andrews and Gordy Andrews, who have supported my writing with encouragement and a beautiful retreat cottage on the coast. For the other mothers whose support was offered so freely, especially Robyn Sowers, Sherry Register, and Diane Utter.

Lastly, Fiorin Finn Greiner, me writing this book has been in the background of your entire life. You have been the most wonderful, kind, supportive, smart, loving human being I could have ever dreamed of having in my life. I remember writing in the attic loft with you playing next to me when you were two-years old, until just this winter when we walked to the café, and I wrote while you worked on your Chinese homework. I am so happy with you as you launch into the world.

Rosie Finn
Olympia, WA
July 2024

Introduction

"Spring is about to spring. Persephone is coming back and the ice is groaning, about to break with the exquisite and deafening roar. It's a time for madness; a time for our fangs to come down and our eyes to glaze over so that the beast in us can sing with unmitigated joy. Oh yes, ecstasy, I welcome thee!"

—J. Christopher Stevens
US Ambassador to Libya,
killed in the 2012 Benghazi attack

T he world is changing. All around cracks in our civilization are getting larger and many of us are waiting for a break down—an implosion— some catastrophic event that turns everything upside down. Plagues, fires, and storms now commonly occur—disasters I felt protected from as a kid growing up in the suburbs in the 1970s. Climate change, storms, refugee crisis, and economic breakdowns are just the beginning. The abundance of fresh air and clean water I took for granted in my twenties is becoming a luxury. A deep underlying uncertainty pervades our current culture. Culture wars, invasions and an economy held up by a tenuous infrastructure seems moments away from collapse.

As an astrologer, I consider it my work to give reassurance and hope to my clients, at the same time holding them in their very real suffering. For seventeen years, I gave monthly talks on the transits, and often the question arose: "When is it going to get better?" As one friend asked in a recent talk, "When is the *everything-is-going-to-get-better* chart?"

In the quest for the *everything-is-going-to-get-better* chart, I poured over tables and books, gave lectures, readings and obsessively studied for years. I found hope in a most unusual place, in the cycle of Pluto and the accompanying myth of Persephone.

By tracking the cycle of the planet Pluto as it moves north and south of the Earth's equatorial plane, I recognized a pattern in history—a cycle that begins with visionaries, leads to dramatic abuses of power and brutal wars, that in turn triggers cries for justice, and finally leads to a time of reformation, rectification of the past abuses, and increased power to the common person. This 248-year cycle has played itself out over and over again. What is more interesting is how this cycle is changing, leading to a final revolution—a revolution to end all revolutions, and even a potential end to all war.

As we head into this time of reformation and revolution from 2025 to 2035, we have a great opportunity to rectify the abuses of power perpetrated in the 1940s. We have a chance at true awakening, not only a chance, more than a chance. This window of time offers itself to reform as it has done so every time for the past fifteen Pluto cycles (since 1700 BCE) and every time, masses of people have stepped into the window, opened it wide, and with courage and strength in numbers, called out authority, beat down the door of oppression, and forced real change.

Within the next decade, people all over the world will rise and claim their power. Movements that yielded little fruit in the past will reach a tipping point into actual transformation. Peaceful accords and agreements of unity have a heightened probability of lasting success. At the same time, revolutions will take down dictators—some through non-violent demonstrations, some through an up-in-arms mob. Systems dubiously set up to protect and manage societies may fail. Collapse, demonstrations, revolution, and a scientific paradigm shift—all potentials evidenced in prior cycles—invite in a new possibility: a never-before-seen global awakening.

This book weaves astronomy, history, myth, and my own hopes for the future into a somewhat complex narrative. When I first set out to write it, I simply wanted to offer the astronomy data of Pluto's cycle alongside a list of historical events, allowing us all to draw our own conclusions. After giving talks and leading workshops, this part of the narrative moved further and further into the background. You can now find it in the appendix, its final resting place. Over the years, interpretation has crept into the discourse arriving at four stages, naming the stages, and finally finding a way to describe each stage. The entry of myth into the picture was initially the recommendation of my first editor, Cameron Steele, and an excellent one, for the myth provides a nodal point where I can integrate the rich history and astronomy. Persephone's story of ascending from the underworld offers us a perfect metaphor we can work with to process the transformation arising in societies throughout the world.

PART I, THE MAP, lays out the foundation of the book, introducing the three components: myth, astronomy, and history. Then we move to PART II, THE PAST, to follow Pluto's mythic journey through a few choice cycles in history. PART III, THE PRESENT, takes us through the current cycle which begins, as I'll demonstrate, in 1863. PART IV, THE FUTURE, offers visions for five potential outcomes—one for each main character in Persephone's drama. Extensive APPENDICES revisit the raw data I used to create my interpretations, so you can work with the material and come to your own conclusions.

In 2003, when I started researching Pluto's journey north and south of the equatorial plane, Bush and Cheney were in the White House declaring war on Iraq, Homeland Security was growing in the wake of 9/11, and hippies in the Northwest were demonstrating with vibrant processions, indie music, buses of supplies to Cuba, community-sustainable agriculture projects, herbal faires, and yoga retreats. I lived at the crossroads of outraged activists and New Age meditators. My eccentric community included leaders in Buy Local programs, a network of extraordinary healers, and some very frustrated political protestors.

With my astrology practice in full swing since 1998, I began using declination (planets as they move north and south of the equatorial plane) after attending a workshop in 2002 with Dr. Mitchell Gibson, a psychiatrist who studied mystical phenomena. His well-researched exploration of planetary transits most likely to correlate with revelatory experiences led to a focus on extreme declination,[1] particularly of Mercury and Venus. This inspired me to look at other planets in extreme declination. When I got to Pluto, I was amazed at the correlation of Pluto in extreme declination with important moments in history, including the beginning of the Roman Empire, the conquests of Genghis Khan, Saladin, King Louis XIV, and most recently the outbreak of World War II. In addition to the conquerors, I found revolutions and reformations, including the reforms of Constantine, the Reformation in Europe, and the American and French Revolutions. This book contains my distilled version of a repeating and evolving cycle that weaves history into the present and offers hope for the future.

---

1. A thorough explanation of extreme declination can be found in Appendix IV.

I hope that reading this book helps you feel aligned with the radical shifts taking place on the globe right now, without cowering in fear or feeling overwhelmed. The myth of Persephone offers a touchstone for traveling back through Pluto cycles of the past. As planets circle round and round the solar system, events in this world spiral with repeating themes. Connecting history and planetary movements is a study as ancient as humanity itself and even amidst continued skepticism, these patterns reveal an ineffable connection between the events on this insignificant globe—the only home we have—and the rest of the universe.

By following the trajectory of one outer planet in one simple facet of its orbit, I hope you will develop a deeper appreciation for not just the connection between life on this planet and the predictable movement of Pluto, but also a sense of awe at how history echoes, evolves, and offers us a lens into understanding our current situation. By the time you weave through the history, our options for the future will appear as plausible outcomes. Just when things seem like they will never change, a new door opens.

Before I launch you into the belly of the book, I want to express my deepest apologies to the many cultures and countries that I have failed to mention. These omissions are due in part to my own limitations and those inherent in the framework of this project. To map Pluto's cycle onto corresponding historical terrain with appropriate precision, care, and depth, having exact dates is vitally important, and some cultures simply do not have the data needed to adequately represent them in this way. In addition, by going deep into a few cultures that I do know how to represent properly, I hope this book serves as an impetus for future writers, scholars, and astrologers to carry this research into areas I could not take it here.

Part I:
The Map

T hink of reading this book like taking a journey through an unknown *temporal* territory. In Part I, you hold before you a map. This map has three components and four stages. The three components are *myth, astronomy*, and *history*. The four stages are VISION, POWER, JUSTICE, and REFORM, and they each contain *myth, astronomy*, and *history*. If you're already feeling disoriented, that's ok. Stick with me, and with each passing chapter, a clearer vision of this material will start to form in your consciousness.

In Chapter 1, I capture our attention with the myth of Persephone— a story that assists us in assimilating the wild ride of history we are about to embark upon. In Chapter 2, I introduce you to the orbit of Pluto and its relationship to our Earth's wobbly spin, an important factor that accounts for why the cycle appears to be changing so radically. In Chapters 3 through 6, I reveal the history that aligns with the dates found in the astronomy. Once these three components are laid out individually, I weave them into a narrative blueprint that will guide us through the rest of the book. Here's where we meet the four stages—VISION, POWER, JUSTICE, and REFORM—more intimately. Each stage has its own part in the myth, its own corresponding astronomy in Pluto's orbit, and its own historical background. Parts II–IV of this book will move our full narrative blueprint through the past, present, and future. But now, let's dive into the underworld and greet our heroine.

Chapter 1:
Myth

"Myth is much more important and true than history.
History is just journalism and you know how reliable that is."

—Joseph Campbell

The Ancient Greek myth of Hades (Pluto's Greek counterpart) and Persephone—a story of abduction and empowerment—holds complex insights for us as we seek to understand, delineate, and interpret the relationship between the planet Pluto's physical movement through space and historical events on Earth.

Hades Becomes Ruler of the Underworld

Chronos (Time) ruled over the worlds of gods and humans for a long time. His desire to stay in power was stronger than his desire to be a father, and he ate his children in fear that they might usurp him at some time in the future. His wife, Rhea, was understandably not happy with this arrangement. When it came to her sixth child, she disguised a stone and gave it to her husband to eat instead of giving him the child. Somehow this worked. Chronos never suspected that he had eaten a stone instead of child, what with gods and their digestive systems being different than us mortals. She sent the child, baby Zeus, away to be raised far from his father's sight. When Zeus came of age, he indeed did usurp his father. With Chronos out of the picture, Zeus freed his siblings from the belly of Time itself. Naturally, Zeus then was in charge and took all the keys to all the kingdoms, doling them out according to his wishes.

For our purposes, we begin the myth of Persephone and Hades here. Zeus gave the keys to the kingdom of the Underworld to his older brother, Hades, who came to rule all that lives under the Earth, including minerals, crystals, metals, oil, and the dearly departed. Hades, perhaps grateful to be freed from the belly of his father, accepted his role without complaint. Thus, it is that

7

the patriarch of all patriarchs, Zeus, bestowed his elder brother, Hades, with the rulership of the dead.

Demeter Gives Birth to Kore (Persephone)

Zeus gave his sister, Demeter, rulership of what that lies above the Earth—grain, nature, trees, flowers, and food. Demeter gave birth to her one and only daughter, Kore (who becomes Persephone during her time in the Underworld). Motherhood came naturally to Demeter. She slipped gracefully into the role of Goddess of Mothers everywhere. Demeter doted on her daughter while the philandering Zeus played the part of absentee dad.

Kore grew into a beautiful teenager. Many gods desired her and asked Zeus for her hand in marriage. Demeter, the hands-on mom, actively protected Kore from these advances from the gods, wanted or unwanted.

Hades Abducts Kore (Persephone)

As Hades, bound to the Underworld, grew lonely, he asked Zeus for permission to marry Kore. Zeus granted permission. However, Zeus' permission was not enough, even in this patriarchal version of the myth. Demeter denied permission in an attempt to protect her daughter from what she saw as an unsuitable marriage. So, Zeus and Hades devised a plan to abduct Kore. Hades saw his opportunity one day when Kore was picking daisies in a field outside of her mother's vision. He placed a sweet-smelling narcissus flower to entice her. When she picked the flower, a chasm opened in the field, and a carriage with four black horses carrying Hades abducted the innocent maiden and brought her to the Underworld.

Scholars differ in their interpretation of Kore's perspective in this story.[1] In

---

1. The Homeric version of the old myths transformed Demeter into this more subservient version of the mother-goddess, bringer of seed, holder of the mysteries of life, death, and rebirth. To get her daughter back, Demeter hits at the vanity of the gods by devastating the human world, depriving them of their offerings. Along with many other aspects of the myth, previous people like the Hurrians, Sumerians, Indus Valley peoples and other cultures accepted the mother goddess as the primary bringer of life and death, as the judge and jury for justice. In the Egyptian version, Isis was already an incorporated aspect of Au Zit (a cobra goddess) and Au Set (who transformed into Set/Seth, following the meta mythical trope of twins). As far back as 3100 BCE, Isis was seen "as giver of grain and the laws of civilization, as healer, Queen of the Dead, and the One who provides the mystery of resurrected life" (Mara Lynn Keller, "The Eleusinian Mysteries of Demeter and Persephone: Fertility, Sexuality, and Rebirth," 36). Astarte, Nana,

earlier myths, Demeter was the goddess of the Underworld and her daughter, Kore, willfully and against her mother's wishes, went down to the Underworld to tend to the dead, whom her mother had been neglecting.[2] In
this matriarchal myth, the interpretation hinges upon Kore's initial act of
rebellion against her mother. Meanwhile, the interpretative principle of the
more recent Greek myth—only about 3,000 years old—is that of patriarchal
abduction and power: Kore was abducted against her will, and the power is
in the hands of the men in her life—her father who gave her away and her
uncle who abducted her.

What ensues in both myths is the grief of Demeter. She plunged deep into
despair, crying and wandering around the Earth in search of her daughter.
When she asked the all-seeing Sun god where her daughter was, he told her
that Kore had gone to the Underworld with the permission of Zeus. Demeter, filled with rage and grief, retreated from Olympus, disguised herself as
an old woman, and roamed the world of mortals searching for relief from her
unceasing pain.

Demeter Begs Zeus to Intercede

In the Underworld, Kore, whether under duress in the patriarchal myth or
through her own will in the matriarchal myth, transformed from a child into
the goddess, Persephone. Not much has been written about what happened
for Persephone while she was held captive, but it is truly the crux of the story
I tell, which is one of awakening despite immense loss. We know that she
fasted, perhaps out of an awareness that eating in the Underworld would tie
her there forever. Abstinence in its many forms is a spiritual practice that can
lead to ecstatic states and conscious transformation. Abstinence supports
us in obtaining a new perspective, one closer to the truth. Living among the
souls of the dead, Kore abstained and waited. Whether compassion for the
dead was a natural gift or whether she developed this in presence of the suffering of the dead, Persephone emerged, compassionate and empowered.

Nut, Anat, Ishtar, Isis, Ishara, Asheah, Hathor…all and many others represent the mystery of re-
production, survival, and death. Oft cited in Sumerian tales, Inanna ruled the underworld when
Gilgamesh pined for the release of his friend Enkidu from the underworld, centuries earlier than
this version of Pluto, Kore, Demeter and Hermes (Merlin Stone, *When God Was a Woman*, 9).
2. Caroline Casey, *Making the Gods Work for You.*

She transformed from victim to empowered leader. This is an inside job, an inside job that lives in the mysterious realms of the underworld, like a secret whispered among the dead.

Meanwhile, Demeter roamed the Earth disguised as an old woman. In the town of Eleusis, she rested in the home of a nurturing mortal family. In the home was a baby boy. Demeter felt so grateful to this family for caring for her in her grief that she began the process of making their child immortal. This process included a ritual bathing in the waters of Eleusis. Unfortunately, the mother walked in during the ritual, freaked out, took the baby from Demeter and, thus, the child never got to be immortal.

From this myth—as myth and history, story and truth blend in mysterious ways—a temple was built in the town of Eleusis during the early Greek Mycenaean time.[3] This temple became a pilgrimage destination for the Ancient Greeks and into the time of the Roman Empire. For over 2,000 years, spiritual seekers traveled to this mecca (before there was Mecca). Shrouded in mystery, people who went never came back the same—it seemed that what happened in Eleusis stayed in Eleusis. Recent theories suggest that the ergot in the nearby barley fields had psychedelic properties, and the pilgrims in Eleusis were experiencing an acid trip of sorts, using psychotropics to induce a spiritual state, or what the animist tradition calls an "entheogenic experience."

As her mother's journey was creating a whole new religion, Persephone was down in the underworld dealing with Hades (Pluto). As mentioned earlier, Persephone's story while she is held captive is left somewhat unspoken, other than that she fasted.

As Demeter grieved, her worlds—the worlds of plants, food, flowers, and grain—went to waste. The Earth became barren, and drought and famine befell humankind. Without humans, there was no one to worship the gods and this naturally concerned Zeus. He and the other gods and goddesses begged Demeter to return life to Earth, entreating her with gifts, but Demeter only wanted one thing: her daughter back. Finally, Zeus acquiesced. He sent Hermes (Mercury) down to the Underworld to retrieve Kore who was now transformed into Persephone. While Demeter gets most of the credit for Persephone's release, Persephone moved from victim to empowered

3. Keller, 27.

10

equal, from conquered to a voice for those conquered, from over-protected child to equal in power to both her mother and her uncle.

Persephone Returns to Demeter and Becomes Queen of the Underworld

Hermes descended into the Underworld to bring Persephone to her mother. But before Persephone left the underworld, she ate some pomegranate seeds. Eating anything from the realm of the dead bound that being to the Underworld for good, and once Persephone ate the seeds, she was tied to an unbreakable vow: a lifelong marriage with Hades.

Pomegranate seeds have long represented sexuality throughout various cultural and mystical traditions, and so, the metaphor goes, Persephone consummated the marriage when she ate the seeds. Once the marriage was consummated, there was no way for Persephone to get out of it; marriage was a form of bondage for women in the time of the Greeks.[4] However, she negotiated a way to return to her mother for part of the year. For every seed she ate, she had to spend that many months with Hades (six or four, depending on who you ask) and the remaining months with her mother on Earth.

When she returns each year to be with her mother, Demeter rejoices and flowers bloom; wheat grows in the fields, and fruit falls from the trees. When Persephone goes down to the Underworld, Demeter transforms the Earth into winter.

In the Greek myths, Persephone and Hades co-rule the Underworld in a long and faithful marriage. Persephone becomes a wise queen and supports human souls through the difficult transition into death.

Persephone's Transformation

One important question that lingers for those of us who study the Persephone myth is "Why did she eat the pomegranate seeds?" In her feminist poem "Persephone Pauses," Carolyn Kizer, who studied with Joseph Campbell, suggests that Persephone feels something for Hades.[5] She writes that

---

4. And unfortunately, marriage as bondage did not end with the Greeks, perhaps a reason that the myth of Persephone is so relevant today as women are finding ways to get unbound from the oppressive aspects of marriage.
5. See: https://www.cornellcollege.edu/classical_studies/myth/demeter/pause.html

Hades "has moved some gentle part of me," signifying that Persephone has perhaps been seduced in an apparent Stockholm-syndrome situation. While Pluto clearly abducts Kore in the myth, he doesn't appear to harm her further, but instead attempts to woo her.

One possibility is that Persephone ate the seeds intentionally, with full awareness of the outcome. Picture a young woman who has had an unwelcome and traumatic introduction to the dark world of power: it is easy to imagine that rage is one of the feelings likely to arise—a rage, not just at her captor, Hades, but also at her father, Zeus, who connived and supported Hades, and maybe even a rage at her over-bearing mother whose protection did not prepare her for the real world. She isn't asked by anyone what she wants. Her mother even takes front and center stage in the myth. Eating the seeds is the only sovereign decision Persephone makes in the myth, and it is perhaps a decision of defiance—a way of claiming her power. Hades is her way out, and, like many young women who get married too young to men of dubious character, it could be an attempt at escape from the control of her parents.

In another possibility, she was tricked into consuming the seeds and her transformation occurred in the aftermath. Often the myth is told with Hades tricking her into eating the seeds or even forcing her to eat the seeds. If this was the case, how then did Persephone find her power? Tricked by her father, over-protected by her mother, and abducted by her uncle, somehow, she found a way to still come into her own sovereignty. While hard to imagine, how we heal from abuse is part of the deep work many people are doing through therapy, and other healing modalities, now available throughout the world. In this possibility, Persephone empowers herself during her experience as queen and her up and down ride from Earth to the Underworld and back again.

As queen, she rules from a place of compassion for others who suffer and die. She has empathy for those who find themselves abducted. We are left to imagine that Persephone was able to forgive, to forgive them all, and claim her own authority amidst her loss of innocence. In some ways, the older, matriarchal myth lends itself to understanding her process better—that it was her idea and longing to dive into the depths of the underworld for her own transformation that led to her calling as Queen of the Underworld instead of a journey and role she was forced to take at the hands of careless and greedy patriarchs. In either case, Persephone's story requires a redemption, a transformative moment when the wrongs of the past are righted through forgiveness, empowerment, and triumph.

What is also left out of the myth is Hades' transformation. How does a lonely misogynist go from abductor to dutiful husband? How does a god give up his power to his wife and allow her to make the big decisions? How does Hades (Pluto) become the one of the only gods in the pantheon of gods that does not start a war, does not kill, does not pillage, incite violence, or cheat on his wife? Again, we are left with our imaginations and the insights of philosophers. In all, that Hades transforms can be taken to be sign that transformation does not only happen for victims, but the story also offers hope for perpetrators as well.

In the end, Persephone became synonymous with hard-won power. She became the Queen of the Underworld, asserting as much authority as Hades. Persephone is one of the few dark goddesses who never grows old, doesn't have snakes for hair, and isn't portrayed as angry or vindictive. It is Persephone who allows Orpheus to leave the underworld with Eurydice. It is Persephone who allows Heracles to leave with Cerberus. It is Persephone who allows Sisyphus to go back to his wife. It is Persephone who allows Teiresias to retain his intelligence.

As we travel through the looking glass of history, we find many ways in which Hades and Persephone transform, with and without the help of Demeter, Hermes, and Zeus. As we witness the myth unfold time after time, possibilities of the future reveal themselves through the transformation of each of these characters.

Chapter 2:
Astronomy

Picture our solar system as a disc flying through space, as if some great plate was sent hurling through the galaxy by Heracles. Most planets stay safely inside the disc, steadily revolving around our one-and-only star, while some wily planets traverse outside our flat, orbital plane. Pluto, the icy dwarf, is one such planet. It dares to travel 17.14° north and south of the orbital plane. Not only does it travel at an incline, but it does not orbit in a circle, nor is the Sun in the center of its orbit. Pluto's eccentric orbit is an oval with the Sun leaning towards one side, as if the orbit was more like the trajectory of a planet trying to leave this solar system than one comfortably orbiting within its natural limits.

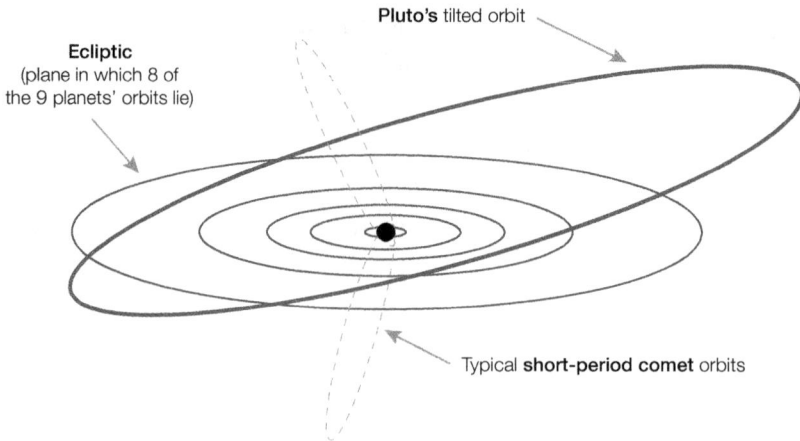

Figure 1: Pluto's tilted orbit.

Declination

Viewing Pluto from our tilting planet, Pluto appears to move up and down. We can track this north and south movement two ways: 1) in relation to the orbital plane of most of our solar system's the planets and 2) in relation to our own planet's equator. The equatorial plane is an imaginary plane that extends from the Earth's equator out into space, which becomes known as the celestial equator. Tracking the movement of the planet's position as moves up and down in relation to the plane of the celestial equator is called *declination*.

Extreme Declination, also called Out-of-Bounds

Standard astrological interpretation understands that a planet exhibits its most extreme behavior when it is in extreme declination. *Extreme declination* is when a planet moves beyond 23.44° north or south of the equatorial plane.

Venus, Mars, and Mercury go into extreme declination frequently—every year or every other year. There is a correlation between Mars, the planet of war and warriors, in extreme declination and terrorist attacks like 9/11, violent murders like the Manson murders in 1969, explosions like Chernobyl, and assassinations like Lincoln, JFK, Robert Kennedy, John Lennon, and Benazir Bhutto.[1]

When Venus, the planet of love and passion, is in extreme declination we are more likely to fall madly and blindly in love (or get very jealous of others falling madly and blindly in love). Notable examples include the romance of Brad Pitt and Angelina Jolie in the summer of 2004 while filming the hot kissing scenes in *Mr. and Mrs. Smith*, or that of Elizabeth Taylor and Richard Burton in the summer of 1962 while filming the steamy scenes on the set of *Cleopatra*. Sometimes Venus in extreme declination leads to great art: Consider the period of spring 1889, when Vincent van Gogh checked himself into an asylum and painted *Irises* (May 1889) and *Starry Night* (June 1889).[2]

When Mercury, the planet of logic, communication, the intellect, and magic, is in extreme declination, our genius shines, and alchemical doorways open into new territories, like during the plague-beleaguered December of 1665, when Isaac Newton started having breakthroughs in physics, or in June 1905,

---

1. The Manson murders occurred in July and August of 1969 when Mars went from 24°S to 25°S. The nuclear power plant in Chernobyl, Ukraine exploded on April 26, 1986, when Mars was at 23°S43'. Lincoln was assassinated April 14, 1865, when Mars was at 25°N. John F. Kennedy was assassinated on November 22, 1963 when Mars was at 23°S54'. Robert Kennedy died on June 6, 1968, a day after he was shot by an assassin, when Mars was at 26°N59'. John Lennon was assassinated on December 8, 1980, when Mars was at 24°S01'. Benazir Bhutto was assassinated on December 27, 2007, when Mars was at 25°N54'.
2. In June 2004, while Brad Pitt and Angelina Jolie were filming *Mr. and Mrs. Smith*, Venus was up to 24°N36'. In June 1962, when Cleopatra was being filmed, Venus got up to 24°N39'. In April 1889, Venus was up to 23°N51', just before Van Gogh moved into the asylum.

when Einstein was writing his relativity papers, or in December 1863 when James Maxwell was hard at work on his paper on electromagnetics.[3]

As we travel farther away from Earth to the outer planets, we encounter the gaseous giants, Jupiter, Saturn, Uranus and Neptune, who orbit neatly within the orbital plane. Saturn and Neptune do not veer into extreme declination, while Jupiter does so infrequently only by a slight amount.[4]

And then there is Pluto, the planet of the Underworld, the overseer of the souls of the dead, the planet of transformation and profound world changes. Separate from the heavens and from Earth, Pluto's world is a world of buried things—gold, gems, oil, our secrets. It is the world of back-room deals and invisible power brokers. Pluto's world scares us and tempts us at the same time. It is the world of monsters and devils, dragons, and dark knights. Pluto in extreme declination is a dark night of the soul for the world—a moment when the energies of the underworld become dominant. Yet, in facing death and destruction, there is an opportunity to face life—and to transform the currently operating paradigm—an opportunity to change the very fabric of what is perceived as reality.

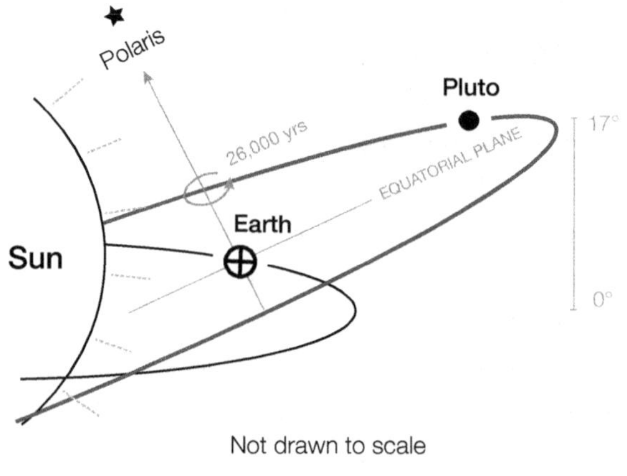

Not drawn to scale

Figure 2: Our Earth spins like a top—rotating and revolving—wobbling on its axis to the tune of a 26,000-year cycle, give or take a thousand years. As the Earth wobbles, its equator, and the plane that extends from the equator, aptly named the equatorial plane, moves north and south, positioning celestial bodies at different angles from our perspective on Earth.

---

3. In December of 1665, Mercury reached 25°S18'. In June 1905, Mercury got up to 24°N41'. In December of 1863, Mercury reached 25°S 27'.
4. Newman, *Declination in Astrology*, 13.

Pluto's Cycle

Astrologers know that Pluto's work brings about radical transformation in any way possible. His work is evolution. His purpose is complete eradication of the old, so something new can be born from the ashes. Pluto's plan for us is death so that a new life can arrive in its wake.

The Irish, known for their sad love songs and happy war songs, celebrate the wake—the transition out of a body and into the next life. One way we can conceive of Pluto is as the mourner at the Irish wake clutching a bottle of whiskey singing at the top of his lungs, both celebrating and accepting the great transition. The Pluto cycle, whether seen in a personal chart or the experience of a society is the transformation from one life to another, from one culture to another, from one paradigm to another, from one world to another.

Pluto's mythic role as the God of the Underworld has been underplayed in recent years due to it being downsized to a dwarf planet by astronomers. However, Pluto's unique relationship with its moon, Charon, gives this tiny dwarf planet an advantage.[5] Charon and Pluto together act more like a binary planet, operating like a barbell spinning through space, processing the debris of all of the suffering psyches in the solar system, sweeping up the souls of the dead.

The rest of this work is focused on Pluto's journey in and out of extreme declination, in and out of the shadow and the work of reaching beyond the suffering of humanity. Witnessing Pluto and the events that occur when Pluto moves out-of-bounds offers us perspective on the work required at this time in history.

---

5. Moons orbit their planet around a common center of mass, called the barycenter, not just around the planet's center of mass. To find the barycenter, add the mass of the planet to the mass of the moon(s) and find the center of mass between them. The larger the moon, the farther away the center of mass moves from the center of the planet. The more moons, the more the center of mass is likely to stay close to center of the planet since those moons are pulling the center of mass in multiple directions. It is the common center of mass of the planet and its moons that orbits the Sun. In most cases, the planet exists as the common center of mass, which is owed to it being significantly larger than its moons. But in the case of Pluto, Charon is a little over half Pluto's size, significantly altering the usual center-of-mass equation.

Chapter 3:
History of POWER and REFORM Times

"History, despite it wrenching pain, cannot be unlived,
but if faced with courage, need not be lived again."
—Maya Angelou

N ow that we know the myth and the astronomy, we look at what happened in the past when Pluto went into extreme declination. There is a notable difference between the events when Pluto went into extreme declination to the north of the equatorial plane and the events that happened when Pluto was south of the equatorial plane. To the north, we see times of dictators, massive wars, innovations in war, and war led by conquerors with unfettered desire for power. To the south, we experience times of revolution, reform, people rising up and taking a stand against an overpowering ruler or a corrupt system.

POWER

Pluto in Extreme Declination to the North

Times of POWER Abuse

In March of 1938, Pluto moved into extreme declination to the north of the equatorial plane. Adolf Hitler took control of the German armed forces and annexed Austria with a show of force so strong that the Austrian military did not resist. Japan had begun its invasion into China in 1937, and the Spanish Civil War was already in full swing (1936–1939), but neither of these wars came close to the devastation that was around the corner. From mid-May of 1938 until January 1939, Pluto tapped *out* of extreme declination and for a brief window, peace talks placated European countries as negotiations over the Sudetenland, a region in Czechoslovakia, were handled with the Munich Agreement (September 1938). Just as Pluto moved back into extreme declination (January 1939), the peace talks fell apart and Otto Hahn announced his discovery of nuclear fission—a scientific discovery

18

that led to nuclear power and nuclear weapons. By September of 1939 and Pluto's full immersion into extreme declination territory, Germany invaded Poland, instigating World War II.

Pluto moved in and out of extreme declination from 1939 until May 1953. By the end, the world was a vastly different place. Cities throughout the world were left in ruins. Countries were carved up into democratic and communist states, leading to more war including the Korean War (1950–1953), the Vietnam war (1955–1975), and continued unrest along the Pakistan-India border. World organizations took center stage, while mass genocide in Russia, China, and throughout Europe laid waste a generation of innocent souls.

At the peak of Pluto in extreme northern declination, in April of 1945, Hitler's bunker exploded, while the Battle of Berlin, one of the deadliest battles in history, raged on, finally ending in May when Germany and Italy surrendered to the Allied Powers. However, more devastation was still to come. A few months later, the US dropped atomic bombs on Hiroshima and Nagasaki instantly killing over a hundred-thousand civilians.

Just as Pluto left extreme declination in 1953, Dwight D. Eisenhower, the newly elected US president, was looking for a way to end the Korean War, and the Russian dictator, Josef Stalin, died after a stroke (March 1953). With new leadership in the Soviet Union and new leadership in the US, the world turned from hot war to cold war, from destruction to some attempt at recovery.

The stunning correspondence between Pluto's extremity and extreme power abuses in history is perhaps best shown in the following chart, a list that cannot possibly encapsulate the drama of these eras, and yet one that nonetheless points to their magnitude.

Table 1: Major Events with Pluto in Extreme Declination to the North

DATES	EVENTS
1771–1724 BCE *Peak Feb. 1744 BCE* (36° N 07′)	• Hammurabi (reign c. 1792–1750 BCE) created a code of law in Assyria, that included the now famous catch phrase "an eye for an eye."[1]

1. In the 3,000 years that people have been finding these tablets, French archaeologists discovered an important source code in 1901. See, J. D. Prince "*The Code of Hammurabi*, et al.," 601–9.

1526–1478 BCE *Peak Feb. 1498 BCE* *(35° N 29′)*	• The 18ᵗʰ Dynasty in Egypt (c. 1539–1075 BCE) focused on war and conquest. It was a time of generals becoming pharaohs, including Thutmose I (r. 1493–1482 BCE), who extended Egypt into Syria.
1280–1232 BCE *Peak Feb. 1253 BCE* *(34° N 50′)*	• Ramses II, Pharoah of Egypt (r. 1279–1213 BCE), developed a new system of warfare, attacked the Hittites at the great battle of Qadesh (1275 BCE), and then arrived at one of the first non-proliferation pacts in history. • Wu Ding (r. c.1250–1192 BCE), the first confirmed emperor of the Shang Dynasty, was raised as a commoner and rose into power through being a great warrior, expanded China to the north and west.
1034–988 BCE *Peak Feb. 1008 BCE* *(34° N 08′)*	• King David of Judea (most likely time is 1000 BCE), known mostly from the Books of Samuel in the Hebrew Bible, united the tribes of Israel and conquered Jerusalem.
788–741 BCE *Peak Mar. 763 BCE* *(33° N 24′)*	• The King of Assyria, Tiglath-Pileser III (r. 745–727 BCE), conquered much of the Middle East. At the end of this time, The First Messenian War broke out in Greece (743–724 BCE) between Messenia and Sparta.
542–497 BCE *Peak Mar. 516 BCE* *(32° N 42′)*	• Darius the Great (r. 522–486 BCE) expanded the Persian Empire into the Caucasus region, extending it into northern Africa and out into the Indus Valley.
290–260 BCE *Peak Feb. 273 BCE* *(31° N 48′)*	• Ashoka the Great (r. 268–232 BCE) expanded the Mauryan Empire, taking over most of India. He converted to Buddhism after witnessing the devastation of war in 266 BCE. • By now Alexander the Great (r. 338–323 BCE) had conquered much of Europe, the Middle East, and into India, where his army mutinied. His early death led his kingdom to splinter into the Seleucid Empire, the Roman Republic, and Egypt. During this time, each empire was getting established by the individual warrior-kings who took over from Alexander.

50–6 BCE *Peak Mar. 25* BCE *(31° N 09')*	• The Roman Republic took over Judea. A year later, Julius Caesar crossed the Rubicon to attack Pompey's army, turning Rome from a Republic into an Empire. Augustus Caesar became sole ruler and emperor in 27 BCE just as Pluto peaked. He continued to expand the empire until Pluto left extreme declination in 6 BCE, after which time he turned his focus away from expansion and towards infrastructure.
197–240 *Peak Mar. 222* *(30° N 20')*	• Ardashir the Great (r. 211–224 CE) founded the Sassanid Empire (modern day Iran). • In China, the Han Dynasty (202 BCE–220 CE), a Confucian dynasty focused on advancements in agriculture, writing, economics, and education, moved into decline and was taken over by the military dictator Cao Cao. His death in 220 CE led to warring factions and three centuries of instability in China.
445–486 *Peak Mar. 469* *(29° N 31')*	• Vandals, Huns, and Goths invaded the Roman Empire. In 443, Attila the Hun (r. 434–453) pulled together an army, invaded Nis (in Serbia today), and began his slash and burn tactics of leave no prisoners or even people. He died before the peak of Pluto in extreme declination, but it was near the peak that Rome fell. By 476, the Vandal leader Odoacer had claimed himself the new King of Italy.
692–731 *Peak Mar. 714* *& Mar. 715* *(28° N 39')*	• Charles "The Hammer" Martel (r. 718–741) fended off the Umayyad Caliphate at the Battle of Tours (732) and expanded the Frankish Empire.[2] Leo III, ruler of the Byzantine Empire from 717 to 741, instituted the Iconoclast time period, when many religious icons and statues were destroyed.

2. Scholars debate about how great a victory this was. The Umayyad Caliphate was in transition during this time. The new leaders were uninterested in continuing expansion into this uncivilized area and felt their focus was better utilized on conquering to the south and east.

940–976 *Peak Mar. 961* *(27° N 47′)*	• The long-lasting Song Dynasty was founded in China in 960, after Zhao Kuangyin, usurped the Zhou emperor and continued to conquer much of the surrounding kingdoms, becoming Emperor Taizu from 960 to 976. • Otto the Great (r. 962–973) consolidated his power through overcoming revolts and expanded the Holy Roman Empire through conquest.
1188–1221 *Peak Mar.–Apr. 1207* *(26° N 54′)*	• Genghis Khan (r. 1206–1227) led Mongolian warriors to take over most of Asia and the Middle East. His conquests began around the time that Pluto went into extreme declination and ended as Pluto left. He was crowned during the peak. • Just prior to this time, Pope Innocent III (p. 1130–1143) launched multiple crusades with the intent to take over Jerusalem. These continued for a century, leaving a lasting impact of war on Europe and the Middle East. One such crusader, Richard the Lionheart (r. 1189–1199) was king of England and died in battle. His brother, King John (r. 1199–1216) took his place, famous for signing the Magna Carta in 1215, a document that gave the barons more power and laid a blueprint for future redistributions of power. Saladin, the Sultan of Egypt and Syria (r. 1174–1193) founded the Ayyubid dynasty and built the Sassanid Empire into a military force that eventually overcame the crusaders.
1437–1466 *Peak Apr. 1453* *& Apr. 1454* *(25° N 59′)*	• The Ottoman Empire (1299–1922) conquered the Byzantine Empire in 1453 under the leadership of Mehmed II, completing with the Fall of Constantinople. Mehmed II closed the trade routes between Europe and Asia, which had the unintentional effect of forcing Europe to build better ships and navigational devices, which in turn began the Age of Discovery. • Itzcoatl (r. 1427–1440) expanded Aztec Empire. Pachacuti (r. 1438–1471) expanded the Incan Empire. Count Vlad (r. 1448–1477) had thousands of people impaled. Cosimo de Medici (r. 1434–1464) expanded the Medici family reach by taking over the finances of the Vatican and nurturing future popes.

1687–1710 *Peak Apr. 1699* *& Apr. 1700* *(25° N 03')*	• Peter the Great (r. 1682–1725) expanded Russia into Sweden. Louis XIV (1643–1715) bankrupted France building Versailles and creating an army that expanded the French borders into Germany, Spain, and the Netherlands. William (r. 1689–1702) and Mary (r. 1689–1694) crossed the English Channel and took over England.
Mar. 1938–May 1938 Feb. 1939–June 1939 Jan. 1940–July 1940 Jan. 1941–July 1941 Dec. 1941–Aug. 1942 Dec. 1942–Aug. 1943 Dec. 1943–Aug. 1944 Dec. 1944–Aug. 1945 Dec. 1945–Aug. 1946 Dec. 1946–July 1947 Jan. 1948–July 1948 Jan. 1949–July 1949 Jan. 1950–July 1950 Feb. 1951–Jun. 1951 Feb. 1952–Jun. 1952 Mar. 1953–May 1953 *Peak: Apr. 1945 &* *Apr. 1946 (24° N 07')*	• This period correlates with World War II, along with global genocide, fascism, the creation of nuclear global threat, and irrevocable climate changes due to postwar industrialization and the United States' export of carbon-fueled capitalism. China fell completely under communist rule. Europe lay in ruins, after losing nearly 10% of its population and many of its landmarks. A world financial banking system was established along with the UN, CIA, KGB, IMF, WHO, and the precursor to the WTO.

POWER

Persephone's Abduction, Pluto Out-of-Bounds North

Pluto out-of-bounds to the north corresponds to the part of the Persephone myth when she was abducted. She was captured against her will. In a moment filled with imagery of innocence, a girl picking flowers in a field, she is seized and stolen into the world of the dead. So begins her time in the world of shadow and the suffering that unfolds. Like the innocent Persephone, during these times in history, the everyday person is abducted by the tyrant who ruthlessly claims power. The fierceness of Pluto unleashed scares us into submission. Pluto out-of-bounds north is a powerful phenomenon—a time when Pluto rises from the Underworld to wreak havoc in the world. It is as if Pluto himself finds a body to inhabit—a form through which he can wield massive, unchecked power. This window of a few years every 248 years brings forth a different-but-same power-hungry tyrant. It is time that inspires legends, not unlike the myth that bears his name.

In 1188 CE, Pluto went into extreme declination at the same time as the young Mongol warrior, Temüjin, started his rampage from one village to the next. People were terrified of his vindictiveness, his willingness to wield destruction, and his ease with torture. Instead of banding together to eradicate him, the tens of thousands of villagers ran away in fear. By the time Pluto hit its highest point of declination in 1207, Temüjin had taken over much of Central Asia, declared himself universal emperor Genghis Khan and founded the Mongol Empire. By the time Pluto left extreme declination in 1221, Genghis and his army of soldiers had expanded the Mongol territory all the way from the Yellow Sea (Pacific Ocean) to the hills of current day Turkmenistan.

King Louis XIV built Versailles and a formidable army during the POWER time that lasted from 1687 to 1710, while Peter the Great expanded the Russian Empire, and William and Mary invaded England in a war that was called the Glorious Revolution but was neither glorious nor a revolution.

Count Vlad (otherwise known as Count Dracula, fictionalized by Bram Stoker) impaled over 10,000 people during the POWER time that lasted from 1437 to 1466. The popular television series *Game of Thrones* is based on the War of the Roses started by Henry VI during that same time period (1437–1466).

King Richard the Lionheart and King John reigned under the guise of Pluto during the POWER time that lasted from 1188 to 1221. During these years the powerful Catholic Pope Innocent III perpetuated the largest of the crusades and supported the eradication of the Cathars (a Christian sect living in Southern France). A particularly prolific POWER time, this period also saw the Gempei Wars of Samurai warrior fame, which introduced the first Shogun in Japan, as well as the reign of the aforementioned Genghis Khan, who conquered more land and people than any other conqueror in history, still to this day.

Pluto takes on forms that shake us to our core—Mehmed II, Otto the Great, Charles "The Hammer" Martel, Attila the Hun, Augustus Caesar, Ashoka Maurya, Darius, Ramses, and Uzziah—all were immortalized on battle fields (and in movies), and all lived during the POWER time. Many found themselves crowned at the peak of the POWER era, when Pluto was at highest degree of declination to the north. The last time Pluto was out-of-bounds, 1938–1949, humanity saw the rise of Hitler, Stalin, and Mussolini, names synonymous with tyrant, dictator, and despot.

When we look to past times of seemingly inconceivable terror, we can struggle to understand why people let such inhumanity happen. During other times in the Pluto cycle, it is easy to judge the people living during the POWER time. It is easy to think we would never allow the horrors of history to happen—the many genocides, the Nazis, the Tiglath-Pilisars, and the Count Vlads—all of which occurred when Pluto was in extreme northern declination. As most of us have never lived through a time when Pluto was in extreme declination, we can only imagine what we would do, how we would behave, how we would feel. We may hope we would be Oskar Schindler, or Varian Fry, or Raoul Wallenberg, but when Pluto is a force unleashed, an overwhelming feeling of disempowerment is more likely. Persephone was an innocent child, protected from harm until her unexpected abduction. She had no recourse. That is Pluto in extreme declination to the north. These are times that chill our bones and push us over the edge...*and, due to its eccentric orbit, Pluto will not go into extreme declination to the north again for the next 3,000 years.*

REFORM

Pluto in Extreme Declination to the South
Times of Revolution and Reformation

"We live in capitalism. Its power seems inescapable. So did the divine right of kings. Any human power can be resisted and changed by human beings. Resistance and change often begin in art, and very often in our art, the art of words."

—*Ursula K. Le Guin*

In late 1773, just before Pluto entered extreme declination to the south, the British government along with the East India Company initiated a series of taxes and punitive measures that riled up the colonists across the Atlantic Ocean. In a state of outrage, the colonists began banding together and committing, at first peaceful, acts of rebellion...dumping tea overboard (Boston Tea Party, Dec. 1773), convening the First Continental Congress (Sep.–Oct. 1774), and forming independent militias (Sep. 1774). It did not take long for peaceful protest to break into skirmishes and then all-out war. By April 1775, the colonists had risen up against the red coats at the Battle of Lexington and Concord. With Pluto solidly ensconced in extreme declination to the south by May of 1776, the colonists, fully committed to independence, began planning the Second Continental Congress, at which the Declaration of Independence was signed (July 1776).

When Pluto finds itself in extreme declination to the south, uprisings from within lead to revolutions, with many people willing to risk their lives for change. These uprisings are usually successful, but not always in an anticipated way. Sometimes, the uprisings lead to a change in heart in the leadership who institutes reforms that benefit the people, as was the case with Catherine the Great of Russia and Constantine after the Christian uprisings. Sometimes the uprisings lead to more chaos and instability, as was the case with the French Revolution. Sometimes the uprisings lead to something entirely new, as was the case with the American War of Independence and the Reformation in Northern Europe. What is consistent with Pluto extreme declination south is that people no longer tolerate the status quo. While dictators may try to subjugate the people, they are no longer successful. Sometimes they implode, as with the Roman Emperor Nero. Sometimes they abdicate, as with Shunzong during the Tang Dynasty (805 CE). Sometimes they focus on infrastructure and building temples, as was the case with Solomon (Solomon's Temple), Justinian (Hagia Sophia 532–537 CE), and Edward the Confessor (Westminster Abbey, 1042–1052).

The people would rather live in revolution and chaos than be subjected any longer to the will of a tyrant. While often a time of revolution and systems collapse, I have named this time the REFORM time as reforms are the outcome, perhaps even the purpose, of these times.

Table 2: Major Events with Pluto in Extreme Declination to the South

DATES	EVENTS
1685–1610 BCE *Peak Aug. 1655 BCE* *(35° S 46')*	• Ammi-Saduqa (r. 1646–1626 BCE) instituted reforms and focused on building temples in a time of relative peace.
1439–1366 BCE *Peak Aug. 1412 BCE* *(35° S 07')*	• Amenhotep III (r. 1390–1353 BCE) focused on infrastructure, including building a large harbor and massive temples.
1194–1123 BCE *Peak Aug. 1166 BCE* *(34° S 29')*	• Multiple large empires collapsed at the same time due to internal strife, climate change, and infrastructure decay, including the Hittites, Assyria, and Egypt.[3]
948–880 BCE *Peak Aug. 922 BCE* *(33° S 47')*	• King Solomon (c. 970–931 BCE) is known for building a great temple in Jerusalem. When he died in 931 BCE, his sons took over and divided the country into two states, Judea and Israel.
701–637 BCE *Peak Sep. 676 BCE* *& Sep. 675 BCE* *(33° S 05')*	• The groundwork for ancient Greece was laid through the formation of a representative government known as the Ecclesia (not official until Solon's Reforms in 594 BCE). In 685 BCE, slaves (helots) in Messenia revolted against the Spartan government in what became The Second Messenian War.

---

3. See anthropologist Eric H. Cline's *1177: The Year Civilization Collapsed.*

455–395 BCE *Peak Sep. 431 &* *Sep. 430 BCE* *(32° S 21')*	• The Peloponnesian Wars, the First from 460–445 BCE and the Second from 431–404 BCE, pitted the two Greeks states of Sparta and Athens against each other. In 431 BCE, Athenian leader Pericles gave a speech, the Funeral Oration, (scribed down by Thericles) as a speech to inspire weary soldiers to fight for democracy. (Athens lost anyway).
210–160 BCE *Peak Aug. 187 BCE* *(31° S 32')*	• Carthaginian general Hannibal led an army across the Alps to invade the Roman Empire from 218 BCE until losing at the Battle of Zama in 202 BCE. He returned to Carthage and took a position as a leading statesman and instituted reforms benefiting the people. He died c. 182 BCE, leaving a legacy of increased Carthage independence from Rome. • The Maccabees, a group of Jewish rebels in the Seleucid Empire, successfully revolted (167–160 BCE) against the empire and took control of Judea. Celebrated to this day as Chanukah.
38–62 CE *Peak Sep. 61 CE* *& Sep. 62 CE* *(30° S 48')*	• The Jewish Revolt in Rome in 70 CE was overcome by Roman forces and led to the destruction of the Jewish temple in Israel. After Nero's death, the empire leadership went into a chaotic time of four emperors. Vespasian, the general that quashed the Jewish Revolt, landed in power. Instead of focusing on expansion of the empire, he turned his attention to internal reforms. Meanwhile, the Christian movement, a movement of the people at the time, was gathering steam through the teachings and deaths of Peter the Apostle and Paul the Apostle, who were both executed precisely at the peak of Pluto in extreme declination.
285–337 *Peak Sep. 307* *(30° S 00')*	• Diocletian (r. 284–305 CE) reformed the constitution, divided the empire into two halves and focused on administration reform. During this time, chaos and Christian uprisings led to thousands of deaths. When Constantine (r. 306–337 CE) stepped into power, he set forth a path for the establishment of Christianity to be a legal religion. The Council of Nicaea in 325 CE led to the initial creation of official Christian doctrine.

533–580 *Peak Aug. 553* *(29° S 10')*	• The year before Pluto went into extreme declination (532), a public sporting event led to an unorganized insurrection in Rome, the Nika Rebellion. Emperor Justinian (r. 527–565) strategically corralled the protestors into the coliseum and had them slaughtered. From this time of chaos, he instituted reforms and focused on internal changes resulting in the Codex of Justinian, a series of judicial reforms that gave increased power to the people, including the right to trial and innocent till proven guilty.
780–824 *Peak Sep. 798* *& Sep. 799* *(28° S 19')*	• Charlemagne (r. 768–814) united Europe and was the first emperor of the Holy Roman Empire. Harun al-Rashid (r. 786–809), ruler of the Abbasid Caliphate, continued to oversee a time of scientific and artistic creativity. In 798, an exchange of gifts between Charlemagne and Harun al-Rashid supported peace between their kingdoms.
1028–1067 *Peak Sep. 1044* *& Sep. 1045* *(27° S 27')*	• At the beginning of this extreme declination time, England transitioned from being ruled by the Danish Cnut the Great (r. 1016–1035) and his successors to being ruled by Edward the Confessor (1042–1066) who authorized the building of Westminster Abbey in 1045. Just as this extreme declination time was ending, William, the King of Normandy, claimed his right to the English throne, crossed the English Channel with an army and attacked King Harold's ill-equipped army in the famous Battle of Hastings. • Meanwhile, The Schism of 1054, tore the Christian church into two separate sects, the western Roman Catholic Church and the Eastern Orthodox Church.
1276–1310 *Peak Sep.–Oct. 1291* *(26° S 34')*	• Kublai Khan (r. 1264–1294) oversaw a time of invention, infrastructure development and failed invasions in China. • The last crusade ended in defeat at the Battle of Acres in 1291. In the same year, three canons in the Alps united in treaty to begin the forming of what is today Switzerland.

1524–1553 *Peak 1537* *(25° S 39′)*	• The Reformation: From 1518 to 1524, Catholic priest Huldrych Zwingli broke with Catholic tradition in his teachings. In 1517, Martin Luther shared his 95 *Theses*, his objections to the Catholic Church. In 1534, the King of England, Henry VIII, broke with the Catholic Church, instituting Protestantism throughout Britain. Near the peak, in 1536, John Calvin published his theological treatise, giving more form to the Reformation and beginning a new religion, Calvinism. By the end of this extreme declination period, in 1555, Lutherans were given permission to practice in the Holy Roman Empire. • In the Americas, the Spanish conquistador, Pizarro invaded the Incan Empire. Hernán Cortés invaded the Aztec Empire. • Suleiman the Magnificent (r. 1520–1566), the Sultan of the Ottoman Empire, instituted economic reforms, judicial reforms, educational reforms, and cultural reforms, bringing the Ottoman Empire into a golden age. His decrees protected Jewish people and supported the empire in being a haven for Jewish refugees for centuries after he lived.
Aug. 1774–Dec. 1774 June 1775–Jan. 1776 May 1776–Feb. 1791 July 1791–Jan. 1792 July 1792–Jan. 1793 Aug. 1793–Dec. 1793 Aug. 1794–Dec. 1794 Oct. 1795–Nov. 1795 *Peak Oct. 1783* *& Oct. 1784* *(24° S 44′)*	• Colonists revolted against the British Empire at a time when Britain was fighting France (1775–1783). The French helped the colonists defeat Britain in the American Revolution, that ends with the Treaty of Paris in 1783. The Articles of Confederation was drawn up in 1781 and laid out the foundation for the Constitution of the US, signed in 1789. In 1789 in Paris, after poor harvests and deepening inequity, an educated and poor population rose up, storming the Bastille. The French Revolution overthrew the monarchy and initiated a time of chaos and terror. At the end of this extreme declination time, Napoleon Bonaparte[4] with a loyal army took over, ending the chaos and beginning a time of expansion. Catherine the Great instituted reforms in Russia.

4. One of the most strategic generals in history, Napoleon Bonaparte may seem to belong in the Extreme North column. His dictatorship began just as Pluto left extreme declination after revolution wreaked havoc in France. His administrative abilities saved France from total collapse, and the reforms he set into motion led to a stable government that valued the people.

Sep 11–Nov 9, 2025	• COLLAPSE (turn to page 170)
Aug 21–Dec 1, 2026	• REVOLUTION (turn to page 181)
Aug 10–Dec 13, 2027	
Aug 4–Dec 17, 2028	• NON-VIOLENT RESISTANCE (turn to page 190)
Aug 2–Dec 21, 2029	• PARADIGM SHIFT (turn to page 204)
Aug 4–Dec 20, 2030	
Aug 7–Dec 16, 2031	• AWAKENING (turn to page 218)
Aug 13–Dec 12, 2032	
Aug 22–Dec 4, 2033	
Sep 4–Nov 23, 2034	
Sep 25–Nov 3, 2035	
Peak Oct. 6–16,	
2030 (23° S 48′)	

• COLLAPSE (turn to page 170)
• REVOLUTION (turn to page 181)
• NON-VIOLENT RESISTANCE (turn to page 190)
• PARADIGM SHIFT (turn to page 204)
• AWAKENING (turn to page 218)

REFORM

Persephone Rises from the Underworld, Pluto Out-of-Bounds South

Pluto extreme declination southside corresponds to Persephone rising from the land of the dead and at the same time taking her place as Queen of the Dead. It is the time when Persephone, goddess of the people (since all people die), empowered and compassionate reforms the underworld from the dark shadow world of Hades to a place where people may find mercy and forgiveness.

Recently, a friend from Seattle said to me that she felt like she was living through the French Revolution. She was referencing the recent demonstrations inspired by the Black Lives Matter and #MeToo movements, which occurred alongside 3%ers demonstrating for gun rights. These demonstrations transpired a decade after the Occupy Movement invited people to live in parks throughout the city and two decades after protesters interrupted the World Trade Organization (WTO) conference.

While hardly the French Revolution, there is a similarity between the uprisings in the US, Israel, Russia, the Middle East, Asia, South America, Africa and well…everywhere…within the last few decades and other revolutions that have happened during past REFORM times. The uprisings *before* the extreme declination time often peter out, are unsuccessful or are quashed. As the REFORM time nears, the revolts, whether peaceful or not, begin to affect real change. I imagine many early colonists, simply doing their best to survive and put food on the table, ignoring some of the signs and being unable to imagine the changes about to unfold. In that way, many people today clamor to return to some pre-pandemic life, or some pre-climate-change life, or some pre-civil rights life. But that life is gone. The clash between political and/or corporate leaders and the populace leaves many of us with a lurking sense that we are on the precipice of irrevocable change. Just as in France, the REFORM time required a massive shift in material and emotional discontent among the public, the upcoming REFORM time urges us to realize the rumblings of our own discontent.

The REFORM time arises in response to the abuses of the POWER time. Like Persephone rising into empowerment during REFORM after being captured during POWER. The French Revolution arose in response to the excesses of the monarchy grossly exaggerated during the reign of Louis XIV during POWER. During the first Pluto cycle of the Roman Empire, Augustus Caesar ruled with an iron fist during the POWER time, and when the REFORM time started, the Roman Empire was in danger of falling apart under the rulership of cruel dictators Caligula and Nero. During the peak of the REFORM time, in 69 CE, four emperors ruled in a chaotic window of Roman Empire history. Vespasian, a general who put down a Jewish revolt in Judea, came out on top and was crowned Caesar. Seeing the writing on the wall, instead of continuing to expand the empire through war, he instituted reforms, saving the Roman Empire from internal dissolution.

When Persephone rises from the dead, either through intervention of her parents, or through her own will, or through Hades loosening his grasp, the transformation changes the landscape of the Underworld for good. As we head into the final REFORM time, uprisings, demonstrations, and worldwide awakening movements have a great chance to change our world for good. As I attempt to offer a few options for how this change may happen, the actual events will likely be unprecedented, unimaginable, and wholly transformative.

Chapter 4:
The POWER and REFORM Times Are Ending
(a little more astronomy)

Yes, the extreme POWER and REFORM times are ending. You read that correctly. Before you brace yourself for the next Alexander or Genghis, know that Pluto's periods of extreme declination are coming to a close—at least for the next few thousand years.

As the Earth wobbles on its axis, its tilt changes. This measurement is known as the *obliquity of the ecliptic,* and the angle has been decreasing. As the Earth's axial tilt changes, its relationship to the orbit of Pluto changes, and thus, the number of degrees that compose Pluto's out-of-bounds period decreases over time. This is the result of the Earth's tilt moving into increasing alignment with Pluto's orbit. As a result, Pluto's time spent in extreme declination is shortening, which holds important implications for the Pluto cycle. It means that the POWER time has ended and one more REFORM time remains.

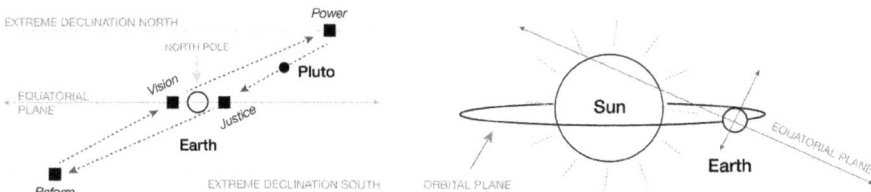

Figure 3: The astronomy of declination and Pluto's cycle.

In 1000 BCE, Pluto went into extreme declination for 47 years. In 1700 CE, Pluto went into extreme declination for 23 years. In 1938 CE, Pluto went into extreme declination for only 11 years. From the following graph, the dates of Pluto in extreme declination show us how much our relationship to Pluto's orbit has changed. The horizontal lines are positioned at 23.44° showing how far beyond extreme declination goes by year.

33

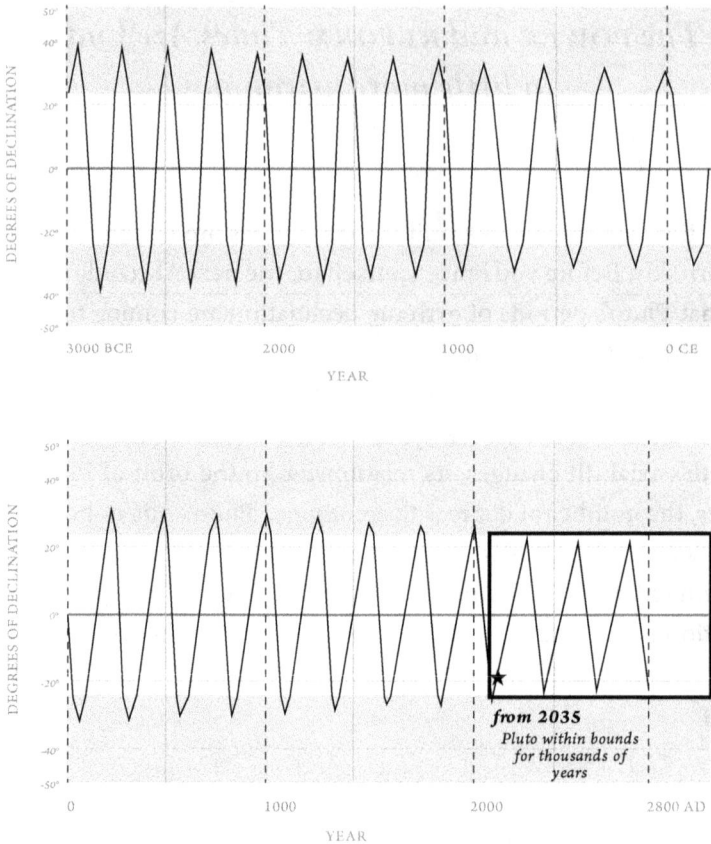

Figure 4: Pluto's declination cycle across time: Top: 3000 BCE to 147 CE. Bottom: 0–2800 CE.

Eventually Pluto will not go out of bounds at all. To be more specific:

The next time Pluto travels out of bounds, from 2025 to 2035 will be the dwarf planet's last period of extreme declination for thousands of years.

As a result, after 2035, the planet Earth, and the beings on it, will not be subjugated to the fearsome effects of Pluto's dark side. Alongside the gradually arriving Aquarian Age, the evidence I found in my research suggests that times of extreme abuse and revolution will recede into history.

Before this utopia occurs, Pluto will move into its last REFORM period of extreme declination. Out-of-bounds to the south, the side that correlates, as we've established, with revolutions and rebellions, reformations and awakenings, Pluto will instigate a global period of fighting and struggle—but one that will ultimately lead to reforms that benefit the people.

The last time Pluto went out-of-bounds north was basically just that. We will not see another extreme northerly declination period corresponding with extreme POWER abuses for thousands of years. It happened between 1937 and 1953, precisely peaking in the summer of 1945, when World War II was at its apex of destruction. At Pluto's final period of peak POWER, August 1945, two atomic bombs were dropped by the US onto Japan, killing hundreds of thousands of people, and devastating the environment for generations. What's remarkable here, astrologically, is that Saturn transited Pluto's discovery degree for the very first time. These nuclear bombs were the realization of our experience of Pluto's power to annihilate.

But as Pluto travels up and down in its orbit and in relationship to the equatorial plane of Earth, there is a trend toward awakening. Through a brief look into human history and humanity's evolution, the POWER to REFORM cycle becomes apparent and reveals a profound hope for our future.

Consider what this means. For all of humanity's recorded history, Pluto has been going into extreme declination, correlating with massive takeovers and violence, abusive dictators, and warlords. Four thousand years ago, Pluto went into extreme declination for almost 50 years. Wars were longer in the past; the fighting was less condensed. Hand-to-hand combat took longer. The last time Pluto was out of bounds, 73 million people died within six years.

Our upcoming experience of Pluto's final out-of-bounds period will be a time of revolution and reform. It is a REFORM period that echoes the texture and feeling of the time cycle that occurred when Jefferson and Franklin were writing the Declaration of Independence. It echoes that of the beginning of "protest"antism. It echoes the time periods of Kublai Khan, the last Crusade, Constantine the Great, and Socrates. While many revolutions have been bloody, there is also the precedent for leaders to emerge in this upcoming out-of-bounds period who institute peaceful reforms.

Chapter 5:
History of VISION and JUSTICE Times

After tracking the POWER and REFORM times, we must explore two other important metrics in Pluto's cycle—the two times when Pluto crosses the equatorial plane. First, as it crosses the equatorial plane from south to north, called the VISION time for reasons that will become apparent. Then, as it crosses the equatorial plane from north to south, called JUSTICE, for reasons that may not be as apparent at first, but will hopefully grow on you. These times of VISION and JUSTICE continue on even as the times of Pluto OOB and its extreme historical correlations discontinue.

VISION

Pluto at 0° of Declination,

Moving from South to North

In 585 BCE, the Ionian philosopher, Thales, accurately predicted an eclipse, a bold leap forward in the field of astronomy. Within his lifetime he arrived at his version of the scientific method, advanced geometry, and mathematics. He is often referred to as the "father of science." He asked the question, "What is the world made of?" not from a mythical, religious perspective but from a physical, scientific perspective. Arthur Herman in his Pulitzer Prize Finalist work, *The Cave and the Light*, argues that the rift between Plato and Aristotle is the root of much of the split thinking in the world. He starts his story with Thales. "The adventure began more than one hundred years before Socrates's birth, in the sunbaked commercial town of Miletus.... In about 585 BCE, a man named Thales amazed his fellow Milesians by correctly predicting an eclipse of the Sun."[1] In Herman's work, Thales, through predicting the eclipse and accurately measuring the pyramids in Egypt, "signaled a major change in Greek thinking and world thinking. A new rational way of understanding reality was born, as opposed to one tied to myth or

---

1. Arthur Herman, *The Cave and the Light*, 12.

religious ritual."[2] Two hundred and fifty years later, that is, one Pluto cycle later, the great philosopher Plato died, and his pupil Aristotle left Athens to explore his own philosophies of life.

New thoughts, completely new thoughts, are rare things. Even John Lennon and Paul McCartney tell us "...there's nothing you can know that isn't known."[3] I heard Deepak Chopra speak once, and he said that most thoughts are spread round and round and that less than 5% of our thinking is original... and I venture that it's even less. But in some rare instances, a person arrives at something new. Charles Murray who wrote *The Bell Curve* calls them meta-inventions, the introduction of an entirely new perspective.[4] These meta-inventions change the world. Once an entirely new perspective is brought to the world, the world is never seen in the same way again. The very nature of reality shifts. From Flat Earth to Round Earth. From Earth in the center of the solar system to Sun in the center of the solar system. From disease as a curse to germ theory.

When Pluto crosses the equatorial plane south to north, a new perspective arrives through the minds of the some of the most revered individuals to walk the Earth. Thales, Aristotle, Ptolemy, Augustine of Hippo, the prophet Muhammad, al-Battānī, Bernard of Clairvaux, Kepler, Galileo, Francis Bacon, Descartes, Darwin, Marx, Pasteur... and the list goes on.

Not all beginnings are scientific or philosophical. Some new perspectives bring forth new dynasties, and new forms of governance including the beginning of 18th Dynasty of Egypt, the beginning of the Tang Dynasty, the beginning of the Rashidan and Umayyad Caliphates, and the pilgrims landing on Plymouth rock. Some beginnings are the work of the dark side of Hades—the reign of the Roman Emperor Theodosius I, who massacred pagans, the first ship bringing enslaved peoples to the shores of Virginia, and most recently the discovery of fossil fuels, dynamite, and the beginning of the Robber Baron dynasties.

---

2. *Ibid.*
3. From "All You Need is Love" Lennon-McCartney.
4. Charles Murray, *Human Accomplishment: The Pursuit of Excellence in the Arts and Sciences, 800 BC to 1950,* 209.

Table 3: Major Events at VISION *time of Pluto at 0° Decl. South to North using an orb of 1°*

DATES	EVENTS
Apr. 1809 BCE, Oct. 1809 BCE, Jan. 1808 BCE Apr. 1811 BCE– Mar. 1807 BCE	• This is the possible time of Abraham and the believed time of the scribing of the Rig Veda (c. 2000–1500 BCE),[5] India.[6] Civilization in India moved from the dried-up Saraswati to the Ganges.[7] • Shang Dynasty began (c. 1800 BCE), China. • Hyksos, a people from north of Palestine, invaded Egypt (c. 1800 BCE).[8]
Apr. 1565 BCE, Sep. 1565 BCE, Feb. 1564 BCE, Apr. 1567 BCE– Jan. 1562 BCE	• The 18th Dynasty in Egypt, the *New Kingdom*, started in 1567 BCE with Pharoah Ahmose.
May 1321 BCE, Sep. 1321 BCE, Mar. 1320 BCE May 1323 BCE– Feb. 1318 BCE	• Ay (r. 1323–1319 BCE), Pharoah of Egypt, for only and almost exactly the Vision time, tore down the religion of Akhenaten and rebuilt Egypt into a military might.

---

5. Georg Feuerstein, *The Essence Of Yoga*, 105.
6. "This is one value of the Vedas to us, that through them we see religion in the making, and can follow the birth, growth and death of gods and beliefs from animism to philosophic pantheism, and from the superstition of the Atharva-veda to the sublime monism of the Upanishads." (Will and Ariel Durant, *Our Oriental Heritage*, 403.)
7. There are several theories about what happened around 1800 BCE in India. What is known is that the Saraswati River dried up, and mass migration to the banks of the Ganges ensued. Climate change is the likely culprit, but other theories include a massive earthquake or invading northerners. "In about 1750 BC[E], town life on the Indus River ended. River mud then buried the remnants of the towns so deeply that historians knew nothing of the Indus people till the 1900s, when archaeologists found the ruins." Found in, James C. Davis, *The Human Story*, 108.
8. The Hyksos were fully in power by 1720 BCE, just at the end of the POWER time. From 1720–1550 BCE, the Hyksos ruled Egypt. As this cycle ends, so does the Hyksos joy ride of the pyramids. This is an early example of what we will see repeated many times over in the rise and fall of empires, precisely coinciding with the Pluto cycle.

Jun. 1077 BCE, Jul. 1077 BCE, Mar. 1076 BCE, Oct. 1076 BCE, Jan. 1075 BCE Jan. 1077 BCE– Mar. 1074 BCE	• The last king of the 20th Dynasty of Egypt, Ramses XI, died (1068 BCE) and the 21st Dynasty of Egypt under the leadership of Smendes I began (1077–1052 BCE). • Zhou Dynasty (1046–256 BCE) under the leadership of King Wen (r. 1100–1050 BCE) began its takeover of the Shang Dynasty. The Mandate of Heaven, giving kings a divine right to rule, began with Wen and the Zhou Dynasty in China. • Samuel, the Seer, Hebrew Bible, had a vision and shared it with the elder Eli. According to bible dates, Samuel would have been about 11 years old at this time, just about the time the young lad was impressing the elder Eli.
Apr. 832 BCE, Sep. 832 BCE, Feb. 831 BCE, Apr. 834 BCE– Feb. 829 BCE	• The Spartan leader, Lycurgus, visited the Delphic Oracle and returned to create the Great Rhetra, a code of conduct not written down as law, but instituted as a way of life, circa 820 BCE.[9] • The Black Obelisk was erected in Assyria. • China moved into a dark age.[10] • Around this time, Greece emerged from a dark age (c. 1100–800 BCE) of drought and depopulation.[11]

---

9. There is some debate was to whether Lycurgus actually lived or is a legend. In either case, this VISION time is the beginning of the Great Rhetra. The Great Rhetra had several main components. Two kings ruled, side by side. Land was divided into 30,000 plots to be farmed by serfs, an early communistic ideal that in practice maintained a caste system where the poor stayed poor and the rich stayed rich. A system of preparation for war was instituted. Boys were sent off to be trained at a young age as warriors, men were expected to continue their training and always be available for war. Even girls and women were expected to do some battle training.

10. On the other side of Assyria, China was moving into a dark age. The nomadic tribes, the Quanrong, overran the largest city, Haojing, and took over the Zhou Dynasty. Instead of being a coalesced force and moving into a new dynasty, China fell into a collection of feudal states for the next five hundred years.

11. C. 800 BCE, people in Greece started planting grapes and olives and other plants that could thrive in arid and warm climate. Life in Greece began to return. A collection of city-states, including Sparta, Athens, Thebes, and Macedon, grew in prosperity and intellect.

Jun. 588 BCE, Aug. 588 BCE, Mar. 587 BCE, Oct .587 BCE, Jan. 586 BCE Jun. 590 BCE– Mar. 585 BCE	• In 585 BCE, the Ionian philosopher, Thales, accurately predicted an eclipse, a bold leap forward in the field of astronomy. Within his lifetime Thales arrived at his version of the scientific method, advanced geometry, and mathematics, and was the first person to ask, "What is the world made of?" not from a mythical, religious perspective but from a physical, scientific perspective. He is often referred to as the "father of science. • c. 594 BCE the leader of Greece, Solon, created new laws for Athens, known as Solon's Reforms, and initiated a new age in Greece.[12] • Sappho wrote poetry around this time.
May 343 BCE, Sep. 343 BCE, Mar. 342 BCE Apr. 345 BCE– May 341 BCE	• Aristotle taught Alexander the Great, logic, strategy, and philosophy. King Philip of Macedonia hired the greatest teacher he could find for his teenage son, Alexander. Philip had developed his army and expanded his kingdom along the Adriatic. He was ambitions without being ruthless. He was a master tactician and an inspiration to his troops. • Chanakya (375–283 BCE) instructed Chandragupta (r. c. 324–c. 297 BCE)—often credited with writing *Arthashastra*, one of the first books on political science and economics. Chandragupta later founded the Mauryan Empire, that covered much of India, in part due to Alexander the Great's incursions. • In China, the philosopher Zhuang Zhou wrote *Zhuangzi* (also written *Chuang-tze),* a foundational work on Taoism.[13]

12. Solon's Reforms are a turning point in Greek history. Solon, King of Greece, was a visionary. His reforms including canceling farmers' debts, leveling out the justice system so that laws applied to all people equally and un-leveling the tax system so that the wealthy paid more. The Senate was elected by land-owning citizens and the heliaea (congress) was elected by all citizens. "All these laws and their punishments Solon made known by having them written in public places for all to see. He made the government promise to obey his laws for 10 years, then embarked on a tour of Egypt and Asia. The government kept its promise." From: http://www.socialstudiesforkids.com/articles/worldhistory/lycurgussolon.htm

13. His back-to-nature philosophy preceded Thoreau and Emerson, who also lived during a VISION time. His theories of evolution are compared favorably to Darwin, also active during a VISION time. (Durant & Durant, 691.) "Zhuangzi's basic claim is that what we take to be facts are only facts in relation to our distorted view of the world, and what we take to be good or bad things only appear to have positive and negative value because our mistaken beliefs lead us into arbitrary prejudices. The dynamic operation of the world-system as a whole is the Dao." From *Zhuangzi: The Inner Chapters*, translated by Robert Eno.

Apr. 98 BCE, Oct. 98 BCE, Feb. 97 BCE, Apr. 100 BCE– Feb. 95 BCE	• A new day dawned in the Roman Republic when the Roman senate banned human sacrifices in 97 BCE. Local uprisings, high taxes, and a growing slave class had caused enough of a threat to the security of fearful free citizens. • The future Senator Cicero (106–43 BCE) studied with Philo of Larissa. Around this time, Cicero was initiated into the Eleusinian Mysteries.[14]
Jun. 147, Jul 147, Mar. 148, Oct. 148, Feb. 149 Jan. 147– Feb. 151	• Claudius Ptolemy (c.100–c. 170 CE) wrote *Almagest,* an astronomy text used for centuries. • Justin Martyr (100–165 CE), a Christian saint, united Greek philosophy with the Christian faith. • Marcus Aurelius studied with Apollonius. (Several years later he wrote his classic work, *Meditations,* 160–170 CE). Marcus Aurelius was initiated into the Eleusinian Mysteries.[15] • Nāgārjuna (c. 150–250 CE, India), just born at this time, went on to write texts on Buddhism and found Mahayana Buddhism.
May 392, Aug. 392, Mar. 393, Oct. 393, Jan. 394 Apr. 390– Apr. 395	• Augustine of Hippo wrote *Confessions* between 397–400 CE after having an awakening experience when his mother died in 387 CE. • The scientist, Hypatia, taught in Alexandria, Egypt before she was executed in 415 CE. • In 395 CE, the Roman Empire split in two, the West governed from Ravenna in Northern Italy and the East governed from Constantinople. • Kalidasa, considered to be the greatest Indian poet to have ever lived, wrote during this time.

---

14. Brian Muraresku, *The Immortality Key,* 71.
15. *Ibid.*

| May 637, Aug. 637, Mar. 638, Nov. 638, Jan. 639 Apr. 635– Apr. 640 | • The prophet Muhammad died in 632 CE, Abū Bakr, Muhammad's close friend, stepped into a leadership position of the newly formed Rashidan Caliphate, the first Islamic caliphate. The Rashidan Caliphate gave way to the Ummayad Caliphate (second Islamic caliphate) that followed the lineage of Alī ibn Abī Tālib, Muhammad's son-in-law (who was married to Muhammad's daughter, Fatima, who died the same year as Muhammad). The Sunni-Shia split in Islam can be traced back to this time, with Sunni Muslims following Abū Bakr and Shia Muslims believing Alī to be the true successor. In 634 CE, Abū Bakr died and Umar (Omar) ibn al-Khattab (r. 634–44), became Caliph. Umar began a series of military campaigns to gain farmable land, a rare commodity in the deserts of Arabia. During this period, the Arabs forced the Romans to retreat from Syria (636), defeated the Persian army (637), conquered Egypt (641), and took over Jerusalem (637).[16] In 638, Umar issued a charter that left the Christian shrines undisturbed and cleared the rubble of the ruined Jewish Temple (destroyed in 70 CE). Upon that site, he contracted Haram al-Sharif, the "Most Noble Sanctuary,"[17] which was to become the third most holy site for Muslims (after Mecca and Medina). Even though he was coopting the site of the temple, he invited the Jews back into Jerusalem, a place they had been barred from since the Bar Kobha revolt.[18] |

16. The surrender of Jerusalem to the Arabian caliphate anchors Islam as the predominant religion for the next three Pluto cycles.

17. Karen Armstrong, *Fields of Blood*, 188.

18. The Bar Kokbha revolt of 132–136 CE destroyed organized Judaism and the Temple in Jerusalem, and expelled all Jews from Jerusalem, save for one visit per year. This forced the Jewish community to Tiberias and created a new center of organized Judaism. "Tiberias became the center of Jewish life and the spiritual capital for Palestine, also of the Diaspora following the mass Jewish emigration from Judea to Galilee." (Judith Bronstein, "Zionism, Medieval Culture, and National Discourse," 123). Coinciding with a rise in support for the new Christian churches, this revolt began a millennium of banishment from Jerusalem for followers of Yahweh.

May 882, Aug. 882, Mar. 883, Nov. 883, Jan. 884 Apr. 880– Apr. 885	• While Alfred the Great was fighting off the Vikings on the British Isle. Abū ʿAbd Allāh Muḥammad ibn Jābir ibn Sinān al-Raqqī al-Ḥarrānī aṣ-Ṣābiʾ al-Battānī (c. 858–929 CE), known as Al-Battānī or Albategnius, was an astronomer, considered by astronomers as the Ptolemy of the Arabs, whose seminal work in trigonometry is quoted in Copernicus' work.[19] We can give thanks to Al-Battānī for the trig tables that we had to rewrite as sophomores in high school. He is the one who invented sine and cosine—derivatives of Hipparchus' chords. While he lived a long life, it is during the VISION time that he began compiling his tables and writing his *Opus Astronomicum*. In this work, al-Battānī supports and extolls upon Ptolemy's *Almagest*, written at the VISION time three cycles earlier.[20] The polymath, Abū Yūsuf Yaʿqūb ibn ʾIsḥāq aṣ-Ṣabbāḥ al-Kindī, Al-Kindi for short (c. 801–873 CE) introduced Indian numerals to the Arabic world in Baghdad. • Thabit ibn Qurra (826–901) founded the field of statics, developing engineering mechanics, and understanding physical systems.[21] • Abū Bakr Muḥammad ibn Zakariyyāʾ al-Rāzī, al-Razi for short (c. 854–925/935 CE), Persia (Iran) wrote foundational works in the field of medicine, discovered sulfuric acid and derived treatments for smallpox. Sometime near the VISION time, al-Razi had a visitor from China, a brilliant physician who quickly learned Arabic and translated Galen from Arabic to Chinese.[22] There is strong evidence for the exchange of knowledge and goods between the Abbasid Caliphate and the Tang Dynasty.[23] • Abu Zayd al-Balkhi (850–934) was one of the first cognitive psychologists. He connected mental, spiritual, and physical health and one of the first to talk about diseases of the soul.

19. Peter Barlow, et al., *The Encyclopaedia of Astronomy*, 494.
20. Giorgio Abetti, *The History of Astronomy*.
21. Muzaffar K. Awan, "The Paradox of Hidden Human History," 30–33.
22. Alain George, "Direct Sea Trade Between Early Islamic Iraq and Tang China," 579–624.
23. *Ibid.*

May 1127, Aug. 1127, Mar. 1128, Oct. 1128, Jan. 1129 Apr. 1125– Apr. 1130	• In 1126, philosopher Peter Abelard (1079–1142) translated Muhammad ibn Mūsā al-Khwārizmī's works on algebra into Latin, helping usher in the Islam renaissance to Europe. In 1128, Bernard of Clairvaux (1090–1153) wrote *In Praise of the New Knighthood*, introducing chivalry to Europe. In 1129, he attended the Council of Troyes (1129) that sanctioned the Knights Templar in the Roman Catholic Church. Hildegard von Bingen (c. 1098–1179) was having visions and writing music.
May 1372, Aug. 1372, Mar. 1373, Oct. 1373, Feb. 1374 Apr. 1370– Mar. 1376	• Francesco Petrarca wrote his autobiography at the end of his life and died in 1374. Giovanni Boccaccio revised his earlier work, *The Decameron* (1371). John Wycliffe sewed seeds for the Reformation, while his student, Geoffrey Chaucer, went on holiday to Florence (1373). Catherine of Siena visited the pope in an attempt to heal the schism in the Roman Catholic Church (1376).
May 1617, Aug. 1617, Mar. 1618, Oct. 1618, Feb. 1619 Mar. 1616– Mar. 1621	• Francis Bacon wrote *Novum Organum* (1620). Johannes Kepler discovered the Third Law of Planetary Motion (1618). Galileo Galilei defended Copernicus. René Descartes worked on analytic geometry. Puritans landed at Plymouth Rock (1620). The first ship carrying enslaved people from Africa arrived in the Americas in 1619, in Jamestown, the colony supported by Francis Bacon. The Romanov Dynasty took control in Russia in 1613.
May 1862, Aug. 1862, Oct. 1863 Mar. 1861– May 1865	• Charles Darwin published *On the Origin of Species* (1859). Abraham Lincoln signed the Emancipation Proclamation in Jan. 1863 and in Nov. delivered the Gettysburg Address. In Oct. 1863, sixteen countries met in Geneva and formed the International Red Cross. In Dec. of 1864, Scottish scientist James Clerk Maxwell presented his paper, *A Dynamical Theory of the Electromagnetic Field*, the root of all technology today. Louis Pasteur discovered bacteria and invented pasteurization in 1863, and Joseph Lister invented antiseptic surgery in 1865. Karl Marx wrote *Das Kapital* (1867). Ramakrishna had an awakening along the Ganges River in India. Bahá'u'lláh had a vision in a garden in Baghdad that led to the creation of the Bahá'í Faith. H. P. Blavatsky fell off a horse in Russia (mid 1860s) and had an awakening. • The US Homestead Act of 1862 (May 20, 1862) offered 160 acres of land for a small filing fee to any head of household willing to farm the land. Promises vyed with perils as the tidal wave of settlers caused wide-scale harm to indiginous populations.

Kore Is Born. Hades Becomes Ruler of the Underworld.

This stage in Pluto's declination journey corresponds to the outset of Persephone's journey. Demeter gives birth to Kore. It is the birth of a goddess of the people. She represents innocence lost and a true desire to help others, to alleviate suffering, and to look death squarely in the face without fear. She represents the journey of the "Everyman," as James Joyce puts it. She is the goddess that goes through the dark night of the soul and arrives empowered, the journey that every human must take in one form or another.

When Pluto crosses the equatorial plane from south to north, inspired individuals share a new vision with the world, like an innocent Persephone, the idea is fresh and harmless. Often, the idea comes through the minds of philosophers, scientists, healers, and spiritual seekers who only want the best for the world. They may have started a religion, new philosophy, a new science, or even science itself. The beginning is not always obvious until hindsight brings it 20-20. People living during the time of the prophet Muhammad may not have realized that centuries later it would become one of the world's largest religions. It is unlikely that the followers of Aristotle thought that logic would overtake the world, or that Thales himself ever thought he would be considered the father of science.

In several important cases, a privileged pupil gained access to this new knowledge and used it to attain power, as in the case of Alexander the Great who used the wisdom of Aristotle for battle strategy, or in the case of Saul who took the visions of Samuel to fight for a Jewish homeland, or in the case of Umar, the prophet Muhammad's close disciple and second Caliph of the Rashidun Caliphate, who accelerated the geographic conquests on the Arabic peninsula and northern Africa that would culminate in the extensive reach of Ummayad Caliphate. Those who study from the masters spread the knowledge—sometimes for many years, even whole generations—but it isn't until the REFORM time, three cycles later, that the multitudes, the people, the mass consciousness, accepts this new thinking, for good or bad. It isn't until the REFORM time that it becomes a way of life, as in the case of John Wycliffe's teachings of reforming the Catholic Church during VISION that led to the Reformation over one hundred years later. This is Persephone being born—the very beginning of a paradigm shift. This is Hades taking over the underworld—the very beginning of a dynasty.

In the Pluto declination cycle, it is the beginning of a new paradigm, a new thought, a new way of being. It is not fully formed—it is still an idea. Michael Faraday, a self-taught scientist, had ideas about electricity and magnetism that he shared with his student, James Clerk Maxwell. Maxwell turned these ideas into useful equations during the beginning of this current cycle. Aristotle had the idea of logic. Al-Battānī came up with sines and cosines. Without knowing what their vision, their idea, their new thought would lead to, the idea spread—first to the wealthy, the educated, the privileged. Aristotle taught his students, including Alexander the Great. Maxwell wrote a paper for other scientists. John Wycliffe taught Chaucer and other privileged students at the University of Oxford.

With students and followers, the new thought spreads to leaders and influencers. Maxwell's equations were used by Einstein and his followers who made the atomic bomb. Aristotle's teachings spread throughout the kingdoms left behind by Alexander and were ensconced in the Library of Alexandria. It was a vision at the beginning, became a power play at POW-ER and by REFORM, an accepted truth known to even the less-privileged, less-educated, and less-wealthy commoners. What John Wycliffe taught Chaucer became the Reformation. What Aristotle taught Alexander became logic itself. What Maxwell inspired in Einstein and Nikola Tesla became… *still to be determined.*

Another beginning in this myth is the beginning of Hades' reign of the underworld—the old ribbon-cutting ceremony—the passing of the keys to the kingdom. This is the beginning of Hades' rule over the dead. During the VISION time, not only are Persephone figures born through new ideas and awakenings, but it also marks the beginning of dynasties, new kingdoms, and a new guard. It is the beginning of the 18th Egyptian Dynasty, the Tang Dynasty, the Romanov Dynasty and more recently, the rule of the "Robber Barons." Civil wars fought over dominions are common, as intrepid individuals dare to upset the status quo out of a desire for power or wealth or both. Sometimes the new perspective, seeping into reality, creates a split—and that split eventually leads to war.

JUSTICE

Pluto at 0° of Declination

Moving from North to South

After the visionaries at the VISION time offer new ideas, and after tyrants have whipped the masses into fear-based control during POWER, Pluto crosses the equatorial plane, north to south, and changes the conversation. During this third stage, a series of events unfold. First, **a leader dies.** This leader is usually someone that has created a sense of security, the kind of security that accompanies loss of freedom but placates most people into submission. As was the case with Augustus Caesar, Ashoka Maurya, and Leonid Brezhnev. When these leaders die, their mortal absence creates **a power vacuum.** A cavern in the world of Hades opens—and it leaves an opportunity for all kinds of upheaval, **crisis,** reactions, underground organizations, intercessions, and interventions. Amidst the crisis, breakthroughs in art, music, and literature accompany a renaissance of reactive and activist thought. The cycle reaches a turning point.

The underlying movement of this time is a *cry* for JUSTICE. Tired of corruption and tyranny, waking up to the possibility of a new world, activists shout from the mountaintops to shake the subdued masses awake. Usually, these activists are killed, the rebellions quashed, and the coups unsuccessful. However, it is the shaking ground that begins the march toward REFORM. It is the crisis that reveals a larger change is needed.

Oftentimes, the reaction is one that tears at the fabric of the empire, and the cohesion that tyranny offers begins to erode. It is a time that correlates with the beginning of the decline of empires.

Take a look at the following table, and then we will see how each time has unfolded in its own unique way, but with a similar theme of a cry for JUSTICE, with a similar kind of upheaval. For years, I have felt uncomfortable with the word *justice*. Sometimes it is used to justify revenge. Sometimes it lacks nuance or compassion. And rarely if ever has a true time of justice existed in history. People have always enslaved other people. People have always been oppressed, wrongly convicted, and so on. Cultures have always been dismissed, bad laws issued, corrupt politicians corrupting, and misguided judges judging. Prisons have always been filled with people whose sole crime was simply to speak the truth. People have always been born into poverty without any avenue for obtaining wealth, success, or even comfort. This JUSTICE time is not a time of justice served, or justice achieved. It is a time when the *cries for justice* begin to be heard. It is a time when the masses *awaken* to the conditions of oppression surrounding their existence and begin to see a way out.

Table 4: Major Events at JUSTICE time of Pluto at 0° Decl. North to South using an orb of 1°

DATES	EVENTS
Sep. 1462 BCE– Jul. 1461 BCE Nov. 1462 BCE, Mar. 1461 BCE, Aug. 1461 BCE	• Hatshepsut died in 1458 BCE after being sole ruler for 21 years. • Thutmose III, her son, took over. While Thutmose was known as a great warrior who invaded Assyria, evidence of the destruction of Hatshepsut's statues suggests a time of unrest and upheaval.
Oct. 1217 BCE–Sep. 1215 BCE Oct. 1216 BCE, May 1215 BCE, Jul. 1215 BCE	• The king of the Hittites, Tudhaliya IV, died in 1209. The Egyptian Pharoah, Ramses II, died in 1213 BCE. Their deaths are often cited as the beginning of the decline of both empires.
Oct. 971 BCE– Aug. 969 BCE Sep. 970 BCE	• King David died around 970 BCE. His son, Solomon, became ruler of Judea in a peaceful transfer of power between kings. • King Zhao (r. 977–957 BCE) of the Zhou Dynasty in China lost a battle in the Yangtze basin (957 BCE), that initiated the decline of the Zhou Dynasty (1046–771 BCE).
Sep. 725 BCE– Aug. 723 BCE Dec. 725 BCE, Feb. 724 BCE, Sep. 724 BCE	• Tiglath-Pilesar III (r. 745–727 BCE), the King of Assyria who nearly doubled its size, died. His son, Shalmaneser V, (r. 727–722 BCE), a weaker leader, took over and was deposed five years later. He oversaw a time of crisis that included attacking Israel and deporting the Israelites, setting the stage for future unrest.[24]

---

24. In 722 BCE, the northern kingdom of Israel was destroyed and most of the Jews dispersed into exile. During JUSTICE times, there is a turning over of power, a discovery, or destruction that upends the current state. This destruction leads to a time of awakening—a call for revolution or reform.

Sep. 479 BCE– Aug. 477 BCE Nov. 479 BCE, Feb. 478 BCE, Aug. 478 BCE	• Both Confucius and Gautama Buddha died, during this time, leaving behind teachings on justice that continue to influence humanity. • After decades of war between Persia and Greece, the Greek states formed an alliance, the Delian League in 478 BCE, a pact that protected Ionia from Persian invasion, a turning point as the empires of Persia and Assyria moved into decline, and Greece began its rise into an epicenter for advancements in science, art, and philosophy.
Sep. 233 BCE– Aug. 231 BCE Nov. 233 BCE, Feb. 232 BCE, Aug. 232 BCE	• Ashoka Maurya, the third and most famous of the kings of the Mauryan Empire (322–184 BCE, India), died in 232 BCE. His grandsons, weaker leaders who fought each other, took over and the empire moved into slow decline. Invaders began to overrun what is today most of India. Fracturing into different kingdoms, the ending of the Mauryan empire spawned a time of religious and devotional development in many parts of India. • In China, the Zhou Dynasty, in power for over 700 years, fell in 256 BCE. An unstable time followed until the Qin Dynasty took over eleven years later in 221 BCE.
Sep. 14 CE– Aug. 16 CE Dec. 14 CE, Jan. 15 CE, Sep. 15 CE	• Augustus Caesar died in 14 CE and his stepson, Tiberius, a weaker ruler, became emperor of Rome. This set the stage for the decline of the Roman Empire and for reactionaries and activists, including Jesus, who was potentially in his early teens at the time.[25]
Oct. 260 CE– Sep. 262 CE Oct. 261 CE, May 262 CE, Jul. 262 CE	• Ardashir I (r. 211-224) founded the Sassanid Empire in the land of Persia (Iran), leaving it to his son, Shapur I (r. 240–270). During the later years of Shapur's reign, the radical mystic Mani (216–274/277 CE), founder of Manichaeism, spoke out against injustice. He and his followers, much like Jesus and his followers during the prior JUSTICE time, were imprisoned and killed. • In the decaying Roman Empire, when Christians were being persecuted and the Temple of Artemis was destroyed by Goths (262 CE), Plotinus (c. 204/5–270 CE), a metaphysical, Hellenistic philosopher, advocated for a new society based on the teachings of Plato.[26]

25. From the Bible of Luke 2:41-52, Jesus, twelve years old at the time, disobeyed his parents and stayed in the temple listening to the religious teachers.
26. Herman, 143.

Nov. 506 CE– Aug. 509 CE Nov. 507 CE, Mar. 508 CE, Aug. 508 CE	• In the Roman Empire, recently conquered by the Visigoths, King Alaric brought together jurists, priests, and nobles to collect a compendium of Roman law, called the Breviary of Alaric (506 CE), a revision of the Roman justice system. • Around 504 BCE, Anicius Manlius Severinus Boethius wrote a new theory of music. An outspoken critic of the corruption of the Roman government, he was imprisoned and executed for conspiracy in 524. • In India, Aryabhata (476–550 CE) wrote the classic work, *Aryabhatiya* (c. 510 CE), an astronomical and mathematical text that calculated Pi, described eclipses accurately and inspired the Arabic numeral system to come (three hundred years later).
Oct. 753 CE– Sep. 755 CE Sep. 754 CE, Jun. 755 CE.	• The English missionary and Benedictine monk, Boniface (c. 672–754 CE), dedicated his life to converting the people of Germania to Christianity. At the time, the lands along the Rhine were loosely part of the Frankish empire recently conquered by Charles Martel and his sons. Boniface set out to unify the lands with Christianity being the glue. He was killed by Frisian (northern Dutch) pagans in 754 CE, possibly for political reasons. • In 1751, at the Battle of Talas, the Tang Dynasty lost ground to the Abbasid Caliphate, who then overthrew the Umayyads leading to the reign of al-Mansur (r. 754–755) who stepped into power with the backing of the Persians and claimed the throne as a descendent of Muhammad's uncle, Abbas. At the end of this JUSTICE time, the tired Tang Emperor Xuanzong (r. 712–756) lost his grip on the empire when the General An Lushan coalesced a large army and attacked his own country. The ensuing war included blockades during a draught and led to over 10 million deaths from famine and war. The emperor did not die but he took his eye off the ball in a time of grief over losing his favorite concubine. While An Lushan's rebellion was not successful, his army destroyed much of the infrastructure of a country in a golden age and initiated the decline of the Tang Dynasty. • In China, during the waning years of the Tang Dynasty, two of the greatest poets in history lived—Li Po (701–762) and Du Fu (712–770).[27]

27. Poets Du Fu (712–770) and Li Po (701–762) were born during POWER and did their greatest work

Sep. 1000 CE– Aug. 1002 CE	• The noblewoman Murasaki Shikibu wrote the world's first novel, *Tale of Genji*, circa 1000 CE in Japan.
Nov. 1000 CE, Mar. 1001 CE, Aug. 1001 CE	• The Persian poet Abul-Qâsemm Ferdowsi Tusi wrote *Shanameh: The Persian Book of Kings* c. 977–1010 CE, in Iran. • The Old English epic *Beowulf* appears. • ibn al-Haytham (c. 965–c. 1040), scientist, published *Book of Optics* (c. 1011–1021). His contributions to science included understanding refraction and reflection through his studies of light, founding the field of optics and the scientific method. • In 1001 CE, Leif Ericson led a contingency of Vikings across the Atlantic and set up camp along the northern coast of North America.
Mar. 1247 CE– Jul. 1249 CE Oct. 1247 CE, Apr. 1248 CE, Jul. 1248 CE	• In 1252, Pope Innocent IV issued the papal bull, *Ad extirpanda*, that exonerated the use of torture in cases of perceived heresy, thus creating the document that would be used to torture and execute thousands of innocent people. His idea of justice, abhorrent to most of us today, was validated by the powers bestowed into the papacy during the time of Innocent III, who lived during the previous POWER time. • 1246: Robert Grosseteste translated Aristotle and developed a modern scientific method. • 1246: Güyük Khan, Mongol emperor, visited Arabia and brought scientific advancement back to China. He died in 1248 and a power vacuum existed for three years until Mongke Khan took over in 1251. • 1247: Inventor and politician Qin Jiushao published the original form of the Chinese remainder theorem. • 1247: Jala Uddin Rumi's teacher disappeared prompting Rumi to write 30,000 verses of poetry. • 1248: Roger Bacon published a formula for gun powder. • 1248: Thomas Aquinas began his work as a scholar and teacher, writing his first works during this time.

around the JUSTICE time, the same period in the Pluto cycle that: Michelangelo and Da Vinci painted (700 years later), Bach and Handel inspired baroque music (850 years later); and Rumi and Rabia were active. In the next cycle, around the JUSTICE time, *Beowulf, Shanameh,* and *The Tale of Genji* will be written.

Sep. 1493– Sep. 1495 Sep. 1494, May 1495, Jun. 1495	• 1492 was a significant turning point in history for more than the Columbus voyage. In April of 1492, Lorenzo de Medici died, leaving Florence in the hands of his son, a weaker leader. Three months after Lorenzo died, in July, Pope Innocent VIII died. The papal enclave elected Rodrigo Borgia to be the next pope, Pope Alexander VI. Savonarola (r. 1494–1498), riled up the people of Florence against corruption in the Catholic Church. • On June 7, 1494, Pope Alexander VI signed the Treaty of Tordesillas, that divided the newly invaded Americas, giving what is today Brazil to the Portuguese and the rest to Spain. This time of upheaval in Italy and Spain spread like a virus to the Aztec and Incan Empires whose leadership was also changing. • Meanwhile, Leonardo da Vinci painted *The Last Supper* (1494–1498) in Milan, Michelangelo sculpted in Bologna, Sandro Botticelli painted *The Calumny of Apelles* (c. 1495), and Raphael cleaned his father's brushes in Urbino. • The governments of both Spain (1492) and Russia (Sudebnik of 1497) expelled the Jewish people from these countries. Many found refuge in the Ottoman Empire.[28]
Sep. 1740– Sep. 1742 Nov. 1740, Feb. 1741, Sep. 1741	• The early 1740s were a turning point in the British colonies in America. The burgeoning city of Manhattan, originally settled by the Dutch at the beginning of this cycle and now overtaken by British colonists, was becoming a hub: Where once stood a wall separating Dutch and British colonists, now was Wall Street where enslaved African hostages were traded as day laborers. In 1741, a series of mysterious fires broke out all over the city— homes of prominent New Yorkers and public builders burned to the ground. With almost no evidence, the city put Black people on trial and sentenced them to death—medieval tortures were resurrected and 16 Blacks and 4 whites were burned at the stake. This eruption of fear and violence initiated a time of upheaval and unrest on the island. • 10,000 enslaved native Chinese people in Batavia, Indonesia rose up against the East India Company only to be slaughtered. • The Jacobite rebellions in Scotland were quashed by the British army (final battle, the Battle of Culloden, 1746). Britain and Spain were at war (War of Jenkins' Ear).

28. Horace Dewey, "The 1497 Sudebnik-Muscovite Russia's First National Law Code," 325–38.

Con't from prev. page: Sep. 1740– Sep. 1742 Nov. 1740, Feb. 1741, Sep. 1741	• A commanding orator and future president of the College of New Jersey (Princeton University), Jonathan Edwards, inspired the *Great Awakening* with his fire and brimstone sermons. This in turn inspired a fervor for freedom of religion. Samuel Adams became interested in politics and Benjamin Franklin started the first police department, the first volunteer fire brigades, a scientific organization, and wrote *Poor Richard's Almanack*. • In 1741, George Frideric Handel composed *The Messiah*. That same year in Vienna, Antonio Vivaldi died, and 9-year-old Franz Joseph Hayden joined the St. Stephen's Choir. Meanwhile in Germany, Johann Sebastian Bach, now in his late 50s, wrote *The Art of the Fugue*. • In 1740, the pope died, Emperor Charles VI, ruler of the Holy Roman Empire (Germany) died, leading to the Austrian War of Succession. Also, in 1740, the Russian monarch died leading to a military-supported coup that installed Empress Elisabeth to the throne. The king of Prussia died, and his son took over.
Oct. 1986– Sep. 1989 Nov. 1987, Feb. 1988, Sep. 1988	• Soviet Union fell in 1991 after policies *glasnost* and *perestroika* opened the country to foreign intervention. Berlin Wall comes down in 1989. Peaceful revolutions in the eastern parts of the Soviet Union, including the Velvet Revolution in Czechoslovakia and Singing Revolution in Estonia lead to independent nations. • Underground organizations formed in reaction to empire overreach include Hezbollah, Hamas, and Al-Qaeda. • Nov 18, 1987: Iran-Contra Affair—US Senate and House charge President Ronald Reagan with responsibility for the affair. • Oct. 19, 1987: Black Monday—Stock market drops sharply. • Afghan-Soviet War: 1979–Feb 1989. • Sep 11, 1988: Singing Revolution—Estonian Soviet Socialist Republic—300,000 people sing the Estonian national anthem to express support for independence.

Demeter Grieves, Protests, and Begs for Intervention.
Persephone Fasts. Hades Loses his Grip.

During this part of the Pluto cycle, Demeter discovers that Persephone is in the Underworld and begs Zeus to intervene and bring their daughter back. She exerts her power in whatever way she can. She allows all the plants to die and threatens eternal winter in what may be considered the first successful boycott. Demeter's grief incites change. It is a cry to be reunited with her daughter and a cry for justice. Zeus is forced to listen.

Something happened to Hades during this time. He didn't just go from all-powerful ruler of the dead to some guy who gives up easily. Perhaps Persephone's compassion healed some wounded part of him (his father treated him terribly), or his loneliness got the better of him, or his obsession with Persephone blinded him, or he really just couldn't go up against Zeus. In any of these cases, Hades is no longer in power. He loses his grip. This mirrors this time in history when powerful rulers die, and kingdoms move into decline—making them ripe for intervention.

Leaders who died and left power vacuums include: Ramses the Great, King David of Judea, Tiglath-Pileser III, Ashoka Maurya, and Augustus Caesar. Other political tides that turned include the end of the Umayyad Caliphate and the beginning of the Sunni-based Abbasid Caliphate, the decline of the Hittites, the Mauryan Empire, a change in tide of the Roman Empire, and the creation of Delian League in Ancient Greece and the Hanseatic League in Germany, leagues that supported cooperation among city-states in the Delian League and among merchants in the Hanseatic League.

The interventions of this time can look like reactionaries crying for justice, like Boethius railing against corruption in the Roman Empire, and Savonarola railing against corruption in the Church that decades later inspired Martin Luther and the Reformation, or Samuel Adams and Jonathan Edwards who set the stage for the upcoming successful rebellion in the colonies, or spiritual activists like Buddha, Confucius, Jesus, Mani, Benedict, Boniface, and Aquinas. The interventions can also appear as times of great creativity—poets Du Fu, Li Po, Rumi, writers Shikibu, Tusi, Voltaire, the Italian Renaissance artists da Vinci, Michelangelo, and Botticelli, and then one Pluto cycle later, the great Classical composers Bach and Handel.

The JUSTICE times reveal the cracks in civilization and open a door for a change that begins at this time but is not successful until the REFORM time. The activists often lose or die, rebellions quashed, and interjections of foreign powers into new lands wind up being difficult at REFORM for both parties. Columbus may have landed in the New World during the JUSTICE time, but the Spanish invasions under the leaders Hernán Cortés (1519–1520) and Francisco Pizarro (1532) leading into the REFORM time never actually benefited the Spanish who went into decline and bankruptcy as the cycle was ending. Leif Ericson may have also landed in the New World during a JUSTICE time, only to return without leaving a trace. Meanwhile, the Spanish Inquisition launched a few years before the JUSTICE time in 1478, moved into full swing when Ferdinand and Isabella, the ruling monarchs of Spain, expelled the Jewish people from Spain in 1492 and the Moors from Granada that same year. The inquisitions gave rise to the Reformation and the radicals that instigated uprisings against the Catholic Church.

In our current cycle, the USSR broke up into fifteen different countries after Leonid Brezhnev died (1982), and the following two Soviet heads of state died within the next three years. Mikhail Gorbachev stepped into power in 1985 with some radical ideas of opening the doors of the closed-off nation. The economic crisis in the Soviet Union, along with mass demonstrations, losing the Afghan-Soviet war, and a severe drop in oil prices and profits after Saudi leaders upscaled production led to upheaval and crisis in the empire that Stalin had brought into power during the POWER time. The Soviet Union is a classic example of a Hades-ruled dominion. During POWER, Josef Stalin abducted, tortured, and killed many of its citizens. During JUSTICE, outside intervention in the form of Saudi oil production, US intervention in Afghanistan, and massive demonstrations within, led to a great fall, a turning point in the history of Russia.

Table 5: Leaders during All Four Stages during the Last 16 Pluto Cycles

0° DECLINATION S TO N: VISION	EXTREME DECL. NORTH: POWER	0°DECLINATION N TO S: JUSTICE	EXTREME DECL. SOUTH: REFORM
Abraham	Hammurabi	Samsu-iluna, Hammurabi's son and king of Babylon died.	Ammi-Saduqa
Ahmose I	Hatshepsut	Hatshepsut died.	Amenhotep III
Bhagavad Gita transcribed. Ay	Ramses II Šuppiluliuma I, Battle of Kadesh	Ramses II died. Šuppiluliuma died.	Nebuchadnezzar, Civilization collapse
Samuel	King David	King David died.	Solomon,
Lycurgus	Tiglath-Pileser III	Tiglath-Pileser III died.	The Ecclesia
Thales	Darius the Great	Confucius died. Buddha died.	Pericles, Peloponnesian Wars
Aristotle	Seleucid Empire (Alexander the Great)	Archimedes	Hannibal
Cicero	Julius Caesar, Augustus Caesar	Augustus Caesar died. Jesus	Nero, Paul of Tarsus, Vespasian
Ptolemy, Saint Justin, Marcus Aurelius	Ardishir I, Han Dynasty falls.	Plotinus, Mani	Diocletian, Constantine
Augustine of Hippo, Hypatia	Attila the Hun, Roman Empire falls.	Breviary of Alaric	Nika Rebellion, Justinian Code
Muhammad	Battle of Covadonga, Charles Martel, Leo III	Al-Mansur, Baghdad founded.	Harun al-Rashid, Charlemagne

Albategnius	Song Dynasty founded. Otto the Great	*Beowulf, Tale of Genji, Shahnameh,* Al-Binini	Battle of Hastings, Movable type invented in China. First crusades
Bernard of Clairvaux, Saint Hildegard von Bingen;	Genghis Khan, Gempei Wars, Saladin, Pope Innocent III, Magna Carta	Pope Innocent IV, Rumi, Hanseatic League	Kublai Khan, Crusades ended.
Francesco Petrarca, Giovanni Boccaccio, Italian Renaissance begins.	Cosimo de Medici, Itzcoatl, Pachakuti, Mehmed II, Byzantine Empire falls.	Columbus, Treaty of Tordesillas, Savonarola, Michelangelo, Leonardo da Vinci	The Reformation
Sir Francis Bacon, Galileo Galilei, René Descartes, Johannes Kepler, The Mayflower, Jamestown	William and Mary, Peter the Great, Louis XIV	The Great Awakening, Jonathan Edwards	American Revolution, French Revolution, Catherine the Great
Charles Darwin, Karl Marx, The US Civil War, Taiping Rebellion	WWII	Iron Curtain comes down. INF Treaty, Tiananmen Square protests	2026–2031

Chapter 6:
Myth, Astronomy, and History—All Together

Now that we have briefly touched on the historical and interpretative framework for the periods of VISION, POWER, JUSTICE, and REFORM, let us take a moment to combine astronomy, myth, and historical evidence as we delve deeper into the Pluto cycle.

In this chapter, I will show you how I've been putting these elements together—the mythic timeline and its main themes with the manifestations of history. I use the cycle that began with Aristotle as an example because most people have heard of Aristotle and Alexander the Great and because it makes my point so efficiently.

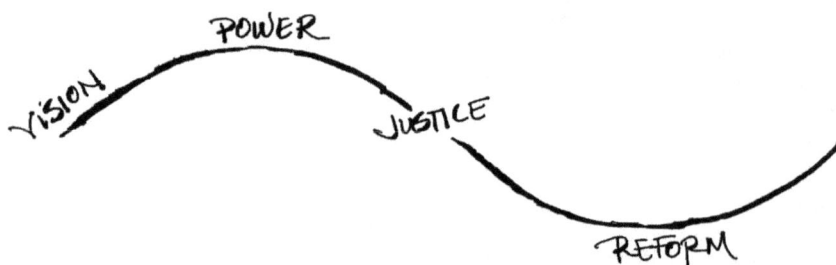

The Four Stages

- VISION times begin when Pluto crosses the equatorial plane moving south to north. For the purposes of our work with the myth of Persephone and Hades, we will call this the beginning of the cycle.
- POWER times begin when Pluto moves into extreme declination north between 23.44° north and a peak declination degree that varies in each cycle but is decreasing over time, and then finally travels back to 23.44° north.
- JUSTICE times begin when Pluto crosses the equatorial plane moving north to south.
- REFORM times begin when Pluto moves into extreme declination south between 23.44° south and a peak declination that varies in each cycle, decreasing over time, and then finally travels back to 23.44° south.

Turning Points, Myth, and History

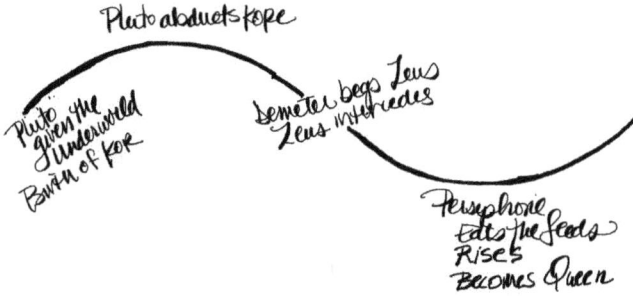

Pluto abducts Kore

Pluto given the Underworld
Birth of Kore

Demeter begs Zeus
Zeus interceedes

Persephone
Eats the seeds
Rises
Becomes Queen

VISION Times

Mythic Timeline
HADES BEGINS HIS REIGN OVER THE WORLD OF THE DEAD.
DEMETER GIVES BIRTH TO A GIRL.

Main Themes
THINK A NEW THOUGHT.

DREAM A NEW DREAM.

At the beginning of the cycle, a new world is born. It may not be obvious at first, but in hindsight, great minds, philosophers, and polymaths live during the time of VISION. The paradigm shift that will require the entire 248 years to complete begins with people who have new ideas. These ideas are like seeds that grow into a new, robust plant. Hades being given the Underworld is not in and of itself a bad or a good thing. He accepts his destiny and perhaps even embraces it, as the Underworld suits his solitary nature. Meanwhile, the birth of Kore was a joyful occasion, especially for the goddess of mothers, Demeter.

As we move through history, the ideas that begin cycles aren't attached to moral judgment at the outset. Most are earnestly shared ideas that are truly inspired. New thinking is first shared with the powerbrokers of the time, be they kings, conquerors, or the wealthy. Our world has a long history of philosophers, scientists, and artists needing patronage from the aristocracy, religious leaders, political rulers, and other members of the powerful elite. The powerful, in turn, have first access to the great minds. *The visionaries share their new thinking with leaders, conquerors, and/or other so-called wealthy powerbrokers.*

59

322-298 BC 298-272 BC 268-232 BC

Chandragupta Bindusara Ashoka

Alexander Seleucus

272 BC

341 BC

Aristotle
Chanakya

Ashoka died

231 BC Punic Wars (Carthage vs. Rome)

Hannibal's
Father

185 BC

Hannibal Maccabean
Revolt
167-160 BC

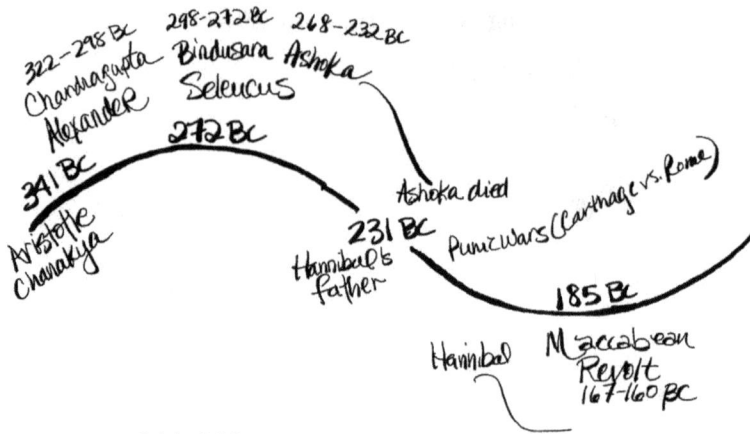

VISION   344–338 BCE

King Philip II of Macedonia, whose reign lasted from 359 to 336 BCE, a brilliant general, amassed a well-trained army and brought Macedonia into a highly functioning society as the great civilization of Ancient Greece fell into decline. He employed the greatest mind at the time, Aristotle, to tutor his rambunctious son, Alexander, in the years from 343 to 337 BCE. This would be like Abraham Lincoln hiring James Maxwell to tutor his son, Robert.

For the few years that Aristotle could tolerate the young Alexander (or that Alexander could sit still) Pluto was exactly at the VISION point in the cycle. Even while Aristotle tutored the boy, the great scholar was developing plans for his new school (The Lyceum, which he would start in 335 BCE) and writing what would become foundational texts for centuries thereafter on logic, metaphysics, physics, biology, botany, and mathematics, to name a few.

Aristotle began a movement—a paradigm shift—that his student then spread throughout much of the world. Alexander's worldly conquests introduced the world to Aristotle's concepts of logic, deductive reasoning, and rhetoric. These ways of thinking in turn influenced the Roman leaders to follow, including Cicero, Varro, and Lucretius, as well as shaping the later intellectual efforts of Augustine, Ptolemy, and the Arabian Golden Age. As Alexander perpetuated his conquering rampage through southern Europe, Africa, and the Middle East, in the fourth century BCE, he brought with him the knowledge that Aristotle bestowed upon him. Instead of burning the libraries and destroying the culture of the people he conquered, he allowed them to continue to flourish. This supported his rise to great power.

POWER Times

Mythic Timeline
HADES ABDUCTS PERSEPHONE.

Main Themes
BUILD AN ARMY.
ABDUCT, CONQUER, DOMINATE, CONTROL, AND AMASS MORE POWER.
DIVE INTO THE UNDERWORLD TO WITNESS DESTRUCTION AND
PROCESS THE SHADOWS OF LIFE.

During this stage in Pluto's journey through the solar system, the most abusive and power-hungry dictators and tyrants live on Earth. The powerful leaders of the time take the new ideas realized during the VISION time and run wild with them, accumulating massive wealth, building armies, and "abducting friends." At the very peak of northerly extreme declination in the past, many such tyrants were crowned. These megalomaniacs wreak havoc on the world and the people they are charged with ruling. Like the lonely Hades, they crave something that is not theirs, and—armed with the new knowledge of the visionaries preceding them—they succeed in conquering and ruling.[1]

It seems that the ordinary people who live during the POWER time are somehow caught unaware, as if they are metaphorically asleep at the wheel— or just innocently picking daffodils. The idea that a distant ruler could wreak personal havoc is not something they've planned for or feel they have any power to do anything about once the tyranny and suffering have begun. They are left with a feeling of helplessness, fear, shock, and trauma.

POWER   296–252 BCE   Peak: 272 BCE

After Alexander the Great had conquered most of the so-called civilized world, including the Middle East and southern Europe into parts of Asia, and with India always evading his grasp, he died a mysterious death at age 32.

---

1. In many ways, Pluto's abduction of Kore is an abduction of the ancient world by the new northern Indo-Greek patriarchal tyranny. Prior to these new Greek myths/stories, Robert Graves viewed the "Great Goddess...as immortal, changeless, omnipotent; and the concept of fatherhood had not yet been introduced into religious thoughts'" (Stone, 23). Like Artemis (goddess-sexual creator of the world converted by Homer into a virgin huntress), Demeter comes from the Potnia Mater (Great Goddess) matrilineal world. Invasions of the northern people and sea peoples brought in patrilineal religions (Dyaus Pater—God Father—is a Sanskrit word via Mycenaeans). The storm god comes from the northern mountains, supplanting the fertile goddess as the central authority.

He spent his entire life fighting and did not get to the ruling part—the time when a king sits on a throne and dictates, organizes, and establishes the kingdom. His companion and general, Seleucus I succeeded him instead, founding the Seleucid Empire in 305 BCE, a rulership that included what we know today as Iran, Iraq, and the Indian border.

When Alexander got to India, his army mutinied, and he retreated, coming up to the boundary of the newly forming Mauryan Empire, founded by Chandragupta. Around the same time that Aristotle was teaching Alexander, Chanakya, an Indian philosopher considered to be the founder of political science, was teaching Chandragupta.[2] This means that while Alexander was being given the keys to one kingdom, Chandragupta was giving birth to a kingdom of his own.

During this POWER time, most of the land from Egypt to India had been abducted by Alexander, and his successor, Seleucus I, was getting down to the business of ruling. Chandragupta died in 297 BCE, handing over rulership to his successor, his son Bindusara. Bindusara went into expansion mode, overtaking much of the peoples in what we call India today. He died just before the peak of the POWER time. During the peak of the POWER time, Bindusara's heirs fought over the kingdom until his son Ashoka killed his brothers (and whoever else laid claim to the throne) to emerge victorious. While not a common name to many of us in the west, in India, Ashoka Maurya's name is equivalent to George Washington or William the Conqueror.

Ashoka continued the expansion mode of his father,[3] Bindusara, battling the Kalingas in the southeastern part of India. On the battlefield, as 40,000 soldiers lay dead, Ashoka had an epiphany, namely, to paraphrase in contemporary language, "War sucks." For most of us, this is not such a grand epiphany, but, in 261 BCE, for a man who became king by killing his brothers, this was huge. In fact, it has gone down in history as one of the most significant epiphanies anyone has ever had. He converted to Buddhism and, in the process, required the entire empire to convert to Buddhism as well. This is akin to Hades abducting Kore, bringing her down to the Underworld, looking into her tortured face, and feeling remorse. Although we don't really know if

---

2. I was not able to find exact dates when Chanakya came into Chandragupta's life. Chandragupta's birth date, also, does not appear to be recorded.
3. It is not clear if Ashoka was Bindusara's son. Most histories consider him to be Chandragupta's grandson, therefore Bindusara's son, but there is some ambiguity about this in other sources.

Hades had a significant awakening after seeing the suffering of Kore, we do know that at some point in the process, Hades allows Persephone to co-rule the underworld. This transformation must have come with some degree of self-awareness. As we look at dictators who rule during the POWER time, there are many ways they transform. Some simply get tired, like Genghis Khan at the end of his life. Some reach the limits of their power. Some commit suicide. Some never transform. Ashoka Maurya is the rare ruler who recognized that a change was needed and followed through on his promise.

Let's turn back to the neighbors of Ashoka, the Seleucids. After Seleucus died, his son, Antiochus I, took over and acquired the name, "King of the Universe." This is akin to Hades abducting Kore and then believing he is awesome for doing it. This is another side to the myth, and more often than not, it is the most the recognizable version, the one we read about in history books.

JUSTICE Times

Mythic Timeline

ZEUS INTERCEDES ON DEMETER'S BEHALF.

THE DARK NIGHT OF THE SOUL AS KORE TRANSFORMS INTO PERSEPHONE.

Main Themes

LEADER DIES. POWER VACUUM.

SEE THE INJUSTICE.

CRY OUT FOR JUSTICE.

Persephone's mother, Demeter, was a force to be reckoned with. She was not going to sit idly by while her daughter lived with the god of the underworld. The first thing she did was cry, and cry, and cry some more. She went on strike, and the plants died; the Earth turned cold, and every place on Earth filled with grief and devastation. She sat in silence at a well for nine days in Eleusis, until the young Iambe came by and made Demeter laugh, breaking the grief spell.

In wanting the gods to suffer, Demeter wandered the Earth in disguise. Landing in Eleusis, she worked as nurse to Demophon and Triptolemus, giving them near immortality and teaching them the secret of blending the new grain with the dying crop. The Mysteries given to her initiates at Eleusis embody the triple-goddess nature (giver of life, death, and rebirth) at the center of Demeter's gift. As "reward" for letting the world die during Persephone's time in the Underworld, the gift of rebirth is an essential Mystery given to those she chose to help survive.

As humans suffered during the endless winter of Demeter's grief, Zeus realized that without the people, he had no realm to rule, no playground to play in, and no one to receive his boons. On behalf of the people (or his own need to be worshiped), he intervened on Demeter's behalf and negotiated with his older brother. Under pressure, Hades agreed to release Persephone.

During this stage in the Pluto cycle, people with courage cry out for justice. Knowledgeable of the vision proposed during the VISION time, they share their outcry publicly. Often there is an intercession, and underground organizations form to fight on behalf of a wronged people.

JUSTICE   230–232 BCE

In many cases, the intercession during the JUSTICE time manifests as the death of the tyrant or conqueror. Ashoka Maurya is one of these cases, ruler of the Mauryan Empire in India. He died precisely during JUSTICE in 232 BCE. After Ashoka's death, the kingdom moved into decline with weaker leaders taking his place.

During this same time, the Seleucid Empire was also falling into decay after taking hits from armies to the east and losing sight of the big picture. As Egypt, Macedon, and Seleucid, the empires that arose in the footprint of Alexander were taking hold, so too was the Roman Republic forming in the land of what is today, Italy.

During this period, alternating treaty negotiations between shifting empires led to in-fighting around the Mediterranean. The Punic Wars (264–146 BCE) were three wars fought between Carthage (Algeria) and the Roman Republic (Italy). At this time, a Carthaginian general, Hamilcar Barca, who fought in the first Punic War (264 BCE) was raising his radical son, Hannibal. While organizations and radicals often begin their work during the JUSTICE time, Hamilcar Barca did not start an underground organization so much as he groomed an underground general. History has long made note of how Hannibal's father instilled in him a hatred for the Romans. Hannibal's cry for justice was a battle cry against the Roman Republic on behalf of the people of Carthage.

REFORM Times

Mythic Timeline
PERSEPHONE IS RELEASED. PERSEPHONE BECOMES QUEEN OF THE UNDERWORLD.

Main Themes
PLAN A REVOLUTION.
EXECUTE A REVOLUTION.
CHANGE EVERYTHING.
ACCEPT CHANGE.
ABSORB THE VISION INTO EVERYDAY LIFE.

Persephone comes to be the co-ruler of the Underworld alongside Hades. Persephone "transforms her abduction experience into wisdom and empowers herself with the mysteries of life, death, and the spirit world."[4]

During the REFORM time, a rectification in the balance of power occurs. What was claimed and hoarded during the POWER time is released. People rise with a new confidence and reclaim their power. With the people no longer caught off guard, monarchs and rulers are forced to institute reforms, or they have to deal with the rebellions, riots, and revolutions that ensue. No longer blinded by the tyrants and wanna-be tyrants, people stand up to the powers that be.

Great landmarks and temples built during the REFORM time include Solomon's Temple in Israel, the Hanging Gardens of Babylon (700 BCE),[5] the Temple of Artemis at Ephesus (430 BCE), the temple to Apollo in Rome, the statue of Zeus by Phidias (one of the seven wonders of the world) in Olympia (431 BCE), the Acropolis and Parthenon in Athens (432 BCE), the Terra Cotta Warriors (206 BCE), the Colosseum in Rome (80 CE), the Hagia Sophia in Istanbul (537 CE), the Borobudur Temple in Indonesia (750–842 CE), and Westminster Abbey in England (1042–1060). The REFORM time gracefully lends itself to the creation of extraordinary art, as well as the radical, out-of-the-box thinking that great works require.

---

4. Ariel Guttman and Kenneth Johnson, *Mythic Astrology: Archetypal Powers in the Horoscope*, 174.
5. The Hanging Gardens of Babylon may be more legend than real, but there is a significant possibility that these are the gardens that were built in Nineveh during the reign of Sennacherib (704–681 BCE) during the next REFORM period.

REFORM   208–150 BCE

With Hannibal fully grown, an army behind him, and a giant chip on his shoulder, he ushered elephants over the Alps to attack Rome. This was an act of rebellion—one fomented by intergenerational scorn for the Romans. The rebellion didn't last long, and Rome survived, but the battle started a series of events that led to the end of the Roman Republic while making way for the Roman Empire (during the next POWER time).

The rebellion during this REFORM time that is more interesting for the purposes of studying the sine-wave cycle of Pluto, however, is the Maccabean Revolt and what that has come to mean to us today. The Maccabees lived in the Seleucid Empire in the vestiges of Alexander the Great's kingdom of Aristotelian thought. During the REFORM time, the Maccabees, a Jewish clan living in the Hellenistic Seleucid land of Syria, took it upon themselves to revolt (exactly at the peak of REFORM).

Judaism, already well established by this time, was allowed in the Seleucid Empire, and even well-supported, until Antiochus IV came to power, ruling from 175 to 164 BCE. He tried to "extort money from the Jews"[6] and did this through converting Jewish temples into Hellenistic centers, threatening their beliefs and way of life. Judas Maccabeus, the leader of the family, initiated a rebellion that successfully put down the armies of Antiochus IV and established Judaism in that area of Syria for the next century.[7]

---

6. Norman F. Cantor, *Antiquity: From the Birth of Sumerian Civilization to the Fall*, 82.

7. When Seleucid Emperor Antiochus IV ordered the apis bull of Zeus installed in the Temple Complex in Jerusalem in 167 BCE, it was part of a Hellenization program aimed at limiting any religious order from dominance. With taxation a fundamental role of the temple (and an essential reason the Romans had a liberal view on polytheism: more temples=more taxes), the Temple in Jerusalem had an inordinate influence on commerce in the region of Judea. Some estimates say that up to 20,000 priests and rabbis worked in the Temple complex, many in administrative and financial roles.

¶ The Seleucid victory of the Ptolemies of Egypt in the Syro-Egypt war of 170–167 BCE enabled Antiochus to shift focus to Syria and the Levant. Humiliation by religious zealots to his chosen High Priest, Meneleus, led to the massacre or enslavement of over 150,000 people—nearly all followers of Yahweh. An already significant dispute between Hellenized and Orthodox adherents to Judaism began a seismic shift in religious and political management of Israel.

¶ The Maccabee brothers (originators of the Hasmonean line ended with Herod Antipas) led a revolutionary reaction to these policies and were briefly successful in defeating a weakened regional outpost until Antiochus shifted significant forces to Judea. Prior, the Levant had been a loosely managed regent of the Seleucid empire. Through a years-long sequence of conflicts, battles, negotiations, assassinations, and religious authorities, the last of the four brothers Maccabee was able to create the Hasmonean kingdom. Aligned with the Roman senate, this "inde-

The Jewish people in this cycle are an example of Persephone in the form of a revolutionary group. When abducted by Alexander and Seleucus I during the POWER time, they adapted to the new empire (Underworld). They grieved. They bargained. They paid their taxes. They learned from the transmission of Aristotelian VISION under this new rule. But all the time, a growing and hidden evolution—an empowerment—was happening out of public view during the JUSTICE time that eventually burst into rebellion during REFORM. They acted in defiance—ate the seeds in defiance of the overlords—and fought for their independence.[8]

This rebellion is celebrated today by Jewish people throughout the world as the holy days of Hannukah.[9] While the Jewish people only ruled the region for a century, the spirit of the rebellion lives on in the celebrations of today. Revolutions that take place during REFORM are usually successful and live on in some form or another.

---

pendent kingdom" sat within the Province of Syria with a Roman Governor (eventually the role Pontius Pilate would play) and a Hasmonean regent.

8. Everett Gendler, "Fellowship."

9. For centuries, the celebration of lights, was held as a rabbinical celebration, as it did not come out of the Hebrew Bible. The militarism inherent in celebrating this victory limited the scope of how traditional Jews celebrated Hanukkah. Rabbinical scholars sought ways to balance militarism with the realities of nonviolence and flight that Jews throughout history have embraced for most of Western history. The militaristic violence inherent in the Maccabean revolt remained a background point until the 20th-century rise of Zionism, when a resurgent Jewish community convinced British, French, and American diplomats to create a modern Jewish state, the country of Israel.

PART II:
THE PAST

In this next part of the book, we will travel through different cycles in history to deeply explore the pattern of Pluto's declination cycle. In Part I, we established the basics through the structure of the myth, the astronomical data, and foundational historical information and graphs. Now we will attend to the intricacies of specific histories to comprehend how each cycle is both a recurring pattern and an evolutionary process: from visionaries, to warlords, to justice seekers, to reformers, on seemingly endless repeat. However, pay close attention and notice that what begins at the VISION time slowly permeates throughout the realm until it becomes the dominant paradigm during and after the REFORM time.

Chapter 7:
Augustine to Justinian, 393–638 CE

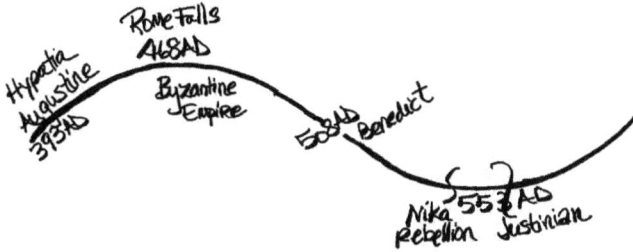

Each cycle stands on the growth and evolution that occurred in the prior cycle. In order to explore the Pluto cycle that started in 393 CE with Augustine of Hippo living on the outskirts of a dying Roman Empire and ended after the Byzantine Emperor Justinian rewrote Roman law, we must take a brief look into the cycle that precedes it. From 147 to 389 CE, Christianity evolved like a crazed cult, with people throwing themselves into fires, preaching from street pulpits, and willingly martyring themselves at the hands of Roman soldiers, while the Roman Empire continued to expand. During the REFORM time (285–337 CE), two well-known rulers emerged: Diocletian and Constantine. During Diocletian's reign, thousands of Christians were killed, and his reforms unsettled the people. When Constantine followed, he saw the need to accept Christianity as a way to quell the disputes and rebellions. He did this by convening the First Council of Nicaea to validate Christianity as a religion. This process resulted in the establishment of Christian creeds, rituals, and holy days. He moved the capital from Rome to Byzantium (modern-day Istanbul), which fractured the Roman Empire into its eastern half (which later became the Byzantine Empire) and the western still-Roman Empire (settled in Rome). Christianity had a monumental influence on cycles to come. While Judaism was a religion of Chosen People, Hellenism a religion that benefited the nobles, and Hinduism a religion of castes, Christianity arose as a religion that one could practice no matter one's station in life or ancestry. This radical openness to all participants was a move towards freedom of worship, freedom of religion, and freedom from wrongful persecution. It started going wrong at the beginning of this cycle.

VISION   389–396 CE

It was into this split empire that Augustine and Hypatia were born. It is unlikely that these two great minds ever met, but their parallel lives during the VISION time aptly reflect the transformation in the Roman Empire during this cycle. Augustine (354–430 CE) lived on the outskirts of the empire, along the southern coast of the Mediterranean, in a town called Hippo in what is modern-day Algeria. He was a curious young man, intellectually and spiritually. His father, a professor, saw promise in his son and went to great lengths to secure young Augustine an education. His parents practiced different religions: his father an intellect and pagan, his mother a devout Christian who ceaselessly prayed for her son.

Augustine moved to Carthage (Tunisia) when he was seventeen to study Latin and the classics—and to sow some wild oats, as it turned out. In the big city, Augustine partied and, like many young folks, experimented with other religions. In his case, the most influential religion was Manichaeism. Mani was a radical teacher much like Jesus, who, one Pluto cycle after Jesus, started a movement that ended in much the same way, with Mani being executed. Mani based his movement on Christian and Zoroastrian theology. Augustine's Manicheistic phase did not last long, but his voracious appetite for learning lived on. Augustine became enamored with the Latin classics, in particular the work of the Roman senator, Cicero.

Cicero (106–43 BCE), like both Augustine and Aristotle, started his seeking during a VISION time (99–93 BCE) and wrote and taught in the time between VISION and POWER (93–50 BCE). Cicero wrote about *"philo-sophia"* (philosophy) as the love (*philo*) of wisdom (*sophia*), a concept that enthralled Augustine. *Sophia* as Cicero conceived it was not just knowledge or intelligence, it was a divine wisdom, an inspiration from on high. Cicero also gets credit for a philosophy of *just war* that supported his use of martial law, while allowing him to maintain a moral high ground. Cicero's justification for violence comes from a belief in natural order. These ideas ignited Augustine, who brought God into Cicero's justification of violence, and were part of the fuel that transformed this party boy into a great scholar.

In a nearby city (if five hundred hours of walking can be considered nearby), along the same southside of the Mediterranean, in the great Egyptian city of Alexandria, lived Hypatia (360–415 BCE), a young woman with a father of means and her own intelligence. Hypatia's father took pride in his gifted daughter and taught her everything he knew. She became one of the leading mathematicians and scientists of the time.

While Hypatia was being tutored by her father in the cosmopolitan city that Alexander the Great founded, Augustine was studying in Carthage. While Hypatia was traveling to Athens to deepen her studies, Augustine was traveling to Rome and Milan to deepen his. In what appears as a mirror, both in terms of place and in terms of studies, Augustine studied philosophy, religion, and Christianity while avoiding math and science, and Hypatia studied math and science while avoiding Christianity.

Augustine's mother followed her son to Milan and there, with her nudging, Augustine found himself inspired by the Bishop Ambrose and his devotion to the teachings of Jesus. As the VISION time began, Augustine decided to return to Hippo and become a Bishop. At the port town of Ostria, while waiting weeks for the ship to arrive, he and his mother together had an awakening experience that changed their lives. He referred to it in *Confessions* as the "Ecstasy at Ostria." His mother came to a place of completion with her life. She felt her work was done. Within days, a fever took over her body, and she died there in Ostria waiting for a boat. Augustine returned to Hippo and began writing his greatest work, *Confessions*, precisely during the VISION time.

Meanwhile, Hypatia at this point had become a teacher herself in the great temple at Alexandria. The Emperor of Rome, Theodosius I, was a Christian who sought to make the empire entirely Christian, as opposed to Constantine's more inclusive approach. During the VISION time, he outlawed the pagan rituals of the Olympic Games and made Christianity the state religion. He disbanded the Vestal Virgins, and in 391 CE he called for the destruction of non-Christian temples and places. One of these sites was the Library of Alexandria, where Hypatia taught, fought, and was ultimately brutally murdered. Over the next decade, Christians utterly destroyed the Library of Alexandria.

Augustine, on the other hand, ended up living a long and prosperous life, writing many great works including the utopian guide for how to get through the fall of the Roman Empire, *The City of God*. Augustine is credited with being one of the first great scholars of the Catholic Church and with establishing the ethos of sin and austerities. Celibate priests have Augustine to thank. Right and wrong, heaven and hell, good and evil—these were all polarities Augustine taught and impressed upon future generations of Christian scholars.

During a time when Theodosius was ruthlessly casting aside the inclusiveness of Constantine and enforcing Christianity as the state religion, one of the greatest Christian scholars wrote his greatest work. That Augustine aligned himself with the ruler who had the keys to Hades' underworld kingdom allowed his work to go viral, as we might say today. And the execution of the Hellenistic wise woman, a Demeter-Persephone archetype, Hypatia, set the stage for the eradication of the Hellenists throughout the rest of this cycle. It even portended the end of the Hellenistic Roman Empire. With Augustine's ideas and Theodosius' power, a Christian ethos governed the underworld of Pluto, while the pagan Persephones, powerless at the hands of the new rulers were easily captured during the POWER time.

POWER   445–486 CE   Peak: 468–469 CE

The Huns had been encroaching on the southern Mediterranean for almost a century by 445 CE. Augustine's *The City of God* had become a veritable bestseller (as far as it could be without a printing press), as people sought hope within his pages, while the Huns ceaselessly raided their homeland. Originally from the area currently located around Kazakhstan, and originally mercenaries for the Roman Empire, the Huns, under the leadership of Attila (r. 434–453 CE), pushed the Goths (originally from northern Europe) deeper into the Roman Empire. Like dominos, the Christian Goths pushed the Vandals (originally from what is today Poland) south, and they both fell upon the western Roman Empire.

In 473 CE, four years after Pluto's northerly out-of-bounds peak, Odoacer, general of the Goths, deposed the last Roman emperor and declared himself ruler, marking the end of the great Roman Empire. A chaotic time in Rome began, while the eastern Roman Empire, headquartered in Byzantium (Constantinople/Istanbul), remained more stable. The reign of Odoacer did not last long. The Byzantine emperor, Zeno, sent Theodoric the Great to invade Odoacer's kingdom, which his army successfully did in 493 CE.

So much has been written of the Fall of the Roman Empire—the Visigoths and the Ostrogoths, the Vandals and the Huns, and all their migrations, battles, and leaders—that it feels unnecessary to go into lengthy detail here.

For our purposes, we will mark this POWER time easily as a time of legendary war and conquering.

The great Roman Empire fell, and the Byzantine Empire officially began its long and prosperous rule, lasting several Pluto cycles. The Roman people were overtaken by the Goths and Vandals, much like Hades overtaking Persephone. While the metaphor is not perfect as the Roman Empire was already in decline and not the innocent child picking flowers, it is not hard to imagine that at least some if not many of the people of Rome did not expect to be invaded, conquered, or, as Persephone was, abducted.

JUSTICE   506–508 CE

After years of warring with border civilizations on all sides, the Byzantines signed what turned out to be a temporary peace treaty with the Persians in 506 CE. However, peace to the east only enabled more troops to go west to fight the Ostrogoths. Meanwhile, disgusted with the wars, a Christian spiritual seeker, Benedict of Nursia (480–547 CE), spent three years in a cave meditating. It is precisely during the JUSTICE time that Benedict emerged from the cave as an enlightened teacher. Within a few years, he formed a monastery, wrote the monastic code known as *Benedict's Rule*, and inspired many people to adopt a more ascetic life. He led his followers into a simple life of moderation and service. Benedict was directly inspired by Augustine and his rules for monastic life. Augustine, the visionary during a VISION time, inspired Benedict, the social justice advocate during a JUSTICE time, to change society by founding the Benedictine order, an organization that still functions to this day with a focus on social justice.

REFORM   533–580 CE, Peak: 553 CE

In 532 CE, the year before Pluto moved out-of-bounds to the south, a devastatingly unsuccessful rebellion took place, the Nika Rebellion. (If only they had waited a year, they might have found help from Pluto's movement into extreme declination, since rebellions during JUSTICE times tend to be quashed). The new emperor, Justinian I, who reigned from 527 to 565 CE, was already unpopular after he increased taxes without getting support from the nobles. During the yearly chariot races in the enormous Hippodrome, amongst an already riled-up crowd, riots broke out, and tensions led to violence. Justinian, afraid that the riots would spread as many were unhappy with his reign, considered fleeing. Justinian's wife, Theodora, talked him into staying, and the emperor ordered his troops to corral and slaughter the remaining rioters. As often occurs during the REFORM time, a powerful wife governs alongside her emperor husband, and this is one such case.

The riots pushed Justinian to consider a change in the way he was governing. With an opportunity to stay in power, he redirected his focus to rebuilding and rewriting the laws of the Byzantine Empire once Pluto moved out of bounds. His famous reforms set up a structure of laws and codes of conduct that inspired centuries of civilizations. Justinian is an example, much like the Roman Emperor Constantine, of a leader who saw a need for compromise and reform during the REFORM time. Both were able to oversee a sea change in their kingdoms and offer the people a greater voice in politics, Justinian through his new laws and Constantine through the First Council of Nicaea.

Summary and Synthesis

During this Pluto cycle, two great visionaries, Augustine of Hippo and Hypatia of Alexandria lived in the midst of a crumbling empire, both Persephones bringing a fresh perspective to life, both living in the realm of Hades' crumbling infrastructure. When Pluto went out of bounds to the north (POWER, 445–486 CE), the Western Roman Empire fell completely, and the Eastern Roman Empire, the Byzantine Empire, took on a larger role in world politics. The transition of power that took place is a textbook example of what often happens during POWER times—massive war on the scale of legends. The Fall of the Roman Empire at the hands of invaders, captors, abductors, left the good, common people living in fear. When Pluto crossed the celestial equator from north to south (JUSTICE, 506–508 CE), a follower of Augustine, Benedict of Nursia, set up a radical new way of living, inspiring centuries of devotees. He didn't only cry for justice; he initiated a path for others to continue crying for justice to this day. The intercession of Demeter and the deep inner work of Persephone is entwined in Benedict's spiritual work of here. When Pluto entered extreme declination to the south (REFORM, 533–580 CE), the Byzantine emperor Justinian established reforms in the judicial system and in civilian life that gave people more political representation, which helped him stay in power and inspired future societies. The societies that took down the Roman Empire, the representatives of Hades in this case, found a new way to rule with mercy.

Each part of the cycle worked to move Roman civilization from the old Empire founded by Hellenists and pagans into a new empire based on Christian tenets. The paradigm shift began with Augustine's doctrines on right and wrong, heaven and hell, during VISION, displayed in full light as Rome crumbled during POWER, when the Goths established a Christian empire. Augustinian and Gothic ideas of austerity and purpose were put into practice by Benedict and his followers during JUSTICE. Then, the Benedictine movement of practice, moderation, and willful regard for the rights of others led to the establishment of a new code of law under Emperor Justinian during REFORM. By the end of this cycle, the Benedictine monasteries were fully established, and the ideas of Augustine, as radical as they were when he was alive, became a regular part of life for the everyday citizen of the Byzantine Empire.

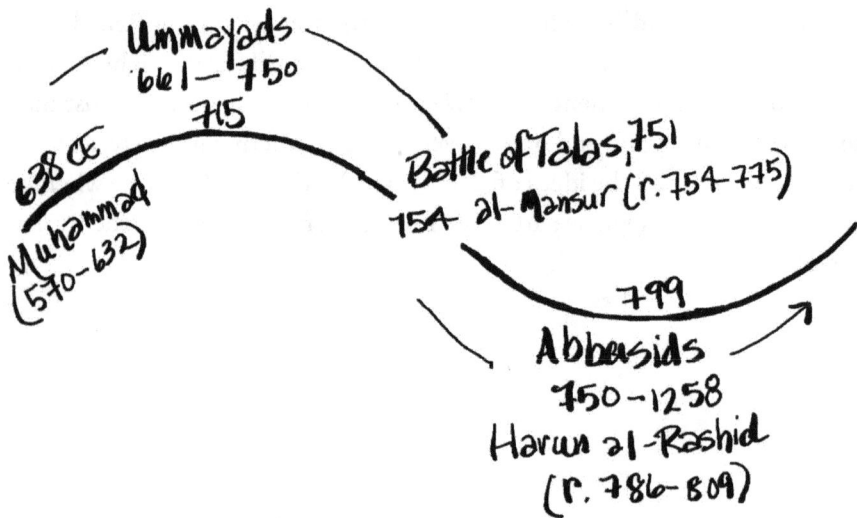

Ummayads
661 – 750
715
638 CE
Muhammad
(570–632)
Battle of Talas, 751
754 al-Mansur (r. 754–775)
799
Abbasids
750–1258
Harun al-Rashid
(r. 786–809)

Chapter 8:
Islamic Golden Age Part I, 638–883 CE

Two centuries after the fall of Rome circa 600 CE, the dry desert land that is today Saudi Arabia and Yemen was processing the aftermath in much the way that Europe was: decaying infrastructure, uncertainty, disorientation, and power vacuums. Europe remained in a "Dark Age" for another few centuries. The Byzantine Empire, less organized than the Roman Empire on which grounds it stood, had been fighting with the Persian Sassanid Empire. One civilization was ending and another beginning. As often happens in the transition from one cycle to another, an opportunity arises for a leader with charisma and vision to step into the limelight. That leader was the Prophet Muhammad.

The Islamic Golden Age, 632 CE–883 CE

VISION   635–641

The Prophet Muhammad (570–632 CE) brought hope and unity to a scattered people during a time when trade was bringing a new abundance to the desert lands, particularly to his tribe, the Quraish. His revelations took 23 years and culminated in the book of Islam, the Quran. During his lifetime, he taught, wrote, and led his followers on a conquest that extended throughout what is today Saudi Arabia. He died in 632 CE, three years before Pluto crossed the celestial equator from south to north. This VISION time began as a new way of life permeated the Arabian Peninsula.

While it is the seed time of a long-lasting religion, it is also the seed time of the divide within Islam. The question of succession arose just after Muhammad died. His followers fell into two camps. One group, the Shias, believed that Muhammad chose his son-in-law, Alī ibn Abī Ṭālib,[1] to be his hereditary successor. The other group, the Sunnis, believed Muhammad did not leave a successor and that a righteous devotee can carry on the Prophet's work; a collective of devotees appointed Abū Bakr to power. Contention between

---

1. Ali was married to Muhammad's daughter, Fatima, a Persephone-type, who adored her father. She died six months after her father in 632 CE.

the Shias, followers of Alī, and the Sunnis, those who live by the model set by Muhammad, continues to this day.

After Muhammad's death, the Rashidun Caliphate (632–661 CE) began with Abū Bakr as caliph seeking conquest of the Arabian peninsula. When he died two years into his reign, Umar (Omar) ibn al-Khattab (r. 634–644) took over and accelerated the campaign of conquest, absorbing two-thirds of the Byzantine Empire and nearly the entire Sassanid Empire. Alī eventually did get to ascend to power, as the fourth in line after Muhammad; he ruled from 656 to 661. After a civil war known as the First Fitna, the Rashidun Caliphate gave way to the Umayyad Caliphate (661–750 CE), which became one of the largest geographical empires in history.

While it may be seemingly contradictory to think of Muhammad and his followers as Persephones, as war already permeated their culture, the essence of Persephone as the bringer of a fresh perspective, the goddess of mercy and wisdom, was interwoven in Muhammad's teachings. Consider Muhammad's daughter, Fatima, whose mythology today takes on the role of purity and compassion. She died six months after her father, entreating her spirit into this cycle alongside her father's. It may be equally strange to think of Muhammad and his followers as Hades, the god of death and the dark underworld, and yet, the division and ongoing divisiveness within Islam, the conquering nature that was part of its beginning, and the way Islam took over the Middle East during this cycle are emblematic of Hades' role.

POWER   692–731   Peak: 715

Similar to the building of the Roman Empire during the time of Augustus Caesar, the reign of al-Malik (r. 685–705, Umayyad Caliphate) during the POWER time introduced a standard currency (the dinar) and a common language (Arabic) throughout the Islamic empire. His son, al-Walid I (r. 705–715), expanded the empire into Northern Africa and conquered the Visigoths in Spain (711). He died at the peak of POWER, when his brother took over for two years until he died in battle. The following caliphs during POWER continued to expand the empire and established the most successful time of the Umayyad Caliphate. Meanwhile, during the peak of Pluto out of bounds, a young warrior began his rule of the Frankish Empire. Known as Charles "The Hammer" Martel (r. 718–741), he expanded the Frankish empire up to the border of the Umayyad Caliphate. Just as Pluto left extreme northerly declination, "The Hammer" fended off the Muslim warriors in the famous Battle of Tours (732 CE).[2] The battle signaled a turning point for both lands, establishing the Franks as a force to be reckoned with and marking a retreat for the Umayyads.

JUSTICE   753–755

During the small window of the JUSTICE time (751–755), as Pluto crossed from north back to south declination, a dramatic twist in history with long-term consequences occurred. Recalling that the JUSTICE time is a turning point in the cycle, this may be the turning point of all turning points.

Internal strife between the conquering Umayyad dynasty and the rebel Abbasids (followers of Muhammad's uncle Abbas) reached a head in 750 CE when the Abbasids won a battle by the River Zab, with the help of Persians. To ensure their victory, the Abbasids slaughtered the entire Umayyad leadership, including women and children, in the middle of the night.[3] On the eastern front, in 751, at the Battle of Talas (somewhere in modern day Kazakhstan), the Abbasids and the Tang Dynasty (China), both lands in times of expansion, reached a stalemate. The battle tide turned when mercenary Karluk Turks, initially fighting for the Tang, changed sides.

The JUSTICE time is a time of intercession, Demeter begging for her daughter back and Zeus acquiescing. It marks the turning of the tide. The shifting alliances during the Battle of Talas supported the rise of the Abbasids and the decline of the Tang. A popular myth comes from a tenth-century Arab historian, Al-Tha'ilibī, who wrote that Chinese prisoners of war taught the Abbasids papermaking. While not true, since paper letters from an angry wife from centuries prior were discovered in the area in 1907, the myth of this transition and the marking of the turning point of this battle lives on in cultural significance.[4] In Manhattan, one of the most comprehensive sources for bookbinding supplies and archival papers is called TALAS (est. 1962).

---

2. Famous because he beat the Umayyads and famous because that might not be true. What is more likely, is that the Umayyads redirected their focus to fending off lands to the south and west and left the less civilized regions of France out of lack of interest and desire.
3. Michael Hamilton Morgan, *Lost History: The Enduring Legacy of Muslim Scientists, Thinkers, and Artists*, 40–41.
4. Mark Kurlanksy, *Paper: Paper through History*, 48–49.

The beginning of the *Translation Movement* is often tied to rise of Abu Jafar al-Mansur (r. 754–775) and the founding of Baghdad (July 30, 762 CE). The Translation Movement, an Islamic Renaissance, valued the translations of the great works from Greek, Latin, Sanskrit, and Hebrew and filled libraries in the new city of Baghdad. The new Abbasid caliph paid handsomely for these translations, making educated scholars wealthy in a way that was usually reserved for mercenaries and kings. This in turn led to many great inventions, advancements in math (algebra), and new healing modalities and medicines.

REFORM   780–824   Peak: 799

At the beginning of the REFORM time (780–824), the great library known as the House of Wisdom was founded in Baghdad (786), under the leadership of Harun al-Rashid (r. 786–809), made famous by Antoine Galland's *One Thousand and One Nights* and then later by a Disney movie. Mathematicians, philosophers, scientists, physicians, and artists gathered in the great halls of the new city of Baghdad, initiating a time of great scientific advancements. Between REFORM and the next VISION time, Abū Mūsā Jābir ibn Ḥayyān (c. 800), known as Geber in the west, considered by some to be the father of chemistry, wrote over 200 hundred books and was "the first to describe systematically the principle operations in chemistry—calcination, reduction, evaporation, sublimation, melting and crystallization."[5] Abu Yusuf Ya'qub Ishaq as-Sabbah al-Kindi (801–873) derived a theory of relativity (not unlike Einstein's), created the foundation for the field of pharmacology through his methods for organizing substances into categories, and introduced Indian numerals to the Arabic world, forming the Arabic numerals used today. A woman in Morocco, Fatima al-Fihri (800–878), founded the first university in the world, the University of Al-Karaouine (f. 859), still in existence today. Finally, we have Muḥammad ibn Mūsā al-Khwārizmī (780–850 CE) to thank for algebra invented during this REFORM window.

Summary and Synthesis

At the very beginning of this cycle, as Pluto crossed from southern declination to northern, the Prophet Muhammad died and left the seeds of a

---

5. Watson, 27.

new religion in the hands of his followers. The rituals and doctrines of Islam are clearly traced to what was established at the beginning of this cycle. The rift between the Shias and Sunnis also began, which continues to play out on the world stage. The teachings of Islam and its interpretations included support for the arts and sciences. The succedent Islamic empires grew into a powerful force, ruling from the borders of India to the Atlantic coast of the Iberian Peninsula, and reaching their penultimate extent as Pluto reached its peak northern declination, out of bounds. As Pluto made its way to cross from northern to southern declination again, the caliphates established not only a new major world religion, but a society that produced great scientists and mathematicians, which by the time Pluto entered extreme declination to the south, sprouted into a Golden Age that later inspired European mathematicians and scientists during the Italian Renaissance.

As William Durant wrote in *Age of Faith*, from 700–1200 CE, "Islam led the world in power, order, and extent of government, in refinement of manners, in standard of living, in humane legislation and religious toleration, in literature, scholarship, science, medicine, and philosophy."[6]

European "Dark Age," 632 CE–883 CE

The dearth of information about this period in European history could be responsible for the epithet "dark age." While we have exact dates for when Pericles gave a speech in 431 BCE, we don't know if King Arthur actually existed. A mini-Ice Age may have been underway in Europe. The teachings of Augustine and Benedict had permeated Europe by this time lending to a strong focus on ascetic living, spiritual atonement, and prayer in the everyday citizen. More faith-based and less intellect-oriented, the early Christians were grounded in good deeds and simplicity. In fact, things got so simple that people forgot how to calculate a triangle.

VISION   635–641

A young Irish Benedictine monk, Aiden, established the first priory in England, on Lindisfarne Island in 635 CE.[7] He is known for converting the

---

6. Will Durant, *Age of Faith*, 341.
7. St. Aiden was written about extensively in The Ecclesiastical History of the English People that was written in 731 CE by Bede (at the end of the POWER time).

Anglo-Saxons in the northern regions of the British Isles to Christianity, thus establishing Christianity in what is today the United Kingdom.

POWER 692–731 Peak: 715

While England may or may not be in the hands of King Arthur and Round Table magic,[8] we know the Byzantine Empire was soon to be in the hands of Leo III (r. 717–741). Within a year of Pluto going into extreme northerly declination (POWER), the Byzantine Empire slipped into a time of chaos and anarchy. From 695–717, a series of weak emperors allowed heavy taxation, chaos, and anarchy. Invading armies from the Umayyad Caliphate took chunks off the eastern region. Confusion and fear were somewhat alleviated with the iron fist of Leo III who usurped the throne in 717 CE, two years after Pluto peaked in extreme declination. Famous for being an iconoclast ("icon breaker"), he issued edicts against the veneration of images and ordered the destruction of statues, relics, and altars throughout the kingdom. His decision was met with resistance and rebellion, all of which were overcome by Byzantine forces.

Nearby and a bit north, the Frankish Empire (France) was mired in a similar state of unrest. Between 715 and 718, civil war broke out after the emperor died without a clear successor. His illegitimate son Charles Martel (going by ancient standards) rose into leadership, usurping the throne one year after Leo III ascended to the throne of the Byzantine Empire. As already mentioned, Charles was known affectionately as "The Hammer," and his legendary conquests included staving off the Umayyads at the Battle of Tours and pushing back the Anglo-Saxons. Anyone whose nickname is "The Hammer" deserves a rightful place alongside Hades.

JUSTICE 753–755

In 754, exactly as Pluto crossed from northern to southern declination, Boniface (675–754), a Catholic activist, with a mission to convert as much of the continent as possible, died a martyr. Living in the Frankish Empire, he had the blessings of the pope and in his early years, Charles Martel. He is

8. A reference in old Welsh literature infers a Battle of Camlan in 537 CE that some conjecture could be a reference to Camelot. See Andrew Breeze, "The Battle of Camlan and Camelford, Cornwall," 75–90.

credited with establishing relationships between the Vatican and the Carolingian family that would eventually blossom into a renaissance. Boniface is a classic Demeter—begging for an awakening of faith during the post-iconoclast period.

REFORM   780–824   Peak: 799

During Pluto's extreme declination to the south (REFORM), Pope Leo III (not to be confused with Leo III, Byzantine Emperor during the POWER time), a man from a humble background was easily elected pope after a series of popes who came from noble birth. He immediately aligned himself with Charlemagne, the King of the Franks (from 768) and Lombards (from 774). Pope Leo III blessed Charlemagne's coronation as the first Emperor of the Romans in over three centuries on Christmas Day in 800 CE, two days after his own. This means that at precisely the peak of REFORM, both Pope Leo III and Charlemagne came into full power, and this began the important alliance between the Carolingian Empire and the Roman Catholic Church that eventually became the Holy Roman Empire, which was neither holy nor Roman, and barely an empire (composed largely of what today is Germany and Italy). The stability achieved by this alliance birthed the Carolingian Renaissance, a time of great art, learning, and cultural advancement, and the first of three major renaissances in Europe.

Summary and Synthesis

Even if the VISION of the visionaries in Europe remains a bit mysterious during the Dark Ages, this cycle established Christianity throughout Europe, beginning with the conversion of the Anglo-Saxons on the British Isles. During POWER, icons were destroyed in an attempt to gain power over the Christians, which backfired when Boniface cried out for justice for Christians during JUSTICE, which then led to a period of stability when the marriage of religion and government, evidenced by Pope Leo III and Emperor Charlemagne, birthed a creative time of REFORM.

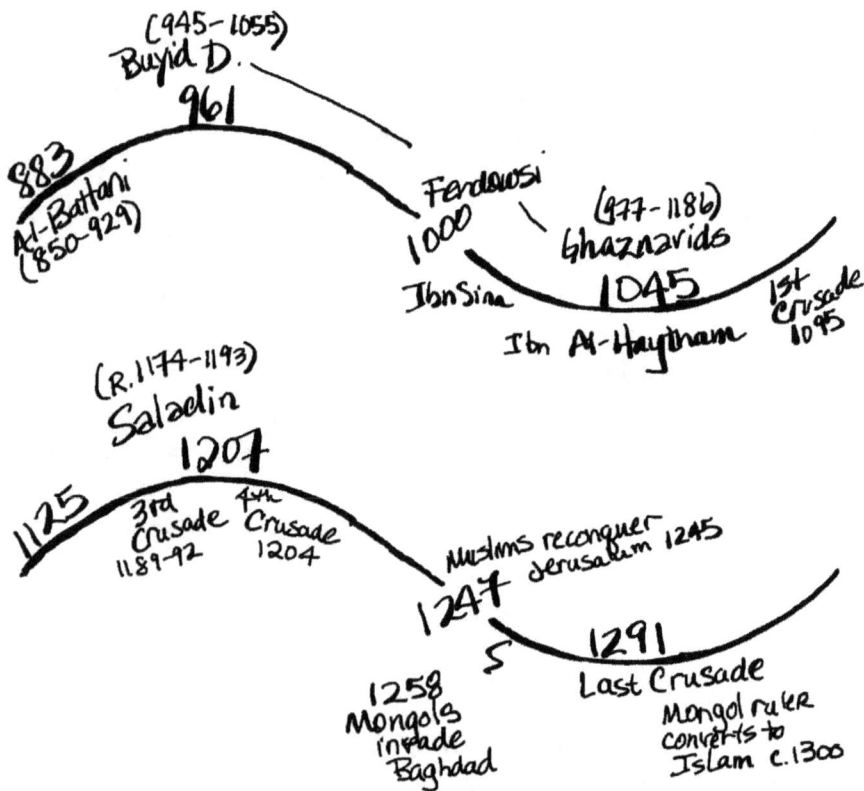

(945-1055)
Buyid D.
961

883
Al-Battani
(850-929)

Ferdowsi
1000

(977-1186)
Ghaznavids
1045

IbnSina

Ibn Al-Haytham

1st
Crusade
1095

(R.1174-1193)
Saladin
1207

1125

3rd
Crusade
1189-92

4th
Crusade
1204

Muslims reconquer
Jerusalem 1245

1247

1291
Last Crusade

1258
Mongols
invade
Baghdad

Mongol ruler
converts to
Islam c.1300

Chapter 9:
Islamic Golden Age Part II, 883–1128 CE

In 880, the desert lands of Arabia and Persia were aflame with new thought. Scientific breakthroughs in math, medicine, optics, astronomy, and chemistry made Baghdad a hub for the exchange of ideas and trade for almost five centuries (two Pluto cycles). Translations of the classic works of Ancient Greece, Indian Sanskrit, Chinese, and almost everything written in Latin could be found in House of Wisdom, the Grand Library of Baghdad. In Arabia, one could have cataracts removed in an air-conditioned hospital while in Europe, leeches and bloodletting were popular healing modalities, heating was a fire pit in the home, and few lived long enough to need cataract surgery. In Europe, Vikings encroached on the British Isles as the Anglo-Saxon tribes began gaining power. While the Islamic Golden Age continued to bear fruit with art, science, invention, and culture, the northern European states began to develop enhanced agricultural practices that laid the foundation for civilizations to come.

The Islamic Golden Age Continues

VISION   880–885

In Baghdad, Thabit ibn Qurra (826–901) founded the field of statics and engineering mechanics. Abū Bakr Muḥammad ibn Zakariyyā᾽ al-Rāzī (854–c. 930), a Persian doctor, discovered a treatment for smallpox. Most notably, astronomer and mathematician, al-Battānī (850–929), took the work of Ptolemy (100–170 CE, who also lived during the VISION time before Augustine) and advanced the field of trigonometry. We have al-Battānī to thank for sines and cosines. (Copernicus, seven hundred years later, cited al-Battānī in his revolutionary work.) Abu Zayd al-Balkhi (850–934) advanced the field of cognitive psychology, connecting mental, spiritual, and physical health.

POWER   940–976   Peak: 961

As the POWER time took hold, strife once again entered the picture and triggered a Buyid takeover. This did not destabilize the region in the way we see other POWER time takeovers. With an iron first, 'Adud al-Dawla (r. 949–983) suspended public demonstrations in order to gain control. Even so, the Buyids continued the path of the Abbasids and invested in infrastructure, dams, and canals, and increased food production.

JUSTICE   999–1002

During the JUSTICE time, ibn al-Haytham published the *Book of Optics* (c. 1011), a book that, in addition to founding the field of optics, laid out a blueprint for the scientific method. This was a particularly creative period in literature—a time of breakthroughs. During this time, Abul-Qâsem Ferdowsi Tusi wrote *Shanameh: The Persian Book of Kings*, a compendium of history and myth, of stories of heroes and warriors fighting for justice. It is a work that preserved the language of Persia (Iran) and offered a poetic view of centuries of Persian history.

REFORM   1028–1067   Peak: 1045

During REFORM, the Persian polymath, Ibn Sina, also known as Avicenna, (980–1037) wrote *The Book of Healing* and *The Canon of Medicine,* a medical encyclopedia used for centuries throughout Europe, Africa, and Asia. In 1037, nine years into Pluto out-of-bounds to the south, the Seljuks, a recent Islamic-converted Turkish tribe, take over and unite the kingdoms stretching from what is modern-day Turkey through Pakistan.[1] Overseeing a time of relative peace, the first ruler, Tughril (r. 1037–1063), transformed the region precisely during this REFORM time.

Summary and Synthesis

By the end of this Pluto cycle, five hundred years had lapsed since the death of Muhammad. The Islamic world was miles ahead of the medieval Europeans in science, education, invention, medicine, and the arts. It is a land ripe with comfort, stunning architecture, modern medicine, and organized systems that support efficient government and higher education. In other words,

---

1. Morgan, 75.

it is ripe for an invasion. Sure enough, at the end of this cycle, Christians, inspired by the battle cry of Pope Urban II in 1095, with a lust for Arabian products and inventions or a pious desire to visit their religious homeland or a fear of the people they called "infidels," initiated a wave of crusades (1095–1291) forcing Muslims to take up arms. Overall, this period demonstrates a more subtle alignment with the Pluto cycle than the previous period.

Over in England

VISION   880–885

The City of London was "refounded" out of the Roman walls of Londinium in 886 CE under the leadership of Alfred the Great (r. 871–899). Alfred is often considered the first King of England. He coalesced the scattered village centers into a unified force through his leadership in fighting off the invading Vikings, much like Muhammad. Alfred, not just a typical meathead warrior, translated *On the Consolation of Philosophy*, a work written by Boethius in captivity in 523 CE (during a JUSTICE time; his appeals for clemency were met with execution), into Anglo-Saxon (Old English). This work espoused Neoplatonic ideas, considered the individual's role in the Christian debates on fate and free will, and became one of the most influential texts in Europe during the Middle Ages. By translating it into vernacular, King Alfred gave the populace an access point to Boethius' once-squashed vision. In 883, Alfred sent emissaries to Rome and India,[2] moving England from an isolated island into a country with international ties. By 886, his army had fought off the Vikings and established a home in London. We can look at Alfred as both Persephone and Hades—both a visionary for spiritual awareness and for initiating out of conquest what would eventually become the British Empire.

POWER   940–976   Peak: 961

After Alfred kicked the Vikings out of Mercia and Wessex (from about Manchester south), they remained in Northumbria (from Manchester up to Edinburgh). Seven years into this POWER time, Eric Haraldsson, an ex-king of Norway (r. 931–933) known in history books as Bloodaxe, came into power in Northumbria (r. 947–948; 952–954). As Pluto was moving into its peak extreme northerly declination, Eric was run out of England and killed on his

2. Caitlin R. Green, *King Alfred and India.*

way out. Æthelstan (r. 927–939), the ruler of Wessex and Mercia took over Northumbria and unified the main states of England and Scotland. Without knowing much about Bloodaxe, we can imagine he wasn't a very nice guy. He was expelled from two countries and nicknamed "Bloodaxe," after-all. After Æthelstan, his brother, Edgar the Peaceful (r. 959–975) took over. Tales of his reign range from entirely peaceful to a tyrannical Joffrey (*Game of Thrones*). As there is little written material from that time, we will have to accept this evidence to represent Pluto's power grab during this time.

JUSTICE   999–1002

During the same time that Ferdowsi was writing an epic story of heroes and kings in Persia and Shikibu was writing the world's first novel in Japan, an unknown writer penned the earliest extant epic in the English language, *Beowulf*. In the poem, the young warrior Beowulf kills the monster Grendel and his mother. The monster and his mother live in a cave, an underworld dwelling, and are depicted as evil, thus the term monster. During a time when Christianity was co-opting pagan rites, the myth parallels pre-Christian goddess myths, including the story of Demeter and Persephone, but with a twist. The young warrior, Beowulf, slays the mother monster, a Medusa-like version of a dark goddess full of rage and venom. As England unifies in alignment with the Christian church in Rome, claiming the ancient Druid stronghold of Glastonbury for their own, a myth about killing an evil mother goes viral. The denigration of the feminine takes root. Not that women were held in high esteem during Roman times. The Greeks were also terrible misogynists. But the pagans of the British Isles traditionally honored the mother and feminine. Queen Boudica, of the ancient British Iceni tribe, led an almost successful rebellion against the Roman Empire in 60–61 CE. But times were changing. The stories of heroes and warriors warding off dark, feminine creatures cir-culated throughout Northern Europe. The patriarchal roots of Christianity planted by Paul and Augustine now infiltrate the mythic tale of Beowulf and the newly formed country of England.

At this stage in the Pluto cycle, Demeter begs Zeus for an intervention. But no intervention comes, the Demeter figure (the mythic mother of Gren-del) is killed off, leaving Persephone in the dark underworld to fend for her-self. With prayers unanswered, Hades' power grows in the REFORM time.

REFORM   1028–1067   Peak: 1045

A decade before the REFORM time, Cnut the Great (r. 1016–1035) invaded England (1018 CE) from his homeland of Denmark to become King of England, Norway, and Denmark. His sons had successive short reigns leaving the kingdom to Edward the Confessor (r. 1042–1066) whose father was the Anglo-Saxon King Æthelred and his mother, Emma of Normandy. With the help of his mother, who happened to be Cnut's widow, Edward returned England to Anglo-Saxon rule. His stable, 24-year-long rule consisted of enacting legal reforms establishing a more unified ruling body, the building of Westminster Abbey, and playing games with successorship. Without a son, he was left to name his successor, sometimes favoring his cousin William of Normandy and sometimes favoring his brother-in-law, Harold. William's ability to take hold of Normandy in 1035 and maintain order, even as an illegitimate son of the prior ruler, provided him experience and contributed to his confidence. When Edward the Confessor died in 1066, Harold claimed the throne, but within the year, William took an army across the English Channel, killed Harold in battle, and claimed the English throne for himself. This battle, the Battle of Hastings, began the long history of Norman rule of England. Since William only spoke French, his court needed to speak French as well. Over the years, the French language blended with the native language to create Middle English. While it may appear that the Battle of Hastings is more in line with what occurs during the POWER time, particularly in the way it has come to be revered, the battle was not a foreign dictator arriving on foreign soil to claim a victory. William was a cousin of the king and had a rightful claim to the throne. He also did not continue his campaign into other countries. He claimed England, changed the language, the governing systems, and established a right of succession to continue into the next cycle.

Summary and Synthesis

From a Viking stronghold to Anglo-Saxon rule, to Danish rule and back to Anglo-Saxon and finally Norman rule, England transformed again and again during this cycle. From a pagan land of small enclaves living in the aftermath of Arthurian legends to an established Christian nation with international connections. From Alfred the Great to the Battle of Hastings, this cycle established Britain as a nation with influence, power, and prestige. From this point on, the Great British Isles, a land thirteen times smaller than India and 42 times smaller than all of Europe, grew in power to become the largest global empire in history. The roots of its strength lie in the visionaries and reformers of this time. Alfred who envisioned a unified nation, the literary genius of the anonymous author of *Beowulf*, who transmitted a vision of patriarchy through poetry, and Edward the Confessor demonstrating the future greatness and the potential for this kingdom with the grandness of the cathedral he had built during his stable, prosperous reign.

Meanwhile in China: The Song Dynasty

Allow me to give a nod to Chinese history during this cycle, since the transition from Tang Dynasty to Song Dynasty that occurred during the POWER time holds significance for the Chinese to this day. During the Middle Ages in Europe and alongside the Islamic Golden Age, China flourished with developments in the arts and sciences. While fighting at the border between China and Persia continued throughout the prior Pluto cycle, during this cycle, Islamic forces withdrew, and China transitioned into a new dynasty.

VISION   880–885

A young rebel and gang leader, Zhu Wen (852–912), rose through the ranks of the Chinese military during the time of the declining Tang Dynasty. His father, a scholar of the Five Classics,[3] taught Zhu Wen before this cycle began, but it was as Pluto crossed from southern to northern declination (VISION) in 883, that Zhu became the military governor of the Bian Prefecture (current day Henan province). From this position, he drew together an army that eventually overthrew the Tang Dynasty in 907, killed the emperor and all his sons in 904, and destroyed the capital. He placed himself on the throne, but that didn't last long. His eldest son killed him in 912. His lineage, the Hou (Later) Liang, didn't last long either, ending in 923.

---

3. The Five Classics is a school of thinking mostly based on the works of Confucius that includes: classic poetry, history, and prose of ancient Chinese rulers; a Book of Rites that includes ancient rites, ceremonies, and social customs thought to come from Confucius; the *I Ching* a system of divination; and a historical record of the State of Lu, Confucius' home state. The Five Classics were adopted during the Han Dynasty and then preserved through times of transition and the Tang Dynasty. It wasn't fully brought back until the Song Dynasty (f. 961) where it became the core teachings and basis for testing, critical for advancement within the government.

POWER   940–976   Peak: 961

From the fall of the Tang Dynasty in 907 to the inception of the Song Dynasty in 961, a complex array of five dynasties and ten kingdoms—with infighting, short-lived rulers, and changing boundaries—transformed China. Just as Pluto went out-of-bounds to the north, the Southern Tang Dynasty invaded the Min Kingdom (909–945). The Southern Tang (937–975), hoping that naming themselves Tang would give them extra staying power/respect, were then overtaken by the Song Dynasty at the end of this POWER time. General Zhao Kuangyin, who had rebelled against his king in 960, founded the Song Dynasty at the peak of POWER in 961. The Song Dynasty began taking over provinces, and by 979 governed most of China. This began a long prosperous rule for China (961–1291). Similar to other leaders during other POWER times, an ambitious general overtook a kingdom, changed his name (to Emperor Taizu, r. 927–976) and amassed great power by conquering region after region until the POWER time ended. The Song Dynasty modeled itself after the Han Dynasty (202 BCE–220 CE) and based its government administration on the teachings of Confucius. The underlying principles of the Song Dynasty cultivated advancements in science, literature, and art.

JUSTICE   999–1002

The Song Dynasty quickly stabilized the region. As the philosophy of Confucius permeated society, the government, and education. Art, science, medicine, shipbuilding, and iron-casting took off. Around this time, scientists discovered the difference between magnetic north and true north. Xu Daoning (fl. 1010) and Yan Wengui (fl. 1007) worked as artists during this period.

REFORM   1028–1067   Peak: 1045

At the peak of Pluto's journey out of bounds to the south (REFORM), Bi Sheng invented movable type (1045). With increasing availability of books, education and science grew. In 1086, Shen Gua wrote technical essays on erosion and sedimentation, centuries before scientists in Europe.[4] While books and science flourished, so did art, including the great Song artists Cui Bo (fl. 1060), Huan Tingjian (fl. 1085), Li Gonglin (fl. 1081), Fan Kuan (fl. 1030),

4. Murray, 39.

Guo Xi (fl. 1041), Su Shi (fl. 1076), Wen Tong (fl. 1059) and writers Feng Yan-si (fl. 1047) and Wang Anshi (fl. 1061).[5] Agriculture produced high yields as farmers benefited from low interest rate loans from the government. Advancements in shipbuilding and navigation supported an industrial revolution.[6] Alongside the growth, however, drought (1047) and rebellion (Song-Xia wars) plagued the Song Dynasty. In 1044, after four years of rebellion led by Li Yuanhao, the Song Dynasty recognized the Xia independence, a western region that stretched from the Yumen Pass to the Yellow River.

Summary and Synthesis

The cycle began with a warrior rebel, educated by a scholar-father, steeped in Confucian philosophy, instigating the decline and fall of the Tang Dynasty. During the POWER time, a new dynasty, through invasion and war, took over China and began one of the most prosperous, inventive, and advanced civilizations on the planet at the time. As the Song Dynasty expanded, it initiated policies that supported growth in the arts and sciences. When the REFORM time hit, revolution—both political and industrial—supported a rise in power to the people. The agricultural advancements and policies that supported centuries of sustainable farming in the Song Dynasty during this REFORM time offer hope for a green revolution during the REFORM time starting in 2025.

---

5. Murray, 543.
6. John M. Hobson, *The Eastern Origins of Western Civilization*, Loc. 692 (kindle).

Chapter 10:
Warriors and Knights, 1126–1372 CE

During this cycle in Europe and Asia, quasi-peaceful, co-existing small cities evolved into great warring nation-states. The crusades turned the lands from present-day France to Jerusalem into constant battlegrounds. The Roman Catholic Church grew in power, while Genghis Khan conquered more territory than anyone in known history. The Shogun was established as the ruler in Japan, while Saladin built an army in Egypt and Syria. It is perhaps no surprise that Baghdad's House of Wisdom fell to invaders and religious warriors, as these kinds of warring exchanges became the new trend. This explosion of war and conquering, particularly intense during this cycle's POWER time, interrupted a time of great science. Faith-based fighting, be it Christian, Muslim, or the Mongolian Tengri, erupted *en masse*. By the end of this Pluto cycle (REFORM), the crusaders limped home from their last campaign, Kublai Khan's failed expansion plans forced China to focus on infrastructure, science, and culture, and a new collaborative form of government quietly grew in the Alps.

The Khans, 1126–1373

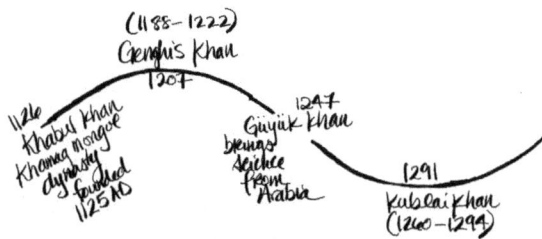

VISION   1122–1128

Exactly when Pluto crossed the equatorial plane from south to north in 1125, the Liao dynasty in the northern region of China fell, and Genghis Khan's great grandfather, Khabul Khan, declared the Khamag Mongol Dynasty, a nomadic tribe, as the new rulers of the land. The natives of the land were known as Tatars (or Tartars), a reference to Tartarus, the abyss of torment deep in the realm of Hades. And so the beginning of this cycle begins with the Khamag Mongol Dynasty taking the keys of Hades' kingdom and, with a Pluto-like thirst for power, becoming rulers of the underworld.

POWER   1188–1221   Peak: 1207

Just before Pluto crossed into extreme northern declination in 1188, a group of bandits abducted Börte, the wife of Temüjin, a fatherless young man dedicated to caring for his siblings, mother, and wife. Temüjin took up a sword, gathered his friends, attacked the village, and rescued his wife. Whatever took place within Temüjin, whatever wildness was unleashed, whatever force within him took over, led to conquest after conquest, led to world domination never seen before (or since). His highly organized and fearsome army declared victory after victory across the plains of present-day Russia, Mongolia, and China. By the time he was done, the new Khan Dynasty ruled from the Caspian Sea to the Pacific Ocean, from Siberia to the Himalayas. At the peak of the POWER time, in 1206, Temüjin declared himself "universal emperor," transforming himself into the legendary Genghis Khan. He continued his conquests until Pluto left extreme northerly declination in 1221. He died six years later, leaving the kingdom to his sons. What began with a typical Persephone-Hades drama—the abduction of a young woman—turned a young warrior into Hades himself, striking fear into village after village.

JUSTICE   1246–1249

Precisely at the beginning of the JUSTICE time, Güyük Khan, Genghis Khan's grandson, came into power. He had a particular desire to take over Medieval Europe mostly under the leadership of Christian churches. The news sent the many political, religious, and aristocratic leaders of Europe into a panic. The Byzantine Church reached out to the Roman Catholic Church hoping for an alliance. The Armenian Church reached out to the Greek Orthodox Church hoping for an alliance. But Güyük's untimely death two years later ended the panic. Without a clear successor, European leaders felt reassured that a Mongol conquest was not imminent, and so they called off their treaties, ending their fake friendships. Möngke Khan (1248–1259), Güyük's nephew, became the next ruler. He turned his attention toward the wealthier Arabian lands, and went on to sack Baghdad, destroying the

House of Wisdom in 1258. This seemingly subtle change in direction shifted dramatically the course of the world. If the Khans had turned their attention toward Europe, still creeping out of the Middle Ages, we might all be living under Mongol rule to this day. Instead, the wisdom of scholars, healers, scientists, and artists in Arabia and Persia disseminated into foreign hands as travelers and warriors returned to China. Whoever intervened on Persephone's behalf was on Europe's side during this JUSTICE time.

REFORM   1276–1310   Peak: 1291

Fourteen years before Pluto went out-of-bounds to the south, Kublai Khan (r. 1264–1294) came into power. He ruled through more than half of this stage, dying at the peak of the REFORM time. His China was described to Europeans very differently than that of his grandfather, Ghenghis Khan. When Marco Polo, previously an Italian tradesman, found himself in Kublai's palace working as a diplomat, he wrote extensively about his time in China, revealing to those back home in Medieval Italy a land of wealth, beauty, and comforts unheard of during the time of European crusades and plagues.

Kublai was not the warrior his grandfather was. In an effort to distance himself from the warlike reputation of his ancestor, he changed the name of the dynasty from the Khan Dynasty to the Yuan Dynasty. Meanwhile, his military campaigns mostly failed. A storm interrupted his takeover of Japan. Heat and disease ruined his invasion of Indonesia. This was a time for REFORM, not POWER. Conversely, his diplomatic efforts were often successful. He peacefully negotiated with the Song Dynasty in southern China, merging those lands into his realm in 1276, just as Pluto went out-of-bounds southward. He built canals, developed a postal system, and invested in science, medicine, and education. The banking system used paper money backed by gold, which was efficient and supportive of trade, an invention of Yuan economists.

Following Kublai Khan's death, his grandson, Temür (r. 1294–1307), ruled for the duration of this REFORM time and continued many of his grandfather's improvements and ideals. He called off all warring expansionism and focused on economic recovery after the expensive failed military excursions of Kublai. Temür, unlike his ancestor Genghis Khan, had to deal with rebellions, particularly in the southeastern part of his kingdom. Temür maintained order, but not easily. Eventually, the Yuan Dynasty was overthrown during the Red Turban Rebellions between the years 1351 and 1368 at the end of this Pluto cycle, just in time for a new VISION to begin.

Looking at the current cycle for our contemporary moment in time, we can look to Kublai Khan and his focus on education, culture, construction, and infrastructure as a potential touchstone for the upcoming REFORM period between 2025 and 2035. It's also interesting to note that his son, Temür Khan, was ill for much of his time as ruler and his wife, Bulugan, ruled the empire in his stead. Perhaps Hades was ill in the myth, and Persephone ruled in his stead; perhaps we can expect to see similar dynamics among world leaders in our upcoming REFORM period.

Summary and Synthesis

The rise and fall of the Khan dynasty mirrors the Pluto declination cycle in action. From the birth of Genghis' dynasty during VISION, his conquests precisely as Pluto went out-of-bounds northward, his crowning at the peak POWER time, the petering out of expansion as Pluto dipped back into bounds, an intercession and tide-turning event during Pluto's crossover into southern declination, to a perfect example of the kind of REFORMS observed during Pluto's extreme southerly declination, with Kublai Khan on the throne. The synchronization is so strong, this may be the only cycle needed to explore how history and Pluto align. But let's keep going.

The Crusades, 1126–1372

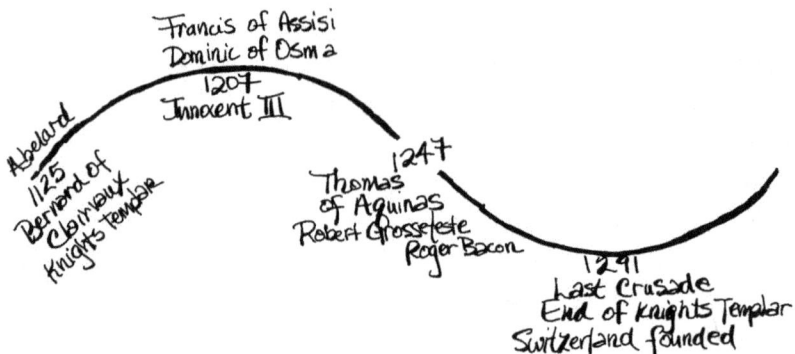

98

VISION   1122–1128

This VISION time began with notable visionaries, including Peter Abelard, a monk known more for his love story with Eloise—and her relatives who attacked and castrated the poor man sending him into monastic life—than for his brilliance as a scientist and theologian. Another visionary is a man named Dmitri, a mysterious Bogomil who barely receives a footnote in history but somehow initiated a major uprising in Kiev in 1125. Consider Ibn Tufayl (c. 1105–1185), a Muslim scholar and physician who wrote philosophical novels and supported dissection for understanding the human body, and Abraham ibn Ezra (c. 1090–c. 1166), a Jewish scholar who wrote a multitude of books on mathematics, religious philosophy, and astronomy, along with a host of other Islamic and Jewish polymaths living in the Iberian Peninsula during this time who ushered in a scientific revolution long before the Bacons.[1]

However, for our purposes, much like the VISION time that began with Augustine and Hypatia, we will focus our attention solely on two notable visionaries. The first is a Christian scholar, proponent of the sanctity of nature, composer, and mystic Benedictine abbess, Hildegard of Bingen (1098–1179, Germany). The other is a Christian scholar, master of austerity, and dogmatic Cistercian monk, Bernard of Clairvaux (1090–1153, France). Both figures were young adults during this VISION time, and both went on to live long and influential lives. And while they did eventually meet through letters, their philosophies were almost diametrically opposed, much like Augustine's and Hypatia's views were.

Hildegard began having visions as a child that took on a life of their own as she matured. In her early thirties, as Pluto crossed from southern to northern declination (VISION), she took on a leadership role at the Benedictine convent in which she had lived most of her life. She arrived at the theological concept of *viriditas* or "greening power," the fruitfulness of creativity.[2] "Viriditas...is God's freshness that humans receive in their spiritual and physical life-forces. It is the power of springtime, a germinating force, a fruitfulness that comes from God and penetrates all creation."[3] Hildegard gave voice to

---

1. Roger Bacon (1219–1292) and Francis Bacon (1561–1626), two unrelated philosophers known for introducing the scientific method.
2. Jean Shinoda Bolen, *Crossing to Avalon: A Woman's Midlife Pilgrimage*, 214.
3. Matthew Fox, "Viriditas: Greening Power" in *Illuminations of Hildegard von Bingen*.

the feminine spirit. She considered the dried-up spiritual convictions of sin that Augustine proposed to go against God and the blessing of life. Jungian psychiatrist, Jean Shinoda Bolen, MD, directly compared Hildegard's thinking to Persephone in her book *Crossing to Avalon.* "The promise of spring and the return of greenness to the barren land is also a psychological possibility symbolized by the return of the maiden goddess Persephone to her mother, Demeter."[4] Consider that Hildegard wrote to popes and bishops, advocating for this Earth-based perspective of spirituality during the same time that crusaders were invading the holy sites, international banking was taking root, and patriarchal systems of government and religion were gaining in power, particularly Catholicism and Islam.

By 1122, the Cistercian monk, Bernard of Clairvaux (1090–1153) was already a well-respected Catholic scholar and diplomat. With friends in high places (the pope), he moved easily through the realms of power and prestige. When Hugues de Payne, his uncle, founded the Knights Templar in 1119, Bernard suggested a council be formed in support of the new organization.[5] As the tale goes, the Knights Templar was originally formed as a religious-warrior order geared towards protecting crusaders, the Christian pilgrims visiting the newly conquered Jerusalem (1099, First Crusade). It was Bernard's sponsorship through the Council of Troyes that gave the Knights the backing of the Catholic Church. It was Bernard who wrote the code of conduct, a handbook of sorts, for the Knights Templar, *In Praise of the New Knighthood* (1129), an idealistic, faith-based compendium featuring knights in shining armor, chivalry, and human nobility—the basis for our contemporary ideas about the romance of this period. That they were written by a celibate monk who never saw battle is just another irony in history.

In 1126, precisely as Pluto was crossing the equatorial plane (VISION), Bernard of Clairvaux wrote *On Grace and Free Choice,* one of his most significant works. During this same time in Bologna, Mater Gratian, also known as the "Father of Canon Law," wrote his compendium, *Decretum,* using the work of Augustine and the First Council of Nicaea to organize and initiate the laws of the Catholic Church. Their theology together inspired generations of Christian scholars.

---

4. Bolen, 218.
5. Freddy Silva, *First Templar Nation*, 83–87.

As this cycle unfolds, these two visionaries and their visions go head-to-head, vying for power as Catholic doctrines launch witch-burnings and inquisitions and the juiciness of Hildegard's teachings and music go underground (to be seriously resurrected during the JUSTICE time three Pluto cycles later in the late 1980s).

One more figure bears mentioning here. While Bernard was writing codes of conduct for soldiers setting out to attack Muslims, Peter Abelard translated Muḥammad ibn Mūsā al-Khwārizmī's mathematical work on algebra from Arabic into Latin. Abelard's efforts sharply contrasted the work of Bernard. Bernard's faith-based idealism in which everything was grace—even human accomplishment—ran contrary to Abelard's reason-based, logic-loving open-mindedness. Bernard inspired crusades against the Muslim lands, while Abelard honored their knowledge. However, it was Bernard who found favor with the pope while Abelard was cast off to the western coast of France to rebuild a crumbling monastery. And so it was that Bernard and the crusaders were given the mythic and historical keys to the kingdom of Hades, a world of violence, destruction, and death.

Despite who started what, who was more violent, who acted in bad faith, be it Muslims, Christians, Seljuk Turks, Mongolian fighters, or bankers making bank, the dark underworld of Hades was well-represented by the secret codes, underhanded dealings, and crusaders willing to kill to gain access to holy grounds. Bernard was sainted in the Catholic Church in 1174, his teachings revered as scripture, and his political acumen regarded as inspirational. It may be controversial to call him a representative of anything resembling the underworld. Yet, his activism with the papacy and support of the knights gave credence to these holy wars, gave credence even to the concept of holy war, that over the next century destroyed cities, cultures, and many, many lives.

POWER   1188–1221   Peak: 1207

This POWER time is filled with intrigue, wars, and the roots of the Inquisition, witch-burnings, unrest in the Middle East, and legends aplenty. Knights in shining armor, Richard the Lionheart fighting Saladin, King John and the Magna Carta, Dominic of Osma and Francis of Assisi starting orders still consequential today, and one of the most powerful popes in history, Pope Innocent III (p. 1198–1216).

In 1184, four years before Pluto crossed into extreme northerly decli-nation (POWER), Pope Lucius III (p. 1181–1185) sent a list of heresies to Europe's bishops and commanded them to root out any heretics in their regions. Instead of using the courts, the pope authorized the bishops to "inquire" the accused heretics about their possible heretical practices—"in-quire," perhaps a nice word for coerce or torture. The power of the Catholic Church at this time, such that it was, held sway over the courts, so this line of inquisition was an efficient way to assure conformity within the church. Whether Lucius had any idea of the avalanche of suffering he was starting, we don't know. It is as if Hades (in the form of Pope Lucius III) perhaps in-nocently, began negotiations with Zeus (the kings and courts) for his daugh-ter (the people) with an "inquiry."

In 1187, Saladin (r. 1174–1193), the Sultan of the Ayyubid Empire (along the Levant and Arabian Peninsula), and his well-trained army of sword-bran-dishing Muslim fighters took back Jerusalem from the Christians. Just as Plu-to went out-of-bounds, Henry II, King of England, died, and his son, Rich-ard I of England, known popularly as Richard the Lionheart (r. 1189–1199), came into power. At the behest of the pope, Richard immediately left En-gland to lead the Third Crusade (1189–1192) in a show of force against Sal-adin's army that resulted in a loss for the crusaders and a short-lasting peace treaty. Famously, Richard died in battle seven years later, and his inept (as the legend goes) brother, John, became king of England. King John, as we might remember from Disney's 1971 movie *Robin Hood*, was not well-loved. The barons rebelled against him and forced him to sign the Magna Carta, a doc-ument that was to become an inspiration for the US Constitution, among other constitutions. The Magna Carta offered the aristocratic barons greater power, more protection from unwarranted arrests, and limitations on how much they could be taxed. While the document only gave more power to a small group of wealthy people, it sowed the seeds for future parliaments and representative governments. Consider that in our current Pluto cycle, we acknowledge the Magna Carta as the beginning of democracy, when what it really did was give power to the Plutocrats, the barons, and the rest of the aristocracy, limiting the powers of the sole Zeus-like monarch.

The year before Richard died, Pope Celestine III died, and a new pope was ordained—a pope who today is still considered one of the most powerful popes in history. Pope Innocent III, whose papacy lasted from 1198 to 1216, extended the powers of the Catholic Church and instigated crusades not just in conquest of Jerusalem, but also against the Cathars in southern France and the Muslims in Spain.

Early in his papacy Pope Innocent III sent Cistercian monks to convert the Cathars, a mystical Christian sect in the south of France, known for their devotion to Mary Magdalene. A young Catholic priest, Dominic of Osma (1170–1221), encountered these monks and was particularly perturbed at their ineffectiveness in converting the Mary-worshipping, peace-loving medieval "hippies." In response to the Cistercians' failure, Dominic began a new monastic order designed to be more austere, more disciplined, and more focused on preaching—basically better at converting. Thus, the Dominican Order began between 1204 and 1206 in Toulouse, France, and was officially sanctioned by the Roman Catholic Church in 1215 at the Fourth Lateran Council, all during the peak of Pluto out of bounds to the north. While Dominic's intentions and spiritual aspirations may have been pure, that the Dominican Order began during a POWER time and focused on conversion in the way it did, it found itself aligned with this new path of harsh inquisitions at the behest of the pope. Becoming the right hand of the papacy over the next few centuries, the Dominican Order is known for ordaining some of the most diabolical inquisitors and torturers, including Tomás de Torquemada (1420–1498).

In 1202, Innocent III recruited an army mostly from Venice to go back down to the Levant and invade Egypt. The Venetian crusaders of the Fourth Crusade diverged from that plan finding it more advantageous for their purposes to invade the rival port city of Constantinople, the capital city of the Christian Byzantine Empire. Naturally, Innocent III was upset hearing that his Christian crusaders had attacked another Christian city against his wishes. He started making plans for another crusade to the Levant. He died in 1216 the year before the Fifth Crusade left (1217), returning unsuccessful in 1221, just as Pluto was leaving extreme northerly declination.

At its peak, in a stroke of POWER that might make Hades jealous, Pope Innocent III, in 1205, issued the papal bull, *Si adversus von*, forbidding legal assistance to those accused of heresy. Then, in the same year, he condemned Jews to perpetual servitude in retribution for their part in condemning Jesus.

In 1206, upon the failure to convert the Cathars, Innocent III claimed all lands in the south of France for the Catholic Church and called on the French lords to convene a crusade to accomplish this. Between 1206 and 1209, French leaders were coerced into fulfilling a crusade against their own people, killing tens of thousands.[6] At the end of this Pluto cycle's POWER time, Raymond VI of Toulouse, one of the main accomplices to Pope Innocent III's crusade for the lands of south France, died, and fighting in France petered out.

In 1212, two alleged Children's Crusades took off for Jerusalem, one from Germany and one from France. Neither were sanctioned by the pope, neither were made up of all children, and neither got anywhere near Jerusalem. However, the legends of the Children's Crusades tell a story so horrific that it could only have happened when Pluto was out-of-bounds north. Stories recount children leaving their homes, and their parents, following vigilantes, being abducted by pirates, and never returning.[7] For those of us who have never lived (and will never live) through a POWER time, a certain fervor takes over that is hard to imagine. The power of an out-of-bounds Pluto correlates with a feeling of fear so profound that we send our children off to war or give over control of our village with the mention of the name of a new and fearsome warrior.

While Pope Innocent III was coalescing Vatican power, the Knights Templar were setting up one of the finest international banking systems. The trail to Jerusalem was a mugger's paradise. In response, the Templars set up posts along the way, places where pilgrims could deposit their money, receive an encoded Certificate of Deposit, and carry that deposit to the next post to retrieve their money. Even though the Templars themselves had taken vows of poverty, as an organization the Templars became wealthy. In part, their poverty vow helped people to trust them. In a parallel to other POWER times, both the extension of power and the increase in wealth in the hands of the few, overrode the will of the people.

By the Fourth Council of the Lateran in November 1215, in the last year of Innocent III's papacy and life, much of southern France had been taken by

---

6. Some French crusaders were more willing than others to follow the pope's orders. The Duc of Anjou and some other French leaders went to Albi and massacred the Cathars willingly and were hardly opposed to dealing brutally with a mystical cult that saw little value in wealth or participation in warfare.

7. Steve Anchell, "The Historical basis for the Children's Crusades, 1212 CE."

the crusades. The Canons (Catholic law) created during this council would exert powerful and terrible effects over the following centuries. Canon 8 advocated the criminal treatment of heretics, which would support the upcoming inquisitions and witch burnings, for example. Canon 68 initiated the rule that Jews and Muslims had to wear badges, a punitive measure meant to outcast them, that eventually succeeded throughout Europe, but especially in Spain when, over the next two centuries, hundreds of thousands of Jews and Muslims were either forced to convert to Christianity or exiled.

During this same POWER time, there's a Persephone counterpoint to the power-mad, marauding crusaders and inquisitions. In the Tuscan town of Assisi, a wealthy merchant's son named Francis was still a teenager when his town attacked the larger town, Perugia. Like many naïve, young men attracted to the glory and excitement of battle, his experience was anything but. The "Persephones," these young men barely of shaving age, are abducted into war—either through coercion, drafts, or false ideas of glory—by a patriarchal society that values war foremost and sees it as the only way to handle a situation. Young male innocence numbed, lost.

The attack on Perugia went badly, and Francis was captured. He spent a year in the dark underworld dungeon of Hades (Perugia), where he almost died. During his dark night of the soul, he turned toward prayer. When he was released, through intercession on the part of the nobles, he was a completely different person. Spiritually awake and with renewed purpose, he visited the pope and unsuccessfully tried to talk him out of the Crusades. Then he journeyed with crusaders and tried unsuccessfully to convert Muslims in the region, returned to Assisi, and founded a religious order, the Franciscans, that focused on prayer and simplicity. Similarly, his friend and follower from another noble family, Clare of Assisi, started an order of nuns, the Poor Clares, who were also dedicated to austerity and service. Francis and Clare offer us a window into the radical acts of spiritual awakening and compassion that can be a result of the POWER time.

JUSTICE   1246–1249

During this JUSTICE time, the very word "justice" was redefined, in a particularly twisted way to the 21st-century mind. It was a time when most legal, scientific, and literary scholars were Christian monks and priests. It was a time when Europe, after decades of pilgrimages and invasions of the sophisticated Arabian lands, was waking up out of its medieval sleep, beguiled with tales of science, medicine, and magic carpets from faraway lands. The Dominican Order, founded in 1215, was gathering recruits and Pope Gregory IX gave the monks authority to examine heretics (1231), particularly the Cathars in southern France. The decree from the pope demanded that such heretics be handed over to the secular arm for "due punishment", another way of saying, since the church does not execute people, we will hand these heretics over to the state who does. "Due punishment" clearly meaning death by fire during that time.[8] These examinations lay the foundation for future inquisitions.

Robert Grosseteste, the bishop of Lincoln, England, was a clergyman credited with developing the scientific method and passing it on to his student, Roger Bacon. He studied optics and nature, was an apt translator of Greek and Arabian, and was a scholar of Aristotle, Avicenna, and Averroes and their work. Meanwhile, Thomas Aquinas, a Dominican monk from Italy, wrote highly sophisticated Catholic doctrines, using the work of Aristotle in his quest to unite logic with the faith-based teachings of Christianity. The field of science was emerging in medieval Europe, finally catching up to advances that were already well-developed in other parts of the world, such as Persia and China. This makes it all the more alarming that the Inquisition, a deeply fanatical movement of killing women and men out of a twisted sense of reason, began at this time and prevailed—for centuries.

Grosseteste had a hand in the Inquisition. His early writings supported "heresy zeal"—as the Catholic Church started to torture and execute those who did not fully support their doctrine. It was his definition of heresy that spread through the region. He defined heresy as "opinion chosen by human perception contrary to holy scripture, publicly avowed and obstinately defended." Understanding his complicated effect on society during Pluto's crossing from northern to southern declination (JUSTICE) mirrors the complexity of exactly what justice is.

We often think of justice synonymously with retribution or even vengeance. Today, justice often conjures thoughts of social justice, fair treatment, and rectification of wrongs. Webster's Dictionary defines justice as

8. Benzion Netanyahu, *The Origins of the Inquisition in Fifteenth Century Spain*, 500.

the maintenance of what is "just", and "just" is defined as reasonable. We can view justice as the process of moving toward reason. And reason is an ever-evolving perception. Robert Grosseteste brought reasoning to a new level with his curious mix of secular scientific method and his views on religious heresy. That his views led to the vigilante and extreme measure of a warped perception of justice by the Dominican monks of Spain, has more to do with the pope at the time. In 1252, Pope Innocent IV initiated the papal bull, *Ad extirpanda*, authorizing torture to elicit confessions. He also began the idea of corporate personhood, where an organization, in this case a monastic order, could act as and claim the rights of a person. Pope Innocent IV's idea of justice, abhorrent to most of us today, was validated by the powers bestowed into the papacy during the POWER time of Pope Innocent III.

REFORM   1276–1310   Peak: 1291

Precisely at the peak of Pluto's extreme declination to the south (REFORM) in 1291, the last crusade ended after a failed, six-week siege of the Mamluk city of Acre—along the coast of modern-day Israel—an important port town for the Christian pilgrims. Once the Mamluks, under the rulership of Sultan Khalil, won in these final crusade battles, chaos ensued. The Muslim Mamluks captured, enslaved, and killed many of the Christians. Others were able to escape to Cyprus and return to Europe.

Some of the knights landed in Portugal, where King Dinis created a ruse and changed the name of the Knights Templar to the Order of Christ. Some traveled up to Scotland to join the Scottish rebellions under William Wallace (1270–1305, r. 1297–1298) and Robert the Bruce (r. 1306–1329). And some knights might just as easily have crossed over southern France into the Alps, precisely when three small cantons were gathering to create a federation, which they named after one of the cantons, Swyss. The day celebrated as the birth of Switzerland, August 1, 1291, is a mere two months after the Siege of Acre. What began as a declaration of independence from the Holy Roman Empire became the seed place of future reformations, including The Reformation under the inspiration of Huldrych Zwingli during the next Pluto cycle's REFORM time, and a mathematical reformation under the inspiration of Swiss polymath, Leonhard Euler (1707–1783) in the subsequent Pluto cycle's REFORM time. In 1291, during the peak of this cycle's REFORM, a few warrior knights planted the seeds of the roots of a new form of direct democracy and the initial breath of a country that sat in the middle of two future world wars and claimed neutrality.[9]

In the British Isles, King Edward I (r. 1272–1307)—who ruled England nearly the entire time Pluto was out-of-bounds to the south—was known as a reformer within England for his focus on the judicial system and administrative functions. Outside of England, he was known as a ruthless invader, forcing the Scottish clans to claim fealty to the crown and forcing high taxes on the Irish, Welsh, and Scottish. Rebellions ensued. Just after the peak of REFORM, William Wallace and Andrew Moray in Scotland raised an army and beat the English at the Battle of Stirling Bridge (1297), made famous by the not-exactly-historically-accurate movie *Braveheart*. The next year, the Scots lost in battle and in 1305, Edward's army captured and executed Wallace. This further incited the Scots under the leadership of Robert the Bruce, who took back Scotland for the Scots through stealth warfare and cunning strategy. For the rest of this Pluto cycle and throughout the next one, Scottish people ruled Scotland.

In France, King Phillip IV (r. 1285–1314) eradicated the Knights Templar, the few remaining Cathars revolted for the last time (1290) before being entirely wiped out, and the pope moved to Avignon in 1309 initiating a schism in the Catholic Church.

Summary and Synthesis

At the beginning of this Pluto cycle, the works of Bernard of Clairvaux, and the battle-rules of chivalry and "just wars," pervaded the lands, while Hildegard's embodied nature teachings went into remission. The "Persephones," the pilgrims along the road to Jerusalem, enticed with messages of salvation, were abducted and thrown into the hell that was the Crusades. During JUSTICE, reason and faith became terribly intermingled and co-opted by rulers to define heresy and begin the brutal process of "bringing to

---

9. While no records prove that the Knights Templar fled to what is now modern-day Switzerland, it is easily conceivable that some ended up there, travelling over the east border of France in their escape. It is known that the Swiss cantons were able to fight off invaders with new weaponry, a sign of well-trained knights. It is also interesting that Switzerland to this day is known for its banking, perhaps a holdover from the Templars banking industry. It could be that the dissolution of the Knights Templar into Switzerland supported future of international banking.

justice" heretics. In the REFORM time, the Crusades met their end, and a new form of government based on collaboration and accords was created in the Alps. While tiny in comparison to the world stage of politics at the time, the birth of Switzerland during the REFORM time displays a country founded by the "Persephones" of the planet.

At the end of this Pluto cycle, filled with war and edicts that allowed for torture, a battle-weary Europe was dramatically transformed by the Black Plague (1346–1353) and the mass death that ensued. As China moved into a time of genuine reform under Kublai Khan, Europe seemed to be stuck in an era of violence and was hit particularly hard. Instead of bowing to the will of the people, European leaders, especially Edward I and Phillip IV, continued policies of torture and expulsions, as if they were Hades unable to loosen their grips on total domination. But plague came anyway. Persephone always gets to co-rule in some way, whether it takes a storm or a plague or a schism to get there. In most cases, wise rulers see the writing on the wall and adapt to the needs of the people. In Europe, superstition and xenophobia increased. In the Holy Roman Empire, anti-Semitism incited violence against Jewish people, blaming them for the plague. This Pluto cycle was Europe's difficult birth into a new age. By the end, Dante's writing, influenced by his experience of the plague, is considered an early entry into the Italian Renaissance. The markers of the new age began in back rooms in Florence, small enclaves in Switzerland, and colleges in England.

Chapter 11:
Renaissance to Reformation, 1373–1618

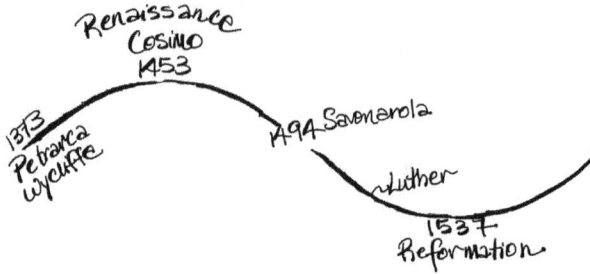

This Pluto cycle begins with the early visionaries of the Italian Renaissance, loyal Christians in a time when the European states bowed to the will of the Catholic pope. Through the power of words and the development of the printing press, a revolution of new thought led to mass protests and a reformation of Christian thought and freedom. It is a cycle when a small country, half the size of Turkey, took down a Christian empire, introduced weapons of mass destruction (cannons), and transformed the Middle East into the Ottoman Empire. It is a cycle that began with two continents (currently called the Americas) of peaceful societies that grew into warring nations and then were destroyed by a small group of greedy, iron-clad soldiers.

Gold, mined from the bowels of the Earth, ruled by Hades himself, triggered an avalanche of desire and gave power to conquistadors. Coin-minting and double-entry bookkeeping enhanced the powers of banking. Navigational tools led to a revolution in travel and global exploration, which, in turn, galvanized an explosion of trade—silk-road textiles and spices—and the requisite labor to mine, make, and transport those treasures. Clocks told time in new ways. Improved compasses told direction. Time and space—now measurable—could ostensibly be controlled. Portuguese and Spanish ships, built to traverse oceans, carried enslaved people. Ottoman cannons broke down walled cities. Mass-produced books broke down centuries of superstition, illiteracy, and informational control. Into a world torn apart by plague, this cycle brought a revolution in trade and travel.

This cycle is fascinating, in part, because of the precision with which historical change links to Pluto's astronomical orbit. In the beginning, as Pluto

crosses from southern to northern declination (VISION), scholars introduced new languages (English and Italian) and new thinking (humanism
and linear perspective)—Persephones. Similar to other cycles, some visionaries, driven by greed and power lust, desired world domination—Hades. In
the aftermath of a plague that traversed the world, universal suffering led to
a breakdown in boundaries, barely perceptible at the beginning, but by the
end of the cycle, all continents were within reach of each other. Gone were
the ideas of flat Earth, and isolated local economies moved towards extinc-
tion. Even during the Roman Empire or Genghis' Mongol Empire, oceans
created natural boundaries and separated worlds. What began in VISION led
to invasions, not simple crusades, or hand soldiers taking over villages, but
invasions of continents for what lay beneath the surface—gold, silver, ore,
and other metals.

Exactly at the peak of POWER, the Ottomans invaded Constantinople, an
essential trading port city. This act of abduction gave the Sultan Mehmed II
control over trade routes, that he used to limit trade and supplies between
Asia and Europe. Cut off from cloth, spices, and food supplies, land after
land fell to the Ottomans and the European nations were forced to find a
work around that escalated ship building, navigation technology, resentment toward Muslims, and ultimately greed and xenophobia.

During JUSTICE, activist monks under the leadership of Girolamo Savonarola called out the Catholic Church on injustices and corruption, moving
Europe one step closer to the Reformation. At the same time, an Italian
merchant, funded by the monarchs of Spain, turned the world upside down
when he captained three ships across the Atlantic. Christopher Columbus
invaded the "New World," brought disease and weapons to these lands, enslaved people living there, and returned to Europe with a ship full of gold,
treasure, and human capital.

Columbus began a wave of conquistadors and other merchant-adventur-
ers who travelled back and forth over the Atlantic, upsetting the balance of
powers in Europe, and enriching Spain. The racist policies of the Church
through the papal bull *Dum Diversas* (1452), written during the prior JUS-
TICE time, now became permission to exploit these lands. The Spanish pope,
Alexander VI, favored Spain over Portugal in the race for world domination,
and through the papal bull *Inter caetera* (1493) and the Treaty of Tordesillas

(1494) split the newly invaded lands between Spain and Portugal, without any consideration of the people already living there. It is another moment when a few small decisions changed the world. Ferdinand and Isabella's decision to fund the journey, Columbus' skill at navigation and his belief in himself, and the election of a Spanish pope, merged continents.

Precisely during the REFORM time, a movement of protests against corruption in the Catholic Church broke down theocratic power structures throughout Europe. Meanwhile, invasions of the Americas, complete with plague, guns, and deception, pushed the Hades agenda into the next cycle.

Europe

VISION   1370–1376

In 1373, the Catholic Church lay in a schism with one pope in Avignon and the other in Rome. Florence, a small, inconsequential city, devastated by the plague with several unfinished cathedrals and a smelly tanning industry, mourned the loss of Dante (1265–1321). Giovanni Boccaccio (1313–1375) and Francesco Petrarca (1304–1374), two humanistic philosophers often credited with initiating the Italian Renaissance, were old men living near Florence. Geoffrey Chaucer (1340–1400), on holiday in Florence that summer, possibly met the elder writers for a drink near the half-built cathedral, longing for its dome. Filippo Brunelleschi, the man who later invented linear perspective and finished the dome with a feat of engineering still a mystery today, was a wish in his parents' minds—not to be born until four years later in 1377. In nearby Siena, a young, devout girl named Catherine climbed the stone steps near the west gate and saw God, a vision that gave her the courage to inspire healing amongst the church's people.

When the Pluto cycle begins, the VISION time is not always an obvious time of initiation. The visions are not always broadcast. The people don't always know that something is starting. In Florence, Boccaccio's book, *The Decameron*, well-read by a small contingency of educated men—by the standards of the time was a best-seller. But without the printing press, most people were illiterate and the ideas of humanism that Petrarca and Boccaccio brought forth were more like a rumor than a movement.

Meanwhile, in England, in the halls of Oxford University, John Wycliffe, Chaucer's professor, influenced a generation of radicals. Wycliffe shared his outspoken views on corruption in the Catholic Church in three significant works: *On Divine Dominion* (1373–1374), *On Civil Dominion* (1375–1376), and *On the Truth of Sacred Scripture* (1378). These three works questioned the authority of the papacy, the authority of the Catholic Church's rule in England, and even the authority of the scriptures. Wycliffe argued the scriptures, rather than being eternally transmitted in Latin, should be translated into English in order that the public might be able to read them. Over a century later, Martin Luther and Huldrych Zwingli read these works and began a movement of protests against the Catholic Church that has come to be known as the Protestant Reformation. Chaucer's writings as a young man critiqued the Catholic Church in tandem with Wycliffe's. His *Canterbury Tales* exhibits a similarity to Boccaccio's *Decameron,* with both featuring tales of wandering minstrels who foreshadow a cycle of exploration and discovery.

During the same time, a fatherless, 13-year-old Giovanni di Bicci de' Medici roamed the streets of Florence. Soon to become the patriarch of the Medici dynasty, Giovanni studied banking under the tutelage of his uncle, the latter himself an early Hades figure in the making.

Threads of an intellectual, artistic renaissance, international banking, an age of discovery, and a growing world movement of religious sects strung throughout the cycle have origins within this brief window of time.

POWER   1437–1466   Peak: 1453–54

Between the VISION and POWER times, Giovanni de Medici grew a meager wool business into a banking empire. He founded the Medici Bank in 1397, that became the bank of the Catholic Church in Pisa, during Anti-Pope John XXIII's papacy (1410–1415). When Giovanni died in 1429, he left a small fortune to his ambitious son Cosimo.

During this POWER time, Cosimo de Medici (r. 1434–1464) amassed great wealth through taxes and his management of the Vatican Bank, that were bolstered by indulgences (people literally paying for their sins to absolve themselves). History credits him with inventing double-entry bookkeeping that led to efficient management of his vast funds. Throughout his tenure as head of Florence, he groomed popes, sponsored artists (Donatello and Brunelleschi), oversaw the building of Pitti Palace, and the completion of the Duomo in 1436. This wealthy banker of a small city knew how to make a mark. The Medici name is synonymous with underworld power, secret handshakes, and the patronage of some the greatest art ever created. It was like Hades learned to live the good life and his abduction (of innocence) in this case was not through an overt invasion but through clandestine meetings, conspiracies, and power deals. Pluto infiltrated the banking system and the corruption through taxes and the selling of indulgences kindled the fire to a radical departure from organized religion.

Right as this was happening, a young German goldsmith, Johannes Gutenberg, crafted block letters into moveable type, creating perhaps the most important invention of the century: the printing press (1436). At the peak of the POWER time from 1452 to 1456, he printed the first bible with his own oil-based ink. He possibly only printed 200 bibles, but it was enough to begin a campaign of literacy, which birthed a movement of Persephones reading pamphlets and broadsides and forming educated opinions about the underworld power structures—opinions normally reserved for priests and politicians.

While Gutenberg introduced printed bibles in the Holy Roman Empire, a conquering king to the south encroached on the Byzantine Empire. Mehmed II, the sultan of the Muslim Ottomans and the leader of a relatively small country (constituting about half the size of modern-day Turkey), hired engineers to redesign cannons. Out of fear of Mehmed's armies, Pope Nicholas V issued the bull *Dum Diversas* in 1452, which authorized the Portuguese to arrest, attack, and kill non-Christians. The bull was aimed at supporting Portugal in suppressing the rise of the Islamic Ottomans by giving them permission to enslave and kill Muslims.

In 1453, precisely at the peak of Pluto's extreme northerly declination, Mehmed II attacked Constantinople. In a dramatic, 58-day siege, the Christian Byzantine Empire crumbled. To say this changed everything may be an understatement. Russia pulled out of the Roman Catholic Church and formed the Russian Orthodox Church. The Ottomans took control of the strategically positioned trading port, Constantinople, and interfered with Europe's ability to trade with the Orient. Silks and tea from China, spices and textiles from India, and other fabrics from Indonesia became almost impossible to acquire. This changed the revenue stream of trade and inspired generations of explorers to find new ways to travel to lands rich in these luxury items. Henry the Navigator, a prince in Portugal, built ships to traverse the stormy seas of the Atlantic in an attempt to get around Africa. The ensuing popes authorized more crusades against the Muslims and issued more papal bulls authorizing torture, which later supported mass executions of women and healers, inquisitions, the slave trade, and the genocide of the native peoples of the Americas.

The popes, to follow the Persephone myth, took on the directives, robes, and desires of Zeus. Without getting their own hands dirty, they inspired and empowered others to torture, kill, enslave, and abduct. Meanwhile, Mehmed II acquired the reputation of a Hades in this drama—a warlord capturing a city of ill-protected civilians. Part of the reason Byzantium fell stemmed from the lack of support from the rest of Europe, whose countries and leaders were all embroiled in wars of their own, much like the gods and goddesses who looked the other way while Persephone was abducted. France and England had finally finished the Hundred Years' War when two families with a claim to the British throne threw the country into yet another war that lasted for an additional 32 years (1455–1487). The House of York and the House of Lancaster families were full of the POWER period's lust during the War of the Roses. With little regard for the British people who were barely able to survive at this time, the war ended when all the male heirs were killed off, and a new dynasty stepped into power, the House of Tudor.

JUSTICE   1492–1498

This JUSTICE time is considered one of the most eventful in modern Western history, a turning point in world politics and art. Leonardo da Vinci (1452–1519) painted The Last Supper (1495); Michelangelo (1475–1564) carved The Pieta (1500); Raphael Santi (1483–1520) began his painting career, while Sandro Botticelli (1445–1510) painted his final works. The cities of Italy bustled with hubs of artists and artists' assistants, tradespeople, and wealth. The Laurentian Library in Florence housed meetings of philosophers, poets, and astrologers alongside politicians and generals.

Just as Pluto began crossing from northern to southern declination (JUSTICE), the fair-minded, art-loving leader of Florence, Lorenzo de Medici, died on April 4, 1492. Remember, there is often a power vacuum that opens during the JUSTICE time, leaving a gap for more radical views, and Florence in 1492 remains an apt example. Into the void in leadership rose the Dominican preacher, Girolamo Savonarola. Charismatic and austere, he whipped up an anti-corruption fervor that would have made John Wycliffe proud. Four months after Lorenzo passed, the Italian Pope Innocent VIII died, and the Spaniard Rodrigo Borgia became Pope Alexander VI (p. 1492–1503). Alexander VI, the second Spanish pope in history, brought to the Vatican a significant amount of baggage—a mistress, a beguiling daughter, Lucretia, and a battle-crazed son, Cesare, giving Savonarola that much more to protest.

Savonarola, railing against excesses in the Catholic Church, moved people to burn their treasures in the main square, what has come to be known as the "Bonfire of the Vanities." He began these bonfires on his own in 1495, around the start of Lent. By 1497, word had spread, and that year's event got the attention of the pope, who excommunicated and later executed Savonarola. Like many justice-seekers during the JUSTICE time, he was burned at the stake with his friends as the Catholic Church sought to keep a tight hold on the power they had amassed through the centuries. However, Savonarola had crossed a threshold. The word was out: The Catholic Church was corrupt and there was no putting that genie back in the bottle. He amassed followers, who spread the word far and wide, eventually reaching the ears of Martin Luther in Germany and Huldrych Zwingli in Switzerland.

However, the world tipped upside down when Columbus captained three ships to the lands across the great sea. The conquistadors, Spanish religious warriors, found gold in the Americas and dove deep into the underworld. Once the Catholic Church had taken over Europe, it moved on to the Americas. The Demeter-like demand for intercession at this time arose from Savonarola, who begged Pope Alexander VI to live simpler and more spiritually. In this case, Zeus does intervene; the pope retracted *Dum Diversas* (1452). However, Hades—represented by the conquistadors and the Dominican order—did not release Persephone so easily. In this myth, Hades found gold. Even with the Church shaming the conquistadors from abroad, they don't give up the gold or the hostages in the new lands. The conquistadors refused to listen to the pope, instead keeping the native peoples of the Americas enslaved so they could keep mining. Later, during REFORM, a precedent-setting trial emboldened the conquistadors.

REFORM   1524–1553   Peak: 1537

The empowerment of the people (Persephone) during this REFORM time was brought about by none other than the Protestant Reformation, a historically acclaimed and much-debated revolution of new thinking. In October 1517, Martin Luther, an Augustinian monk in Germany, wrote a paper outlining 95 grievances against the Catholic Church. Most of the issues presented railed against the practice of selling indulgences, the pope's way of raising funds by making people pay to have their sins exonerated, a fancy word for bribery. Earlier in 1517, the poet and art-loving second son of Lorenzo de Medici, Pope Leo X, increased the sale of indulgences to help complete the building of St. Peter's Basilica. This fiscal abuse of the scriptures and an already impoverished society sent Luther into a writing frenzy. With the aid of Gutenberg's printing press, Luther's writings littered northern Germany. When Pluto entered extreme southern declination in 1524, a group of peasants in southern Germany rose up against the church in a move that Luther condemned. With the protestants outnumbered five-to-one, the Holy Roman Empire soldiers easily quashed the uprising. Nevertheless, the protest enflamed a fever for peasants' rights against the overreaching Catholic Church.

In England, a country that managed to largely avert the inquisitions, Thomas More (1478–1535), King Henry VIII's advisor, wrote a proto-communist manifesto of sorts, *Utopia*, in 1516. More was an austere, Catholic lawyer whose writings envisioned a world of liberation, a land of public housing, universal healthcare, religious toleration, six-hour workdays, and the abolishment of private property (as long as everyone believed in an afterlife). More refused to go along with rising anti-Catholic sentiments. But King Henry VIII—so notorious for his six wives that it almost needs no mention—saw an opportunity for himself in breaking ties with the Catholic Church. In addition to giving him permission to divorce, he confiscated the lands and treasures of the churches and monasteries, which bolstered his depleted coffers. He had More executed (1535) and gave the world a daughter, Elizabeth I, who would later become an inadvertent founder of capitalism when she backed the first mega-corporation, the East India

Company.[1] And so it was that Henry VIII kicked the Catholic Church out of England undoubtedly for self-centered reasons, but nonetheless thereby empowered and paved the way for a Persephone-type, Queen Elizabeth I, whose four-decade rule began in 1558 and lasted until near the end of this Pluto cycle.

In the newly formed Swiss Confederation, another radical rebel roused the people. Huldrych Zwingli, inspired by Savonarola and Luther, led a campaign against the pope. He was not as lucky as Luther and was captured and burned to death on a dung heap. This did not stop the revolution in Switzerland. More cantons joined the Swiss Confederation, and more people joined the protests.

In the field of science, a few radicals during the Reformation changed the way the world understood itself. Nicolaus Copernicus (1473–1543) polymath, mathematician, and astronomer from Prussia (now Poland) figured out (again) that the Sun is the center of our solar system. When Copernicus wrote *On the Revolutions of Heavenly Spheres* (1543), most people in Europe believed the Earth to be at the center, with the stars and Sun revolving around it. Though Copernicus did not share his work openly out of fear of the churches, the shift from a geo-centric to a helio-centric universe was occurring. Beliefs were changing about the nature of humans, the stars, and the soul.

The field of medicine also took a great leap forward during this REFORM time. Paracelsus (c. 1493–1541), Swiss (al)chemist and "father of toxicology," wrote about "the body as a chemical system subject to specific ailments."[2] Girolamo Fracastoro (Italy, c. 1476–1553) hypothesized that microbes and germs caused infectious disease. Ambroise Paré (France, 1510–1590) innovated treatments for traumatic injuries. Andreas Vesalius (Brussels, 1514–1564) compiled a scientifically exact anatomy text based on his work dissecting cadavers.

---

1. In response to the growing interest in new markets combined with the perils of the high seas, the East India Company was founded on December 31, 1600, with a charter from Queen Elizabeth, as a "terminable stock" company. Stocks were sold on a voyage-to-voyage basis and initial investors totaled approximately 220 people in 1600, growing exponentially over the next two decades. The returns were manifold and new wealth poured into England. Ranging from dukes to cooks, the list of investors represented a blend of new and old money that helped influence British policy for nearly the next three centuries. (Vahé Baladouni, "Financial Reporting in the Early Years of the East India Company.")
2. Murray, 314.

This REFORM time led Europe into the next cycle, replete with the beginning of corporate power, capitalism, industry, Newtonian physics, and colonialism.

Summary and Synthesis

From 1373 to 1619, Europe pivoted from focusing on the activities of murderous Medieval knights to a realm where the arts and sciences took center stage with the support of wealthy bankers and the Roman Catholic Church. From pilgrims walking miles across Europe to pilgrims sailing across the Atlantic; from hand-written books for a small population of monks and scholars to mass-produced books laying the foundation for new religions; from regional wars to multi-continental invasions. The cycle began in the aftermath of the Black Death that killed over a third of the population of Europe. The visionaries during VISION brought forth new ideas of literacy via Italian and English, of art, of governance, and of religion. Persephones whispered insights of new ways of conversing with God, slipped into the world by preachers and writers. Hades claimed a new kingdom in the aftermath of the Knights Templar in the form of banking and gold. During POWER, the Medici family stood in the center of money, politics, and art, emboldening the Italian Renaissance. As the Ottomans grabbed the trade capitol of the world, inventors and their benefactors in Europe got busy finding work arounds and sail-arounds. An Age of Discovery changed the landscape of countries, religions, and continents, while education and literacy took one giant leap forward with the invention of the printing press. During JUSTICE, the town criers called out corruption within what had become a Catholic theocracy infused with money. Beating the drum of change, these anti-corruption advocates inspired a wave of protests that crested at the peak of this period, leading me to christen this part of the cycle REFORM. The Protestant Reformation forever changed power dynamics within Europe.

The Ottoman Empire

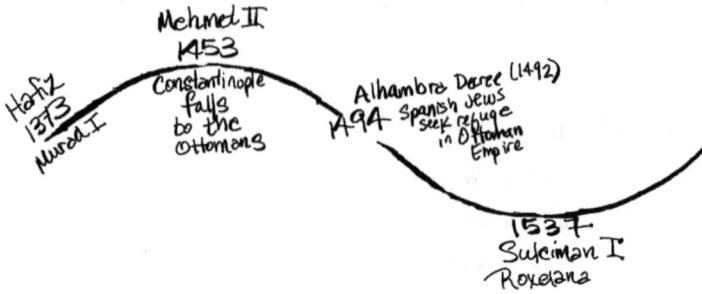

Mehmed II
1453
Constantinople
falls
to the
Ottomans

Hafiz
1373
Murad I

Alhambra Daree (1492)
1494 Spanish Jews
seek refuge
in Ottoman
Empire

1537
Suleiman I
Roxelana

VISION   1370–1376

While Chaucer and Petrarca were rustling the leaves of Europe, Hafez was shaking the trees in Persia, what we now know as modern-day Iran. Hafez (also spelled Hafiz), (1350–1390), was Sufi, a member of a mystical branch of Islam. His spiritual and ironic poetry took political aim at the status quo. While Hafez inspired many in the Islamic territories at the time, he is not the significant visionary of this cycle. Instead, in the Ottoman lands this Pluto cycle began with a different vision—a vision of an army.

To set the stage, the Islamic Golden Age had come and gone. The House of Wisdom in Baghdad, founded in the 700s and a precursor to the British Royal Society, the Laurentian Library of the Renaissance, and the high-powered think-tanks of today, was destroyed by the Mongol army in 1258. For more than six-hundred years, scientists and philosophers were revered in Arabia and Persia, bringing to the world significant breakthroughs in math (algebra), chemistry (al-kalis), and astronomy (seeing and recording the stars Al-gol, Al-genib, Al-cyone, etc.).

After a century of Christian crusades, Muslims developed warring skills and lost focus on the sciences and philosophies that had flourished from 632 to 1258. The Ottoman Empire was founded in 1301, ten years after the last crusade in 1291. At first it was relatively small, only occupying a part of what is today Turkey. Along its western border the Christian Byzantine Empire declined and crumbled.

Murad I (1362–1389) was given the keys to the Ottoman Kingdom during the VISION time. It was his vision (or one of his advisors) to form a standing army. This was one of the first paid standing armies in history. In the beginning, the soldiers were enslaved people gathered by the sultan as a tax on the wealthy. Because it was illegal to enslave a Muslim in the Ottoman kingdom, mostly Christians were enslaved, spoils of war from the crusades and the Ottoman incursions into the Byzantine Empire. The young Christian boys were trained with great discipline. The Janissaries, as they were called, developed a unique culture. Originally formed as a type of secret service for the sultan, the outfit grew into an army of thousands. They were held to a stricter standard of conduct, not allowed to marry, and forced into brutal training. Unlike other enslaved peoples, they were paid and paid well, treated extensively with medicine, and were highly regarded. In the absence of war, they served as policemen, firemen, and guards. The Janissary soldier became a coveted position, and poor Christian families willingly began to give their young sons to the Janissary cause.

POWER   1437–1466   Peak: 1453–54

During the POWER time, Mehmed II came into power after his father died in 1451. Mehmed followed the work of Hades perfectly. Mehmed had been in exile since he was a boy and was comfortable with the underworld. From a young age, he had his heart set on conquering the legendary city of Constantinople. Between the well-trained and loyal Janissary army and advanced weaponry, the ambitious Mehmed's army conquered Constantinople, the stronghold of the Christian Byzantine Empire. That it was Christian soldiers who took down a Christian empire for a Muslim nation is one of the ironies of history—and likely what angered Pope Nicholas V so much that he wrote the prejudicial *Dum Diversus*.

Mehmed's victory marked a turning point in conquering. His abduction of Constantinople, born out of an obsession from a young age, is a classic Hades/Pluto power play. Before 1453, stone-walled cities like Constantinople were considered impervious to destruction. No manmade element had ever been able to destroy the thick fortresses that surrounded many of the medieval cities of the time. The large-scale cannons and the destruction of these walled city marks for many historians the end of the Middle Ages and an introduction to the age of weapons of mass destruction.

By the end of the POWER time, the lands of the Ottomans had grown into an empire spanning from Belgrade to Aleppo. Controlling the strategic port city that Constantine had christened the center of Europe over a thousand years ago helped the Ottoman Empire maintain a stronghold in Europe and the Middle East up until the mid-1860s (the start of our present Pluto cycle).

JUSTICE   1492–1498

During the JUSTICE time, the Spanish Inquisition—given power by a papal bull from Pope Sixtus IV during the POWER time—was ramping up. While Ferdinand and Isabella were funding Columbus, they were also expelling the Jews. These Jewish refugees found a new home in the more religiously tolerant Ottoman Empire, which was willing to receive them. The immigrants brought with them trade, knowledge, and skills in banking. Injustice in Spain spilled into justice for the Turks. With new intellectual talent and in a more open-minded society, the upcoming REFORM stage went well for the Ottomans—and poorly for the Spaniards.

REFORM   1524–1553   Peak: 1537

Just before Pluto entered extreme southerly declination (REFORM), Suleiman I (1520–1566), nicknamed Suleiman the Magnificent, came into power. Suleiman was a ruler with a classical background: a lover of the arts, an intellectual, and a supporter of great architecture. His reign occurred at the same time in the cycle as other great reformers: Like Solomon who built a temple during a REFORM time after David created a nation during POWER many centuries prior, Suleiman built the Sulaymaniyah Mosque and rebuilt the Dome of the Rock, after Mehmet II turned the Ottoman Empire into a superpower during POWER. Suleiman's reign is known as the Golden Age of the Ottoman Empire, a time when the arts flourished there. He significantly reformed the judiciary system and surrounded himself with wise advisors. His reforms supported an advanced culture, during the same time that the Reformation was taking place in Europe.

Suleiman's wife, Roxelana, was not noble born. She was plucked from the daisies of his harem into the role of queen. Roxelana, as we can see, is a perfect parallel to Persephone. She started as an innocent girl, found herself abducted by a prince, and became a co-ruler of an empire. She found her own personal power and moved into a position of advisor. She is given credit for many of the reforms and prosperity of the Ottoman Empire at this time. As the story goes, their marriage was a happy one of respect and mutual support.

Summary and Synthesis

From its humble beginnings as a small kingdom between the Black Sea and the Mediterranean to a nation that expanded from modern day Hungry throughout the Middle East, the Ottoman Empire established itself as a force to be reckoned with for centuries to follow. The greatest sultans of this cycle ruled while Pluto ventured out-of-bounds. Their nicknames reveal the nature of the times—Mehmed the Conqueror during POWER and Suleiman the Magnificent during REFORM. While Mehmed invested in the arts and Suleiman doubled the size of the empire, their reputations follow along Persephone's myth with perfection. A two-month siege of a walled city as Pluto peaked in extreme declination north forced Europe to invest in shipping and exploration, while Suleiman and his Persephone-wife, Roxelana, ruled over a time when culture and infrastructure set down roots for a prosperous empire throughout the next cycle.

Invasion of the Americas

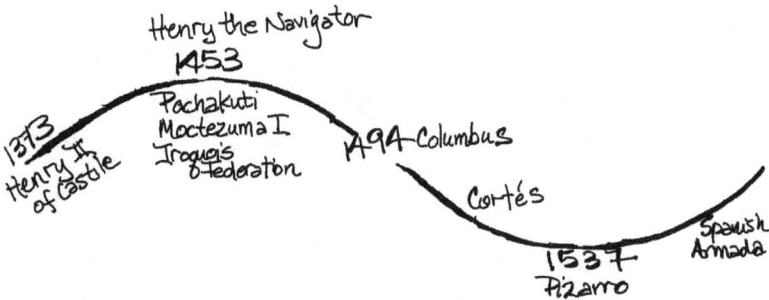

VISION   1370–1376

The story of the invasion of the Americas begins in the Iberian Peninsula. During the VISION time of 1373, the Iberian Peninsula, what is today Spain and Portugal, was divided into the territories of Navarra, Aragon, Castile, Granada, and Portugal, a modern-day melting pot. Jews, Muslims, and Christians living side-by-side. The Catholic Henry II ruled the largest region,

Castile, with the blessings of the pope. To the north, the Catholic Peter IV ruled Aragon, without the blessings of the pope. To the south, the Sultan Muhammad V ruled the mostly Muslim region of Granada. The kingdom of Navarre, abutting France, was ruled by the Catholic Charles II, nicknamed Charles the Bad for his cruel suppression of uprisings. By JUSTICE, Castile, Aragon, and Granada would become one kingdom under the rulership of the historically familiar Ferdinand and Isabella.

During the cycle from 1373 to 1618, what started as a region of states grew into the most powerful nation, destroyed the populations of two continents (the Americas), deported the Jews and Muslims, and wreaked havoc on its own citizens through the Spanish Inquisition. In the beginning of this cycle, the Iberian Peninsula was a land rich in diversity and exceptionalism. For men, it was a land of freedom, where healers and philosophers gathered in architectures of stunning beauty. As leaders leaned into violence and states merged through marital unions, contracts, and battles, the culture narrowed. In a case where the victors tell the history, this time is often called the Golden Age of Spain, a time of brave conquistadors and great strides in travel, navigation, and invention. The power of the empire expanded, and, for a brief period, Spain was probably the most powerful country in the world. But Spain is also a cautionary tale. Its alliance with the Catholic Church and its increasing intolerance for diversity slowly strangled the economy and the freedoms the people enjoyed at the beginning of the cycle. At the end, in 1588, England took down the Spanish Armada, and the once most powerful nation moved into decline. To this day, Spain suffers as one of the poorest countries in Europe.

The notable visionaries in Spain during the VISION time were almost all Jewish scientists, physicians, and philosophers. These included, to name a few, the philosopher Hasdai Crescas (1340–1410), the author, Rabbinical scholar, astronomer, mathematician, and physician Simeon ben Zemah Duran (1361–1444), the physician Profiat Duran (Isaac ben Moses ha-Levi) (1350–1415) and the humanist Catalan writer Bernat Metge (1340–1413).

Another visionary had hate-filled intentions. Reigning from 1334 to 1379, Henry II of Castile went to great lengths to fight his half-brother, Pedro, for the crown—engaging in battles all over Europe. Finally, he succeeded and, with his brother dead, he ascended to power. Henry was strongly anti-Semitic. That he was given the keys to the kingdom, beating out his open-minded, half-brother, remains a deeply misfortunate turn in the pages of history. Seemingly following in the footsteps of another ruler—Theodosius I of Rome, who cast out the Hellenists to make way for an entirely Christian empire—Henry II began to label and cast out a population of "others" within and from his kingdom. He ordered the Spanish Jews to wear badges and change their names. He penalized them financially by ordering that debts paid to Jewish bankers only needed to be repaid at two-thirds of the principal. At the end of his life, he made it illegal for Jews to hold public office. Many Jews left the peninsula, including all the great thinkers mentioned above. Most left for the more open-minded Ottoman Empire.

When the visions during VISION are filled with hatred, it does not bode well for the rest of the cycle. Spain's Henry II was an embodied foreboding of dark times ahead. Meanwhile, England and Portugal formed an alliance, the Anglo-Portuguese Treaty of 1373, precisely in the middle of the VISION time. Portugal and England agreed to be perpetual allies, and like many things that begin when Pluto crosses the equatorial plane from south to north, the treaty has not been broken to this day.

While Henry of Castile was casting out the Jews, in the lands across the Atlantic—lands that would later be named after the Italian explorer Amerigo Vespucci—a brewing shift was taking place. Like animals before a storm or warriors before battle, the people of these lands established nation states and developed armies. It was as if they felt the oncoming European invasion and started preparing. After centuries of tribal coexistence, leaders began to emerge. Both the Incan Nation (Peru) and the Aztec Nation (central Mexico) were "upstart empires, erected with astonishing rapidity, from small regional states, in a few generations."[3] In the region we call Peru today, people had been living in communal villages for centuries. Sometime around 1200 CE, people began to congregate in Huchuy Qosqo (Cusco in Spanish) to form a larger state, which grew over the next century. During the VISION time, the Inca community was still relatively small and peaceful. In the region we call Mexico today, people had coexisted peacefully in tribes for centuries. The great Mayan civilization had come and gone. In its wake,

---

3. Felipe Fernández-Armesto, *1492: The Year the World Began.*

the city of Tenochtitlan was built in the early 1300s. The first Aztec king, Acamapichtli, the ruler of Tenochtitlan, began his reign in 1376, precisely at this VISION time. It was a reign that lasted for nineteen years and initiated a time of building and expansion.

POWER   1437–1466   Peak: 1453–54

Incas

As Pluto entered extreme declination to the north, a squabble broke out between the Inca people and the nearby Chanka. Viracocha, head of the Incas vowed to conquer half the world, but when it came time to the fight, he and his three elder sons ran away. His youngest son stepped into the battle and, with only a handful of warriors, defeated the Chanka. Viracocha refused to honor his youngest son, Inka Cusi Yupanqui. Yupanqui was a great warrior, and this slight did not settle well with him. Viracocha plotted to kill his youngest son, but the plot went awry, sending Viracocha into exile as Yupanqui became the leader of the Inca (r. 1438–1471).

Yupanqui had great ambition. He turned one victory into another and went on a rampage with his army. He changed his name to Pachacuti. Often just the sight of the army arriving sent villagers into surrender mode. This worked well for Pachacuti who had no interest in plundering or destroying these settlements. Instead, he brought gifts for the people in exchange for allegiance. Under his leadership, the Inca nation grew from a small settlement into the largest empire on the planet at that time.

In 1463, just at the end of POWER, Pachacuti gave his son Topa Inca charge of the military and turned his focus toward infrastructure. Historical accounts hypothesize that Machu Pichu was built between 1450 to 1460 under Pachacuti's leadership. He died peacefully in 1471, a mere five years after Pluto left extreme northern declination.

Aztecs

To the north of the Inca Empire, the Aztec Empire also grew. Before the POWER time started, in 1427, a triple alliance was formed between Tenochtitlan, and two neighboring cities, Tlacopan and Texcoco. This alliance cemented the beginning of a new empire, and Itzcoatl, reigning from 1427 to

1440, became its first emperor. Several years after Pluto went into extreme declination, another powerful leader took over, Moctezuma I, who reigned between 1440 and 1469. Not to be confused with his descendant, Moctezuma II, who was emperor when the Spanish arrived. Moctezuma I expanded the empire in true POWER style, taking over Oaxaca in 1445.

Iroquois

In 1451, during the peak of POWER, six tribes far to the north of the Aztecs formed an alliance. The Haudenosaunee Confederacy, more commonly known as the Iroquois, comprised a tribe formed perhaps as early as 1100 CE, such that, at this time, the civilization was already centuries old. 1451 is the traditionally accepted historical date of a treaty between six tribes: Mohawk, Onondaga, Oneida, Cayuga, and Seneca, largely settled in what would become New York State around the lakes named after them. This treaty inspired Benjamin Franklin and other later settlers in these lands to create a new nation. It is another example of power coalescing, as if preparing for an inundation.

Back in Europe

The Ottomans capture of Constantinople in 1453 at the peak of Pluto's extreme northerly declination (POWER), blocked direct overland trade routes to Asia, so European countries now needed to find a water route to Asia to access to spices, salt, china, silk, and other goods. This blockage angered Pope Nicholas V, who, in response, gave King Afonso V (1438–1481) of Portugal permission to conquer anyone who was not Christian. The pope's intention was mostly directed at the Ottoman Empire, but Portugal and Spain followed this "opportunity" and later applied it to dwellers in other lands, which ultimately meant, the two continents in the Western hemisphere they were about to "discover" by sea.

A bit of background: Henry the Navigator, the Prince of Portugal, student of all things nautical, and the grandson of John of Gaunt (who sponsored both Chaucer and Petrarca), is credited with initiating the Age of Discovery—a time when Europe began an era of shipping, travel, and exploration. The larger and more powerful carrack ships, first made in Genoa in the 1400s, bypassed the Ottoman Empire by sailing around Africa. Portugal began two underworld businesses—gold and slavery. Just as Pluto moved into extreme declination, Afonso V became king and the first shipments of gold arrived. Portugal set up its first gold-coin minting operation in 1441. Seven years later, the first Portuguese fort built to house enslaved people was completed.

While Portugal was becoming rich and powerful, the Spanish states of Castile and Aragon formed an alliance. Just after the end of the POWER time, one of the greatest historical alliances through marriage was consummated—Isabella I of Castile married Ferdinand II of Aragon—and the two states were united in 1469.

JUSTICE   1492–1498

As Pluto began crossing from northern to southern declination (JUSTICE) in 1492, an Italian from Genoa, who had been living in Portugal, petitioned the Spanish royal court for funds for a voyage across the Atlantic. Isabella agreed. In an effort to find a new trade route to the orient, Christopher Columbus led three ships that landed in Hispaniola. Finding gold, he enslaved the people of the island and amassed as much treasure as the ship could carry. It is estimated that over 600,000 native people died under the hands of Columbus. They had no way to cry for justice then, but we cry for justice for them now, during our own JUSTICE period.[4]

In 1493, Thupa Inca, the emperor since Panchakuti, died. He had around sixty sons with multiple wives and an unclear succession. At the exact same time as Lorenzo de Medici's death left a power vacuum in Florence, a power void in the Inca Empire led to infighting. When Wayne Quapaq became the next emperor, he didn't know that across the continent to the north, Christopher Columbus was enslaving the native peoples on the island of Hispaniola.

When Isabella died in 1504, Spain was in the midst of a Golden Age of Exploration. Joanna the Mad took over as regent from 1504 to 1519 until her son Charles I came of age to rule. In 1520, Charles I had just come to the throne, Cortés beginning to conquer the Aztecs, and Martin Luther, an upstart in Germany, was excommunicated for his writings against the Catholic Church. The reformation was beginning.

---

4. In the US, Columbus Day is still celebrated, but in 1992, people in San Francisco started to transform Columbus Day to Indigenous Peoples' Day. As of 2024, 23 states and 195 cities honor this new holiday.

When Zeus interceded on behalf of Demeter's wishes, he sent Hermes down to get Persephone. While the myth focuses on Demeter, Persephone's transformation in the Underworld bears conjecture. Something occurred there to transform a teenage girl into a queen equal in power to her abductor. What often transforms us is suffering, a dark night of the soul, or a deep inner quest. Hades is the guardian of the underworld and as such also governs over everything that exists under the Earth, like gold, petroleum, coal, crystals and the hot molten core of the planet. The conquistadors found gold, a metal that the Inca, who did not use currency, valued only in personal adornments and figurines—and water pipes![5] Atawalpa, the Inca leader when Pizarro entered, offered the Spaniard as much gold as he could carry. This pillaging of Pluto's realm rarely serves in the long run. It is as if during this intercession, Mars snuck in and started stealing underworld treasures from Pluto, and in return Pluto started stealing souls from the Earth—some estimates suggest that over 60 million people died of smallpox in the Americas between 1520 and 1619.

REFORM   1524–1553   Peak: 1537

Columbus's journey inspired a movement of explorers seeking fortune in the new world—de Soto, Vasco de Gama, Pizarro, Amerigo Vespucci, Vasco Nunez de Balboa, and Ferdinand Magellan to name a famous few. Ship after ship left the Iberian Peninsula, stopping at the Canary Islands to pick up the good current and landing in the new world. Amerigo Vespucci made several voyages between Europe and the lands named after him between 1497 and 1502. In 1523, Giovanni da Verrazzano journeyed along the coast from North Carolina to Maine and described a heavily populated area with visible smoke plumes throughout the trip.

Hernán Cortés and his troops landed in Vera Cruz on April 22, 1519, and by 1521 he had completely overtaken the great city of Tenochtitlan. He was an ambitious businessman/warrior, a conquistador. In addition to winning through fear tactics, Cortés brought smallpox with him, like other voyagers from Europe to the Americas. Just as Pluto entered extreme declination to the south (REFORM), the first smallpox outbreak obliterated the populations of the Aztecs and Incas.

5. Carol Schultze and Charles Stanish, "Copper Metallurgy in the Andes."

Pizarro and 168 Spaniards landed in Inca territory in 1531, and in a similar fashion to Cortés, take the Inca by surprise with their European guns, steel, and horses and in a short period of time the Inca surrendered. In 1533 and 1535, two more smallpox outbreaks took more lives.

By the time of the peak of REFORM, millions of native peoples had died in epidemics and war with the Spanish. In May of 1539, another Spanish voyager arrived in the Americas, Hernando De Soto. He travelled along the Mississippi River and through the lands of the southeast part of the North America—up to North Carolina and through Florida, over to Texas, and then he left. He found a heavily populated area. He brought along three hundred pigs and it is believed that the pigs brought Hepatitis A that brought another horrific fatal, biological threat to the native populations.

In Spain, during the REFORM time, the cruelty of the Spanish toward the Aztecs, Incas and other Native Americans was troubling for some of the clergy. Even before Cortés or Pizarro had landed in the Americas, a young monk, Bartolomé de las Casas was advocating for reform of the enslavement policies of the Spanish. In 1542 (just after Pluto peaked in southerly extreme declination in REFORM) after Cortés and Pizarro had pillaged and destroyed the Aztecs and Incas, King Charles V began to listen to Las Casas' argument that the newly conquered people could be converted to Catholicism and become loyal subjects of the crown—without the abuse and torture of the Spanish. Charles V put forth a decree called the New Laws, ending further enslavement of the peoples of the so-called New World. This did not go over well with the conquistadors. For the next ten years, the conquistadors rebelled.

Usually during the REFORM time, the rebellions are of the oppressed people seeking to reclaim their power. In this case, with Spain, the rebellion was of the warriors against a decently fair-minded reform from the monarchy. The conquistadors were greedy for the abundant silver and gold being mined in the Americas, and it took many victims of slavery working in horrible conditions to mine those treasures. The conquistadors' and merchants' wealth relied on the subjugation of the indigenous people, and when a shortage of people occurred (because they were dying of disease as well as the harsh conditions in the mines), they turned to Africa, to enslave new people and transport them across the Atlantic. In this frenzy for wealth, the armed soldiers and wealthy merchants rose up against these New Laws. This led to a trial in 1550. On one side, Las Casas represented the Native Peoples and argued they could be converted and deserved rights to land and to their life. On the other side, Juan Givés de Sepúlveda used the work of Aristotle to argue that there was a biological inferiority of the enslaved people and that they should be happy to be the subjects of the noble and sophisticated Spanish.

The world would be a very different place if Las Casas had won this trial, not that that was even a possibility in the climate of Spain at the time. Sepúlveda earned himself the nickname "father of racism." Ironically, all this gold and silver did little to help Spain. The loot was used in trade and supported the wealth and growth of other European countries, while Spain went into decline under the weight of inflation. Charles V's fierce loyalty to the Catholic Church led to several expensive wars, one with the Turks in Eastern Europe, another against Holland and the reformers and others around the Mediterranean. By 1558 (end of REFORM), Spain was almost totally bankrupt, and Charles V was totally dead. The final nail in the coffin of Spain's Golden Age was in 1588, when the Spanish Armada, a fleet of ships considered invincible, was defeated by the British. Limping home after the defeat, Spain moved deeper into debt and decay. Spain declared bankruptcy in 1607—at the very end of the cycle.

Summary and Synthesis

The Hades-Persephone myth plays itself out during this cycle, as merchant Hades types with a lust for gold, mined from the bowels of the Earth and invaded continents. The Persephone types, all of the people throughout the world who lived close to the land, transformed from illiterate servants of theocracies to literate protestors choosing new religions. Nations separated by oceans grew closer with advances in ships and navigation.

In the continents of the Americas, the Persephones at the beginning of this cycle lived in villages peppered over 17 million square miles. Villages merged into nations during the POWER time, poised for an invasion that began during JUSTICE, and overcome by guns, germs, and steel during REFORM. This chapter in history is a cautionary tale of when a country—Spain in this case—becomes greedy and allows Pluto to out-rule Zeus. The monarchy and the intelligencia in Spain lost control over the inquisitors and conquistadors, who are the unfortunate reformers during reform. Eventually, these angry and greedy reformers destroyed their own homeland and the people living in the lands they conquered.

We don't know who the visionaries were for the Incas or Aztecs at the beginning of this cycle, or least I wasn't able to find them, but something stirred in someone because both cultures simultaneously established new dynasties that became warring nations. During the time of Persephone's abduction (POWER), the leaders were raiding village after village. While remaining far more peaceful than Genghis or Augustus, they still amassed power and created empire. During the time of the intercession (JUSTICE), the Spanish arrived and began capturing and enslaving the people of the land. The indigenous people projected god-like status onto the new arrivals and like deer in headlights succumbed to their power. This intercession is a fate like no other fate in history. A foreign invader, backed by a country, but with a small contingency of sailors, set out for wealth. The goal was trading. It wasn't a government army that landed to conquer. It was greed for wealth—particularly gold—that motivated the conquistadors. The invasion was secondary. By the time of REFORM, the European invaders had infiltrated the Americas, forever setting down roots. Perhaps during the upcoming REFORM, a rectification of some of the atrocities of this time may happen. A friend of mine who works for a Catholic organization in Olympia, WA recently told me that in Washington State (and perhaps elsewhere), the Catholic Church is actively returning land to the local indigenous tribes. In addition, the Catholic Church recently repudiated the Doctrine of Discovery, "Inter Caetera," that allowed the conquering of land from any non-Christians.[6]

6. Holy See Press Office, "Joint Statement of the Dicasteries for Culture and Education and for Promoting Integral Human Development on the 'Doctrine of Discovery.'"

Chapter 12:
The British Empire, 1619–1862

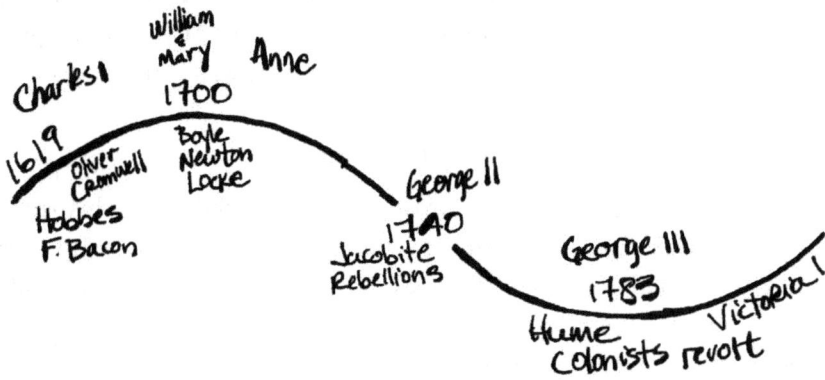

Persephone is us, the people, the commoners, the "everyman" of James Joyce's *Finnegan's Wake*, the person ensconced in society. In the beginning of this cycle, ships carry passengers back and forth over oceans. Commoners, not just soldiers and explorers, traveled across the Atlantic to settle into a new culture. For this cycle, we will assign the dubious role of Hades, not to a person, but to the first international corporation, the East India Company (EIC). While many members of this elite group of merchants may have been well-meaning, simply trying to make a living in this crazy world, many members saw an opportunity to take advantage of people living close to the land, coexisting in empires governed by naïve or corrupt rulers. What was about to befall the people and lands of India, China, Japan, and Indonesia, was a tidal wave of greed and abuse that eventually infiltrated and devastated them.

By 1619, the world was shrinking. Ships circumnavigated the globe. What used to be relegated to a few traveling merchants along the silk road had become a highway of investors, missionaries, and sightseers. Cities protected by walls with their own customs and languages found themselves vulnerable to invasions. The Catholic Church that had wielded so much power throughout the 1400s and 1500s, was losing its grip as the Reformation enticed many into newly formed Christian religions. The New World beckoned to many seeking a new life. Doors were opening and group of merchants in England saw an opportunity. In 1600, Queen Elizabeth I granted the group a charter to form The British East India Company (EIC). Complete with shareholders, a board of directors, and its own governor, the company set out to make boat-loads of money by bringing goods from Asia, starting with India, to sell in Europe. Two years later, a group of merchants in The Netherlands established a sister corporation, the Dutch East India Company (VOC). By the end of this Pluto cycle, both corporations merged into the empires they forged.

Industrial Revolution

Other visionaries in this time arose from the backdrop of this shift in power. René Descartes pondered the seemingly opposing views of the faith-based Catholic Church with his interest in logic-driven science. His philosophies inspired a French awakening. In England, Francis Bacon, considered the prophet of the scientific revolution, published *Novum Organum* (1620).[1] Bacon was an advocate of reason while at the same time offering a utopian ideal. He assisted and partly funded the colonies of Virginia and Newfoundland, earning him a place on Newfoundland's postage stamp. Galileo saw the moons of Jupiter (1609), openly shared Copernicus' heliocentric model of solar system (1613) only to be banned by the Catholic Church (1616). Nevertheless, both his work and the work of Copernicus spread among European scientists. In literature, Cervantes in Spain and Shakespeare in England died in the same week (April 1616) leaving behind great works of literature that only became more popular posthumously.

What comes of this cycle is clearly seen in the beginning of it. The scientific revolution began with the ideas of Bacon, Kepler, and Galileo, exploded with Newton's and Boyle's equations during the POWER time, came into integration with the math of Euler, with Newton-inspired Voltaire's philosophies, and John Kay's flying shuttle that improved weaving looms during JUSTICE, and emerged into full-blown Industrial revolution during REFORM when James Watt improved Newcomen's steam engine and James Hargreaves improved Kay's flying shuttle into the spinning jenny. With the ready availability of coal to fuel the steam engine and machines that improved weaving outputs, textiles could now be mass produced in factories. The steam engine powered locomotives. Nicolas-Joseph Cugnot created a self-propelled vehicle (1769). In North America, Oliver Evan's automatic flour mill (1785)

---

1. Thomas S. Kuhn, *The Structure of Scientific Revolutions*, 18.

innovated material handling leading to increased production and reduced contamination of flour and other raw materials. Eli Whitney's cotton gin (1793) significantly reduced the labor required to remove cotton seeds. This led to the prosperity of the South that led to the hubris that initiated the US Civil War during the VISION of the next cycle.

VISION   1615–1622

The gold coming from the New World during the prior cycle had unexpected effects in England. Until the late 1500s, peasants rented land from the gentry in exchange for services rendered. They lived off the land that they farmed. In years with good harvests, they lived well. The gold, though, lit a fire under the merchants, who mostly traded in wool; they became rich and encroached on the kind of power reserved for the gentry for the past five centuries. This newly empowered merchant caste disregarded the old customs of fixed rents and *noblesse oblige*. The land once farmed for food transitioned into sheep grazing pastures through what came to be called enclosure, a series of laws that supported sheep farming over food farming, that began with an act of parliament in 1603. The local sheriffs supported the land-owning wool traders who had the money to bribe authorities. The lower classes in England began to starve.

The merchants then turned their sights on Ireland for more sheep grazing land, beginning a centuries-long exploitation of the Irish people.[2] Coinage became the new god, and those who valued gold considered themselves a more enlightened species than those who lived close to the land. Roots grew of the cultural values that supported corporate greed and capitalism, values of money over land, trade over farming, and handshakes over hard work. Alongside the Catholic Church's decrees that supported racism, enslavement, and murder of the native people in the Americas, a growing culture of snobbery of the wealthy over the poor, of landholders over the people who worked the land, and of English over Irish permeated the British Isles.

The beginning of the East India Company is the beginning of the first publicly traded stock, the first stock exchange, the Amsterdam Stock Exchange (1602), and the first limited liability company. For centuries, guilds functioned to support tradespeople. To be part of the guild and reap the financial benefits of collective negotiations, one had to be a tradesperson. To be a member of

---

2. John Mohawk, *Utopian Legacies*, 145.

the tanners' guild in Florence, one had to be a tanner. The EIC, started with a group of wool merchants, was unlike any of the trade organizations from the past. They opened the doors to anyone who had money. If you had money, you could invest in the EIC and become a shareholder.

Trade with the orient was growing and a desire for cotton, silks, and spices blossomed within the aristocracy of Europe. The English obsession with hot beverages started when tea and coffee were imported from India and China sometime at the end of the 16th century. As English merchants became wealthier, the poor grew poorer, and the growing divide set the stage for civil war. James I tried to hold onto the power of the monarchy by dissolving parliament for seven years, from 1614 to 1621, precisely during this VISION time. This is particularly interesting, as what happens during VISION plays itself out throughout the cycle. In the absence of parliament, the monarchy struggled while the EIC began its commercial enterprises in India. In August of 1608 the first EIC representatives landed in Surat (Gujarat), India. Four years later, the ruler of the Mughal Empire, then encompassing much of modern-day India, granted the EIC permission to build a factory, then more of a staging area for trading goods than a place of manufacturing.

With Spain bankrupt, the English, French, and Dutch took advantage of the power vacuum in the New World. English settlers founded Jamestown (1606) and Plymouth (1620). The French settled Quebec (1608). The Dutch settled in New Amsterdam (Manhattan, 1612) and Henry Hudson sailed up the river that still bears his name (in 1609). The first slave ship from Africa to America landed in Jamestown in 1619, beginning a horrifying practice that enabled settlers to increase tobacco and cotton crop yields, that brought more wealth and power to the merchants and landowners in the Americas. The shift in power from monarchies and theocracies, represented by Zeus in our myth as metaphor, to capitalism and corporate greed, represented by Hades, that began during the prior cycle, took a giant leap forward during this VISION time.

POWER   1687–1710   Peak: 1700

Kicking off this POWER time, William and Mary and their army crossed the English Channel from Normandy to England and claimed their right to the throne (1688). As soon as they got settled in, the French King Louis XIV (r. 1643–1715) declared war on them and everyone else in Europe including

Spain, England, the Dutch Republic, the Holy Roman Empire (Hapsburgs), Portugal, and Savoy. King Louis XIV had become the most powerful monarch in Europe at the time, through both the accumulation of wealth through taxes and fur trading in the Americas and by spending a lot of that money on infrastructure, the military, and his palace. The Nine Years War, also known as the first world war, lasted until 1697 when the depleted French accepted the small gain of Alsace and recognized William as the ruler of England.

At the peak of this POWER time, in 1700, the Spanish King Charles II died childless and left a vacancy on the Spanish throne. King Louis XIV was quick to install his grandson, Philip, whose grandmother was Maria Therese of Spain (1638–1683), Infanta of Spain. The Holy Roman Empire wanted their pick for the throne and another war broke out, The Spanish War of Succession (1701–1715). In the end, over a million people died and Philip of Anjou became king of Spain.

Meanwhile, EIC and VOC trading posts littered Asia. In the early years of Louis XIV, the French got in on the orient trade, forming the French East India Company (f. 1664). The empire of colonization through corporation was in full swing. Trading posts in Japan, Korea, Australia, China, Indonesia, and India were divided among England, France, and the Netherlands. In the 1680s, the Chinese Qing Dynasty "lifted restrictions on foreign trade, leading to a surge in exports of tea, porcelain, and Chinese sugar."[3] Madras and Bombay, port cities for goods from China, grew into international trade centers. The Moghul Empire that encompassed much of India, including Madras and Bombay, at first welcomed the EIC traders, but as time went on, corruption in both the Company and the Empire incited squabbles.

The last Moghul emperor, Aurangzeb (r. 1658–1707), was a Sunni Muslim who started his reign with accommodating the Hindus. As Pluto moved into extreme declination, he became increasingly tyrannical, imposing Sharia law and invading the Maratha Empire during the reign of Sambhaji (1680–1689) in central India. In a show of extreme force, he killed the last emperor of Maratha by publicly torturing him for a week.[4]

In 1686, a ranking EIC official, Sir Josiah Child, tired of the hoops and bribes and squabbles, decided to put the Mughal Empire in its place. Nineteen

---

3. Peter Frankopan, *Silk Roads*, 262.
4. William Dalrymple, *The Anarchy*, 29.

warships with 600 soldiers sailed from England and attacked the Indian army. This did not go so well for the English, who barely made it ashore. The Mughals confiscated the factories and sent the EIC packing—but the EIC repented and submitted to Mughal rule. By 1690, Aurangzeb had forgiven the invasion and returned the factories that were not destroyed to the EIC. Ironically, this failed invasion by the EIC just prior to Pluto transiting out-of-bounds to the north may have contributed to the ongoing success of the Company. With these renewed relations, one EIC representative bought a small settlement between the villages of Kalikata and Sutanuti, that grew into the large trading port of Calcutta. While Aurangzeb ruled, the EIC took over the European markets, oversaw most of the trade routes throughout the world and invested in infrastructure.

When Aurangzeb died in 1707, the empire collapsed. The EIC took advantage of the chaos. By 1712, 15% of British imports came from India and almost all through the Company.[5] India, splitting into smaller and weaker states, gave the EIC cause to begin arming itself. As impotent rulers tried to keep the Mughal empire going, Company representatives navigated the realms of power through bribes and backroom handshakes, all the while lobbying England for the right to build an army.

Textile factories, early sweat shops, consisted of over a million Indian workers pushing looms in horrid conditions. Tobacco and cotton farms worked by enslaved people abducted from Africa produced mad profits for land-owner gentry. Meanwhile, the EIC began arming and training local soldiers to fight in their mercenary army.

JUSTICE   1739–1742

As often occurs during JUSTICE, the scales of power tip, and this cycle is no exception. The Mughal Empire hung on in Dehli, a city larger than Paris and London combined. In 1738, Nadar Shah, the leader of the Afsharid dynasty in the region of Iran, invaded the northern territories of India. When Nadar Shah's forces sieged the city, killing over 100,000 people, the Mughal leader fell on his sword and made a deal allowing Persians to continue to loot the city if they stopped the massacres. The Persians were mostly interested in the money—money needed to fund the army to ward off Ottoman and

---

5. Gordon Kerr, *A Short History of India*, 94.

Russian invasions. The more the dynasties fell, the more the EIC and VOC saw opportunity. By 1740, the EIC had hired and armed more soldiers than the entire British army. Only one in seven soldiers was British—the other six of seven were Indian men known as sepoys. With advanced weaponry and money to pay troops, the EIC became a superpower, military-industrial complex. If England had tried to invade, the EIC had enough weapons and manpower to overtake them.

The Dutch East India Company lost a critical battle to the Travancore Kingdom in 1741. Travancore was a small kingdom in southern India that held a critical spice port. After the battle, the kingdom took over the black pepper trade and the VOC moved into decline.

The most famous freedom-loving advocates at this time were Voltaire in France, Jonathan Edwards in the colonies, and David Hume in Scotland. Voltaire advocated for free speech, freedom of religion, separation of church and state. Leaders from all over the world were fans. Hume published *A Treatise of Human Nature* in 1740, his most famous work that explored the nature of human psychology. His political views, not concretely expressed in his writings, included "seeing governments as a struggle between authority and liberty, with the best of them achieving a balance between the two."[6] Hume inspired his friend, Adam Smith, who during REFORM wrote *Wealth of Nations*, both an admonishment of corporate monopolies and praise for corporate politics. Voltaire inspired Catherine the Great to address oppression in Russian during the REFORM time. And Jonathan Edwards, the original fire and brimstone preacher of the first Great Awakening, inspired colonists to fight for freedom of religion. In London in 1738, John Wesley experienced a spiritual awakening that is commemorated in the Methodist church, which he went on to found.

The Jacobite rebellions during this window of time led to a devastating loss of the Scottish rebels on the fields of Culloden. These battles had the side effect of training and emboldening the young British soldier, Robert Clive, who then went to work for the EIC, becoming a governor in 1757. Clive is given almost sole credit for building the EIC army. His apparent suicide in 1774, after years of opium addiction, opened the door for new leaders.

Rebellions during this window of time, such as the Stono Rebellion, a revolt of enslaved people in South Carolina in 1740, a revolt in Batavia that resulted

---

6. Neil McArthur, "Hume's Political Philosophy."

in the death of thousands of Chinese Indonesians, and an insurrection of enslaved people in New York City in 1741, were all quashed by military forces.
The cry for justice, usually from loud individuals, was now being heralded by
collectives. As we move into the REFORM time, one revolution, in particular,
succeeds.

REFORM   1774–1795   Peak 1783–85

In 1770, just before Pluto headed out of bounds to the south (REFORM),
drought in India destroyed two years of harvest. Millions died and the EIC
fell into debt. The British government saw the EIC as "too big to fail."[7] Without the Company, the people of Britain would not have easy access to cotton
and silks, and perhaps more importantly, tobacco, coffee, and tea, to which
much of the population was addicted. In order to bail out the EIC, England
instituted the Regulatory Act of 1773, that took control of the management
and financial oversight of the Company. From this point on, the British Empire increasingly took over control until the end of the cycle, when the EIC
dissolved completely into the British government, and Queen Victoria became empress of India (1870). Three years after the Regulatory Act, in 1776,
Adam Smith wrote a severe critique of the EIC monopoly. This critique, *The
Wealth of Nations*, has become an anthem for capitalism—an economic system that took off in the next cycle.

Parliament looked to the colonies for the extra funding needed to save the
EIC, and enacted a monopoly on tea sales. The colonists, already frustrated
with having no representation in parliament, began boycotting EIC products. When a group of protestors calling themselves Sons of Liberty board-
ed three British ships laden with tea that were docked in Griffin's Wharf in
Boston and tossed into the bay crates and crates of tea, they triggered more
protests and then more revolts, until a group of colonists declared independence from England on July 4, 1776, just as the REFORM time began.

The unfolding of the American Revolution (or the American War of Independence if you are in Britain) is a tale well told. By the peak of this REFORM
time in 1783, the colonists had worn out the British Empire and founded a
new country based not on blind fealty to a monarch, but on the rule of the
people. Shortly after, the French, who largely funded the colonists, started

7. Dalrymple, 233.

a revolution of their own. The French, without the benefit of Pluto heading toward its peak extreme declination to the south, fared not as well as the colonists. As a time of terror ensued, the French fight devolved as Pluto was heading north again, reentering the bounds in 1795. In the chaotic aftermath of the revolution, a young general rose into power to bring order and another wave of conquering success to France in the waning years of the cycle. By the end of the cycle, even France had become a parliamentary system.

Summary and Synthesis

Starting with a world ruled by kings and queens, we emerge from this cycle with a world ruled by parliaments with prime ministers and presidents. We began this cycle with slavery, the inquisition, serfdom, and oppression through religion. We leave this cycle with many countries having freedom of religion, freedom of speech, freedom from slavery, and freedom from wrongful persecution (at least according to law, if not in practice). We began this cycle with the inventions of telescopes and microscopes and end the cycle with anesthesia, pasteurization, dynamite, and the electric motor. We begin the cycle with horse-drawn carriages and end with transcontinental railroads. From Shakespeare to Dickens, from Elizabeth I to Victoria, from Galileo to Maxwell, from Descartes to Pasteur, the world moved from local economies into global markets of trade where one corporation changed everything.

Persephone and Demeter, the commoners of this cycle, rose in power as books and newspapers supported a rise in education and political savvy. The revolutions of the REFORM time gave rise to the power of the people through one of the most powerful documents to ever be written, the US Constitution. The Hades-like corporation that enslaved workers throughout Asia, started with less than forty men, ruled the world during POWER and fell into the British and French Empires during the REFORM time. Zeus, representing the monarchies of Europe, moved into an advisory role, while parliaments and corporations rose to power. Religions, so powerful in prior cycles, took a back seat to politics, as new and competing religions gained devotees.

PART III:
THE PRESENT

We are currently in the Pluto cycle that began in 1863. In Part II: The Past, you saw example after example of how the VISION portion of the cycle informs the developments that take place throughout the cycle and leads to the next VISION time. In natal astrology the beginning (the chart) is the seed that contains all the potentials for the life. Even though it doesn't have a chart in the same way as a person or entity, the beginning of a cycle in history contains the seeds for the garden that will grow over the course of the cycle.

Think about 1863. Consider that everything that happened in that year is a seed that is unfolding into a fruit-bearing tree. While I share my own interests and what I think is relevant in breakthroughs in medicine, travel, technology, and spirituality that was occurring the middle of the nineteenth century in Part III, you may have other areas that add to the fullness of this picture. I invite you to think about your own interests, your knowledge of history, and see what you discover that may be relevant to the upcoming REFORM period of 2025 to 2035. The more we understand the roots of the conflicts set up in the early parts of the cycle, the more we can understand what needs to be done in the final stage. What this also means is that the Civil War is not a thing of the past, it's still a current event. Everything since 1863 is a current event.

Also, remember that the current Pluto cycle is the final cycle in which Pluto will travel into extreme declination. Pluto will continue to orbit the Sun, but the Earth's changing axial tilt means that Pluto no longer appears to be as high or as low in the sky as any time in the last 4,000 years. We are about to enter new territory.

In this final cycle we will explore visionaries in a different way. I will link the visionary figures most like each main character in the myth of Persephone and Hades. We will meet the Zeus visionaries, the Persephone visionaries, the Hermes visionaries, the Demeter visionaries, and the Hades visionaries. Through associating these visionaries with these mythic archetypes, we can see that not all visions are clear, helpful to humanity, or full of joy. Sometimes the visions are seedy, self-serving, and dark.

Rather than casting judgment, as with all other VISION times of the past, we observe and take note of what began during the VISION time. Who or what was empowered during POWER? And who or what was (or was not) called into question during JUSTICE? The answers to these questions will allow us to tune into the ultimate unfolding of the cycle's concluding pattern during the REFORM time, which I discuss at length in PART IV. Through expanding and deepening our perspective on the past, we become empowered in the present and prepared for the future. Using myth as a doorway into understanding, we can watch the Hades-types of the world fall and the Zeus-types step aside, while Hermes-types incite change, the Persephones rise, and the Demeters bring back spring.

At the wrap of our present cycle, as planet Pluto moves neatly into our perceived view, his rule dwindles, and Persephone is redeemed. Pluto's last extreme declination will occur between 2025 to 2035, bringing ten years of the Ruler of the Underworld positioned extremely low on the south side of the equatorial plane, and thus bringing about a time of reform, revolutions, and, for the last time, leaving us all with Persephone's ultimate rise into lasting power. Let's see what has gotten us to this point.

Chapter 13:
The Current Cycle, 1863–2110

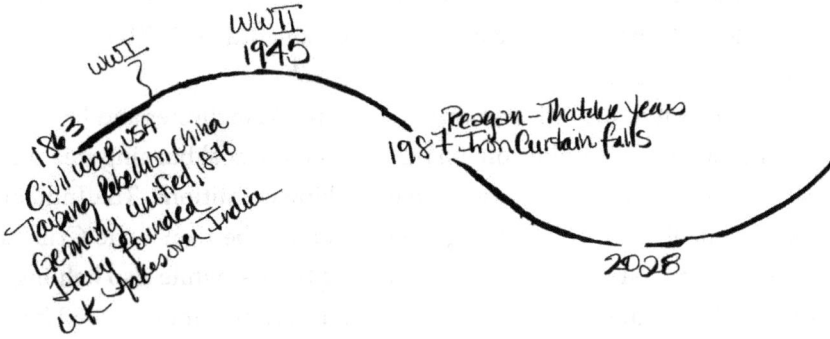

The world in 1860, like the world millennium's, was divided into separate nation states with borders decided by treaties written at the conclusion of wars. The nation state organized civilization. Borders determined after battles, after bloodshed, defined a nation. These boundaries, then, determined the language, economic system, political machinations, and customs of the people. With few exceptions, national boundaries waxed and waned in this way for thousands of years prior to our contemporary moment. The largest nation states in 1860 were the United Kingdom under the reign of Queen Victoria, Russia under the reign of Tsar Alexander II, France, under the reign of Napoleon Bonaparte III, the Ottoman Empire in the last year of the reign of Abdulmajed I, and China in the last year of the reign of Qing Dynasty Emperor Xianfeng. This was also the time when the Sun never set on the British Empire, after Britain colonized much of Africa and Asia.

In the early 1860s, the transition from agrarian life to industrial life was in full swing. Advancements in trains and shipping began to upstage wagons, still a popular mode of transportation. Telegraph cables, both submarine and overland, were traversing continents while most posts were still handwritten letters delivered by horse drawn carriages. In homes throughout the world, lamps lit by whale or nut oils provided light, soon to be replaced with fossil fuels. While most food was bought and sold through local merchants and grown by local farmers, early refrigerated shipping cars, called reefers, transferred dairy products from the New York countryside to Manhattan. In 1854, when Henry David Thoreau wrote *Walden*, he lived in wilderness a mere mile and a half from the busy town of Concord, MA. There were no streetlights, no cars, no planes, no televisions.

It was different in the cities. In urban areas like Manchester and Mumbai, factories created noise, pollution emanated from the coal burning steam engines, and laborers endured abominable working conditions. The Industrial Revolution, already in full swing, helped wars to be won—the Crimean War, the Opium Wars far from the least among them—while also helping to squash rebellions globally—including the Southern rebellion in the United States, the Sepoy rebellion in India, the Taiping Rebellion in China, and the Warsaw Uprising in Poland. Industry was taking over, and the titans of industry had usurped considerable power away from the political rulers. For the first time in history, the merchants were coming into real power, and the nation state was showing cracks in its armor. Leaders were rising through the ranks rather than being born into nobility, including Benjamin Disraeli in England and Otto von Bismarck in Germany.

The industrialized world (Hades) needed a new form of government to suit its takeover of the aristocracy (Zeus), and it chose a parliamentary system. This was a government system by the people, for the people, and with the people, where politicians could be bought, and money was the ruling doctrine—basically an arrangement where capitalism and industry could thrive.

Finally, systemic oppression based on skin color, background, gender, sexual orientation, ability, and other prejudices was just beginning to break down. In the United States, Abraham Lincoln issued the Emancipation Proclamation in 1863, freeing the enslaved—one step in a long ongoing battle for racial equality for Black Americans. In Russia, Tsar Alexander II freed those in serfdom in the Emancipation Reform of 1861, a step towards class-based equality. In the mid 1800s, the first suffragist organizations were formed in the United States, eventually succeeding seventy years later. While France and Italy had already taken the death penalty off the table for sodomy in the late 1700s, the British Empire did so in 1861, three years after the Ottoman Empire entirely decriminalized homosexuality (1858).

Hades

While the Persephones were having new visions, Hades seized the keys to the kingdom. Enterprising industrialists rose into power during this VISION time. Cornelius Vanderbilt built up his railroad business, John D. Rockefeller Sr. saw the future of oil in the 1860s and founded Standard Oil in 1870. Andrew Carnegie invested in steel, and Jay Gould planned his stock market scheme, all aptly assuming the dubious honor of being called the "robber barons" of their time. The modern-day corporation took great strides forward. With the North winning the Civil War, government had the back of industry. Incorporated during this VISION time were The Union Pacific Railway in 1863, the Michigan Car Company that would later become Ford Motor Company in 1863, Cargill, Inc. foods in 1865, and The Keystone Bridge Company in 1865.

The US was not the only country witnessing the birth of the new corporate economy. In 1865 in Germany, a goldsmith and dye-maker founded BASF, still the second-largest chemical company in the world. That same year, Hong Kong saw the establishment of The Hongkong and Shanghai Banking Corporation, still the largest bank in Hong Kong. In Sweden, the explosives company Dyno Nobel was founded in 1865. A year later, the Nestlé corporation was founded in Switzerland. In 1863, a dyer and a dye salesman founded Bayer in Germany. In fact, 1863 was a big year—brothers and chemists Alfred and Ernest Solvay formed Solvay S.A. in Belgium and in England the Staveley Coal and Iron Company got its start. Concordantly, Dynamit Nobel AG, an explosives company, was founded in Germany around the same time that The Deutsche Bank (1870) came into existence.

Corporations have had an incredibly powerful effect on society and the environment, and in these early days, the greed of these wealthy companies and their shareholders was wholly unregulated. Established throughout the prior Pluto cycle (1616–1863) through the colonizing East India Company, these corporations grew in power during the 1940s POWER time, before corporate regulations were established. This allowed companies all over the world to prosper with the sole aim of making money for their shareholders. Without oversight, these corporations polluted, abused their workers, and destroyed environments with impunity.

Other Hades/Plutos were the money lenders in Europe who funded the Suez Canal and bankrupted the Ottoman Empire,[1] the British politicians who found it a worthy cause to send soldiers to China to fight a war on behalf of drug lords in the Opium Wars, Boss Tweed and the Tammany Hall politicians of New York City who combined politics and business with cunning adeptness, and the corporate mercenary army that oppressed the people of India and installed Victoria as empress of a land she had never visited.

Speaking of mercenary armies, while not a new thing in the world, "security companies," armed guards for hire, were on the rise. The Pinkertons were hired by United States President Abraham Lincoln to protect his inauguration and Wells Fargo was hired to protect the building of the Transcontinental Railroad. Other private security firms were getting started at the VISION time, like Brinks (1859), and American Express (1850).

Meanwhile, the invention of dynamite in 1867 boosted mineral mining, particularly the mining and exportation of diamonds in and from Africa. The first oil wells were drilled during this time. It was like the underworld of Pluto was opened for the first time, and entrepreneurs, whose sole focus was on building personal wealth, bounded in. Much in the way that Hades perceived Persephone as his right to abduct after being given permission from Zeus, ailing monarchies throughout the world gave their blessings to the new Plutocrats to abduct mineral rich lands and the peoples living on them.

---

1. European, mostly British and French, banks lent money to the Ottoman Empire, first to fund the Crimean War against Russia, defending an advantageous port city for both European traders and the Ottoman Empire. European money lenders continued to lend the Ottoman money for infrastructure projects that continued to benefit both travel and trade for Europeans. When the lenders started calling in the loans, the Ottoman Empire found themselves too deep in debt to repay. The sultan committed suicide and bankers formed the Ottoman Public Debt Association, under the leadership of Gabriel Aubaret. Aubaret, who fought in Crimea (a lieutenant during the Siege of Sobastopol), who helped take down Peking during the Opium Wars, who had been part of the Siamese King Mungkat's adjustment to Western ways (*The King and I* king) and had managed to have a very public love affair with a French actress who was the ex-lover of Napoleon III, stepped in behind the scenes to levy taxes on the Muslim people of the Middle East. (And we wonder why they were so mad.)

¶ This all left a bitter taste in the mouths of the Ottomans who secretly sided with the Germans in WWI against the British. This did not go so well for them. When the Central Powers lost, a plan to divide up the Ottoman Empire was led by two diplomats, Picot (French) and Sykes (British). The Sykes–Picot lines through the Middle East are like deep cuts in the skin of a living organism, still painful, still bleeding.

Zeus

As the Plutocrats were taking over industries and human capital, Zeus, holders of the reigns, were in a shift of their own. In prior cycles, the aristocracies, the theocracies, and the monarchies that represented the Zeus energy had extraordinary wealth and governing power. In this cycle—for the first time in four thousand years—the aristocracy was falling, all over the world. While Zeus represents royalty, he also represents patriarchy—a path still heavily tread even while it is being questioned and called out through large scale demonstration movements of modern times.

While Marx and Engels were suggesting a form of government that did not include kings and queens, many countries were forming republics. Abraham Lincoln in the US, Benito Juárez in Mexico, Bartolomé Mitre in the Argentine Republic, and José Joaquín Pérez in the Liberal Republic of Chile were democratically elected presidents of new republics. In 1864 in South America, Venezuela formed a republic, The United States of Venezuela. France, too, formed a (third) republic in 1870. This and more all points to a fall of the mighty Zeus during the upcoming REFORM time in this final cycle of Pluto in extreme declination, a unique outcome during a cycle that began with the fall of monarchies.

Even while Pope Pious IX was declaring popes infallible—an act of a Zeus feeling the ebbing tides—the Catholic Church continued to lose ground as a powerbroker in the world, particularly as Italy unified and established itself as a nation. With Italian governance separate from that of the Vatican, Pope Pious IX, in protest, never left the Vatican. His protest made little difference.

Other Zeuses were not faring well for other reasons. Queen Victoria was in grief over the loss of her beloved Albert in 1858. Tsar Nicholas I was backed into a corner to free the serfs, and Maximillian was kicked out of Mexico in 1867.

The kings and queens of the world were not having a good time. The Zeuses of the world were finding themselves, for the first time in recorded history, moving toward dreaded irrelevancy. One could argue that the upcoming World War I was a last gasp of the royalty, as the grandchildren of Victoria, King George V of England and Wilhelm II of Germany fought each other to stay relevant. With the rise of the Bolsheviks in Russia, Tsar Nicholas II rightly feared for his life along with his cousins, Wilhelm II in Germany and

George V in England. When Archduke Ferdinand, the heir apparent to the Austrian throne, was assassinated it sent a ripple of foreboding through the aristocracy of their imminent demise. Wilhelm II was the last emperor of Germany, and in the aftermath of WWI, the parliaments of other European countries took on larger leadership roles.

In China, the Empress Dowager Cixi, a low-level concubine of the past emperor, staged a coup, known as the Xinyou Coup, and established herself on the throne while her five-year old son waited to step into power. Her policies lifted China up out of debt to England, kicked opened the doors of trade to the west, and established universities in China by bringing in science professors (Hermes) from Europe and the US. While she held the role of a Zeus, her past as an abducted concubine reveals that she is more like Persephone. As the cycle unfolds for China, the dual leadership of a Persephone and a Zeus at the beginning of this cycle supports the increased influence of China during REFORM.

Zeus is the god that maintains the self-benefiting hierarchy in the heavens. His role as Persephone's father is the ultimate expression of the self-aggrandizing, patriarch. While plutocracy is on the rise, by the time of the JUSTICE period of this cycle in the 1980s, the great monarchies will be either ousted or relegated to superficial figureheads.

Demeter

Demeter is the voice for Persephone, the goddess who takes a stance on her behalf, the mother who boycotts so that her daughter can be free. She wields her power passionately and destructively. She is willing to take down the whole system, the whole lot of humanity, to get what she wants—and to rectify an injustice. She is the voice for the Earth and for nature itself. She offers seeds to those who respect her and withholds seeds when she feels dismissed or disregarded. Her grief permeates both the world of humans and the world of the gods. She is the essence of the emotional life—in one moment sad and the next enraged. She shows compassion in one breath and in the next destroys an entire season of crops.

Demeter represents those in positions of power who advocate for the underprivileged, for the people who do not have the power to advocate for themselves. She is fierce and often her methods are confrontational and caustic. During this VISION time, she becomes the force behind the early suf-fragists and the labor unions, the activists for the environment, for social jus-tice, for equal rights, and for civil rights. She is the advocate for the oppressed everywhere and the ability for large groups to affect real change. She is the voice for the enslaved, those captured by the plutocrats who steal and torture without conscience.

Hermes

Hermes is the scientist and philosopher who spreads information about how things work, and inventors who spread thoughts about how things are made. Hermes represents the new ideas, and the paradigm shifts that arise from those new ideas, the inventions that change our perspective. A change in perspective is the beginning of a revolution in thought—a consciousness shift that becomes a new way of living.

At the beginning of our current cycle, a wave of new science erupted all over the globe. Scottish James Maxwell's equations on electricity and mag-netism have governed all modern technology since he presented his paper in 1864. English Charles Darwin published his paper on evolution in 1859, allowing a theory that has been construed to mean "survival of the fittest" to spread extensively during this VISION time. French Louis Pasteur had his epiphanies about bacteria and developed a method for fighting infection. Austrian Gregor Mendel introduced genetics. American John Lister invented antiseptic surgery. Russian Dmitri Mendeleev designed the periodic table of elements. This is just the beginning of a long list of scientific beginnings.

Persephones

The Persephones are people everywhere. Persephone does the deep in-ner work to transform from abducted victim into empowered queen. Tran-scending from her role as the daughter Kore into a wise and compassionate ruler, she takes responsibility for her own life and accepts her fate. Without malice or role models, she finds a way to collaborate and share power. She moves beyond both the fear of dying and the dark underworld of death. She becomes a Goddess who travels between the worlds effortlessly, honoring both life and death.

Visionaries such as Ramakrishna, who inspired Gandhi, Helena Blavatsky, who founded theosophy, Bahá'u'lláh, who founded Bahá'í, and Hawthorne

Wodziwob, who led the first Ghost Dance ceremony for the Northern Pai-ute, all had significant visions during the early 1860s. Add to this the early pioneers of psychology and sociology, hypnotherapy and homeopathy, na-turopathy and osteopathy, evolving fields during the VISION time. They are part of the spiritual movements of the mid 1800s that forged a path for the evolution of the inner work needed for humanity to both survive and thrive during this final and upcoming REFORM time.

From VISION to POWER, 1866–1937

In the previous part of the book (Part II: The Past), I covered the four key turning points in Pluto's declination cycle, so I could present you with a cou-ple thousand years of history succinctly. For this cycle, I want to take more time to flesh out the history between these decisive periods to orient us more thoroughly for the next part of the book (Part IV: The Future).

Thirty years into this cycle, the United States quietly became a plutocra-cy. J.P. Morgan controlled much of the banking and investment world. He spent his time destroying inventors, such as Tesla, and boosting profits for friends. Corporations and monopolies grew. Companies like General Elec-tric, IBM, and Ford Motor Company, using new technologies, boosted their market share and put the US in a position of potential world dominance. The market-state was getting legs, as wars over country boundaries took war to a new level.

In 1896, the robber barons even figured out a way to exert their financial power to buy the presidency. The election was between William Jennings Bryan, a great orator who was passionately against corporate interests, and William McKinley, who favored the gold standard and was adequately vague around his economic policies. With money pouring in from Rockefeller, Car-negie. and J.P. Morgan, McKinley outspent Bryan five-to-one and went on to win the election with a wide margin.

As the Hades-backed plutocrats grew in power between the VISION and POWER times, the Zeuses lost further ground. World War I cut up the Otto-man Empire and left the Second German Empire in ruins. Russian rebellions during the Bolshevik Revolutions in 1905 and 1917 killed off the last of the tsars and veered away from Marxism-Leninism, becoming steeped in a fascist form of communism. In China, the Ming Dynasty monarchy was overthrown in 1912 by rebels under the leadership of western-educated Sun Yat-sen. It was not a good time to be a monarch.

Meanwhile, the Demeters were growing in power. Women's suffrage grew roots in many countries throughout the world, including New Zealand, Australia, many countries in Europe, Russia, England, and the US. The labor movement was growing with the birth of the AFL-CIO and other labor organizations. However there were a few disastrous setbacks, including the Homestead steel workers strike that ended when the private Pinkerton army showed up with guns to kill demonstrators. Prohibition fueled an underground bootleg alcohol industry and reinforced other Hades-type industrialists including Joseph Kennedy whose family came into power later in this cycle.

Science and technology made leaps and bounds. Hermes flourished with figures such as Thomas Edison, Alexander Graham Bell, Nikola Tesla, and Albert Einstein making breakthroughs with inventions and equations that changed the world. The Wright Brothers invented flight: Hermes literally got his wings.

In 1929 Hades took a hit when the stock market crashed, sending the US and most of the Western world into depression. China and Russia moved deeper into communism, and Europe struggled to stay relevant. In response to breadlines, suicides, and suffering, charismatic leaders made big promises. Winston Churchill, Franklin Delano Roosevelt, Josef Stalin, Adolf Hitler, Benito Mussolini, and Mao Zedong moved into influential positions. Arising with the support of corporations and bankers, this new brand of leadership was full of loud declarations and pledges. In a land growing in fear and lack, any promise was better than no promise. In the midst of this fear, Pluto went out of bounds to the north.

POWER 1938–1949

Zeus and Hades Wage War

Precisely as Pluto crossed into extreme declination in November 1938, the German Gestapo began incarcerating Jews in the infamous Night of Broken Glass, *Kristallnacht*. The abduction of the Jews into the underworld of concentration camps and genocide was an abduction unlike any other in history. People were conscripted into war, kidnapped into camps, killed, or forced to work to build an excess of goods with little use outside of wartime. Women and children were called in. All the world was mobilized in service of the great plutocrats, and they were playing both sides and could not lose in this rigged system.

While 37 million Persephones screamed in death and millions more in suffering, the plutocrats and Zeuses made deals and plans. The dictators at the time, Stalin, Hitler, Mao Zedong, Hideki Tojo, and Francisco Franco, took over lands where desperate populations felt impotent. While many of the republics in Europe were conquered by Germany and Italy, the republics of England and the US stepped up war preparation. FDR, born into a long line of wealthy merchants, stayed in power long past the usual presidency in part due to his policies that supported war. Churchill, also coming from a long line of wealth and aristocracy, returned to power through his use of strong language in support of war.

As Pluto moved into its point of maximum declination during the summers of 1944 and 1945, agreements of a new world order were formed (The Bretton Woods Conference, July 1944) and enforced (atomic bombs dropped on Hiroshima and Nagasaki, August 1945). The extraordinary change that took place during this POWER time cannot be underemphasized. In the aftermath of war, leaders of the Allied Countries formed world organizations including the World Bank in 1944, the IMF in 1944, the United Nations in 1945, the World Health Organization in 1948, and in 1947 GATT, which was the General Agreements on Tariffs and Trade, the precursor to the World Trade Organization.

The victors of WWII carved up Germany, Korea, and Vietnam, and created new divisions between Pakistan and India. New constitutions were implemented for many countries, including Italy, West Germany, Japan, and China. Indonesia declared independence from the Netherlands in 1946. A year later, India declared independence from Great Britain. And just one year after that, the formation of Israel brought a radical change to the Middle East in 1948.

Finally, while Pluto was still in extreme northern declination, the underworld took on new forms as intelligence agencies throughout the world were formed. The National Security Act of 1947 established the intelligence organizations within the US, including the CIA. The FBI grew in power under the leadership of J. Edgar Hoover from 1924 to 1972, when FDR gave the FBI power to incarcerate Japanese Americans within internment camps during the war. In England, MI6, Military Intelligence, Section 6, grew out of the earlier versions of MI. In Russia, the precursors to the KGB expanded in influence until the KGB became well-established in 1954.

Demeter and Persephone: Fasting for Peace

While Nazi Germany was still a burgeoning effort, and the US lie deep in Depression, a young Mahatma Gandhi, inspired by Ramakrishna, led a group of demonstrators on a march to voice opposition to a British law that prohibited people in India from making their own salt. In an act of civil disobedience, Gandhi and 60,000 other protesters picked up handfuls of salted mud and were arrested. This peaceful protest galvanized a movement for Indian independence, which became a successful reality in 1947, at the end of POWER. Moreover, Gandhi, who went on extreme and public fasts in his acts of political protest (particularly during the time when Pluto was at its most extreme of declination), inspired Martin Luther King, Jr. and a host of other later nonviolent demonstration leaders.

Gandhi, as a true representation of Persephone, stood in the underworld and took the power he had, the power to fast, just as Persephone fasted in the underworld, and just as Demeter fasted upon the Earth in protest. In doing so, Gandhi changed the world. This extraordinary act changed the entire Hades story for this cycle. India was let out of the underworld, was freed from Zeus—no Hermes intervention or begging from Demeter. Persephone herself changed the course of the story. This act of empowerment can perhaps give us great hope as the nonviolent demonstration movement gains power, strength, and popularity going into the REFORM time.

In addition, the war took many men into military service and opened the doors for women to step into working positions. For the first time, women en masse proved to themselves and the world they could do work traditionally assigned to men. Patriarchal assertions of the inferiority of women lost significant ground, even if they still linger to this day.

While Zeus and Hades destroyed much of the world with bombs, Demeter grieved. At this point in the myth, Demeter is wholly lost. The grief is too much to bear. She feels powerless and takes on the form of a mortal search-ing the world for her love. While the Persephones were abducted, the Deme-ters wailed. Few were unscathed. The destruction of the environment from atomic weaponry and forces unlike any that came before drove many into despair—a time of searching for meaning and love—a time of loss. Wives lost husbands. Children lost parents. Parents lost children.

Meanwhile, oil was discovered in the Middle East and plane and car travel took leaps and bounds. Highways across the US were designed and built in a grid pattern beneficial for cars and careless for the environment. Manufac-turing for war goods—tanks, helicopters, guns—increased, as did the de-struction to the environment that this manufacturing caused. Demeter is the grief cry of the environment, that even while greenhouse gas emissions were already detected, the world of commerce and its ensuing destruction grew.

Hermes

Perhaps, the most important Hermes to arise during WWII was British mathematician and inventor, Alan Turing. While working to decode cy-phers in WWII, he applied his theories of computation to invent the first programmable, automated digital computing machine. Meanwhile, Ameri-can physicist and inventor Percy Spencer developed microwave technology and scientists at Lost Alamos, under the leadership of Robert Oppenheimer, developed the atomic bomb. During this time of abduction, the electro-mag-netic equations of the visionary James Maxwell led to inventions that have overtaken the world in one form and another.

From POWER to JUSTICE, 1949–1986

The 1950s included an entrenched blame game with people reeling from the after-effects of WWII. With Hades' all-encompassing fear beginning to dissolve in the cessation of world war, there was a desire to point fingers. A fear of communism and rising tensions between the Soviet Union and the US were the result. Hades figures rarely take responsibility for their ac-tions. We can view the aftermath of WWII as analogous to the rest of the Olympian gods and goddesses finding out about the abduction and blaming solely him rather than taking responsibility for their part—whether it was their part to look the other way or to actively participate. When US Senator

Joseph McCarthy went on a witch-hunt for communists, people within the country moved into paralyzing fear—as soldiers had to deal with the likes of post-traumatic stress disorder from WWII. However, his movement did not last in the way the Nazi's had. Instead, the Red Scare, not unlike the Gestapo, found resistance and was successfully dismantled in part because of the courage of journalists. Without Pluto in extreme declination, his fear-based tactics did not last.

As Hades lost power, Demeter grieved and the Persephones started to feel empowered—even if or while they were still captured. Demeter's boycott laid siege to the world. As such, civil rights movements flared like a bright, inspirational light into the world under the leadership of Martin Luther King Jr., Malcolm X, Rosa Parks, Nelson Mandela, Desmond Tutu, and Angela Davis, to name a few. While these movements steered some policies in the direction of freedom for all, the leaders were often assassinated or imprisoned. Persephone was still under Zeus' reign.

Other Demeters who moved the world toward justice were women's rights activists, including Gloria Steinem and Betty Friedan. Meanwhile, Harvey Milk, a gay rights activist, became the first openly gay mayor of San Francisco in 1978—and was assassinated before the year was up. Cesar Chavez, a labor movement activist inspired by Gandhi, became an integral part of starting the United Farm Workers (advocating for fair working conditions for the agriculture laborers, 1962).

Between POWER and JUSTICE, tensions between capitalist states and communist states rose into a crescendo where for a few brief hours the world stood on the precipice of annihilation during the Cuban Missile Crisis in 1962. The Cold War between the two reigning empires, the US and the USSR, took hostages all along the way: Cuba, Turkey, Venezuela, Afghanistan, Iran, Guatemala, Vietnam, Korea, Hungary, Laos, Haiti, Ecuador, Brazil, Indonesia, Greece, Congo, Bolivia, Uruguay, Cambodia, Chile, El Salvador, Nicaragua, Honduras, Panama, and much of Eastern Europe found themselves under the thumb of one or other of the two global empires.

To paint a broad scene of the temporal moment: while the Beatles were busy practicing in Liverpool, John F. Kennedy fired the first director of the CIA, Allen Dulles, in November 1961, just shortly after the Bay of Pigs Invasion failed to take down Cuba's Communist Leader Fidel Castro. Kennedy's assassination a year later followed by the assassination of his brother Bobby, the arch nemesis of J. Edgar Hoover, did not stop the movement toward justice. Lyndon B. Johnson followed and signed into law civil rights bills that continued the effort toward social justice. During his presidency, the Vietnam War brought with it a wave of anti-war demonstrations that served to push war underground and away from the public sight of Americans.

In the meantime, hidden organizations like the CIA and corporations increased in power. Government regulations intended to stem the tide of corruption of the robber baron monopolies became a model for the modern corporation, which found new ways to subvert democracy. Companies like Coca-Cola, Nestlé, IBM, Ford, Chase Bank, and Standard Oil profited from WWII and found themselves on solid ground coming out of the devastation they enabled.

JUSTICE 1986–1989

The JUSTICE period is often a complex time in the Pluto cycle when movements for civil freedoms and fairness begin at the same time as underground organizations are established. In both cases, a shift in power occurs. Often rulers die and weaker rulers take their place. These weaker leaders often begin subversive organizations in order to stay in control. Ultimately these organizations fall during the REFORM time but can gain strength between JUSTICE and REFORM while people gradually become more aware of what is really going on.

The late 1980s saw the Iron Curtain lift, the Berlin Wall fall, perestroika, and the breaking apart of the Soviet Union into fifteen separate countries. Peaceful demonstrations in Latvia, Estonia, and Lithuania (The Singing Revolution), and Czechoslovakia (The Velvet Revolution), led to new countries. Meanwhile, US leaders finally outlawed genocide. The People Power Revolution in the Philippines led to a new government there. For the first time in history, the Catholic pope visited a synagogue. And justice was served in 1987 when German S.S. Operative Klaus Barbie was found guilty of war crimes committed during WWII.

As the AIDS epidemic spread along with misunderstanding and misinformation, gay rights advocates gained traction. In 1987, ACT UP (AIDS

Coalition to Unleash Power) galvanized activists and initiated a wave of gay pride including the first National Coming Out Day in 1988.

At the same time, the fall of the Soviet Union left the US as the only surviving superpower. During the late Reagan years, an ailing president oversaw policies that shoved issues underground. "Trickle-down" economics turned out to be Orwellian double speak, trickling up to serve the wealthy at the expense of the poor. The "Just Say No" campaign shoved drug addiction underground. In 1983, a group of Republicans from Tennessee launched The Corrections Corporation of America and began the process of privatizing the prison system in the US at the same time as policing of nonviolent drug crimes increased. This put many people with minor drug infractions into the prison system that was making a profit for the plutocrats. The Persephones were incarcerated and fasting, doing time, and secretly building coalitions.

In the Middle East, Islamic extremists, tired of overreaching Western supremacy, created underground organizations, namely Hamas, Hezbollah and Al-Qaeda. Muslim Palestinians formed Hamas to help their people acquire arms and other accoutrements for acquiring independence. In response to Israeli incursions into Lebanon, Muslims formed Hezbollah. And in 1988, in response to the US and Soviet presences in Afghanistan, Osama bin Laden formed Al-Qaeda. Hamas, Hezbollah, and al-Qaeda are all contemporary militant Muslim organizations that arose out of conflicts stemming from boundary decisions made during WWII. Their terrorist tactics mask a cry for justice for the people they claim to represent. It can be very tricky to discuss this nuance in the current political climate, so I will stop here.

While Europeans and Americans were distracted by Princess Diana's love life and the Iran-Contra scandal, China was in a complicated time of its own. An Open Door policy from 1978 opened the country to the growth of business and financial gain in China; by 1989 its export volume had doubled in size. This also meant increased awareness of other nations and their values: free trade leading to calls for free speech. Peaceful protests advocating for free speech in Tiananmen Square and throughout China were violently quashed by the Chinese government. An unknown number of justice seekers were killed or arrested. Protest movements went underground.

From JUSTICE to REFORM, 1990–2025

In the period between JUSTICE and REFORM, Demeter begs Zeus and Persephone finds her power. It represents a time of a movement from the dark mysteries to the renaissance spring. It represents a time of movement from people who sacrifice their lives advocating for their causes amidst ridicule (and worse) to masses of people aligning with the cause. It represents a time when monkey after monkey wakes up to the new way until, just at the dawn of the REFORM time, the hundredth monkey wakes up. Once that hundredth monkey picks up the cause, everything changes. Structures that were thought to be solid dissolve. Organizations that seemed to have long-lasting, all-embracing power fall from grace. It is a disorienting time when anything can happen, and the only constant is change.

During the Roman Empire—during a JUSTICE time—a young lad named Jesus started turning over the tables in the temple. He championed for a new age of love, for taking down the hierarchy of status that had developed in Rome, and for seeing all people as worthy of respect—even prostitutes and tax-collectors. He was a voice against the machine. He was executed midway between JUSTICE and REFORM. But by the time of the REFORM period, Paul and Peter had started a movement in his name.

One cycle after Jesus, Mani did the same thing. He taught about love and compassion and was executed, in the same way, at the same time in the cycle. Other mystics and radicals that lead movements of awakening between JUSTICE and REFORM include Benedict of Nursia, Rabia, Thomas Aquinas, Rumi, and Martin Luther. Sometimes the movements are more political, as in the last cycle, when Samuel Adams riled up the North American colonists in Massachusetts. The voices that speak truth to power during this time get things going, but often to their personal detriment. Martin Luther may not have been executed, for example, but he lived much of his life in hiding from the authorities.

In our current cycle, the last cycle of Pluto in extreme declination for thousands of years, political dissidents are struggling to share their truths. Chelsea Manning, Edward Snowden, Julian Assange, and Greta Thunberg are viewed with varying degrees of disdain and adulation. Malala Yousafzai, a Pakistani human rights activist, was shot in the face for speaking out in

2012 (she miraculously survived). Mohamed Bouazizi set himself on fire in public and started a revolution in Tunis. Monks in Myanmar have done the same. The Arab Spring, a time of revolutions throughout the Middle East, started in 2010 and with various outcomes in 2012, was the beginning, a run-through. Revolutions that begin before Pluto goes into extreme southern declination often fail, like the Nika Rebellion and the Christian uprisings during the time of Diocletian. Revolutions that occur during the peak, succeed, like the American Revolution and Constantine's reforms. Revolutions that take place late during Pluto's period of extreme southern declination have a harder time getting established, like the French Revolution.

While the 1960s, during the time before JUSTICE, had many notable social justice advocates, many assassinated for their radicalism—Martin Luther King Jr., Malcom X, Harvey Milk, and JFK, as mentioned above, their movements led us into JUSTICE and serve as fuel for the reforms and revolutions of today.

Right now, increasing numbers of people are awakening to the truths laid down during the VISION time: the truths of climate change and social injustice, movements of nonviolent demonstrations and self-help, religions that are open to all religions, and open borders between countries. Whether we can fully see it or not, people are beginning to awaken to the patterns of abuse, control, and corruption at work in our societies.

REFORM   2025–2035

As we move into the last time Pluto goes out-of-bounds for thousands of years, we may discover that this relatively short period of extreme declination might be more intense than REFORM times that came before. Since the POWER time was shorter and more intense (WWII), the REFORM time may mirror that intensity. However, it mirrors it with a great Up-Rising instead of a great world war.

As of this moment of writing—early 2024—unrest in the world is becoming more evident. A white-supremacist-led insurrection in the US had Congress officials cowering under desks, leaving five people dead. The deadly COVID-19 pandemic has killed millions worldwide, but has also not stemmed the tide of demonstrations, from both left and right, in the wake of the insurrection's symbolic rupture. Russian leaders look to take over other countries. Market competitions between US and China intensify. The destabilized Middle East continues to fester. Refugee crises mount. Climate change triggers droughts, floods, more intense storms. Health care systems operate in name only, failing those they're meant to serve. Airwaves are polluted. New technologies create new problems. Rich get richer. Poor get poorer. These are the typical issues that happen just before the REFORM time. How we move through the apex of this time depends on us. We have options.

PART IV:
THE FUTURE

Our strategy should be not only to confront empire, but to lay siege to it. To deprive it of oxygen. To shame it. To mock it. With our art, our music, our literature, our stubbornness, our joy, our brilliance, our sheer relent-lessness—and our ability to tell our own stories. Stories that are different from the ones we're being brainwashed to believe. ❡ The corporate revolu-tion will collapse if we refuse to buy what they are selling—their ideas, their version of history, their wars, their weapons, their notion of inevitability. ❡ Remember this: We be many and they be few. They need us more than we need them. ❡ Another world is not only possible, she is on her way. On a quiet day, I can hear her breathing.

—Arundhati Roy

In this final Part, we will look at the five possible outcomes of the upcom-ing REFORM period and draw again upon some histories that inform why each outcome would take place.

Chapter 14:
Five Potential Futures

How we as a world, as a society, as humanity, move into and through the upcoming REFORM time has a lot to do with all of us. Looking back at history, we have multiple options. Unlike POWER, a time of war and explosion, expansion, and force, REFORM, as a time of implosion, presents a host of opportunities. In my own research and analysis, I have narrowed it down to four options based on history, and added a fifth, because history does not always repeat.

1. Collapse
2. Revolution
3. Non-violent Resistance and Benevolent Rulers
4. Paradigm Shift
5. Awakening

Potential 1: Collapse
Outcome of the Hades Visionaries

What defines the collapse of a culture, country, or society is relative and somewhat arbitrary. We often define collapse by the ruins and stories left behind—the Mayan ruins, the Anasazi ruins, the Roman ruins, the ruins of the burned down Carnegie mansion on the property where I once lived in Western Massachusetts. For our purposes, collapse is not only physical, but also the destruction of conceptual systems and agreements about what is civil, what is truth, what is right, what is beneficial.

The causes of collapse are varied—greed, invasions, climate change, freak disasters. Sometimes a civilization—a system of organization of, for, and through people—collapses, and people are better off. Sometimes it leads to chaos and anarchy. Regardless, collapse is a time when the current perspective on "reality," the shared consensus on what is true and right, radically changes, for better or worse.

As Persephone rises into power, the agreements that have kept her out of power need to change. This requires a paradigm shift, an entirely new way of seeing the world. As this shift takes place, the systems that do not also adjust their perspectives fail. The collapse occurs as people see a new truth about the conditions in which they live and act to change those conditions. Economic systems like capitalism and communism, law-and-order systems where torture is acceptable, agricultural systems that deplete the soil, and environmental systems that destroy forests for short-term gain at the expense of the long-term need for clean air and water—these systems come into question during times of REFORM, and, as such, are improved or destroyed.

For guidance into our nearing REFORM time, we will look back to the time of Egypt and the Hittites, the time of Ramses the Great and Moses. On first glance, Ancient Egypt may seem like a long time ago or an arbitrary period to look back on. Consider that, much like today, heading into the REFORM period of 1190 BCE, there were superpowers (Assyria, Egypt, the Hittite Empire) and there were world trade agreements and treaties. Even without our contemporary technology, 1190 BCE saw countries that were well-developed with complex organizational systems. And then they all collapsed, simultaneously, within a decade. For generations, archeologists have rummaged through the ruins for clues and arrived at multiple causes. Most causes point to human decisions—an unsustainable way of life that mirrors our current condition.

The visions of the plutocrats, the Hades of our current times, leads to an inevitable collapse as these visionaries cared little for the environment, for the Earth and for other people. Without consideration or empathy, Hades invariably finds himself demoted and sitting impotent beside his queen, has little to say in future episodes of underworld stories.

Potential 2: Revolution
Outcome of the Zeus Visionaries

For this option, we need only look back to the prior cycle, the time of the American War of Independence and the French Revolution—bloody, uncomfortable, and irreverent times of destruction that, out of ruins and violence, birthed new civilizations. Most of the battles fought during REFORM times have been uprisings by people revolting over an oppressive system. Sometimes these were successful and lead to new governments as in the American War of Independence. Sometimes they were successful but lead to a new authoritarian regime as in the French Revolution. Sometimes they were unsuccessful like Boudica's rebellion against the Roman Empire circa 60 CE or the Jewish Revolt in 70 CE.

Uprisings and revolts are likely during the upcoming REFORM period. Deeply entrenched rulers will need to be ousted. Governments that do not adapt will be overthrown as the people establish new governments. Persephone will take out a sword and slash her way to the throne.

When Zeus-like power is held in an iron-clad grip, revolution is often the only option for the Persephones demanding power. Riots, uprisings, and sabotage ensue to take down controlling patriarchal power. In the myth, Zeus gives in to Demeter out of a desire to keep people from experiencing the devastating effects of a year-long winter. Without people to rule, Zeus loses his kingdom. Uprisings are a path toward power, a way to let Zeus know that without the people he has no kingdom, no one to rule. He has nothing.

Potential 3: Non-violent Resistance & Benevolent Rulers
Outcome of Demeter Visionaries

In this scenario, the rulers and governments make changes in response to the non-violent demonstrations that erupt with a passion heading into the final REFORM time. A wise ruler will notice the change in direction and adjust accordingly. There are many examples of this in history during past REFORM times.

Revolts in Ancient Greece led to the creation of the Ecclesia, extending government participation to most male citizens—an early form of democracy. Constantine was aware of the Christian uprisings and the massacres that were taking place. Seeing the writing on the wall, he instituted reforms, in particular the freedom of religion. He then supported the creation of the Christian sect at the Council of Nicaea. In another example, after the Nika Rebellion was vociferously put down, Justinian, the emperor of the Byzantine Empire, turned his sights inward, instituted reforms at home, and dealt with a decaying infrastructure. More recently, Catherine the Great of Russia, a follower of the Enlightenment philosophers, tried to outlaw capital punishment and institute other voting reforms, after Pugachev's Rebellion.[1] Other examples of REFORM benevolent rulers are Solomon, Harun al-Rashid, Suleiman I, and Kublai Khan. Once they were in power, they reigned over times of creativity, internal restructuring, and support for the arts and sciences, bowing to the desires of the people they governed.

Demeter leaving the Earth to rot is the original boycott. Demeter is the resistance movement personified, or rather deified. Demeter wields her goddess power through the destructive act of passive resistance—she withdraws support, retreats into grief and in a grand act of defiance, stops working. As demonstrations, both violent and non-violent erupt throughout the world, like a massive wave of Demeter intercessions, elected leaders in republics and democracies with clear vision have the potential to institute reforms that support all people and the environment that supports life for all people. Even non-elected leaders can rise to respond to the wave of boycotts, sit-ins, bed-ins, walk-outs, and run-outs that transpire in the mid 2020s—addressing climate change, work-place inequities, racism, civil rights violations, and crumbling infrastructure with regulations, reparations, and restructuring.

Potential 4: Paradigm Shift
The Result of Hermes

In the prior cycle during REFORM (1770s), a scientific revolution led to massive industrial progress. By the 1860s, pollution, a biproduct of industry, was already a problem in many places in the world. Coal-burning furnaces, factories, and sweat shops produced greenhouse gases as scientists John Tyndall and Eunice Newton Foote pointed out right at the beginning of this cycle.

Technology—as we have come to know it—was in its infancy. The Massachusetts Institute of Technology (MIT), founded in 1861, used the word "technology" in its very name, the first institute to do so, bringing the concept, rarely used, to the forefront.[2]

---

1. In a twist with repercussions to Russia in the current cycle, Catherine gave more power to land-owning nobility who helped put down the Pugachev Rebellion.
2. Jon Agar, "What is technology?" 377–82.

For a look into the future of the coming technological paradigm shift, we will go back to the prior cycle and explore the scientific revolution that brought us industry in the first place. What started at the VISION time in the 1610s as science itself, became industry at the late 1700s REFORM time. What started at the VISION time in the 1860s as technology itself, leads to anti-industry and remarkable advancements in sustainable technologies.

The new thoughts of both times initiated new paradigms. Bacon, Galileo, Descartes, and Hobbes brought science to the forefront and spread ideas that inspired the inventions of the Industrial Revolution. In our current cycle, Maxwell, Lyell, Darwin, Mendel, Pasteur, Lister and a host of others brought technology and new sciences to the forefront and spread ideas that will inspires a new scientific revolution that brings technology into a new age.

Potential 5: Awakening

Gleaning insight from the Pluto cycles laid out in this book, we will look at the uniqueness of this time, and arrive at new possibilities for the upcoming REFORM period. It is likely that each option will occur somewhere in the world. Different countries have different pasts and will go through the final REFORM differently. However, the world is one world, and we are all interconnected. This interconnectedness will matter more in this REFORM time than ever before. When one country falls, it affects all other countries. One economy crashes, and the ripples create tidal waves in a land far away. One natural disaster in one place could wreak havoc in another place. Likewise, one country reforms, and others are inspired to reform as well. One movement adapts, and that adaptation becomes a template for all other movements.

The possibility for a new world—a world of peace, compassion, and shared prosperity—is more than just an elusive dream. When Persephone becomes queen, the Underworld changes. No longer the dark place of suffering, Persephone brings in the light. Her compassion permeates the Underworld. She shares her wisdom and becomes a benevolent ruler alongside her husband. Hades does not go away, as much as many of us would like. He stays and sits beside her, and this is a radical transformation of its own. The plutocrats of today, the patriarchy of today, the power dynamics of today must change—must make way for the greater good of all people.

Hades becomes not only faithful to Persephone, he also becomes sub-missive—allowing her to take the lead. Often, we think of submissiveness, particularly in men, as a loss of power and a negative quality. However, sub-mission to compassion is greatness. Looking at our options, we will explore the ways that Persephone steps into power, the potentials for the very near future, and possibilities for us to move forward with wisdom and kindness.

Potential 1: Collapse

It isn't hard to find books on world collapse these days. Many are seeing it in the not-too-distant future. Since World War II, it seems that the world has been on a building spree. Coalitions are building. Skyscrapers and strip malls continue to be built long after the need exists. Technology, science, medicine, and weaponry have made unfathomable strides in the past fifty years. But in spite of—or perhaps because of—this, collapse seems to be a likely course for our future, and it is deeply unfamiliar to most of us.

The word "collapse" can conjure many different images. Barbarians tram-pling through gardens and burning villages. Soldiers in riot gear locking us in our homes. Tear gas and biological weapons used with ease. Nuclear melt-downs and bombings of public buildings. Zombies and alien invasions. All these visions are believed by some people to be the Armageddon future to-ward which we are headed. Yet, history suggests a different kind of collapse.

Noted British archeologist, Colin Renfrew, described systems collapse as the collapse of a central administrative organization, the evaporation of the ruling elite, the fall of a centralized economy, a refugee crisis, and population decline. Once central systems breakdown occurs, power falls to smaller or-ganizations, local tribes, and states.[3]

---

3. Cline, 161.

A Story of Collapse from 1177 BCE

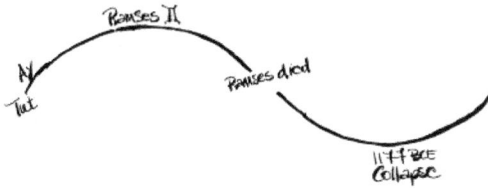

To explore this, we look to a time many centuries ago. The young Pharoah Tutankhamun had just died, ending the great 18th Dynasty of Egypt. Meanwhile, the cult of the Sun God, Aten, was being dismantled by the new occupant of the palace in Giza, the Pharaoh Ay. The Hittites (Turkey), Assyria (Syria), Mycenae (Greece), and Minoa (Crete) were major superpowers with armies, trade agreements, economies, and industry.

VISION   1322–1316 BCE

When Tut died at the end of the prior cycle (c. 1323 BCE), he left no heir. This situation happens often with monarchies, and a typical trajectory is war. Siblings fight each other. Murder and coups become commonplace. This time was no different. As VISION began, Ay, an elder mystic and general, married King Tut's widow, his own granddaughter, and usurped the throne. His vision was to release Egypt from the cult of Aten and return the empire to the old, pantheistic ways of worship, where multiple gods and goddesses accounted for the machinations of the physical and spiritual worlds. Ay turned his attention toward the military, beefed up supplies, weapons, and training for soldiers. But he died of old age shortly into this VISION time, and the general, Horemheb, declared himself pharaoh. Horemheb followed Ay's vision and levelled the temple of Aten. As a military leader, he installed his army buddies into positions as priests and restored the old religion.[4] of Amun that was the main religion prior to Akhenaten.

In the Hittite Empire (modern day Turkey), a similar fate was unfolding. A year after Tut died, the Hittite emperor, Šuppiluliuma I, died. Under his

---

4. The old religion of Amun included the worship of multiple gods. During the prior cycle's REFORM time, Akhanaten III and his son Akhanaten IV instituted a series of reforms that led to a new religion that worshipped one god, the Sun god, Aten. When Ay came into power, he began dismantling the new religion of Aten.

leadership, the Hittites expanded the empire to the south into Mittani, much like the American presidents prior to the current VISION time expanded the reach of the United States far west, taking over the land of the indigenous occupants. His son, Muršili II, followed in his footsteps. It was Muršili II who reigned during the VISION period and oversaw a time of building and expansion of the Hittite Empire.

A third superpower, Assyria, already a developed nation for centuries, may have been the largest nation-state at this time. Evidence of correspondences between Egypt, Assyria, the Hittite Empire, and Mycenae (Greece) exist. Trading documents, including horses, lapis lazuli, and chariots between Egypt and the Hittites were found by archeologists in the 19th century. Much like the British Empire in 1863, Assyria was at its peak. Both were the go-to empires for financing, weapons, and armies, and both had policies of expansion based on commerce,[5] a Hades theme to the collapse potential.

In 1316 BCE, five superpowers were on a building jag. In addition to Egypt and Assyria, the ancient Greeks during the Mycenaean time, the Hittites that occupied what is Turkey today and the Minoa, also in Greece, were developing civilizations that we mythologize to this day. It was the time of the Trojan War and the beginning of the Eleusinian Mysteries, the building of ancient temples. In a parallel moment, in 1865, the entrenched empires of Britain, France, and Russia alongside the burgeoning empires of the US and China, were on building sprees where new inventions of steam engines, train travel, and telegraphs were beginning an international era. The underpinning negotiations of underworld figures making backroom deals infuses both VISION times with a strong Hades influence.

In our current cycle, the assassination of the newly re-elected President Abraham Lincoln upset the plan, much the way that Tut's early demise may have upset the continuity of leadership in ancient Egypt. Andrew Johnson moved into power and led the US into a reconstruction that demoralized the South. Like Pharoah Ay and Horemheb, who destructively dismantled the old institutions, Johnson's reconstruction policies destructively dismantled much of the South, setting the region back decades. The early Robber Barons took advantage of the war to amass fortunes unheard of among the merchants of yore. Even today, the millions acquired by Rockefeller and Carnegie outdo

5. Cline, 161.

the Gates fortune when adjusted for inflation. Not only did the titans of industry, the corporate entrepreneurs of the 1860s, amass Hades-like fortunes, they did so with Hades-like industries—those industries that come from under the Earth. Oil and steel. The beginning of industry based on underworld products was in its early inception.

Hades also rears its head in the story of China. Opium was a product grown and processed in India and Turkey that British merchants, today we call them drug lords, bought in India and sold in China, feeding an opium epidemic. When the emperor of China tried to eradicate the epidemic, the British Empire backed the East India Company merchants and attacked. While keeping opium illegal and out of Britain, they insisted that China allow opium and its British merchants inside its walls. Along with opium, the British Empire was also insistent on Christian missionaries being allowed to set up posts in China. The Opium Wars (1839–1860) devastated the Chinese economy, heavily indebting them to Europe. European and US financiers were staging a coup on the rest of the world.

POWER	1280–1233 BCE	Peak: 1252 BCE
	1938–1949	*Peak: Summers of 1944, 1945, and 1946*

During POWER, the focus is often on battle strategy and advances in military weapons. In our current cycle, for example, the atomic bomb was used for the first time. Chemical weapons and spy rings, computers and communication systems all contributed to new war technologies during World War II. While spies were nothing new, two powerful spy organizations came into full form during the war, the CIA in 1947 and the MGB/KGB in 1946.

In May of 1274 BCE, during another POWER time, Egyptian and Hittite armies used advances in military strategy and weaponry at the famous Battle of Kadesh. Pharoah Ramses II used the new war technology of special chariot warfare, battle strategy, spies, and counterspies in the well-documented battle. Drawings on temple walls in Giza tell stories of the victorious Egyptians, when the battle was really a draw and the boundary between the two superpowers remained the same. Ramses was a master of self-promotion, much like the dictators of WWII, Hitler, Mussolini, and Stalin. Massive statues and buildings erected in Ramses' image littered Egypt, an apt reminder to the people who was in charge.

Meanwhile, in what later became Greece, the city of Mycenae was building fortification walls in 1250 BCE to keep out invaders. Archeological evidence points to this POWER time as being the most likely time of the Trojan War, if indeed the war happened. Made famous by Homer and his students, occurring during the same period as Ramses II's reign, the legend goes that Mycenaean troops from mainland Greece entered Troy by disguising themselves within the belly of a large wooden horse. This trickery gave them inside advantage and easy victory. The city of Troy, excavated and re-excavated over the last century, points to a great possibility of this war.[6]

In our modern era, atomic bombs were the ultimate Trojan Horse, flown in on planes high out of view. The whole of World War II was the ultimate battle of Kadesh, with the computer industry arising out of a need to decode spy messages. The Axis Powers and the Allied Powers rearranged the world, fighting over boundaries, control, and dominance. A century later, the boundaries determined during WWII remain unchanged.

Corporations that view profit as their sole purpose, the Hades of our modern times, invested through bankers, other Hades, in the building of work camps for mining precious minerals in the economically depleted but minerally rich lands of Germany and Poland. Corporations including IBM and Ford Motor Company invested with the Brown Brothers Harriman & Co. who in turn funded the rising Nazi party, through the industrialist Fritz Thyssen, and the infrastructure that was to become concentration camps for mass genocide.[7] While these corporatists may not have intentionally funded or supported the horrors to come, and even regretted their decisions (as with the case of Fritz Thyssen and Henry Ford), nevertheless, it was their money that helped a radical politician, who had a dubious grasp on reality, rise into a maniacal dictator.[8]

---

6. Cline, 127.
7. The steel industry was an early supporter of the Nazis, led by "Emil Kirdorf, the venerated but dreaded God Wotan of German heavy industry, Albert Voegler, Fritz Springorum, of the Hoesch steel group, and also by Paul Reusch, of the Haniel group, and August Thyssen, father of Hitler's later financier Fritz Thyssen." (Hallgarten, "Adolf Hitler and German Heavy Industry," 252). Without the support of the steel, shipping, and transportation industries, Hitler could not have financed his political machine. See also Milner, "National Socialism."
8. Before the 1932 election, Thyssen donated 3 million marks to the Nazi party's campaign (Milner, 52). On Jan. 27, 1932, he introduced Hitler at the Industry Club in Dusseldorf, in front of most of Germany's wealthiest industrialists, for a speech that—according to Hallgarten—turned the tide for Hitler and moved these industrialists firmly into the Nazi economic program.

For Egypt and the Hittites, in one era of history, and for the US, and the Soviet Union in another, the POWER times solidified their presences on the world stage, with the creation of massive war machines, policies of expansion, and powerful leaders. In our contemporary era, the US, under the leadership of FDR and Truman, Generals Patton, Eisenhower, and MacArthur, and the rest of the country's military might, expanded the powers of the nation, particularly in the treaties that were signed in the aftermath of WWII. Fred Vinson and Dean Acheson created a world banking system at the Bretton Woods Conference and put themselves in charge, while advancement in atomic weapons—and the willingness to use them—made the US a military might. The National Security Act of 1947 established the CIA, the National Security Council, and reorganized the Department of Defense. This began a policy of expansion through covert wars and untransparent takeovers.

While Stalin oversaw a genocide that Ramses never dared, both men stepped over their rivals and wreaked havoc over their lands to establish themselves on the throne. Both men erected massive statues to enhance public perception of their self-proclaimed god-like status. While the mining of petroleum goes back to Peter the Great in 1700, petroleum as a state-led industry began during World War II, under Stalin's rule. The Plutonic abduction in all cases was of the monetary systems, the war industry, and the Pluto-ruled natural resource of oil.

In the same time period, FDR met with the Saudi Arabian king, Abdul Aziz ibn Saud to shore up an alliance over oil. Meeting on a cruiser in the in the Suez Canal, the two leaders shook hands, bonded over wheelchairs, and began a friendship that only lasted a few months, until FDRs death, the repercussions of US intervention in Middle East oil were just beginning.

During WWII, Japan, already an industrialized nation, occupied much of China and provided a breeding ground for Mao Zedong and his radical form of communism to spread. Distrust of other countries, already sewn into the fabric of life China for centuries and further entrenched by western incursions during VISION, gave Mao a platform into leadership.

JUSTICE: 1216–1214 BCE

Ramses II died in 1213 BCE and Tudhaliya IV, King of the Hittite Empire, died in 1209 BCE. The transition of power, particularly after powerful leaders die, is a vulnerable time in a country. When Ramses II died, Merneptah, his elderly son, stepped in to fill his shoes. His weak leadership contributed to the end of the age of the great pharaohs.[9] This marked the beginning of infighting and decay within the superpowers of the ancient world.

During our current cycle, during JUSTICE, the Soviet Union fell, and its effects were like that of a powerful leader dying. In its wake, new countries formed with new constitutions, much in the way a new leader—a weaker leader—would take the place of one that had just died. While the US under Ronald Reagan and England under Margaret Thatcher, continued to appear to thrive, policies initiated during this time instigated decay. Trickle-down economics served the wealthy at the expense of the poor and middle class, a trend that has still not been reversed. A "Just Say No" to drugs and sex campaign decreased education and understanding on both drugs and sex, which did nothing to help the AIDS epidemic that was sweeping through the world. The Iran-Contra Scandal furthered eroded trust in the US, when the government was caught trading guns for hostages and funding unrest in Nicaragua. While not obvious at the time to many people, a certain deterioration in integrity and in compassion was taking place through these government policies, a kind of death of leadership that had started when Richard Nixon had resigned in shame from the US presidency in the prior decade.

Perhaps more deleterious and less obvious to US politics was a realignment of party policies of both Democrats and Republicans. In 1985, after Reagan's second win, a Midwest journalist Al From formed the Democratic Leadership Council (DLC) in an attempt to revive a sagging Democratic party. The DLC was set up as a think-tank, policymaking, fundraising arm of the Democratic party. Their focus was to change tack from liberal policies to more conservative policies, accepting Reagan's trickle-down economics, and aligning with corporate interests while maintaining the appearance of being the social justice party. Mr. From recruited Bill Clinton in April 1989, and the DLC moved into power, increasing the stronghold of corporations in the country and across the world in the increasingly global economy.

Meanwhile, Newt Gingrich as House Minority Whip (1989–1995) along with the Heritage Foundation, a conservative think-tank organization founded in 1973, incited a new wave of Republican policies based on

---

9. Edward Mahler, "The Exodus," 33–67.

Reagan's 1985 inaugural address. These policies advocated a vigilante-type patriotism that favored white men and blamed feminists and other minority groups for the country's growing problems. Concurrently, conservative personality Rush Limbaugh started his radio show in 1984, syndicated nationally in 1988, that broadcasted Gingrich's politics of fear and derision.[10]

Both parties veered away from the needs of the people during this time and took adversarial courses that have contributed to a long-lasting breakdown in bipartisan decision-making in Congress. This investment in injustice, the shadow of justice, mirrors other JUSTICE time politics explored in this book, when corruption eroded governing bodies from within.

Pluto's domain of oil became the true currency of the world as air and car travel ballooned. Oil reserve states increased in power and influence. The creation of the Organization of the Petroleum Exporting Countries (OPEC) in 1961 included Saudi Arabia, Iraq, Iran, Kuwait, and Venezuela. OPEC gave these countries, all devastated at the end of WWII, increased power over their own lands after colonization and the fall of the Ottoman Empire had taken so much away from them. Meanwhile, other oil states, Russia and the USA, continued to dominate oil policies. While Demeter begged for an intercession on behalf of the planet, human-made disasters shed light on the toxicity of the current energy industry. The Exxon Valdez ship crashed leaking 11 million gallons of oil into the ocean and the nuclear reactor in Chernobyl exploded releasing over 50 metric tons of uranium into the atmosphere.[11] Zeus (Jupiter) had lost so much power that only Hades (Pluto) was in charge. The rule of astrological Pluto during this cycle knows no limit, and, for this reason, we are in a precarious time.

In addition, the financial marketplace, a particularly ripe breeding ground for Hades-like characters, rooted a few powerful institutions. Blackstone Inc. (1985), BlackRock Inc. (1988), Enron (1985), and Vanguard (1975). An article in 1986 in the *Institutional Investor* inspired the hedge fund movement when it spotlighted the double-digit success of Julian Robertson's Tiger Fund (started in 1980). The growth of "hedged funds," a financial concept coined in 1949, during POWER, by financier Alfred W. Jones, intoxicated brokers after the economic downturn of the 1970s. With

10. Jared Yates Sexton. *American Rule*, 239.
11. Erin Blakemore, "The Chernobyl disaster: what happened, and the long-term impact."

the growth of fast and faster computers, financial derivatives and corporate trading went on steroids.

This is an example of Hades coming into more power, while Demeter boycotts the planet and Zeus begins begging Hades to release Persephone. With Hades refusing to free Persephone, destruction and collapse becomes a more likely scenario during REFORM.

REFORM   1194–1124 BCE   Peak: 1165–63 BCE

"The economy of Greece is in shambles. Internal rebellions have engulfed Libya, Syria, and Egypt, with outsiders and foreign warriors fanning the flames. Turkey fears it will become involved, as does Israel. Jordan is crowded with refugees. Iran is bellicose and threatening, while Iraq is in turmoil. AD 2013? Yes. But it was also the situation in 1177 BC, more than three thousand years ago, when the Bronze Age Mediterranean civilizations collapsed one after the other, changing forever the course and the future of the Western world." —Eric H. Cline

Not only are the two scenarios described in the epigraph above similar, as archeologist Eric H. Cline points out in his work *1177 BC: The Year Civilization Collapsed*, but both scenarios occur in the same point in the cycle, in the few years approaching the peak of REFORM. Large cities, climate change, earthquakes, global trade agreements, and massive empires all existed then, and all exist now.

The Mycenaean culture collapsed during this time, with an approximate date of 1180 BCE, when the palace in Pylos was destroyed. The Hittite Empire collapsed when the last king, Šuppululiuma II, died in 1178 BCE. The international port city of Ugarit burned down. And in 1155 BCE, Ramses III, the last pharaoh of Egypt died, signifying the end of that empire.

There are many theories about this period in history. Up until the last forty years, the most popular theory was that sea peoples invaded without settling in the area. However, historians such as Eric Cline, Jared Diamond, and others suggest instead the collapse came about as a result of a constellation of internal systems decay, climate change, and invasion.

To understand this collapse, let's go back to the POWER time, when international trade developed and treaties among empires were signed. With international trade increasing, merchants and ship owners gained power.

Much like the relationship between today's modern corporations and national governments, the merchants had to be appeased by the rulers and governments of their time. As the merchants' power grew, piracy and breakdowns in communication also grew. The treaties became more complex. Ugarit was in the middle of it all, being the largest trading city along the Mediterranean—much in the way New York City, London, and Shanghai are at the center of trade in our current world.

As a world civilization developed, agriculture also developed and practices that supported short-term growth rather than long-term sustainability became more prevalent. Cline suggests that when a system is complex, it might only take one simple thing to set into motion a collapse, like the flap of a butterfly wing causing a tidal wave.

Indeed, if complex relationships between countries and the breakdown of systems due to internal strife among merchants, rulers, infrastructure, and agriculture were the cause of the Mycenaean collapse, then our time—with its much-increased level of complexity—may be well served by studying this collapse, especially as it occurred precisely during the REFORM time, the same stage in the cycle into which we are headed.

It seems possible that a simple event could unravel treaties, contracts, boundaries, and alliances in a world of crumbling infrastructure. Current merchants, corporate CEOs and boards, have complicated affiliations throughout the world. Current agricultural practices, using toxic fertilizers and genetically modified seeds, are as short-sighted in terms of sustainable food production practices as the agricultural monocrops of the early 1100s BCE.

As we head more deeply into an era when a few thousand votes in one area of one country can elect a leader that destabilizes contracts and security throughout the world, it might well take just one small event to trigger a collapse. During a time when eight billion people live on a planet that is perhaps designed for a smaller population, one natural disaster, perfectly timed and placed, could lead to a breakdown in commerce, travel, and peace.

What appears as a consistent feature of REFORM times, including past and present eras, is the transformation of world "superpowers" into smaller powers, locally driven leadership, and a chance for the creation of new societies.

In the wake of the collapse of 1177 BCE, the refugees of Egypt—the Jewish people who came to land in the Levant and called themselves the followers of

Yahweh—developed a civilization, a religion, and a way of life that continues to this day, amidst dozens of diasporas, genocide, and continuous anti-Semitic sentiment throughout the world.

While a zombie apocalypse or an alien invasion may trigger visions of a fantastical future, more likely something that has happened time and time again will transpire. The collapse of one civilization will allow for the creation of a new one. The survivors will adapt. and there will be room for something new.

That this upcoming REFORM is the last time that Pluto goes into extreme declination at all, north or south, supports a grand finale of systems collapse in a complicated world that will happen in a unique, if somewhat recognizable, way. Computers that function not only to serve the economy but that *are* the economy in the form of cryptocurrencies might break down, for example, with cyber warfare becoming the new chaos. Crumbling roads and bridges may derail transportation of goods forcing populations to rely on local supplies.

As we prepare for this upcoming decade of REFORM, it may be helpful to consider that it was the refugees that were able to adapt and create a new world. Countries that support refugees may find themselves in better shape, more available or ready for something new, than countries that wall off their borders and look to short-term gains.

To try to avoid collapse, we need to focus our collective and political energies more intently on infrastructure. Countries that are valuing sustainable technology and agricultural practices will be better positioned to make the REFORM transition. Countries that have allowed the merchants to run the show may find themselves in a bit of a pickle as alliances show their true colors, break down, and trigger systems collapse.

Potential 2: Revolution

All over the world, demonstrations are erupting and forcing administration changes and reforms, some with success and some without. In 2011, a man in Tunisia set himself on fire protesting the authoritarian government, thereby setting off a storm of protests and demonstrations throughout the Middle East. Between 2011 and 2012, revolts in Egypt took down the old regime, and military leaders pushed into power. Rebellions in Bahrain, Libya, Syria, and Yemen, during the same window of time, destabilized the region. Throughout the Middle East, demonstrations led to reforms, coups, or social changes. The Arab Spring lasted from 2011 to mid-2012, ending when either the military took control or large-scale conflicts arose, from civil wars in Syria and Libya to an ongoing crisis in Yemen. It is unlikely that these crises will move into peace anytime soon. As we near 2026, it is more likely that another round of protests and rebellions will break out in the region, possibly more focused in countries that were not as strongly affected by the Arab Spring, such as Saudi Arabia and Iran.

In other parts of the world, mass demonstrations may lead into revolution in places where protestors have been killed or imprisoned. China, a place where past demonstrators have been killed, may wake up into revolution if that is what is needed to interrupt the tyranny of the current Communist state. While Russia adapted during the JUSTICE time, which is promising for peace in the future, ongoing large-scale demonstrations against an unpopular war in the Ukraine may lead to revolution if the current administration does not change its ways.

To explore the potential of revolution, we need only to retreat to the prior cycle. Precisely as the REFORM period started, in the early 1770s, colonists in the states started dumping tea and writing declarations. At the peak of REFORM during this past cycle, leaders of the new US democracy wrote the Constitution, established a new government, and signed a peace treaty with England. Not only in the Americas, revolution in France ousted the monarchy and eventually led to the formation of a new republic. The death of Zeus created an opening for Hades to have more power in our current cycle.

Colonization and Revolution, 1619–1863

VISION   1615–1622

This VISION time is the beginning of world colonization by the Dutch, the French, and the British. Spain was moving into decline after bankruptcy spurred by their defeat by Great Britain, the revolt of the Dutch, and poor decision-making. The Catholic Church, in the time of waning inquisitions and the rise of Protestantism, was also losing strength. The northern European countries were poised for world domination. In Queen Elizabeth I of England's final years, she set up a charter for the East India Company (established in 1600) that backed the risks of world travel with government funds and launched one of the first international corporations.

As 1615 rolled around, the East India Company representatives were negotiating trade deals all over the globe—shopping for textiles, spices, tea, and drugs from other countries. Emissaries landed in the Ottoman Empire, in China, and throughout the Orient. The Dutch East India Company that was formed in 1602 on the heels of the British company sent agents into Japan in 1613 and set up shop in Batavia (Jakarta).

In 1607, funded by the East India Company, a group of British settlers landed in the territory of the Algonquin tribe, settled down, and started farming tobacco. In 1619, the white male farming community paid traffickers to capture and transport people from Africa to be enslaved laborers in order to increase tobacco yields and sales in the new colonies in Virginia. Thus, this VISION time is also the traumatic and racist beginning of African slavery in the colonies.

In 1609, Henry Hudson, the British sailor on a Dutch-funded voyage sailed the river that later bore his name. Along that river, on the Lenape island of Manaháhtaan (Manhattan), the Dutch settled and set up trading posts long before they set up churches and government buildings (1624). After establishing such a nice settlement, which the Dutch called New Amsterdam, the British started arriving. A wall was built dividing the two settlements, until it was taken down exactly during the peak of POWER in 1699, and that area then became the epicenter of the trading of enslaved peoples in the Northeastern colonies. Today, it is now the trade capital of the world, called Wall Street.

The Mayflower arrived, hit a rock in 1620, and set up a colony on Massachusetts land. Barely making it through the first year, the Mayflower arrivals celebrated their first meager harvest with the original occupants, a story we know well today as the somewhat mythic root of Thanksgiving celebrations throughout the US. Incidentally and perhaps synchronistically, Lincoln declared Thanksgiving a national holiday in the US when Pluto was exactly at 00 degrees declination one cycle later.

During the same time that colonizers were travelling across the Atlantic, British merchant ships were travelling around Africa into Asia. In 1614, the East India Company built the first factories in India in Surat and Masulipatnam. Initially these "factories" were warehouses for goods of trade, mostly cotton. It was the beginning of the fashion industry. Before 1614, the people of the British Isles wore wool in drab colors and basic, functional styles. Clothing for the masses was strictly utilitarian. Now, with richly dyed and affordable cottons and other fabrics from India, new trends in clothing bourgeoned through Northern Europe.

The keys to Hades' kingdom were handed over to the European settlers who farmed the land for the cash crop of tobacco and then cotton and the to the merchants that launched the fashion industry. The British Empire was growing, building a vast network of ships. France was expanding their own shipping empire. An early form of capitalism was taking root in the newly formed Dutch Republic.

Leaping ahead to our current cycle, the keys to Hades' kingdom were handed over to the Americans who drilled for oil and built the railroads. The robber barons, not unlike the early entrepreneurs of the East India Company and its Dutch counterpart, were initiating a new world of commerce. New Plutonic goods took front and center on the world trading stage during both VISION times, oil and steel in our current cycle, and tobacco, cotton, gold, and silver in the early 1600s.

In our current cycle, Charles Darwin and the social scientists of the time instigated a belief in survival of the fittest, which in turn, supported an economic system based on competition. Meanwhile, Marx and Engels spread ideas of collaboration and communism as an alternative economic system. These systems, at odds with each other, funded future cold wars and contentious rivals. While it often appears that revolutions begin with the town criers and erupt instantaneously and impetuously, the true seeds of revolution are often found with the visionaries living over a century prior. The revolutions of the late 1780s arose in reaction to the policies of the early colonizers and were inspired by philosophers of the early 1600s. The revolutions of the late 2020s may also arise from the policies and beliefs laid out by the philosophers and colonizers of the late mid-1800s.

POWER   1687–1710   Peak: 1700

The East India Companies, both British and Dutch, launched a new era—an era of trade, amassment of wealth through government-sponsored monopolies, and economic competition. As the POWER time began, England and the Dutch Republic saw a dramatic change in leadership. The Dutch protestant, William of Normandy, crossed the English Channel and staged a successful coup in 1689 against the Catholic James II, the last Catholic to reign over England. With the Dutch William on the throne of England, the trading companies were greatly supported.

War between England and France (an ongoing feud that raged on, in one form or another, for centuries) reached the shores of India, and the East India Company militarized itself, buying arms and ammunition and hiring soldiers. At one point, it amassed 260,000 soldiers, twice the size of the British army.

In both cycles, banking took a great leap forward. In 1690, a couple of Quaker goldsmiths founded a bank known as Barclays today. In 1694, the Bank of England, a privately-owned central bank, was founded with the support of King William, who wanted to borrow funds from the wealthy stockholders to build a better shipping fleet so he could beat the French. Meanwhile, in our current cycle, stockholders, and economic advisors the world over formed a central bank in 1945, the World Bank, during the peak year of the last POWER time.

While the Nine Years' War (1688–1697) remains a near-forgotten, pale comparison to the vast death and destruction of WWII, it is nevertheless sometimes referred to as the first world war. France, under the direction of the opulent King Louis XIV, was in expansion mode. As a result, France found itself in conflict with the rest of Europe. It ended with a peace treaty. While Louis XIV and Hitler had little else in common, both of them were charismatic dictators who started world wars. Both believed that their people were superior to other people, engendering a virulent form of patriotism and xenophobia.

JUSTICE   1739–1743

The cry for justice did not come from within the Dutch or East India Companies. The cry came from voices living in the colonized territories. In the occupied Americas, preachers, including Jonathan Edwards, were roaming the countryside setting up tent revivals, stirring up conversations about freedom of religion. In China, in 1740, an uprising among the sugar-mill workers against the Dutch East India Company killed 50 Dutch soldiers and led to a horrific massacre of at least 10,000 ethnic/indigenous Chinese people living in Batavia (Jakarta). It is common that uprisings during JUSTICE periods end up being unsuccessful and overcome by the powers in charge, as in the case of Savonarola in the previous JUSTICE time, whose overt hostility toward the Catholic church led to his execution in the streets of Florence, as in the case of Jesus, many JUSTICE cycles prior, whose anti-establishment teachings led to a public execution just outside of Jerusalem.

It may be helpful to mention that also during the JUSTICE time, the unsuccessful Jacobite rebellions were taking place. The Scottish were attempting to bring back the Catholic, Bonnie Prince Charles, in the hopes of having more say in the governing of the British Empire. Many Scotts left Scotland for the Americas both voluntarily and through banishment by the British. These same Scotts played on both sides of the American Revolution.

Evidence shows that the time when revolutions are most successful is when they take place during the REFORM time in the cycle. Revolutions during the JUSTICE time serve to awaken people to an issue, but rarely serve to transform the issue. The intercession of Zeus is just an intercession. Persephone is still down in the Underworld held captive. The Scottish people were held captive.

In France, Voltaire was stirring the flames of revolution with his radical writings on Isaac Newton and John Locke, inspiring the people and nobles alike to move toward greater freedom, even while writing shockingly racists tracts. In Boston, Samuel Adams, the loud town crier, and an early advocate for revolution, was transitioning from failed businessman into journalist.

In 1748, he and a few friends started a weekly newspaper, *The Independent Advertiser*, filled with subversive essays against the crown. In Philadelphia, Benjamin Franklin turned his attention from his lucrative publishing business toward politics. In 1743, he formed the American Philosophical Society for men of science. His career as a politician was taking wings and, in 1748, he was elected to his first political post as city councilman.

In our current cycle, the late 1980s were a mixture of quashed rebellions and various underground organizations set up to both empower and takedown. This mixture is a growing powder keg in our world. On December 9, 1987, for example, when Pluto was exactly at 0° of declination, a truck crash unleashed an uprising in the Gaza strip, and Palestinians protested against the Israeli government. A series of nonviolent protests, including boycotts, strikes, refusals to pay taxes, and demonstrations, erupted into violence that resulted in Israeli military killing 1100 Palestinians and incarcerating thousands more (1991). Named the First Intifada (a word that means civil uprising in Arabic), this began a movement that emboldened the Islamic military organization, Hamas (f. 1987), into power.

The successful and largely peaceful revolutions during the late 1980s, including the Velvet Revolution and the Singing Revolution in Eastern Europe, positively portend future reforms and peaceful changes during the upcoming REFORM time. These newly created countries emerged from the dissolution of the Soviet Union and instituted democracies in the wake of communism. Fifty years later, they have the footprint of peaceful transitions of power, the heart of a people ready to sing in protest, and an eye toward the future environmental and political changes that will be necessary. Even as the US beefs up army bases in Poland, the people of Poland welcome Ukrainian refugees with open arms. This is perhaps an apt comparison between a people that participated in a successful revolution during the 1980s and a people that remained largely oblivious while their government instituted dramatic changes to the rest of the world.[12]

For an upcoming revolution, the places in the world that were destabilized, and where authoritarian regimes clamped down instead of adapting,

12. Speaking for myself: I was in college studying abroad at the University of Leeds, England in 1985. Being pro-Reagan from a conservative family, I was ill-prepared for the barrage of anti-Reagan sentiment that pervaded the British universities at the time. Invariably, the British, German, and Swiss students I encountered knew far more about American politics than I did.

are places most likely to see violent uprisings during REFORM. The US invasions of Panama and Granada in 1983, for example, led to instability in Central America.[13] The US military under the leadership of President George H.W. Bush, invaded Panama in 1989 and imprisoned the Panama President Manuel Noriega.

The rest of Central America may fair differently. Under the leadership of Costa Rican president, Óscar Arias, a coalition of heads of state from the countries of Central America, including Nicaragua, Honduras, El Salvador, and Guatemala, signed a treaty, the Esquipulas Peace Agreement I (1986) and II (1987, precisely when Pluto was at 00 degrees of declination). In an effort to bring more stability to the region, the country leaders agreed on free and fair elections, open door policies of refugee support and an end to hostilities between the countries and an agreement to not fund any destabilizing groups.[14] This focus on social justice as explicitly stated in a letter to the UN directs the focus of Costa Rica, Honduras, El Salvador, and Guatemala towards a more peaceful transition of power to the people during the REFORM time. Nicaragua may find themselves headed into revolution as unresolved issues with the US tear at their ability to adapt. President Daniel Ortega, a US trained and installed leader who went rogue, still clinging to power and turning a deaf ear to the times, may lead the country straight into unrest.

Underground organizations formed in the late 1980s are more likely to transform into above-ground organizations in the next few years (2023–2026). Hamas, Hezbollah, and Al-Qaeda were all formed in the late 1980s as activist organizations, willing to use force to rectify the abuse of Western overreach.

---

13. In Panama, Manuel Noriega was the *de facto* ruler, a CIA-planted, School of the Americas–trained friend of Columbia drug cartels, a dictator who got too big for his britches. In 1985, when he encountered resistance from a political dissident and physician, Dr. Hugo Spadafora, Noriega had him tortured and beheaded, and sent the decapitated body to the US government. President Reagan and Vice President George H.W. Bush (the prior head of the CIA) began to turn against him, after initially supporting his leadership. Noriega then joined forces with the peace-centered Contadora group (1983–1985), a coalition of Central and South American countries who tried to stabilize the region through a peace treaty. In Nicaragua, then (and again in the 2020s) President Daniel Ortega, a member of the socialist party, the Sandinistas, in a fight against the US backed Contras, further destabilized the region.
14. UN General Assembly Security Council. August 27, 1987. Letter dated 27 August 1987 from the Permanent Representatives of Costa Rica, El Salvador, Guatemala, and Nicaragua to the United Nations addressed to the Secretary-General.

REFORM   1776–1795   Peak: 1783–1785

As Pluto went into extreme declination in REFORM for the last cycle, the Scottish philosopher, Adam Smith, wrote the well-known book, *An Enquiry into the Nature and Causes of the Wealth of Nations*. He wrote this book out of reaction to and disgust with the overwhelming power of the East India Company through the monopolies it enjoyed and that were bestowed upon the company by the British government and the noble Royal Charter of Elizabeth I. Adam Smith was anti-monopoly. His idea was to create "an obvious and simple system of natural liberty" in which the pursuit of self-interest was guided by "an invisible hand" that benefited the whole society and raised its standard of living.

Even before Adam Smith published his book—what has now been deemed the starting point of capitalism—the British government was finding itself frustrated with the power of the East India Company. The Regulating Act of 1773 was set up to begin some modicum of oversight over the trading company by the British government, but it was too little and ineffective. When the peak of REFORM came around in 1783, the British parliament was ready to take more drastic action. The East India Act of 1784, otherwise known as Pitt's India Act, set up a Board of Control, and real reforms were put in place to curtail the overarching power of the company.

To throw another arc into the picture, just prior to the REFORM time in 1770, there was a significant famine in Bengal, India, with about a third of the population dying of starvation. As a main stronghold of the East India Company, this affected their ability to hire workers, and profits subsequently took a dive. To raise funds, the British parliament set a tax on tea, directly benefiting the trading company. As most school children in the United States know, that tea tax angered the local colonists of Boston, setting them into a frenzy of tea dumping and initiating the rebellion that would eventually lead to the American War of Independence.

With Samuel Adams crying in the streets of Boston for revolution and Thomas Paine writing pamphlets about common sense, with a crazy and out-of-touch King George III raising taxes, and with years of religious revival meetings notwithstanding, the colonists were ripe for revolution. The Declaration of Independence was written and signed just as Pluto went into extreme declination—offering the colonists a great chance of success in the revolution. Persephone—the freedom of people to worship as they wish, the freedom of people to speak as they wish, and the creation of a constitutional republic—was rising into power.

After the REFORM time peaked and representatives from the thirteen colonies met in Philadelphia to form a new government, the people of France stormed the Bastille and took the king and queen hostage. Taking down the monarchy in France was bloody business, and a time of anarchy ensued (1789–1799). Because this revolution took place later in the REFORM time, the force it took to overcome the traditional rulers was intense, and the aftermath led to more confusion. Once the REFORM time had ended, people lived for a while in fear of the new revolutionaries as a general rose through the ranks and gathered a loyal following. France thus sank into the apparent safety and control of Napoleon. The Dutch Republic also was dealing with a revolt during this time, the Batavian Revolution, which successfully moved the Dutch Republic into the Batavian Republic.

In our current cycle, the Middle East and Central America have been targets of US colonization in one form or another. Oil in the Middle East, with its vast power to bring wealth to nations and individuals, is a bargaining tool in today's markets. Bananas and other foods that Americans have become dependent on, along with drugs, coffee, and chocolate, are exports from Central and South America, making them valuable lands for US intervention. During JUSTICE, the Soviet Union fell leaving the US as the sole reigning superpower of the world—a power the CIA and US government used to destabilize both Central American and Middle Eastern regions through coups and invasions. But, as in 1776, continued overtaxing and domination can lead to revolution in these areas and US-aligned leaders both of government and industry in Central America and the Middle East may fall to leaders that support the people. Persephone can—and will have the opportunity to—unsheathe her machete to break apart the banks and financial institutions that have rendered much of these two regions powerless. These corrupt rulers may be cut down in ways that are unexpected. The rebel militias of 1776, for example, were ill-trained and didn't follow the rules of war laid out for centuries, yet they were successful. These new rebels will also follow their own path. Cyberattacks on a vulnerable system of zeros and ones, targeted destructions of places most have no knowledge of but that hold great influence and significance, and assassinations of key underworld players may play important parts in the upcoming revolutions. Like the stealth army of Washington lying in wait for the British, people throughout the world are lying in wait, looking for ways to take down the great oil-fueled empires of the US and Russia, or, at the very least, retrieve their own freedom.

Revolutions that begin prematurely can end disastrously. Looking back to the time of Justinian and the Nika Revolt that broke out unexpectedly, almost randomly, just prior to Pluto going out-of-bounds ended with Justinian corralling the rebels and slaughtering them in the coliseum. Today, a profoundly unfortunate event is mirroring that time. When young Hamas fighters broke through Israel's walls, violence erupted and Israel, backed by US funding, is corralling, killing, and starving the people trapped in Gaza. On a much larger scale than Justinian, the Palestinians fight for their lives, but are not succeeding (January 2024). If they hold out until 2026, there is hope for a two-state solution like during the time of Solomon's sons, but more likely, Israel will do just as Justinian did—let half the people go and force the other half into submission or death. Then Israel will restructure, rewrite laws, and elect new leadership.

Potential 3: Non-violent Resistance & Benevolent Rulers

Nonviolent resistance as a path to REFORM represents both a new and an old way of affecting change. For centuries, passive resistance has been a path for reform in India. Citizens actively disobeyed as a form of protest. The early Christians willingly martyred themselves rather than fight. Protestants during the Reformation protested through education, writings, and willful acts of disobedience rather than violence. However, in most of these cases, violence ensued from the opposition. At least 100,000 people died in the Peasants' War during the Reformation. Huldrych Zwingli, one of the main initiators of the Protestant Reformation, died in battle protesting in Switzerland. The Christians, after a few centuries of protests, with thousands of people executed by the Romans and many more martyred, finally won the right to worship, even if seventy years later, Christianity became a religion supported by tyrants.[15] In most cases, the protests led to either a

---

15. Roman Emperor Theodosius instituted Christianity (391 CE) and executed non-adherents.

violent quashing or a leader who listened and instituted at least some of the changes that people needed.

Protests are more likely to be successful during the REFORM time and the inspired ideas at VISION are most likely to become common knowledge during the REFORM time. For these reasons, this cycle poses a new potential—a path for society to transform without violence. The ideas during VISION do not just support new ideas in science and commerce, but significant leaders in the non-violent resistance movement wrote and spoke during the current VISION time. These ideas and the way this movement has evolved throughout this cycle lead up to the REFORM time where people rise up with strength and conviction to overturn corruption, corporate greed and the debilitating destruction of the environment. The twin paths of environmental awareness and social justice blend into something beyond a movement that forces leadership to listen and administer changes or brings in direct democracy—a path without leaders.

Demeter is the goddess of protests. Her boycott of nature forcing Earth into an eternal winter is the boycott to end all boycotts. Demeter may be the first and only goddess to use non-violent resistance to get what she wanted. As such, Demeter is the guide for this path. The lands that listen to the protests of the people arise into new forms without violence.

VISION: 1860–1865

As often occurs, when an idea's time has come, it appears in multiple places, initiating a kind of intellectual synchronicity of the moment. Alexander Graham Bell and Elisha Gray, for example, famously applied for a patent for the telephone on the same day. Just in this way, the idea of nonviolent resistance awoke in multiple people in the mid 1800s. Three people announced this idea clearly: Ramakrishna in India, Leo Tolstoy in Russia, and the American economic philosopher Henry George. All three men directly influenced Mahatma Gandhi in his nonviolent activism, and all three experienced pivotal spiritual breakthroughs in 1863.

Ramakrishna

Ramakrishna, born Gadadhara in 1836, was a spiritually oriented child who had visions that began at age seven. In 1858, his older brother, seeing Gadahara's spiritual proclivities, brought him to meet his friend, the wealthy widow Rani Rashmoni. By this time, Rashmoni had already built a massive temple complex dedicated to the goddess Kali in Dakshineswar, a town outside of Calcutta along the Ganges-tributary Hooghey river. It was in Dakshineswar from 1858 to 1866 that Ramakrishna committed to focused meditation practices. In February of 1861, Gadadhara fell into grief when Rashmoni died. A few months later, a new spiritual teacher entered his life, Brahmani, a woman steeped in the path of Tantra. She stayed at Dakshineswar from 1861 to 1864, the exact time period of the VISION stage. She taught devotional Tantra and Bhakti practices to Gadadhara, now Ramakrishna, whom she had recognized as a great soul. For months he sat in meditation without moving, flies coming in and out of his mouth as if he were dead. One devoted monk force fed him morsels of food to maintain his body. Ramakrishna emerged out of this state when dysentery brought him back into his body. His devotion and great compassion brought attention from other spiritual masters who observed Ramakrishna and determined him to be an avatar, an actual embodiment of God. This did not matter to him. He continued his humble and devotional practices. At the end of 1864, after Brahmani left, another spiritual teacher arrived, Tota Puri, who taught Ramakrishna the path of Vedanta. In the eleven months that Tota Puri was in Dakshineswar, Ramakrishna achieved mystical union with the divine.

After the VISION time was done, Ramakrishna integrated Islam, Christianity, and Buddhism into his spiritual practices. Ramakrishna is a perfect representative of a visionary during a VISION era. Not only did he experience his great awakening precisely during the VISION part of the Pluto cycle, but he also brought together within his teachings most of the major religions of the time. This kind of integration is the spirited beginnings of a non-denominational, non-dogmatic, leaderless awakening that can erupt into a movement during REFORM that is non-denominational, non-dogmatic, and welcoming of all faiths and all people. His close relationship to women including his mother, his benefactor, and his spiritual teacher, support the inclusion of women as equals in this cycle's path toward healing.

Two Henrys

Two important Henrys started this cycle—one most of us have heard of and the other who was famous while he lived but rarely makes it into the history books. The more obvious Henry was American activist—Henry David Thoreau, who wrote *Civil Disobedience* in 1849. *Civil Disobedience* is often cited as an inspiring work for many activists. Thoreau, who died during the VISION time in 1862 and whose work became widespread after his death, was a quiet activist, intentionally anti-involvement. He is credited with starting the environmental movement and the civil disobedience movements from his cottage in the woods along Walden Pond. After his death, his work reached Tolstoy in Russia and Gandhi in India, who both were more proactive in their activism.

For our purposes, we will focus on the lesser-known Henry, Henry George. He picketed and fought for unions, ran for New York City mayor, and helped start the United Labor Party. In 1863, George was an unemployed father of two children. Historians recount how, after his second son was born, he had a pivotal moment. At the time, he was starving and begging in the street. In a destitute state, he decided to rob someone for money, committing himself to violence if it were to become necessary. The man he approached, instead of rejecting George, opened his wallet and gave him a five-dollar bill. Even though violence was not necessary, George realized his capacity for it, and the harm it could have potentially caused a generous-hearted person. This moment changed his life. George finally found a job at the *San Francisco Times*. In 1867, the newspaper promoted him to managing editor. In 1879, he wrote *Progress and Poverty*. The book became an instant bestseller and is often credited with sparking the Progressive Era. Based on his life during the VISION time, George wrote a new theory of economics, called "Georgism." Georgism is critical of capitalism, pointing out that progress benefits the wealthy at the expense of the poor. His solution was a single tax. Tax the landowners based on property and wealth. In this way, only the wealthy are taxed, and the poor have a chance to improve their situations. Today, signs of "Tax the Rich" litter protests. A simple solution to complex problems of inequity and poverty.

Leo Tolstoy

While Ramakrishna was meditating with the flies and Henry George was begging on the street, Leo Tolstoy was settling down into writing his great work *War and Peace*. Tolstoy published this book as serial, sharing a section at a time through a Russian magazine. Tolstoy's writing about and research of Napoleon's conquests sent him deep into an existential exploration of violence and the counterbalance of peace. It was not until 1894, after reading Henry George's best seller, that he wrote *The Kingdom of God is Within You*, a philosophical writing that included his nonviolent demonstration thinking, he called "nonresistance to evil." This is the work that most inspired Gandhi.

The coalesced effort of George and Tolstoy to inspire people toward active non-violent demonstrations to affect change for the oppressed masses is not new, but the scale of its effect during Gandhi's lifetime and the aftereffect of Gandhi's success as it inspired civil rights movements throughout the world *is* new. The visionaries that upheld the possibility of change through peaceful means is a radical departure from other cycles. In prior cycles, the visionaries shared new thinking that was specifically for the elite—for those educated enough to understand their writings. They wrote and taught in ages when small portions of the population could read. Aristotle, Augustine, Ptolemy, Petrarca, Descartes and Francis Bacon wrote their great works during the VISION time, but only those with an education could access these writings. Prior to the 1600s less than 20% of the population were literate. That number doubled between 1600 and 1700. Currently literacy rates throughout the world hover around 90%. *Poverty and Progress* and *War and Peace* were bestsellers among the everyday person and were translated into many languages. When Descartes said, "I think, therefore I am," or something like that, less than 20% of the people could even read it and even less than that would have had access to his intellectual writings on geometry and philosophy. This presents a unique opportunity for this cycle and the upcoming REFORM time—a chance for true reform through non-violent demonstrations. The everyday citizen has access to these writings. We don't need an extra interpreter or scholar to help us understand Aristotle or Descartes. Instead, *Poverty and Progress* and *War and Peace* are readily available at used bookstores and online.

The Labor and Women's Movements

A decade before the VISION time in 1848, over 300 women and men gathered in a church in Seneca Falls, New York and wrote *A Declaration of Sentiments*, a plea for equal rights for women. These early visionaries seeded the suffragist movement in the US.[16] In attendance were the scientist Eunice Foote, Frederick Douglass, and Elizabeth Cady Stanton. By the 1860s, Stanton and Susan B. Anthony were forming the National Woman Suffrage Association (1869) months before Wyoming gave women the right to vote in local elections. When Wyoming became a state in 1890, it was the first state to give women the right to vote. Sweden was the first country to give women the right to vote in local elections in 1863.

Anna Filosofova, Nadezhda Stasova, and Maria Trubnikova founded the *Society for the Organization of Work for Women* in Russia that provided training and advocated for women in the workforce while Tsar Nicholas was instituting education reforms. Millicent Garrett Fawcett started the *London Society for Women's Suffrage* in 1866.

While unions had existed for centuries, the first international labor organization, the *International Workingmen's Association*, was founded in Europe in 1864. Two years later, in 1866, the National Labor Union (an early iteration of the AFL-CIO) was founded by William Sylvis, kicking off the labor movement in the US, twenty-two years after unions were officially legalized in 1842. Shoemakers' unions, teachers' unions, cigar makers' unions and railroad workers' unions were all formed during the VISION time in the US and Europe.

Meanwhile, activists for social justice were also beginning their campaigns for human betterment, including Walt Whitman, an early advocate of the LGBTQIA movement in the US, Henry Dunant, who founded The International Red Cross and instigated the Geneva Conventions in Switzerland, Frederick Douglass, a Civil Rights leader who spoke in front of US Congress

---

16. The women's rights movement had many people advocates long before this VISION time. During the prior cycle's REFORM time, while revolutions were breaking out and breaking down current forms of governance, a British woman, Mary Wollstonecraft, wrote *A Vindication of Women's Rights*, an anthem for the upcoming women's movement. As a kind of Persephone herself, she went to the underworld that was the reign of terror in France at the time to write pamphlets on the rights of men and women, on education and on free speech. Her demands for equality were a dream at the time, but her thoughts were an inspiration for future generations.

for citizenship and voting rights for all people in his country, Florence Nightingale, who famously founded the nursing movement in England, and Henry David Thoreau, whose writings on transcendent environmentalism would represent some of the first steps toward climate action in the United States.

Additionally, there were visionaries who wanted to map out a new way of equitable living, labor, and leisure, like Karl Marx and Friedrich Engels in Germany, whose dreams of a communist revolution hoped to wrest the means of social production and labor out of the hands of the powerful elites, and John Stuart Mill in England, whose significant works on the ethics of utilitarianism offered a perspective on the potential for happiness through service.

POWER   1938–1949

In the spring of 1930, six months after the Stock Market Crash of 1929, the Empire State Building and the Chrysler Buildings were being erected in NYC with great speed. As Henry George had pointed out, the rich were getting richer, and the poor were destitute. On the other side of the world, Mohandas Gandhi galvanized eighty followers to walk to the sea to protest the tax on salt. The march ballooned into thousands, ending with the arrest of over 60,000 non-violent activists and an increased awareness throughout the world of the desire for India to be free of British rule. It was the beginning of the end. The Salt March inspired Martin Luther King, Jr. and the Civil Rights movement in the US. As the POWER time was heating up and WWII was beginning in 1939, Gandhi began to fast for independence for India. His most significant fast lasted for 21 days and took place towards the peak of the POWER time from Feb 10–Mar 3, 1943. His fasting along with other demonstrations and a sympathetic Labour Party in England led to an independent India in August of 1947. This independence was bittersweet, however, as the partition line drawn by the Brits to create two countries—India (mostly Hindu) and Pakistan (mostly Muslim)—left many living in a country misaligned with their religion and values. Riots broke out along the line as people panicked and fled, uprooting thousands of multi-generational homes. Thousands died, and 850,000 Muslims migrated eastward, and 650,000 Hindus migrated westward. Drawing a straight line from Ramakrishna who taught Swami Vivekananda who taught Gandhi, Ramakrishna's awakening during VISION directly influenced the non-violent demonstration movement.

196

It is impossible to underestimate the power of WWII and the changes that occurred from that war. Henry George's economic projections became truer over time. As industry and progress increased, "the 1%," a phrase he used back in the late 1800s, have grown in power. The Robber Barons of today continue to look out for themselves, buy elections, and craft laws to support their wealth. However, in 1938, just as Pluto went into extreme declination, after worker strikes at General Motors and US Steel led to the formation of unions, the Fair Labor Standard Act was passed. This act instituted forty-hour work weeks, eight-hour days, the minimum wage and abolished child labor, a major win for the working person. An uncharacteristic blow to the wealthy during Hades' abduction of Persephone. Not to worry, though, Pluto's power plan was only just beginning.

By the end of the war, six million American workers from the steel, railroad, trucking, and oil industries, fed up with war and the sacrifices that went with it, went on strike. While some of their demands were met, this massive strike led to a blowback by the Plutocrats who found a way to get the Taft-Hartley Act passed in Congress in 1947. The Taft-Hartley Act rolled back many of the provisions that supported unions. Inbred into the act was the fear of communism. The communist Soviet Union, allies to the UK and US during the war, were now seen as threatening. The US needed a new enemy to maintain the progress and keep the wheels of industry turning. Built on the backs of the American worker, the benefits went to the corporations. Hades' abduction of Persephone is an apt metaphor for the Plutocrats abduction of the American worker. The Taft-Hartley Act prohibited secondary strikes and boycotts, wildcat strikes, and strikes by federal employees. It allowed states to pass "right-to-work" laws, laws that allow workers the option of joining the union or not. While this may sound like freedom, the non-union workers benefit from the unions without paying dues, weakening the power of unions.

During the POWER time, even when the people gain there is often a setback. In the case of Russia, while winning the war and becoming a communist state, ideally beneficial for people, Stalin's genocidal practices caused more people to die in the Soviet Union than in any other country at any other time in history. The Labor Movement, which made great strides in the decades leading up to POWER, experienced a major setback with the Taft-Hartley Act. The Indian people cast out British rule only to find themselves with a boundary that causes strife to this day. While workers throughout the world contributed to industry, the making of weapons and transportation vehicles and technology, they found themselves with less power at the end of the war. Financial institutions created during POWER with an intention to support the people, the World Bank and the IMF, have continued to serve capitalism and the wealthy who benefit from it.

Even with the setbacks and horrors of WWII, there are signs of Demeter's intervention going according to the mythological plan. With many men drafted into the military to fight in WWII, women went to work and proved that they could do the work previously set aside exclusively for men. Taking a step backwards after the war when men came home and reclaimed their jobs, women's movements all over the world erupted with new force and conviction two decades later. The intensity of worldwide grief, unlike any other grief in history, supports the power of Demeter—and helps her find the strength to boycott Earth and send a strong message to Zeus. Demeter will not be overpowered again. Her daughter must be returned. Such is the case with this cycle. WWII will not happen again. People will not be fooled into another way. Protests are a new way of life and only continue to grow in size and passion as we head into REFORM.

JUSTICE   1986–1989

There were movements that started before the JUSTICE time that used non-violent activism with success. Inspired by those inspired by Gandhi, particularly Martin Luther King, Jr, non-violent demonstrations took the form of marches, sit-ins, and bed-ins. Rosa Parks non-violently refused to give up her seat. Harvey Milk non-violently became the first openly gay mayor of San Francisco. Martin Luther King, Jr. non-violently gathered thousands of people together to March on Washington in 1963. Starhawk gathered people together to non-violently celebrate the Goddess.

Non-violent demonstrations led to desegregation and the passage of several Civil Rights Acts outlawing discrimination based on race and gender. Antiwar demonstrations against the Vietnam War pushed President Johnson and Nixon to withdraw troops. Women's rights, Gay rights, and rights for the differently abled all benefited from the work of Gandhi.

During JUSTICE, peaceful transformations of power occurred throughout

the world as nonviolent demonstrations restructured countries and governments. Gorbachev, an open fan of Tolstoy, supported Russia in opening its
doors (glasnost), and restructuring the Communist party (perestroika), investing in the people of Russia. In Eastern Europe, Soviet satellite countries
used peaceful demonstrations to attain their independence. Four years of
singing in Estonia, Latvia, and Lithuania, from 1986 to 1991, led to their
sovereignty from the USSR. The Velvet Revolution gave Czechoslovakia independence from the Soviet Union in 1989. The Peaceful Revolution, also
in 1989, led to the dissolution of the socialist German Democratic Republic
and the unification of East and West Germany under the latter's model of
parliamentary democracy. The People Power Revolution in 1986 peacefully took down Fernando Marcos in the Philippines. The Orange Revolution
peacefully transitioned Ukraine into independence. Demonstrations in
South Africa from 1986 to 1991 led to anti-apartheid legislation in 1990 and
the release of Nelson Mandela from a decades-long stay in prison. These
countries radically transformed from oppressive governments into parliamentary democracies. This kind of transformation was unprecedented in
history. Zeus's intercession on behalf of the people alleviated Demeter's grief
and offered the promise of Persephone's awakening. The power of the people became a tangible option for many people in the world.

Meanwhile, Demeter's boycott forced leaders to reconcile with environmental issues. Two environmental disasters with far-reaching consequences brought energy awareness into the larger conversation. In April of 1986,
a combination of human error and design flaws triggered the explosion of
a nuclear power plant in Chernobyl, at the time part of the Soviet Union.
While the direct death toll is a poor indicator of the destructiveness of this
disaster (less than 100 people purportedly died), a clearer indication is that
in 2022, Russian soldiers fighting in Chernobyl, Ukraine, died from radia-
tion poisoning as they mistakenly ventured too close to the site.

In 1989, just three years after Chernobyl, the oil tanker, the Exxon Valdez,
crashed into the Alaskan shore and spilled over 10 million gallons of crude
oil into the ocean. Fish and birds washed up on the shore for years and were
a constant reminder of Demeter's need for intercession.

Elsewhere during this time, Zeus's intercession was just beginning in a
way that was not as visible or as immediately successful. In the United King-

dom, Margaret Thatcher was Prime Minister. Her pro-capitalism policies supported the banks and large corporations in England. Demonstrations and riots against a poll tax (a tax for voting) eventually succeeded and ultimately contributed to her downfall. In 1987, a community center dedicated to supporting gay and lesbian rights in New York City formed the activist organization, ACT-UP. An act of civil disobedience at the New York Stock Exchange was successful in getting the pharmaceutical company, Burroughs Wellcome, to reduce the prices of AZT, the main drug for treating AIDS.

However many non-violent demonstrations were crushed. In 1989, a peaceful student-led protest in China lasted for six weeks before the Chinese government sent in troops to violently clear out the protestors from Tiananmen Square. In 1988, peaceful protests in Burma led by Buddhist nun, Aung San Suu Kyi, led to the ousting of General Ne Win, an oppressive dictator. However, the protests turned violent when Burmese police open fired on the gathering killing almost a hundred people, and the democracy that the people wanted did not materialize. Even though these demonstrations led to violence and devastation, during JUSTICE, they offer an indication of future places of successful protests during the REFORM time on the horizon.

REFORM   2026–2031

In my research, the words "benevolent" and "ruler" have never actually gone together. Even Demeter is not always helpful. Her willingness to cause suffering to humans through an endless winter to save her daughter puts her benevolence into question. Every ruler has their dark side or at least some historian who has demonized them. Sometimes a ruler is considered benevolent if he or she benefited the elite and was terrible to the people. Other times a ruler is considered malevolent if he slaughtered the elite but benefited the people, such as Ivan the Terrible. Sometimes a ruler is benevolent if they benefited the people of their country but treated their enemies atrociously, as did the Roman Emperor Sulla. For our purposes, we will define the benevolent rulers of the past as those whose reigns were focused on benefiting or uplifting the people of their own country. These are rulers whose reforms were geared towards improving the lives of their people rather than simply lining their own coffers or increasing their power, including Catherine the Great of Russia, the Roman Emperor Constantine, Suleiman I of the

Ottoman Empire, the Arabian ruler Harun al-Rashid, and the Mongol leader of China, Kublai Khan. Note that all these leaders ruled during REFORM periods.

Catherine the Great, a provocative "benevolent ruler," expanded the Russian empire into the Crimean Peninsula (modern-day Ukraine) and was not above having friends executed. Yet, to many, she ruled over a time of great reforms that benefited the people of Russia. Kublai Khan, Harun al-Rashid, and Suleiman I were controversial figures. In some books, historians cast them as the most benevolent of rulers, while other writers focus in detail on the executions they ordered, the people they enslaved, and the alliances they formed with unsavory individuals. As an interesting aside, George Washington is the only US president who has held office during a REFORM time, and he is a president who has attained an almost godlike status in the US. But even he has a checkered past, enslaving people on his land and leading soldiers into questionable battles, like the Battle of Monmouth.[17]

Thomas Hobbes in his unprecedented work, *Leviathan*, argues that the best form of government is the benevolent dictatorship, whereby a ruler is given absolute power and uses it, without hesitation, to benefit the people. However, there are many arguments against this form of leadership, in that most people given that much power have little real understanding of the people they are tasked with ruling. They are often out of touch with the real needs and concerns of the populace, and while perhaps they do not mean to be abusive, they nevertheless often become tyrants out of a sense of privilege and entitlement.

Still, there is a noticeable difference between rulers during POWER and REFORM periods, and it might have less to do with their innate nature and more to do with the political climate. During POWER, the ruler is pushed to conquer, to expand the empire, to initiate war for the purpose of empire-building. Augustus Caesar, who ruled during a POWER time, is sometimes considered benevolent as a ruler, however much he expanded the empire and ruled with an iron fist. Even still, during POWER periods, the background vibration of explosion and domination offers the ruler an opportunity to wage war on a grand scale.

---

17. The Battle of Monmouth on a hot summer day with an ill-prepared army was almost certainly unwinnable from the start.

During REFORM, by contrast, uprisings and revolts, vigilantes and radicals pepper the land, and the ruler is forced to focus internally and adapt to the implosive nature of the country. It is unlikely that Constantine gave freedom of religion to the Roman people out of the kindness of his heart. The Roman Empire was being torn apart by persecutions, which were only radicalizing more and more Christians. His reforms were a necessity. Instead of policies of expansion, the policies focused on improving roads, sanitation, education, building safety, and general welfare. In this way, Catherine the Great, Harun al-Rashid, Kublai Khan, and Constantine all focused their attention on the people of their country. More to the point, leaders who do not focus on helping the people during the REFORM time often die tragically. King Louis XVI, his wife Marie Antionette, and the Roman Emperor Nero are famous examples.

In our current cycle, the years between JUSTICE and REFORM have been filled with the typical unrest, instigations, and wake-up calls that often occur between JUSTICE and REFORM. Twelve years after the JUSTICE time, members of Al-Qaeda, an insurgent group of Saudi nationals formed during JUSTICE, in retaliation to Western anti-Muslim sentiments, attacked New York City with planes that took down the World Trade Center. This singular act of terrorism changed US politics. The Homeland Security Department was formed. The president gained extra power, and the people of the US went on high alert.

At the same time, meditation became mainstream. The Self-Help section became the largest section at major bookstores. Non-violent demonstrations became a popular form of activism. Police brutality in New York City sparked a non-violent protest that ballooned into the Occupy Movement in 2011. In cities throughout the world, protestors camped out in city parks, ate together, and created new ways to communicate and collaborate. While little changed, the subtle new infrastructure of communication and communal living laid a foundation for future movements. The Black Lives Matter and #MeToo movements that sprung up in 2013 and 2017 inspired many people to access the tools of non-violent demonstrations of the past. Social media, a radical new tool for this cycle, unlike anything available in prior cycles, offers an ability to bypass power structures and create successful movements instantaneously across the globe.

As of 2022, movements to protest the inequity of the 1%, gun violence, racism, war, genocide, climate change, and corporate domination have produced little true reform. This is often the case. The movements between JUSTICE and REFORM galvanize, activate, and inspire, but they do not produce results. They awaken and motivate. The change comes during the REFORM time. In past cycles, due to the relationship between Pluto and Earth's orbits, the REFORM times have lasted much longer. This upcoming time will be fast and intense. The ideas of the 1860s, the start of our current grand Pluto cycle, finally come to fruition in the late 2020s.

In 2019, BBC journalist David Robson declared that "nonviolent protests are twice as likely to succeed than armed conflicts" Based on research by Erica Chenoweth, a political science professor at Harvard University, it only takes 3.5% of the population to rise up and create change.

The largest demonstrations known in history have occurred the last five years. The Women's March that erupted the day after Donald Trump was inaugurated gathered millions, an estimated 1.5% of the US population. Potentially over 26 million people took to the streets to protest police brutality and racism after George Floyd was killed by a policeman in Minneapolis in 2020. Also in 2020, over 250 million people in India protested corporate-friendly farm laws that were eventually repealed. While systemic injustice remains, and these early adjustments do not go far enough, future movements hold great promise for a more significant overturning of oppression.

As the REFORM time approaches, demonstrations are getting larger. The tipping point of 3.5% is within reach. Gun control, equal rights, environmental protections, corporate regulations, and fair treatment of all people are within reach. The early teachings of Thoreau, George, Tolstoy, and Ramakrishna blossomed into home rule for India during POWER and democracies during JUSTICE. During REFORM, worldwide massive demonstrations for peace and unity can bring a wave of joy unlike anything ever witnessed in human history. This is the last time Persephone rises from the dead and claims her throne. This is the final episode of Persephone's awakening. We could even argue that all of the past sixteen (or so) Pluto cycles have been leading to this one—this radical ten-year window of peaceful protests into peaceful coexistence with each other, with nature and with all life.

Potential 4: Paradigm Shift

When physicist Thomas Kuhn wrote *The Structure of Scientific Revolutions* in 1962, the term "paradigm shift" was not in common usage. Today, all over, we hear the term used to describe any myriad of crimes and potentials. We hear it used to cover up issues or give hope for change. *Paradigm* as Kuhn used the word was focused on a scientific paradigm—the popular, universally-accepted scientific theory currently perceived as truth, examples are atomic theory and germ theory. *Paradigm shifts* as defined by Kuhn are unprecedented achievements of scientific research that shake up the scientific community, drawing scientists away from the competing and currently accepted scientific theories. The new theory is open-ended enough to allow for the new adherents to make their own contributions[18] and often creates an entirely new field of science.

Kuhn also coins the phrase *scientific revolution*. To get from one paradigm to another, a scientific revolution occurs. This revolution comes about when the current paradigm starts to hit its limits. Research begins to show the holes in the current understanding and anomalies arise in such abundance that they cannot be overlooked anymore. Something is wrong with the paradigm, the equation or the perception of reality, and the break down is too apparent to be ignored. In its place, something new arises—an entire new way of thinking. Light moves from particles to waves. The Earth moves from flat to round, from being the center of the solar system to being another planet rotating around the Sun. His work focuses on the examples of Ptolemy, Aristotle, Francis Bacon, Galileo and Charles Lyell—all visionaries during VISION times.[19]

Charles Murray (who wrote the *Bell Curve*) uses the term *meta-invention* to describe a similar phenomenon. In his work *Human Accomplishment*, he delineates *meta-inventions* as shifts in perspective and as an "introduction of a new cognitive tool for dealing with the world."[20] A meta-invention is similar to a paradigm shift—both involve a radical shift in perspective large enough to change an entire culture.

---

18. Kuhn.
19. Copernicus is another example, but he wrote his great work in the midst of a REFORM time. His work remained unkown until Galileo popularized it in the subsequent VISION time.
20. Murray, 209.

Hermes is the god of science. S/he walks between the worlds of reason and magic, between understanding and concrete data, between the real and the imagined. He is the messenger whose winged shoes traverse both time and space. His role in Persephone's journey is barely mentioned. However, as time progresses, and science becomes the reigning religion for many, the role of Hermes must be examined. Like an insider who relays information with their own twist, changing the destiny of many, how Hermes influences Hades is relevant to our current times—when the pharmaceutical industry is measured in trillions of dollars and pesticides decide crop outcomes and technology is money.

Allow me another journey back in time to set the stage for one fantastical potential for a paradigm shift. For this potential, we need to understand certain aspects of the Industrial Revolution and the roots of our current practice of science itself, both in its positive and negative implications. In particular, the connection between science and money that has its roots deep in the early 1700s.

VISION   1615–1622

Prior to the 1600s, belief and thought were interchanged throughout Europe. Science and spirituality were intertwined. Just as a new Pluto cycle began, a new thought arrived—the thought of science itself, or what we have come to understand as science. This thought arrived in the minds of several great natural philosophers in several countries, simultaneously.[21]

Between 1608 and 1609, two Dutch eyeglass makers who lived next door to each other in Middelburg, Zacharias Janssen and Hans Lippershey applied for patents for the telescope and microscope. Galileo Galilei took Lippershey's notes and improved the telescope to see the moons of Jupiter. Galileo's work confirmed what Copernicus and Avicenna had written—the Sun was in the middle of the solar system and not the Earth. Regardless of who and how, in the 1610s the simple invention of putting two lenses together,

---

21. During the middle of the 20th century, Robert K. Merton, a renowned sociologist, often credited with founding the field of sociology, coined the phrase multiple discovery, also known as simultaneous invention. Many inventions have been invented at the same time by multiple people in different parts of the world. This theory flies in the face of most current thinking which subscribes to heroic invention, where an invention is the unique brainchild of one scientist. The multiple discovery theory aligns well with Pluto's cycle and with astrology in general.

one convex and one concave, opened a whole new world. What was too far away for the naked eye to see became visible. Equally visible became dust particles and germs. Observation was no longer limited to the seen realms; the unseen realms moved into observable view. Jupiter had moons. Skin had cells.

Other great thinkers of this new science were also having visions and dreams at this time. Notably, in France, Rene Descartes during the short window of the VISION time, had a series of dreams and from these dreams developed analytical geometry. In Germany, Johannes Kepler, known for his work as an astronomer, envisioned the laws of planetary bodies, that Isaac Newton, the predominant scientist during the POWER time, used to derive his formulas of gravity.[22] In England, Francis Bacon wrote *Novum Organon* (published in 1620), a book that describes the scientific method, using observation, experimentation, data collection, and logic to arrive at truth. Woven into this movement of science was not only rigorous reasoning and meticulous experimentation, but a belief in the separation of people from nature, a thinking that a person could be separate from their environment in a way to be able to objectively observe this environment. This concept that began as an idea developed into a unified belief system throughout this cycle by infiltrating the intelligentsia, the government, and the economy. While the Catholic Church clamped down on this form of heresy by imprisoning Galileo and executing many others, this new brand of thinking, this new way of life, was spreading rapidly throughout Europe. Consider the extraordinary consciousness shift that occurred. Prior to the early 1600s not believing in God was near impossible. The first person to publicly confess to being an atheist was Matthias Knudsen and that was in 1673.

By the end of this cycle, people were fighting for their right to practice religion as they desired. As we look at how this new paradigm launched a new era, fiscally and politically as well as scientifically, we must turn toward one philosopher in particular, Thomas Hobbes, who is credited with launching the Enlightenment Era.[23] While Galileo, Descartes, and Bacon never met,

22. Kuhn, 30.
23. Hobbes returned to England from his trip to Italy in the 1630s as Oliver Cromwell's reign of terror was beginning, which sent him packing to Paris, where he wrote his major treatise, *Leviathan*, in which he shared his take on the social contracts of society. Living during a civil war, when the monarchy was overthrown for a tyrant, his views were shaped by the horror of it and he

Hobbes met them all. When his book *Leviathan* came out it changed the perspectives of many people throughout Europe. His book was revolutionary in that it was one of the first books to talk about a person's natural rights. He maintained that the monarchy was necessary to supply security and peace, but not as maintained by God, but because people needed this form of government. It is a radical and simultaneously subtle shift. The divine right of kings had been unquestioned before this time.

VISION   1860–1865

Just like at the VISION time of the prior cycle (1616–1621), and like the VISION time of every time before, there is a dramatic sea change in philosophy, a new world view emerges, inspiring a paradigm shift that culminates during the REFORM time. At the beginning of this cycle, Charles Darwin had just published his controversial work, *On the Origin of Species* (1859), and it was having an immediate impact on the scientific community, among both the anti-Darwinians and the pro-Darwinians. His name became synonymous with evolution, "survival of the fittest," and a theory that suggests competition breeds growth, success, and accomplishment. His paper overshadowed the work of Alfred Russel Wallace, another biologist working at the same time as Darwin. Wallace saw the same evolutionary aspect of species, but to him life evolved *in relationship with* the environment. His own world view inspired a different theory. Wallace was a feminist, social activist against capitalism, an environmentalist, and a spiritualist. He saw the path of evolution as one of cooperation and integration between species and their host, nature itself. His viewpoint is but a footnote in the hard sciences, where Darwin has become a household name. Just because Darwin is more popular does not mean that he is right or that his theory is the one that will

---

landed on the side of the divine right of kings, or his scientific version of the divine right of kings. The idea of a social contract moved from philosophical to practical during this age, and Thomas Hobbes' *Leviathan* offered a moral defense on the necessity of a strong central authority. Necessary to maintain stability and control, but susceptible to the approval of the people (mostly landed men), an authority figure is only as divine as the contract he has with the people. Linking with Bacon's *Novum Organon* and Descartes' *Passions of the Soul*, Hobbes helped establish a political philosophy based on empirical evidence, where the results become the responsibility of humanity, not God. Though the beast of state may be big, it is not immortal and can be changed. His ideas in a Catholic world of faith were outrageous and he would have been executed if his protestant friend, Charles II, had not intervened.

culminate during the upcoming REFORM time. Sometimes the quiet vision-aries are the ones remembered in the long run.[24]

Whether or not they were Darwin's ideas, or whether we have complete-ly misinterpreted him or whether he even existed, is irrelevant. The myth of Darwin, like a god on Mount Olympus, exists in the framework of reality and the blueprint of our current paradigm. It validates capitalism and the Pluto-crats. It supports the Ayn Rand philosophy of "everyone for themselves" and "may the best man win." Darwin, whether he meant to or not, launched a paradigm of scientific thought that fed the corporate machine, gave credence to the Robber Barons and continues to validate a value system where the rich get richer, and the poor are left to scrape by with the leftovers.[25]

While new corporations, including Bayer, were getting their start and launching the pharmaceutical industry, the Swiss Alfred Nobel invented dy-namite in 1867. Around this time, Henry Bessemer's new way to process steel was making Carnegie a wealthy man. The industrial revolution was on steroids, even while environmental scientists warned of its dangers.

In the same year that Henry David Thoreau published his back-to-nature treatise, *Walden*, John Tyndall, an Irish scientist, presented a paper to the Royal London Society outlining the effect of CO2 emissions, what we now call greenhouse gas emissions. However, the Greenhouse effect was first proposed in 1856, a few years before Tyndall, by Eunice Newton Foote.[26] In addition to being a brilliant scientist, Foote was a suffragist who lived in Seneca Falls and attended the first women's rights convention there in 1848. She presented her paper at the American Association for the Advancement of Science conference on the connection between CO2 emissions and the heating of the planet. During this same period, the American diplomat George Marsh wrote a book, *Man and Nature* (1864). He revealed the im-pact of human behavior on the ecology of our planet, in particular the con-nection between deforestation and desertification. His message is that if we

---

24. In tandem to the works of Darwin and Wallace, Charles Lyell published wrote *Geological Evidences of the Antiquity of Man,* launching the field of *geology.*
25. Also during this VISION time as part of the new science, Austrian and Augustinian monk Gregor Mendel experimented on peas and found an invisible component to heredity. His paper, "Experiments on Plant Hybridization," was published in 1866. His work took forty years to be assimilated when many scientists started coining terms like: chromosomes, genes, and DNA.
26. Ayana Elizabeth Johnson and Katherine K. Wilkinson, eds., *All We Can Save,* xvii.

humans do not take care of Earth, Earth will not take care of us.[27]

All these people were bringing to light the connection between growing industry and pollution, mostly from coal burning at the time, with a potential for rising temperatures on Earth. The separation of humans from nature that rapidly accelerated with the early scientists of the 1600s was coming full circle at this next VISION time, when scientists proposed that the divorce from nature that had taken place throughout the prior Pluto cycle was now having a deleterious effect on Earth.

Contrary to the increasing environmental awareness, the development of the exploitative practices of oil drilling and explosive mineral mining, and equations harnessing electricity and magnetism were amplifying the devastation of human-made pollution. This means that even while the awareness of the effect of greenhouse gases was becoming known, the foundational theories of the technologies that would vastly increase greenhouse gases were also becoming known.

In the same year that George Marsh's book came out, James Maxwell, a Scottish scientist, presented his ground-breaking paper "A Dynamical Theory of the Electromagnetic Field" at a gathering of the Royal Society on Dec. 8, 1864. Maxwell's theories and equations paved the way for electric power, atomic power, and nuclear power. It is the foundational work for the current technological era. As Nobel-prize winning mathematician Richard Feynman put it, "From a long view of the history of mankind, seen from, say, ten thousand years from now, there can be little doubt that the most significant event of the 19th century will be judged as Maxwell's discovery of the laws of electrodynamics. The American Civil War will pale into provincial insignificance in comparison with this important scientific event of the same decade."[28]

Maxwell's equations illuminated the esoteric field of electricity. His equations took pragmatic scientists in the direction of technological innovation and the cornucopia of inventions that ensued using electricity—lights, phones, radio, record machines, and eventually computers—all inventions that use material objects to detect and process the invisible forces of electricity and magnetism.

---

27. https://publicdomainreview.org/collection/man-and-nature-1864
28. https://www.goodreads.com/quotes/342999-from-a-long-view-of-the-history-of-mankind-seen

POWER   1687–1710   Peak: 1700

Between the VISION and POWER times in this cycle, the East India Company, whose headquarters resided in London, was circumnavigating the globe
and planting flags of commerce in the name of king and country. Against
this backdrop, a group of intellectuals in London formed the Royal Society.

The blending of science, commerce, philosophy, and politics took hold in
England in a new way during the 1600s. In the past, benefactors—be they nobles or merchants or political leaders—funded scientists and artists, as in the
Islamic Golden Age when the caliphate gave great support to its intellectuals.
The inventions of Leonardo da Vinci would not have been possible without
the support of the Catholic Church nor the commerce of the Medicis, not to
mention how the Ancient Greeks blended philosophy with politics. However, the Royal Society of London was created to make England the epicenter
of great thinkers. Its members were often politicians *and* scientists *and* philosophers. Its formation during a time of growing British world domination
set the stage for a particular brand of the blending of science, commerce, and
politics that is at the heart of the dilemmas we find ourselves in today.

Formed as a think-tank type organization where intellectuals smoked
Turkish cigars and early corporate (The East India Company) traders influenced markets, the Society was formed by King Charles II, a protestant
with intellectual curiosity who supported science. One of its founders was
Robert Boyle, an Irish aristocrat and scientist who benefited from Oliver
Cromwell's politics. During the early 1660s, Boyle built a lab in London and,
together with his assistant, Robert Hooke, arrived at the aptly named Boyle's
Law, a law that tells how the pressure of a gas increases as the volume of
the gas decreases. As Boyle did his great work prior to the POWER time, the
fusion of faith and reason, religion, and science, was still active in him. He
was on the board of the East India Company and worked tirelessly to bring
Christianity to foreign lands.

Meanwhile, the Great Plague of London 1665–1666 took the lives of 15%
of the city's population, followed by the Great Fire of London in 1666 which
destroyed much of old London. A young Isaac Newton took those two years
of isolation and dove into the work of Johannes Kepler to arrive at his equations and thoughts on gravity. As his work offered him fame and fortune,
Newton transformed from scientist to politician. It is this slippery move from

inventor to businessman that is so intriguing during this POWER time. New-ton lived during a particularly important moment in British politics. Just as the POWER time was beginning in 1685, King Charles II, protestant friend to scientists, died. His openly Catholic brother, James II, was crowned king. The Royal Society in addition to much of British society was not happy to have a Catholic back on the throne. Three years into his reign, James was tak-en out in a coup d'état, the Glorious Revolution. James' protestant daughter, Mary, and her husband, William, the Prince of Orange in the Dutch Repub-lic, pulled together an army, went into England and before the army attacked, James surrendered after his own soldiers were no longer loyal to him. James was allowed to leave the country and William and Mary took over.

Queen Mary died young, felled by smallpox in 1694 at 32 years of age. King William didn't last that long either, dying in 1702 at the age of 51. Their reign however established Protestantism as the official religion of England, which would never again return to Roman Catholicism, and entrenched the philosophies of science and its powers into the life of the common citizen.[29] Meanwhile, in 1696, Newton stepped into the role of warden of the Royal Mint, where his brilliant mind developed the politics of money.

It was during this POWER time that Boyle's laws inspired the inventor of the cook stove, Denis Papin, who in turn inspired a young Thomas Newcomen to invent the steam engine circa 1712. The steam engine and its ability to power machines is often considered the beginning of the Industrial Revolu-tion. Newton presented *Principia Mathematica* (1687) to the Royal Society,[30] during the same time that John Locke, another Enlightenment philosopher, was inspiring a new liberal movement—a step apart from Hobbes. John Locke had a more optimistic take on people. He called for a total break with the monarchy and the divine right of kings. He felt that people were driven to protect their property, and that laws should be upheld in secular courts and not through a monarch.[31]

Simultaneous to the rise in power of the Royal Society and its influence of the economics of the Royal Mint, the infamous French King Louis XIV was

---

29. Anne, Mary's younger sister, became queen in 1702 and ruled over a unified Great Britain, that valued science over religion.
30. Official website of the Royal Society: https://royalsociety.org/about-us/history/
31. Watson, 504.

building Versailles and spending the people's money with abandon. Louis XIV was deeply invested in creating a great society, building a massive army, and making France the envy of all the world. In some way, he succeeded. Versailles is still one of the greatest palaces ever built, and the French influence on culture throughout the world cannot be underestimated.

Farther to the east, Peter the Great, in stark contrast to Louis XIV, was a simple man with simple tastes who, at times, tried to pass as a commoner to get a sense of what was going on in his country. However, the contrast ends there. Peter was equally interested in making Russia a great nation. He built up his army, erected palaces, and founded St. Petersburg at the peak of POWER. He successfully invaded Sweden and expanded the Russian Empire east into Scandinavia and the south, fighting off the Ottoman Empire for a port city along the Adriatic where he could develop Russia's naval power.

POWER   1938–1949

Between VISION and POWER during our current cycle, Maxwell's equations inspired a frenzy of inventions. Thomas Edison (built a better light bulb), Alexander Graham Bell and Elisha Gray (telephone), and later Nikola Tesla (alternating current) and Guglielmo Marconi (radio) launched a technological renaissance. Once Edison's lights illuminated the White House in 1881, electric lights became quickly available to the masses. Inventions in transportation—trains, cars, planes—one after another, followed the innovative wave, and the materialist value of the growing capitalist society. From Maxwell's equations, machines that could compute, conductors and semi-conductors, circuits and switches all became possible, leading to Herman Hollerith's tabulating machine (1890) that became the prototype for IBM's early business machines.

Between VISION and POWER, Einstein, enabled by the work of Maxwell, had a year of creativity, his *annus mirabilis*, 1905. His theory of relativity led to atomic theory, atomic energy, and atomic bombs. At the same point in the cycle as when Boyle's equations on gas made their impact, Einstein's equations were picked up by the military and used for the war machine that was growing the US empire.

Werner Heisenberg's *uncertainty principle* (1920s) and Erwin Schrödinger's *observer effect* (1920s) circled scientists back around to the realization that the observer cannot be removed from the equation. With the advent of quantum physics, science is returning to inclusivity. These pioneers were not just inaugurating a scientific shift, but a deeper, massive shift in perspective that can be truly assimilated in the upcoming REFORM time.

During this POWER time, these scientific breakthroughs supported and were supported by war. War provided the impetus and funding for Alan Turing to invent an early computer and launch the modern technology movement. The field of genetics took a quantum leap forward when Ernst Mayr wrote *Systemics and the Origin of Species* (1942) and bridged the gap between Darwin and Mendel. Chemist Albert Hofmann took the first intentional acid trip (1943) after he synthesized LSD for the first time in 1938, laying the foundation for a shift in the pharmaceutical industry. Genetics, hallucinogens, and technology explored during the war of POWER are poised to explode during the REFORM time, much in the way that the Industrial Revolution took off during the prior REFORM time.

JUSTICE   1739–1743

Between POWER and JUSTICE, science took a step forward with Benjamin Franklin's experiments with electricity and with John Kay's flying shuttle invention—the precursor to the spinning jenny that revolutionized the textile industry.

During the JUSTICE time, the science of the POWER time became assimilated into the education system. Newton's and Boyle's equations were now taught in universities throughout Europe. In 1742, Franklin invented a more efficient stove for heating, making very practical use of the science he learned.

In France, Leonhard Euler developed the analytical geometry of Descartes of VISION, with the calculus developed by Newton of POWER and arrived at a voluminous body of work in mathematics, mechanics, and dynamics. Euler was part of the new generation of scientists who were free to publish and share their work in the world without condemnation.

Perhaps one of the most significant people of the JUSTICE time was a French man, Voltaire. Voltaire spent a few years in the 1720s in England and was greatly inspired by the work of the scientists in the Royal Society. He, in turn, inspired many nobles, in particular Catherine the Great of Russia, as she ruled during the later REFORM period.

During JUSTICE, David Hume (1711–1776) wrote his great work, *A Treatise of Human Nature* (1739–40). What Hobbes and Spinoza bring forward between VISION and POWER, that Locke advances in POWER, Hume makes accessible in JUSTICE. Hume and Voltaire evolved concepts of justice and inspired freedom of the press, freedom of religion, and free-thinking radicals.

In colonies across the pond from Europe, the preacher Jonathan Edwards (1703–1758) traveled the country setting up tent revivals and preaching the message that direct communication with God was possible. This time was named "The Great Awakening" and exactly corresponds to the JUSTICE time. While Edwards was a man of the cloth and an intellectual, later becoming president of what was to become Princeton University, he was a man of the people. He was stirring up the masses with his teachings. All at the same time, Voltaire was inspiring the French to think for themselves, Hume was inviting the British to think for themselves, Edwards was getting the colonists riled up about freedom of religion, and Samuel Adams was taunting British soldiers.

The interweaving of politics, science, industry, invention, and philosophy was in full bloom. Voltaire, Franklin, and Hume blended science, philosophy, and politics seamlessly. Only a century prior, science and the crazy talk of Galileo had been outlawed. Two centuries prior, Copernicus kept his work secret for fear of Catholic condemnation and imprisonment. Fast forward to the 1740s and preachers were running the universities, politicians were inventors, and philosophers were inspiring politics.

JUSTICE   1986–1989

Between the POWER and JUSTICE times, the computer industry, the car industry, the gadget industry, and the financial market industry exploded. Microsoft and Apple launched their platforms in the 1970s. The early imprint of the internet that the military began during WWII, found its way into homes as early as the 1990s.

At the beginning of the JUSTICE time, scientists around the world were in the planning stages of the Human Genome Project—a worldwide, publicly funded project to map the human genome. The ethics of mapping human DNA were brought into the picture and resulted in Health Insurance Portability and Accountability Act (HIPPA) designed to protect a patient against discrimination by giving them the right to use their health information as they choose (1996). In 1984, just entering the JUSTICE time, a controversial experiment by Danish scientists, Steen Willadsen, successfully cloned a sheep. In 1987, cows were cloned.

As Hermes is sent into the underworld to retrieve Persephone from the land of the dead, the questions arise: "what is life?"; "what is death?"; and "how permanent are either of these things?" These are apt questions asked as cloning mammals became possible. What is life? What is death? Can we go to the land of the dead and then return?

Persephone says yes. She journeys between the underworld and the upper world every year. While she is a goddess, she is also a compassionate guide for humans. During this JUSTICE time, genetics takes a turn and brings forward issues that begin to divide the public. Faith-based people, perhaps with little scientific knowledge, decry cloning and all the science that goes along with it. While intellectuals and atheists may have less of an issue with cloning, many easily became afraid of this new technology, and perhaps for good reason. Scientists playing God didn't sound like such a good thing.

REFORM   1776–1795   Peak: 1783–85

During this REFORM time, science experienced a revolution paralleling the American and French political revolutions. In 1765, the Scottish James Watt improved upon Newcomen's steam engine making it reproducible and usable. In 1793, Eli Whitney invented the cotton gin, improving on its precursor, the spinning jenny, invented by James Hargreaves in 1764. In 1806, Henry Fourdrinier was granted a patent for an efficient paper-making machine after Louis-Nicolas Robert invented a paper machine in 1799. The sewing machine, the lithograph, the hydraulic press, the first vaccine, the telegraph, the threshing machine, and the power loom were a cascade of inventions that ushered in the Industrial Revolution. Factories were built. Textile manufacturing, paper mills, railroads, coal mining, and shipbuilding were all developed through the new sciences using Boyle's Law and Newton's laws of gravity. The original ideas of the visionaries of the cycle, Galileo, Bacon, Descartes, and Kepler were now dispersed, taught, applied, and accepted as truth in the world of the early Industrial Revolution.

As innocuous and noble as these inventions may have seemed at the time, the development of humans controlling nature, or believing that such a thing was possible, stood at the center of the new paradigm. Forests were felled for paper. More people were enslaved to keep pace with the cotton gin. Steam-propelled travel inspired a building spree of railroads and ships. Children toiled away in textile factories. All this because one small island nation turned the import-export business into an empire. Science and commerce, married in the name of progress, precipitated an inventing craze of the late 18th century that inspired humanity's intensified divorce from nature, from our environment, and from our bodies.

REFORM   2026–2031

During REFORM, the very nature of science itself may go through a revolution. The word science from the Greek word *scindere*, meaning to separate, becomes *enontitence*—the act of unity derived from the Greek word *enontito*, meaning unity. Or perhaps a word that isn't derived from the patriarchal land of Ancient Greece. This new *enontitence* reveals the connections between different fields of study. No longer can we separate psychology from sociology, geology from meteorology, astronomy from mineralogy. Focused fields are blended studies.

A new interdisciplinary paradigm has the potential to erupt suddenly and intensely. Much like Thomas Newcomen's engine was barely used until James Watt improved it, the breakthroughs during the 1900s, especially the ones that have not taken off yet, can be revived through breakthroughs that could happen in the late 2020s. When Nikola Tesla worked on a free-energy device between VISION and POWER, he laid the foundation for the concept of free-energy—a direct threat to the wedlock of science and money. Understanding that energy is available in the invisible realms and can be harnessed through technology to provide power for heat and light was a radical concept that threatened the Pluto-based industries of oil and coal that provided bankers like J.P Morgan and industrialists massive fortunes. Like all ideas, once they exist, they can never *not* exist. The idea breeds more ideas, and today inventors are working in their garages—out of reach of the prying eyes of industrialists—on free-energy devices. When our infrastructure collapses, people will be in positions to find solutions, and these inventions, without patents, without global banking funding, can become available and shared freely. Part of systems collapse means that while surveillance has only increased through intelligence organizations worldwide, their actual ability to track breaches, with sufficient personnel to follow-up properly, will decay internally, opening the field for inventors to thrive with solid solutions to the energy crisis and climate change.

I think it is interesting that Tesla, who died penniless and disrespected in Manhattan in 1943 during the POWER time, has become a household name because a car is named after him. Every time we say the word Tesla, we are inviting in what he stood for, the esoteric inventions of healing coils and alternating currents. After Tesla's death, many of his files landed in the offices of the CIA. In 2017, President Obama declassified many of Tesla's files including hundreds of pages Tesla had written himself. The simple access to those files can inspire many people to create new inventions based off Tesla's ideas that have been hidden away under lock and key.

Moving to chemistry, while Mendeleev's periodic table of elements is still in use today, as more elements are added the awkward linear nature of the table may be replaced by the three-dimensional periodic table designed by Walter Russell in the 1920s. His table includes harmonics, and the connection between light and sound, spirituality, and electro-magnetism. In the new world of *enontitence*, understanding the elements requires more than an antiquated model of s and p shells. It requires an embodied understanding of dimensions beyond the fourth one, and the ability to integrate quantum physics with technology.

In medicine, as of 2024, many people continue to dismiss the health benefits of energy work and the health injury of invisible rays coming from Wi-Fi and cell phones. Unity-conscious enontitests bring forth awareness of the very real effects of things invisible to the naked eye. No longer a subject of debate among New Age hippies, but a real conversation among learned natural philosophers, industries profiting from this denial are going to be forced to adjust their policies and practices.

I predict the new paradigm will become undeniable. Corporations that began during the VISION time, like the early roots of the pharmaceutical, the fossil fuel, and the pesticide industries, fall. No longer able to spread false information, the awakening brings out not just new technology, inventions, and breakthroughs, but an entire shift in consciousness—one that untethers lucre from thought, profits from productivity, and capital from creativity.

Potential 5: Awakening

To redeem: to free from what distresses or harms[32]

Persephones' actual transformation from abducted victim into queen, from tricked into empowered, is omitted from the myth. We are left with our imaginations, our psychological musings, and our spiritual perspectives to suss out exactly how this happened. Without a role model or support system, she found a way to become kind and wise. This is where the older, matriarchal myth offers more insight. Persephone is born with a desire to support the dead. She witnessed her mother being neglectful to the dead and in an act of rebellion dove into the underworld to serve.

In the Vedic story of the god of the dead, Yama, also the Sanskrit name for the planet Pluto, the feminine and masculine archetypes are interwoven, and there is no abduction. According to the Rig Veda, Yama and Yami were twins—brother and sister. Yama volunteered to be the first god to die. He then became the ruler of the dead—both of heaven and hell. Yami grieved for her dead brother. To help with her grief, Brahma, the god of creation, birthed night and dreams—a time of relief for Yami for the depth of her sadness. Both of the earlier myths, constructed prior to the dark, patriarchal time we find ourselves in now,[33] omit any abduction and therefore no awakening is required. One could argue that over the past four thousand years, a certain amount of "bad karma" has accrued within the human condition. I am not talking about murder and violence on an individual level. I'm talking about the bad karma of a society that believes that war is just, that turns a blind eye to genocide, and institutionalizes racism. Littered throughout recorded history are societies and crowds that have cheered for the suffering of others. Leaders have felt backed into a corner by the people to go to war. This aspect of humanity is not over. Still today, people in the US are arguing to incarcerate immigrants, torture Muslims for no reason, and outlaw services that would alleviate suffering in many. This aspect of humanity did not need

---

32. Merriam-Webster. (n.d.). Redeem. In Merriam-Webster.com dictionary.

33. Many people consider that we are in the time of the Kali Yuga, a time of darkness, wars, and evil. While the dates of the Kali Yuga are controversial, I postulate that as we enter and leave the final time of Pluto in extreme declination, the Satya Yuga, a time of peace and prosperity where human bodies become lighter and brighter, may begin.

to be addressed in the pre-patriarchal myths as perhaps it did not exist. In the archeological digs of the ancient Harrapan society, there is a notable lack of weapons and instruments of war. Our modern-day myth (if we can call the Ancient Greeks modern day) of Hades and Persephone offers a potential for healing, for equality and for unity needed in a world where violence is acceptable and even, at times, condoned. As we enter a time in Pluto's cycle when healing and unity is possible, it is time to dive into the Underworld, discover our inner resources and emerge merciful and wise.

For a year I had a boyfriend who was an activist. Not just a roadside, lip-service activist, but an in-your-face one, involved in organizing the WTO demonstrations in 1999 in Seattle, drove buses to Cuba with computers for kids, started a non-profit for education about events around the world that go underreported, and helped refugees in Nicaragua. A hands-on confrontational activist, he taught me a lot about history and the workings of the world. We had a recurring disagreement. He was angry that so many hippy activists of the 1960s turned toward meditation and gurus, toward self-help and therapy, instead of continuing to demonstrate in the streets. He was mad at the New Age Movement for absconding with so many brilliant minds. And there he was dating me. I never really identified with the New Age, until I looked up the definition and laughed at myself. I was the New Age personified—a crystal-wearing, guru-following astrologer. I argued that we needed to do our own inner work to clear the hatred, resentment, and desire for revenge to truly activate change in the world. I postured along with many friends and teachers that violent demonstrations and angry vitriol left nothing really changed. It just substituted one form of governance with another, one form of righteousness with another. It continued to perpetuate the same underlying issues that were the root cause of the problem in the first place—people wanting things they don't have and don't need, and people being afraid of, even hating, things and people they don't understand. Desire, greed, hatred, and fear, the basic human foibles and ilks, with the addition of that nebulous and indefinable concept of evil, the desire to simply do harm for harm's sake.

In the end, I like to think that we activated each other. I pushed him to look at his stuff, and he pushed me to get out into the streets. I still think that the New Age detour of the hippy activists was essential. The French Revolution led to Napoleon's autocracy for a reason. Violence can only get us so far and eventually leads to more violence. The success of the American Revolution may be placed not just on the activists who killed the redcoats, but also the peace-loving, non-violent Quakers who played such a large part in creating the new country.[34] This combination of revolt, non-violent resistance, and listening leaders intwined the prior REFORM time into a transition where collapse was not the main outcome, not just in the US, but also in the Netherlands, Russia, France, and Peru.

If we can't get along with our partner, our kids, and our neighbors, how can we create a new world? How can we change the deep underpinnings of greed and hate if we can't do it within ourselves? I am not suggesting that we need to be perfect. We just need to be better. Persephone found a way to be better. No one did this for her. It isn't even mentioned, as most inside jobs are not.

Since the JUSTICE time, the 1980s, hordes of people have gone underground to do the inside work. Therapy is a mainstream word now. Meditation and non-violent communication are practiced by millions, certainly enough people to turn this humanity ship around. While the external work of community-building, demonstrating, and funding non-profits has continued to grow in free countries throughout the world, a simultaneous transformation from within has been happening. Post-traumatic-stress-syndrome is understood, diagnosed, and treated in those who have suffered from war and abuse, offering an end to the repeating pattern of trauma—victim to perpetrator to victim and so on.

This is the secret doorway, the unexpected reveal, the game-changer that no one anticipates or expects. As consciousness triggers more consciousness, as more peace-lovers find themselves ready for activism, one small ripple initiates a movement that crests into awakening.

Awakening is a course correction, a change in direction that rectifies past abuses. Persephone's awakening in myth is her rise to power. It is also the compromise, the acceptance of her fate, and her transformation from a victim into a wise ruler. She herself now decides the fates of others with greater justice and compassion than was shown to her.

In a viral video made during the George Floyd protests, Kimberly Latrice

---

34. For example, William Penn was a Quaker and the founder of the Pennsylvania Colony including the original capitol, Philadelphia.

Jones ended her moving speech, a speech using Monopoly as a metaphor for the oppression of Black people in the US, with the quote: "And they are lucky that what Black people are looking for is equality and not revenge."[35] This is a Persephone quote. Mythology is full of gods and goddesses seeking revenge. It is seen as both a human and godlike characteristic, but Persephone does not seek revenge. She moves into power and finds equality. It is this trait in this goddess that comes to the fore during REFORM, the absence of revenge. Persephone forgives and moves into equality.

In our current cycle, the roots of awakening that started during the VISION time, the 1860s include a combination of spiritual and psychological probing—a time when introspection and healing became something not just for monks and healers. It was a time when spiritual healing and deep internal exploration became available to the everyday person. This outreach that has emerged and strengthened throughout this cycle is one that gives hope for awakening. No longer is religion itself the only way to evolve or be redeemed. No longer does one need to be born into the right sect, or be educated, or meditate on a mountaintop. The mountaintop has come to humankind. Education and awareness are shared with greater and greater ease—both through the equanimous sharing of generous people and through freely available technologies.

VISION   1860–1865

In addition to the beginnings of electro-magnetism, genetics, and evolutionary biology, during the 1860s, there was another way that the intangible, the invisible, the esoteric was becoming tangible and that was in the understanding of human beings—our behavior, what makes us tick and how we got that way—whatever that way is. It was the beginning of a conversation about the *unconscious*—what lies invisibly within human beings that influences or perhaps directs our actions, feelings, thoughts, and beliefs. While the Greeks certainly investigated the soul and religions everywhere talk about the spirit, Ibn al-Nafis wrote about the body-mind-spirit in Arabia, and Indian texts as far back as the fourth century BCE describe Ayurveda, the blending of science and spirituality took root during this VISION time precisely when monarchies and theocracies were falling.

---

35. Kimberly Latrice Jones, *How We Can Win*.

Phineas Quimby (1802–1866), a hypnotherapist and founder of the *New Thought* movement in the US, inspired William James, the recognized "father of psychology" and Mary Baker Eddy, the founder of *Christian Science*. The *New Thought* movement was the origination of the New Age Movement—a non-denominational belief system centered in mind-over-matter, the power of positive thinking, and the body-mind-spirit connection. The blending of science and spirituality, of faith and reason, of healing and thought began right at the beginning of this cycle. While Helena Blavatsky was in Russia falling off a horse and having her first visions; and Ramakrishna was meditating with the flies; while Walt Whitman wrote transcendent poems from his time nursing during the Civil War; while Bahá'u'lláh went into a garden and two weeks later emerged with a vision for bringing all religions together; the New Thought movement idea launched the very field of psychology.

In Heidelberg, Germany, William Wundt, the father of experimental psychology and the first person to set up a psychology lab (1870s), wrote *Lectures on Human and Animal Psychology* in 1863–1864, one of the first scholastic papers to explore consciousness in human behavior. On the other side of Germany, retired military lieutenant Eduard von Hartmann worked on *Philosophy of the Unconscious,* a work that laid the framework for Sigmund Freud's dream work analysis. In nearby Bonn, Germany, a young Friedrich Nietzsche began studying theology. His existential views were another nick in the machinations of religion. While Nietzsche was a critic of von Hartmann and Wundt, the deep discussions of what is life and what is consciousness were no less a part of his work.

In Russia, Fyodor Dostoevsky wrote *Notes from Underground* (1864), a critical response to Chernyshevsky's bestselling book, *What Is to Be Done?* (1863). Chernyshevsky's book is a utopian novel, depicting a woman finding redemption in a communal lifestyle. Dostoevsky, ever the realist, countered *What Is to Be Done?* with his dour, life-is-hard attitude that inspired Nietzsche. All of these writings, whether in support of communism or against it, whether idealist or realist, explore the person behind the person, the face behind the mask, the very essence of "personality," a term that only started to be used at the beginning of this cycle.

It is the beginning of self-reflection as a science, as a field of medicine, as a construct for transformation and the roots of changing civilization itself.

The generally accepted father of sociology, Herbert Spencer (1820–1903) coined the term "survival of the fittest." He took Darwin's theories and applied them to the human condition.

These fields of science—psychology and sociology—began studying human behavior, creating an underlying wave throughout this cycle that supports a crest into a redemptive self-awareness at the upcoming REFORM time. This cycle shows us that humans are becoming increasingly self-aware of our ability to change our behavior and to not always feel cast about by the forces of fate or an all-powerful God. Even the exploration of environmental determinism, a field that proposes that one's lot in life is cast by the physical circumstances one is immersed in, began to find popularity. Scotland's Samuel Smiles wrote a book in 1859 called *Self-help* that proposed a "pull yourself up from your bootstraps" kind of thinking, popular in Victorian times. Amongst the greed and competition that kicked off this current Pluto cycle, we can find the early signs of awakening in the labor movement and women's rights movements, Persephone visionaries at the time, as they were getting started in meaningful ways. The ability to protest peacefully and change the world from within requires the deep inner work that spiritualists, psychologists, and philosophers were advancing at this time.

Alcoholics Anonymous

Another arc to awakening as a potential outcome started in 1858 in England, when William Boardman published a book, the *Higher Christian Life*. This started the Higher Life movement, an evangelical Christian movement still alive and well today. The Higher Life movement, focused on healing fear and selfishness, inspired Frank Buchman to start the Oxford Group in the 1920s, another Christian organization. Through the teachings of the Oxford Group which focused on surrender to God, followers experienced remarkable levels of success healing from alcoholism in a time when prohibition and the end of prohibition was putting a spotlight on alcohol consumption. In 1938, just as the POWER time began, one member of the Oxford Group, Bill Wilson, was invited to write a book, which became *Alcoholics Anonymous*. Since its publication, millions of people throughout the world have benefited from the 12-step process of recovery outlined therein. This example of a non-denominational, anonymous, inclusive recovery process taking

root during the POWER time is like Hermes offering Persephone an antidote
as she was being captured—beginning a different path to recovery that was
not about her being saved, but about her doing the work she needed to do
to save herself. During JUSTICE, A.A. reached Russia just as the Iron Curtain was falling. While not without scandal and criticism, today, the 12 Step
movement is often the first step for many into healing. Having an anonymous, group-led, democratic process to step toward healing the deep issues
of addiction and the traumas that often lead into addiction is one indication
of a worldwide healing process that can unfold as we hit the REFORM time.

Drugs

Ingesting, snorting, injecting, or somehow taking in a substance in order
to change one's state of mind or a condition of the body is not in any way
new. Drugs have been ingested since—well, when did humans start living on
this planet? Even taking drugs for awakened states is ancient. The Eleusinian
Mysteries, based on rites that took place in an ancient Greek temple dedicated to Demeter and Persephone, included ingesting a psychotropic barley
plant.[36] Pilgrims, including Plato during the Greek times and Cicero during
Roman times, report experiencing life changing visions in their once-in-a-
lifetime visit to Eleusis.[37] During this last Pluto cycle, the drug movement
has taken a turn—both helpful and harmful.

At the beginning of this cycle, the pharmaceutical business moved from
local apothecaries to corporate industry. John Wyeth and Brother, a drug-
store founded in 1860 (later became Wyeth, LLC) developed a rotary
compressed tablet machine in 1872, making the mass production of pills a
lucrative business. In 1863, two friends in the dye business founded Bayer
and two brothers in Belgium started the chemical company, Solvay S.A., the
largest multinational corporation in the world prior to WWI and still one of
the largest corporations in the world. In 1867, three brothers in Missouri,

---

36. Muraresku.
37. Eleusinian rites used the mushroom *panaeolus papilionaceus*, meaning the "light whose
name is splendor." Many Dionysian cults in the Greek lands used the fly cap mushroom, *ama-
nita muscaria*, for their rituals. The purpose of transmigrating the soul, from living to dead and
back, known as metempsychosis, is an essential element of the mysteries. Utilizing psychotropic
crops like mushrooms and fermented barley were tools that actualize the migration of the soul
between the realms of being and not-being. (Graves; Miles, "Entering Demeter's Gateway.")

sons of an immigrant from Germany, started G. Mallinckrodt and Company as both a metallurgic lab and a drug company.[38] These companies started as cocaine was first isolated from cocoa leaves in 1860 and John Lister started the age of antiseptic surgery in England, particularly the use of phenol as a disinfectant. Microbiologist Louis Pasteur, after inventing pasteurization, created the first laboratory-produced vaccine (1872) and Charles Gabriel Pravaz invented the hollow hypodermic needle, allowing for the ease of injections. William T.G. Morton and John Collins performed the first successful use of ether anaesthesia during surgery in Massachusetts in 1846. Nitrous oxide followed, being used as an anaesthetic in the mid 1860s. Local anaesthesia in the form of cocaine started in 1877. Anaesthesia, pain relief drugs, and antiseptics all took great strides forward at this VISION time and may I speak for everyone who has ever had surgery, this is a tremendous blessing and a noble beginning to what has become a less-than-noble industry, today.

Meanwhile, opium addiction permeated China like the plague, as corporate raiders of the East India Company profited. The Opium Wars (1839–1860), an invasion by Britain and France to keep the opium trade alive and well, killed thousands and devastated the economy of China, putting them heavily into debt to Europe, which in turn forced open the doors of China to European and American commerce, religion, and politics.

POWER   1938–1949

Between VISION and POWER, the work of Sigmund Freud and C. G. Jung moved the field of psychology to the main stage. Pharmacology, psychology, sociology, geology, technology and many other "ologies" made great strides between 1865 and 1938. Many history books focus on this period as if everything of consequence took place in this time—from the work of Einstein and Freud to Edison and the Wright Brothers. Inventions, studies, experimentation, and scientific development was on steroids. Surgery went from saws amputating limbs of awake soldiers on the battlefields of Gettysburg and Solferino with the likes of Walt Whitman and Florence Nightingale holding their hands, to pristine hospitals of finely tooled equipment with patients under anesthesia served by well-trained nurses. By the time of the battlefields of WWI, soldiers were treated to life-saving surgeries from

---

38. See https://www.mallinckrodt.com/about/our-story/

the newly formed Red Cross, tended to by educated nurses administering new drugs of pain relief and antibiotics. The field of psychology became valid with the work of more scientists, while homeopathy grew in Europe, and John Scheel and Benedict Lust spread a new healing modality called naturopathy. Acupuncture, an ancient form of medicine, experienced a resurgence during the 1800s and spread through Europe and America through the late 1800s and early 1900s. Other East-meets-West disciplines crossed the oceans. Ramakrishna's most famous student, Swami Vivekananda, left India in 1893 and gave a groundbreaking speech at the Chicago Parliament of World Religions. He received a two-minute standing ovation after his first sentence. Vivekananda[39] is credited with bringing Vedanta and yoga itself to the US and Europe.

In a dark twist to the pharmaceutical movement, in 1925, Bayer merged with five other companies, all founded in the mid 1860s, to form IG Farben. Funded by this pharmaceutical conglomerate, Nazi scientists and doctors performed horrific experiments on humans. IG Farben is most well-known for providing Zyclon B gas for the gas chambers in the Nazi concentration camps. After WWII, IG Farben was forced to dissolve, and Bayer, BASF (f. 1865), Hoechst (f. 1863), and Agfa (f. 1867) all went back to making drugs and chemicals in their unique and separate companies.

During WWII, Edward Mallinckrodt, Jr., the director of Mallinckrodt Chemical Works and son of his namesake founder, was invited to supply the Manhattan Project with refined uranium. The company mass produced weapons-grade uranium from 1942 to 1957, putting waste in steel drums that gradually leaked into the ground and water in St. Louis, Missouri. The EPA declared West Lake Landfill in St. Louis a superfund site in 1989, during JUSTICE.

While IG Farben and the chemical companies wreaked havoc on humanity, psychology entertained new ideas, new methods of healing, and new understandings. Before WWII, psychotherapy was largely an intellectual discipline for scientists developing theories through experimentation. With both the psychological trauma to soldiers and the advent of psychological warfare during a war that encompassed the world, multiple responses in the field led to the practical application of psychology. In 1942, Carl Rogers, in his book

---

39. Mahatma Gandhi counted Vivekananda as a significant inspiration to him, as did Nikola Tesla and many others.

Counseling and Psychotherapy, introduced client-centered therapy, applying the work of Freud and Jung to a more accessible form of therapy. In 1943, Abraham Maslow published a paper sharing his theory of the hierarchy of needs. In New York City in 1943, the Intersociety Constitutional Convention of Psychologists unified separate factions into one organization, contributing to the reorganization of the American Psychological Association (APA) that was originally founded in 1892.[40] The US government instituted The National Mental Health Act (1946) which led to the formation of the National Institute of Mental Health, increasing available research funds and exponentially growing the field of mental health. In 1943, Leo Kanner first described infantile autism. A year later, Hans Asperger presented a paper describing a pattern of behaviors we now call Asperger's syndrome. Alfred Tomatis, a young Ear, Nose and Throat doctor in France, focused his studies of sound healing, developing a theory that the voice does not produce what the ear does not hear. His work started with the traumas of war and led to the creation of the Tomatis® Method that connects hearing and phonation that has led to electronic ears. I bring up Tomatis as an example of one of the many scientists and healers who initiated breakthroughs in healing from experiencing the trauma of WWII. It is Persephone after being abducted beginning the deep healing work necessary to become empowered during her time in the underworld.

While consciousness seemed to leave the planet for the war, the work of psychologists and healers quickly began looking and finding ways to recover from trauma. Unlike any war before, the need for deep healing was not only apparent but it was taken seriously by scientists, doctors, and governments—who invested money in research and advocacy for those suffering from mental distress.

JUSTICE   1986–1989

After the POWER time, the Cold War between the US and the USSR left a chilly feeling in the air between the two countries. McCarthy's communist witch hunt inspired distrust and fear within US society and Stalin's capitalist witch hunt bred fear and distrust in the USSR. Arising out of these conflicts, a movement of self-empowerment and self-responsibility stirred people in the US to action. The Civil Rights movement inspired millions to demonstrate

---

40. J. E. Anderson, "Outcomes of the Intersociety Constitutional Convention," 585–88.

that led to the Civil Rights Act that LBJ signed into law in 1964. The women's movement gained traction with the creation, but not the passing, of the Equal Rights Amendment. The 1960s brought a wave of East-meets-West spiritual awakenings, along with the destigmatizing of sex and drugs, while rock and roll took off. Meanwhile, in the US, leadership underwent a transformation of its own. A slew of assassinations of powerful leaders (JFK, MLK, RFK, Malcolm X, Harvey Milk) followed by one significant resignation (Richard Nixon) left much of the US demoralized or distrustful of leadership.

At the same time, the spiritual self-help movement was growing wings. Precisely as Pluto was at 0° declination in 1987, José Argüelles inspired thousands of people to gather for peace in what he called the Harmonic Convergence. While most people dismissed the ideas of harmonic gatherings and group meditations, astronaut, Edgar Mitchell, and an investor, Paul N. Temple, started the Institute of Noetic Sciences, a non-profit organization that supports parapsychological research. While it is considered fringe to many, it hosts the Global Consciousness Project, a data gathering and assessing organization of scientists and mathematicians originating at Princeton University in the late 1990s that uses random number generators to correlate synchronicity with world events. With statistical analysis, the GCP asserts that during times when large groups of people are focused on one event or experience, there is increased synchronicity throughout the world.

The term synchronicity bears exploration at this point. Freud's protégé, C. G. Jung is credited with first using the term, which he defined as "meaningful coincidences." Coincidence is normally defined as seemingly related events occurring without apparent cause. Understanding patterns and then being able to transform old patterns into new patterns is a game-changing superpower in a world where random evil has seemed an insurmountable hindrance to world peace. The ability to witness synchronicity and avail oneself of its inherent power is a new development in the consciousness of human beings. Jung's work and those who have come after him have set the stage for the development of a new paradigm that is both scientific and spiritual.

As theoretical physicists arrive at unified field theories, string theories, and quantum explorations, at least ten dimensions are determined. Multi-dimensional living is not just for the meditators and fringe scientists. Understanding our own culpability and power even while we watch the embers of the dying toxic patriarchy lash out its last sparks, leads to the fifth poten-tial—a time of universal awakening, compassion, and re-integration of our physical selves with nature.

The JUSTICE time also brings an intercession, a mediation, and some sort of spiritual awakening, rarely obvious at the time. In the Roman Empire, Jesus preached during JUSTICE, interceding on behalf of the people, sharing compassion for the oppressed. He became famous after his death through the work of his disciples. In the next cycle, Mani, a follower of Jesus' teach-ings, preached compassion. Both were executed. Finding an apt comparison to Jesus in our current cycle is not easy, but just as Jesus became the founder of a major religion centuries after he lived, it will be interesting to see who among us during this time emerges as the leader of a new religion—or even if it is about religion at all. Popular spiritual leaders during the late 1980s in-clude Deepak Chopra, Ram Dass, the Dalai Lama, Pope John Paul II, Moth-er Teresa, Li Hongzhi, and Princess Diana. The loosely defined New Age Movement also took off during the 1970s and grew roots during the 1980s.

However, one person who established herself as an inspiration precisely during this JUSTICE time was a young Oprah Winfrey, who started her syn-dicated talk show in 1987. Oprah introduced people throughout the world to many of the modern-day prophets, preachers, healers and, yes, celebri-ties. Her work as a compassionate conduit helped to empower and reassure people while the world became increasingly complex and uncertain. She offers us a glimpse into the tone of the upcoming REFORM time, a potential-ly non-denominational, non-dogmatic, and, hopefully, non-divisive time. Oprah interceded on the behalf of women and people of color, without alienating the power elite—a tricky dance during a time when it was needed. While many may be offended at the comparison between Oprah and Jesus, I invite you to consider the impact of both during the periods in which they live(d). Who Oprah becomes in the next cycle will depend on who follows in her footsteps. Spiritual leaders and talk show hosts may seem worlds apart, however other spiritual leaders during JUSTICE times were also political with a penchant for the dramatic, like Jonathan Edwards in the 1740s and Savon-arola during the Italian Renaissance. Since this is the last time Pluto goes into extreme declination, the followers may not be vigilantes like Peter and Paul, but a movement of many people rising together. Like Oprah—whose endorsement offered instant fame and whose voice consistently supported the underdogs—Jesus gave voice to the underprivileged and to the shamed in society. Without judging either about their spiritual natures, but instead viewing them from a historical vantage point, we can identify the subtle shift both figures have offered during JUSTICE, which, in turn, did and can lead to radical changes during REFORM.

The Dalai Lama in 1987 addressed the US Congress with a Five Point Peace Plan for Tibet. His vocal activism for the people of Tibet won him the Nobel Prize for Peace in 1989. He was not alone in this intentional blending of activism and spirituality. Starhawk, after writing the Spiral Dance in 1979 and becoming a "prominent voice in modern earth-based spirituality and ecofeminism,"[41] launched an activism Goddess movement with her book *Truth or Dare: Encounters with Power, Authority, and Mystery* in 1988. Other spiritual activists initiated important movements during the JUSTICE time. Desmond Tutu, after becoming the Archbishop of CapeTown in 1986, launched consensus decision-making and in a radical act included women into the priesthood. His active stance against the death penalty, apartheid, and other social injustices, brought non-violent resistance as a path to many throughout the world. Alice Walker who wrote *The Color Purple* in 1982 became a household name after Steven Spielberg made the book into a move in 1985. Deepak Chopra brought ayurvedic medicine to the west in the 1980s, writing his first of many books, *Creating Health*, in 1987. Ram Dass started the Living/Dying Project in 1986. Maharishi Mahesh Yogi, guru to the Beatles, brought Transcendental Meditation to many through his work in the 1970s and 1980s.

The cracks in the East-meets-West movement began to show during JUSTICE when the FBI raided the spiritual community of popular guru, Bhagwan Shree Rajneesh, later named Osho. Just as the JUSTICE time began in 1985, a mass-poisoning in the surrounding town led to the arrest of several community members including Rajneesh and his personal secretary. The community fell apart and the publicly aired abuses, including embezzlement and conspiracy to evade immigration sent a dark ripple through the yoga world. Since Rajneesh, many other spiritual teachers have been outed for sexual and fiscal crimes, including the founder of Ashtanga Yoga, K. Pattabhi Jois, the

---

41. Starhawk's official website: https://starhawk.org/about/biography/

founder of Iyengar yoga, B.K.S. Iyengar, the founder of Kripalu yoga, Amrit Desai, and the founder of Bikram yoga, Bikram Choudhury. Alongside the uncovering of sexual abuse hidden by the Catholic Church that began to be exposed in the 1980s, the fabric of devotion as a spiritual ideal dedicated to the worship of a guru or priest unraveled during JUSTICE.

While the Reformation (1500s) took away the overarching power of the Catholic Church, it gave a few people with charisma a chance to form new religions. These new religions gathered influence during the following cycle (1619–1863). In our current cycle, some of the visionaries during VISION initiated a wave of awakening without gurus, priests, and teachers. Ramakrishna studied all the major religions and concluded that all were both right and wrong. During this JUSTICE time, the veil is further peeled away as teachers begin to be exposed as the human beings they are. It is important that Persephone recognize that it is not just her mother's love that sets her free, but that she must free herself. She must see behind the curtain and recognize her own ability to direct her spiritual life amidst the power of the gods and goddesses that have ruled her life.

In a twist to this JUSTICE time, another spiritual mediation of sorts was brought to us by the pharmaceutical industry. Eli Lilly and Company, founded by a Civil War veteran in 1867 during the VISION time introduced the antidepressant drug Prozac (fluoxetine) in 1986. Mallinckrodt, also founded during VISION, first produced Oxycodone in 1988. Oxycodone, a highly addictive opioid, used for pain relief, is one of the issues of the drug revolution of this cycle. While helpful to many in extreme pain, the addictive nature of the drug has caused many drug-related deaths.

The introduction of these new designer drugs during JUSTICE is like Hades (pharmaceutical corporations) drugging Persephone to get her to eat the seeds with the support of Hermes (scientists), while Zeus (the Reagans) launched the impotent "Just Say No" campaign. While Persephone still weilds power in the end, her path may now have an added challenge. The drugs can serve two purposes: In one case, the drugs have helped her transform and become empowered through the process of the dark night of the soul. In another case, the drugs have anesthetized her core strength, and she will need to go through a difficult detoxification before emerging into power.

Chapter 15:
Intro to the Upcoming REFORM Time

At the REFORM time, people rise up. What has lain hidden, comes to the surface. Persephone rises from the dead. While it is easy to pull the wool over our eyes during POWER, it won't work during REFORM. While we may be complacent during JUSTICE, listening to the Savonarolas and Samuel Adams' of the world and then resorting back to our old tricks, in the RE-FORM time there is revolution. There is reformation. There is change.

The potentials during the upcoming and last REFORM time are unlike any other in history. From the beginning of this cycle, the new thoughts were of a new state of consciousness in humanity. Consider that what befell during past REFORM times included the shift from monarchies to democracies, from agriculture to industry, from the divine right of kings to freedom of speech and religion. Sitting with the vast perceptual changes that these shifts required offers us a sense of the enormity of the transition we are about to go through.

Looking at the seeds that were planted during VISION, not just the obvious Darwin, Maxwell, Lincoln, Victoria seeds, but Ramakrishna, Walt Whitman, the transcendentalists hanging out in Concord, Massachusetts, George Marsh and Oliver Wendell Holmes, Sr. and Jr., Eunice Foote and John Stuart Mill—the feminists and abolitionists, the environmentalists and theosophists, who offered a counterpoint to the fear-based, dis-information movement that was prevalent then and appears to be growing in the world today. Based on other cycles, the old paradigm gets riled up just before it is transformed. Before colonists took to the streets, the monarchy bore down with added taxes and rules. Just before the Reformation, the Spanish inquisition rippled through Europe inciting fear and panic. Just before the reforms of Constantine, thousands of Christians were executed. It always looks like fear and panic just before the REFORM.

In our current cycle, the belief that we can dissect and interpret objectively has been disproven and disavowed even while it finds its last wind in the pro-science, pro-technology craze of fancy Tesla cars and designer drugs. True transcendence of evil is an inside job that we all must attend to—

healing our desire for revenge, destruction, and harm. Many have laid down a path for just such a transformation. Nelson Mandela spent 27 years in prison transforming a desire for revenge into empowerment and the ability to govern without hatred.

As Mother Nature in the form of Demeter shows us that we cannot tame, control, or dominate her, the environmental movement emerges as a worldwide unifier, which in turn offers us an ability to adapt to the corruption in the environment that the core beliefs of our separation from nature instilled. New ideas and inventions, new ways of living and adapting to our changing environment are spread like germs. Instead of the fear-induced misinformation that so easily distracts us from our true purposes today, a wave of enlightened healing practices presents us with options. Already, people are turning away from social media and environmentally harmful technology to find peace and harmony within. Mass movements that support this new paradigm can take off quickly and decisively as soon as Pluto goes into extreme declination.

As decriminalization of marijuana and psychotropic mushrooms ripples throughout the world, the availability of natural medicines to assist with conscious living and conscious dying emanates a new perception—not only the lack of fear of death, but the embracing of the dying process. Without the fear of death, people all over the world find a way to break free from the prisons of addiction. Without the fear of death, people gather in the streets to take down abusive governments and corrupt politicians.

Using synthesized substances to experience altered states, a practice popularized by LSD pioneer Albert Hofmann, began during the POWER time. Now, micro-dosing mushrooms is replacing the need for expensive pharmaceuticals. Meditation is overwhelming the desire for devotion to a charismatic religious speaker. Somatic methods integrating body, mind, and spirit offer deeper healing experiences. EMDR, NLP, Core-Energetics and Bio-Energetics, holographic breathwork, Cell-Level Meditation, books about belief and biology, scientists merging with New Age healers, so long at the fringe, now offer support for redemption for anyone and everyone. No longer plagued by the repeating patterns of our ancestors, by stories of revenge-seeking, family-feuds and long-held secrets come out into the open and are put into the past. Without fake enemies and oppressive taboos, light shed on old issues offers redemption and frees people to pursue their true passions and purposes.

Different Regions and Countries

Like meteorologists that see a storm system forming in the Atlantic, journalists and political pundits are seeing storm systems forming in the political climate, climate scientists are seeing storm systems forming in the geosphere, and biologists are watching storm systems forming in the microsphere. Like meteorologists, we are focused on predicting the future based on evidence gathered from the past. Like the weather, not everything is predictable. The wild card, the outlier, the anomaly, a deviation in the path of the storm, an unexpected wind, an unpredictable heat wave, a collision of other events, turns the storm in a new direction to expand or contract or move sideways. The past is not always prologue, even with astrology. For awakening, we considered a fifth option—the option that nothing that is about to happen has even happened before. The fifth option is the wild card, the black swan—a chance at true redemption.

Given the trajectory of this cycle that began with the Geneva conventions, the Women's Rights movement, government policies that took steps to end slavery in many places in the world and the beginning of an East-meets-West spiritual movement, all events that have never happened in recorded history (at least for the last four thousand years), it is entirely possible for redemption—for an entirely different REFORM time, an entirely new ending to the Pluto out of bounds story. Even the vast destructiveness of the most recent POWER time (1940s) led to never-before-seen world dynamics. Consider that WWII was more harmful, more horrifying, and more disastrous than any other war in history. While the seeds of suffering continue to be planted, wars, famines, and disasters continue to plague this planet, we have not repeated the crimes of the 1940's. Atomic and nuclear weapons have been on the planet with many countries having access to this technology, and yet, the United States continues to be the only country to use this weapon for mass destruction.

Sometimes what it left out is more important than what is left in. Cycle after cycle, the story of Hades and Persephone seems to work as a barometer for the events of history. Visionaries lead to tyrants and abductions, which lead into an intercession, people begging for change, and then into a co-rulership, a time of reform.

As we head into the final REFORM time (2026–2031), what is absent from prior REFORM times may be the best indicator for what is to come. Absent are the dictators that have no remorse—the Hitlers and the Genghis Khans.[1] Absent are the great wars, where superpowers fight each other to devastation. Absent are the land grabs, the times of expansion and domination. With few exceptions, the times of REFORM are ruled by leaders who see the writing on the wall—know that they must adapt, transform, and reform—to stay in power. With few exceptions, prior REFORM times have included movements where the general population, the general masses, the everyday people, *gained* rights and power.

In all the prior cycles since 1800 BCE, men have been in power. Even when women ruled, the common woman had few rights. This cycle began with a wave of visionaries that initiated increased freedoms for people with darker skin, allowed women greater equality, and after centuries of diaspora, a voice for a Jewish homeland began as whispers in the halls of British parliament. The freedom to love who you want to love and be who you want to be slowly established itself. The radical ideas that were birthed and spread throughout the world during our current VISION time laid the groundwork for the accomplishments and transformations that are about to occur. This leads me to explore one final visionary who launched a worldwide peace movement.

The World

In 1859, as the VISION time was just beginning, Henry Dunant walked into the aftermath of the Battle of Solferino (Italy) and was horrified at the conditions of the wounded:

> Here is hand-to-hand struggle in all its horror and frightfulness; Austrians and Allies trampling each other underfoot, killing one another on piles of bleeding corpses, felling their enemies with their rifle butts, crushing skulls, ripping bellies open with sabre and bayonet. No quarter is given; it is sheer butchery; a struggle between savage beasts, maddened with blood and fury. Even the wounded fight to the last gasp. When they have no weapon left, they seize their enemies by the throat and tear them with their teeth.[2]

---

1. Trump, Putin, and Erdogan may have dictatorial aspirations, but according to this cycle, it is unlikely that they will succeed.
2. Dunant, *A Memory of Solferino*, 19.

In 1862, during the exact VISION time, he wrote the book *A Memory of Solferino*, containing his reactions to the battle and his ideas for creating a voluntary medical support organization, along with new agreements for war. These ideas led to the birth of two significant things: the International Red Cross (1863) and the Geneva Conventions (1864) that instituted an agreement between nations for acceptable behaviors of war—including acceptable treatment of prisoners of war and the wounded.[3] These agreements were revisited and reworked in the aftermath of World War II, creating the Geneva Conventions of 1949 (end of POWER time), still in use (and being violated by some regimes) in the 2020s.

Another interesting fact about the Battle of Solferino was that it was the last time that all sides were under the direct command of a ruling monarch. War has changed greatly since 1859. In one cycle, we have moved from muskets to semi-automatic machine guns, from cannons to nuclear weapons, from binoculars to unmanned drones. The distance between the person making the decisions of war and the actual war has increased exponentially. In the US, soldiers fight from computer screens using drones, while superiors in command strategize targets and civilian casualties like a numbers game. Even so, the percentage of people involved in war has significantly decreased in the cycle. After the war and genocides of the 1940s, deaths from war have been declining from nearly 20% of the population directly affected by WWII in 1945 to less than 1% in 2020.[4] Even while it is easier and safer to attack and kill others, current war tactics are used with diminished effects. Trade wars, boycotts, financial maneuverings, and cyber-attacks are the current weapons of mass destruction, and there are ways around these weapons. Living simply, finding ways to move off the grid, divorcing ourselves from capitalist practices, and healing the greed within are subversive tactics for the individual looking to circumvent violence and war. This isn't to say that everyone has these options, in fact most do not. Most of us have to participate in the capitalist, energy-consuming, soil-depleting, ozone-destroying world. We don't have the option to live on a self-sustaining, sovereign farm

---

3. Henry Dunant is credited with founding the International Red Cross in Switzerland in October of 1863 when Pluto was precisely at 0° of declination. To this day, the Red Cross is the largest aide organization in the world.
4. Bastian Herre *et al.* "War and Peace."

in Idaho or Costa Rica or Switzerland. We live here—right where we are—trained for work that is part of the here and now. Most of us need our cell phones and cars. We have few options to buy products that do not feed corporate politics and pollution-increasing industries.

Pluto's last pass through extreme declination can bring an end to these environment-destroying practices. A combination of all five future options creates the perfect storm. As systems collapse, those in power find it difficult to stay in power. Rapid changes of people in power lead to opportunities to create new systems led by grassroots organizations and collective movements. Non-violent resistance overwhelms decaying infrastructure. Chaotic policies offer windows for revolutions and movements that support new ways. Corporate corruption of capitalism breaks down when supplies are exhausted, and travel becomes more challenging. Countries like Cuba are test cases for the future offering solutions from their experiences of being cut off from the world.

As companies get bought and sold with increased rapidity, trust and loyalty erode offering a chance for workers to take advantage of the power of collective bargaining. At REFORM, the labor movements started during VISION reach a pinnacle of activity and success. Divisiveness is a natural response at the beginning of collapse, something we are seeing today, but as the collapse continues, neighborhoods and communities bond together, sometimes out of necessity, to find local solutions. The authority of behemoth governments erodes from within, moving from one stalemate to another until the process, fueled by kickbacks and other financial incentives, grinds to a halt. When nothing works anymore, people—having looked within, having gathered together, having put aside petty differences—find a way forward that only appears once the dust has settled. In the US and other first-world countries, where comforts, addictions, and technology have anaesthetized large parts of the population, the collapse will be the end of access to the dulling provided by video games, binge-watching tv series, and social-media scrolling. The collapse provides the impetus for change—whether people rise into violent revolution, or move into non-violent resistance, or something beyond imagination awakens within enough people so that a new consciousness of inclusiveness floods the world. The Visions are all there. The Power has succeeded. The Cries for Justice have been loud. There is no reason to anticipate anything other than Reform—other than the scales tipping into a world-wide emergence movement.

The paradigm shift that moves technology into a new age accelerates the other four options. Taking us away from industrial practices and into sustainable energy sources, new technologies disrupt the financial markets that thrive on consumption, triggering a fiscal collapse. Alternative energy sources become available and affordable, even free in some countries. Towers that turn smog into diamonds, already built in Shanghai and the Netherlands, become available throughout the world. Tiny homes, down-sized living, and nomadic traveling become sustainable options as the patriarchy, without foresight, thrashes about, waving its power flags as it takes down the very infrastructure it needs to live. Land ownership, water rights, and crop trading replace oil as the underpinnings of the economy. Places where people can work together and have inner and outer harmony begin to thrive—creating a community of peaceful co-existence that becomes the new economy.

One uprising within an oppressive military triggers a chain reaction of soldiers putting down their weapons in other militaries. While not about world war and with a decrease in country-to-country fighting, war within a country may make obsolete certain practices. Take Russia, now at war with Ukraine, and in some strange twist of fate losing. Putin's expansionistic practices for whatever purposes, oil or other resources, is not working. As often happens, leaders who try to make their countries larger fail. Putin will be out by 2026 unless he changes.

Even with nuclear weapons, there is no option for expansion. The US with its expansionistic *Manifest Destiny* way of life that has benefited from CIA led coups and destabilizing other countries to benefit oil barons and the military-industrial complex, lacks the ability to continue along its tried and tired trajectory. Persephone rises into power and these organizations, most of whom began during the last time Pluto was out of bounds, fall apart from within. Infighting makes them less effective. Communication breaks down and systems fail.

War within countries is another thing. Skirmishes between towns and states, over borders and among neighbors is likely to increase in certain places. To avoid these situations, attention to our neighbors' problems and issues can alleviate much suffering. In towns where people know each other and support each other, this kind of violence will likely be minimal. This is regardless of town size. Even in a large city, a block can coalesce to work towards a common goal and find connection. In places where people are turning a blind eye to the suffering next door to them, these are the areas likely to find implosive violence. Suburban neighborhoods that still follow a "keep-up-with-the-Jones'" commercial competitiveness, where substance abuse takes the form of prescribed narcotics, and exercise takes the form of shopping, may fall into a final stage of dystopian decay. While this way of life, so popular a few a decades ago is receding into the background, in places where it still exists, a hard knock is likely around the corner.

United States

Throughout most of the world, guns are hard to come by and mass murders rare, with the notable exception of the reigning superpower, the US. Even with the most lenient gun ownership laws in the world, gun ownership has hovered between 38 to 45% since the 1970s, with a peak in 2011 at 45%.[5] These statistics suggest that no one is converting to gun ownership, but the rise in mass shootings suggests that unstable individuals are feeling more empowered to use their weapons, particularly their semi-automatic weapons. Even in Yemen, second to the US in gun ownership in the world, a citizen cannot buy a semi-automatic weapon. So while violence between countries is at an all-time low, violence within countries, particularly within the US, a country that has perpetrated violence and instigated instability in many other countries throughout the world is now imploding with not just the random acts of violence by unstable individuals, but a rising fear and instigation of fear by unstable individuals. In other words, people are walking around afraid of each other—in schools, libraries, and churches, places usually considered safe havens. The rise in fear itself has an implosive potential. Leading to a potential breaking apart of the states, states that make it difficult to buy and sell weapons and those that make it easy. Even though cross state travel is easy at this time, the division between states may make for border patrols and increased states' rights as centralized government becomes less and less effective.

---

5. Lydia Saad, "What Percentage of Americans Own Guns?"

The wild card in the picture of war in the US and in other unstable countries is the military. Will the military side with the right-wing anti-immigrant pro-gun stance or will they side with a more centrist leader or a socialist or a pro-corporate stance? In the US, there are two militaries. The military as we usually think of military—the army, navy, and air force, the soldiers that enlist to be part of a disciplined, focused machine where they receive benefits, education possibilities, and training. Then there is the mercenary military—underground, invisible, with less training, less oversight, and fewer benefits. Troops for hire like Blackwater (now called Academi), contractors like Halliburton, and policing organizations like Homeland Security, the DEA, and ICE. More and more these organizations are used for war. Less disciplined and potentially less loyal, these mercenary military and intelligence organizations are wild cards—unpredictable. Their people could be trained to be more loyal to their leaders than to any sense of patriotism or pride in country, making them willing and able to turn on their own citizens. The common citizen of the US reacts to violence and war much like congress during the January 6th insurrection instigated by former President Donald Trump—run and hide. Without any wars on our home turf to condition us toward bravery, our comfortable lives have set the stage for many attempting to look for a way out. Many people I know today are looking for a way out of the country, looking to other countries like Costa Rica and Portugal, for safer havens. In the process of revolution and collapse, fear can trigger increased violence in a country that was built on violence.

I'm not talking about the Revolutionary War. That was violent and that was the beginning of a stable republic. The violence most karmic is the genocide of the original occupants of the land whose lifestyle and beliefs radically differed from the European invaders. Instead of working together, adjusting, or adapting to the environment and the First Peoples of these lands, a total invasion and eradication of their lives and livelihoods has polluted the very soul of America. Pull-yourself-up-from-your-bootstraps thinking, wild-west shoot-outs, and the continued glorification of violence pepper the faith of many in the US and lead to the ultimate decay of society. I saw a meme the other day that said, "If you value freedom, but not for everyone, what you really value is privilege." This is the essence of what has built much of the wealth of the nation and is what will also take it down. Live by the sword, die by the sword. Value violence and violence will find you. As harmony becomes commercially valuable, the values that built the country fall away. Different regions of the country will have different problems. The country may fracture in the process. States may successfully cede the union. State governments may begin to act like countries, enforcing different laws, negotiating with other countries separate from the federal government, and establishing stronger border boundaries. One state makes the move, separates from the union, and the toppling begins. One state may outlaw semi-automatic weapons and then set up border patrols to search cars for weapons. Already, some states are outlawing abortion and setting up ways to enforce the law while other states are embedding the right to an abortion in the constitution.[6] The deterioration of continuity, at first chaotic and troubling, ultimately triggers the movements, demonstrations, and actions that bring about new societies. At first, working underground, and then, as Pluto hits the peak of extreme declination in 2027 to 2028, the underground moves above ground and becomes the new system itself.

On the other hand, climate change may unify the country. Storms ravaging the southeast force consciousness shifts with so many learning the painful lesson of non-attachment. Climate refugees within the US turn the focus to infrastructure. The election process, if protected, allows for new leadership that sees the big picture. In a country founded on demonstrations, mass movements can begin in the US. Effective non-violent movements that are inclusive, loving, and creative, start popping like popcorn throughout the country. The connection between food and art, between water and breath, between land and peace, permeates an awakening. For true reformation, a meaningful acknowledgement and support of the Native peoples and of descendants of enslaved peoples is necessary and entirely possible. With this deep healing, an awakening is not just conceivable, but likely.

---

6. CA and VT, Nov 2022 elections.

China

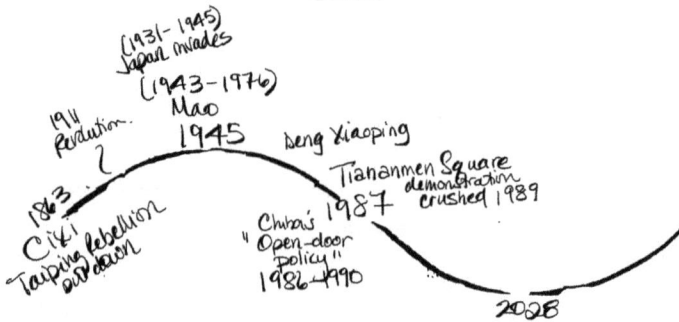

While living in the US, my focus has naturally been centered there. How-ever, in order to arrive at any insight into the upcoming REFORM time, at least a cursory look at China is essential. China is a land all unto itself. Surrounded by walls, with a culture and government uniquely its own. Its history unlike Europe and the US appears as a contiguous movement from one dynasty into another dynasty starting with the Shang Dynasty as early as 1800 BCE. Silk, paper, gunpowder, and moveable type were all inventions that originat-ed in China. This is a land with a long history and deep roots. At the begin-ning of the current cycle, the age of dynasties was coming to an end and a new age was arriving in China.

While the US was embroiled in civil war, the Qing Dynasty (1636–1912), that took hold at the beginning of the prior Pluto cycle, was dealing with two wars. One was a British invasion in support of an open corporate drug mar-ket including an open door to Christian missionaries, the Opium Wars, and the other was a homegrown insurrection, the Taiping Rebellion.

At the end of the last Pluto cycle, in the late 1840s, a charismatic Chinese man, Hong Xiuquan, met a Christian missionary and converted to Christian-ity. He became a preacher himself mixing Christian religious views with his own form of communism, especially a value for shared property. The pover-ty and oppression that was prevalent at the time was an apt backdrop for his popularity. Thousands flocked to his teachings. Hong Xiuquan had a vision of a heavenly city, called Taiping, and his followers were willing to fight for the possibility of this utopia. Gunpowder and weapons were stock-piled and by 1851, rebellion had moved into war. The Taiping Rebellion (1850–1864) took the lives of over 20 million people. As if this all wasn't enough for the

Qing Dynasty to deal with, the British burned down the beautiful and elaborate Summer Palace (1860) as a parting gift in the Opium Wars.

At the beginning of the VISION time, the Qing Emperor Xianfeng died (1861). His successor was his five-year-old son, Tzongeng. At this point, you might be wondering where the vision is in all of this. Many thought of Hong Xiuquan as a visionary, much in the way that people in southern US thought of Jefferson Davis. Ultimately, they lost, but their ideas have breath to this day.

There was another visionary for China at this time, Cixi, the concubine and mother to the new child emperor. Cixi, and Empress Zhen, first wife to the late emperor, were dear friends and raised Tzongeng together. When their husband died, they staged a coup. "...two months after her husband died, the twenty-five-year-old Cixi completed her coup with just three deaths, no bloodshed otherwise and no turmoil."[7]

From behind a screen and without ever being able to visit the great palace (women were not allowed there), Cixi called the shots. With the support of her friend, Empress Zhen, they opened ports and increased trade with the West. With the Opium Wars done and treaties signed with England and France, Cixi accepted the offers of these countries to help put down the Taiping Rebellion.[8] In July 1864, around the same time that the North was beginning to defeat the South in the US, the Taiping Rebellion was put down.

Cixi formed alliances with several westerners who helped reorganize the customs office, which brought in the revenue that paid off Chinese debt to the invading empires. Universities were built to teach western science with imported European professors.

At the beginning of the VISION time, both the US and China were poor, under-educated and under-developed nations in internal chaos. By the end of VISION, an alliance between China and US, changes in government in both countries and an increased value on industry and science kicked off the building of the two most powerful empires in history.

Two people who barely get a footnote in the history books began the empire building process: Empress Cixi and Anson Burlingame (a New Yorker

---

7. Chang, *Empress Dowager Cixi*, 49.
8. Cixi turned down the offer of troops, thinking that she did not want an army of westerners fighting in China—but did accept other forms of help. The Chinese army was trained and armed by British soldiers.

and abolitionist, appointed to the post of Minister to China in 1861—the first minister to China from the US). Burlingame and Cixi became a dynamic duo, transforming both countries into powerful allies.[9] This ally-ship collapsed over time, particularly after WWII when China became a communist nation under the leadership of Mao Zedong.

I think it worth remembering this relationship as what begins at the VISION time is like a seed that grows and bears fruit during the REFORM time. The alliance between China and the US is akin to a throw away seed that blew in the wind and grew in some abandoned corner of the garden. However, at REFORM, it is entirely possible that this tree, ripe with fruit, may find itself the most abundant and a China-US bond may be a saving grace for both countries. Already, the deep economic interdependence between the two countries is incontrovertible. The two nations have never directly been at war. This bodes well for some kind of alliance that benefits both nations and throws an unexpected twist into 2026.

POWER

Between VISION and POWER, Sun Yat-sen, known as the "Father of China," inspired the overthrow of the Qing Dynasty and founded the Republic of China (1912). His attempts at making China into a democracy were challenged by the lack of support he received from democratic nations. Sun Yat-sen died soon after the Republic of China was formed, leaving China in the hands of the military leader, Chaing Kai-shek, a controversial figure. Having risen through the military, his focus was on war, in particular overcoming the encroachments of Japan and Russia. As World War I was ending, Japan claimed areas of China that were under contention. The Treaty of Versailles was weak in returning those lands to China. This led to demonstrations and uprisings, including a student revolt, the May Fourth Movement. While Chaing Kai-shek was establishing a representative republic in China, a young revolutionary, Mao Zedong, was educating himself in communism, inspired by the May Fourth Movement. From 1937 to 1945, Japan occupied China—overcoming the Nationalist forces. Meanwhile, Mao built support in the countryside. By the time a defeated Japan left China at the end of WWII, Mao Zedong had built an army and a following. Mao's army pushed

---

9. Chang, 76–80.

out the Nationalists under Kai-shek. Those nationalists emigrated to Taiwan to establish a new democracy. The split between China and Taiwan in 1949 is one of the many rifts that occurred during that time.

JUSTICE

Mao (1949–1976) and his policies may be responsible for up to 80 million deaths, a genocide possibly worse than what Hitler and Stalin perpetuated. His death in 1976 left the Communist Party, the de facto ruling organization of China, in the hands of Deng Xiaoping, who orchestrated China's emergence into market-capitalism.

Precisely during the JUSTICE time, from 1986–1989, China instituted their "Open-door policy" inviting in foreign investment, tourism and private-sector, corporate relationships. Similar to Russia during perestroika, China reached out to the US and Europe to support their economy and bring in development. However, things changed in 1989. Where the transparency under Gorbachev was able to take hold in Russia (for a little while), in China, demonstrations in Tiananmen Square in 1989 lead to the public massacre of thousands. The violent quashing of the revolts in 1989 lead to a further entrenchment of autocratic communism.

While the transformations during JUSTICE supported the financial viability of China, its human rights records were weak, to say the least, and it is in this that the coming revolution may be challenging in China. Revolutions are often easier to put down during any time of the cycle other than the RE-FORM time. From 2026 to 2031, citizens of China are likely to revolt. During VISION, POWER and JUSTICE times, there were major upheavals and revolts. During VISION and JUSTICE, the revolts were unsuccessful, leaving the people to return to the dictatorial rulers in power. During POWER, the civil war led to an even more oppressive government than the one overthrown.

REFORM: *Non-Violent Resistance and Revolution*

During REFORM, there is likely another revolt coming in China. The oppressed masses, the overworked farmers, factory-workers already working in abhorrent conditions, are likely to rise up again. This time, as the anti-dote to the POWER time, revolution will likely be successful, even though it has great potential to be violent. In the case that the Communist Party, the governing body in China, is prepared for this revolution, and there are signs that they are, reforms may circumvent a bloody war. Xi Jinping, the current general secretary of the Communist Party and the leader of China, has been in power since 2012. A brilliant politician, he appears to be leading a strategy of sacrificing part of China to save part of China. Industry, coal mines, Apple computer factories and nuclear power plants are focused in the eastern half of China, where the oceans are rising above land level and pollution is so high its condensation forms oil slicks in the street. The many may rise up, this time to be successful.

China's interest in maintaining control in Tibet, to the outrage of much of the rest of the world, at first glance seems unnecessary. However, if China is indeed playing a long game, then shoring up resources and land in the western and northern areas makes sense, and Tibet is key to that. China has a long history, much longer than the European states and much much longer than the newbie on the block, US. It is more likely to invest in the future, understanding that die-offs in the form of plagues, famines, and wars are part of life on this planet. Their interest is less likely to be in trying to avoid disaster, but in planning for the eventuality of it. Factories currently polluting southern China are making solar panels and other forms of sustainable energy for the future West.

Another option for REFORM includes China seeing the long game and finding itself governed by a benevolent dictator or a wise communist council willing to reform and adapt. Instead of further entrenching oppression, the Chinese government could make way for new ideas and new values.

The challenge for China will be civil rights. Their military, probably the second largest in the world, is powerful enough to quash a revolution. However, if massive worker-strikes ripple along the east coast, the economy could tank forcing China to institute reforms. Remember, it can take as little as 3.5% to spell success.

What is unlikely is ultimate control and further police state politics. Pluto in extreme declination is a breaking point—a time when people have had enough. Willing to risk their lives, whether through demonstration or refusing to work, people no longer accept the over-arching control of a tyrannical regime.

Russia

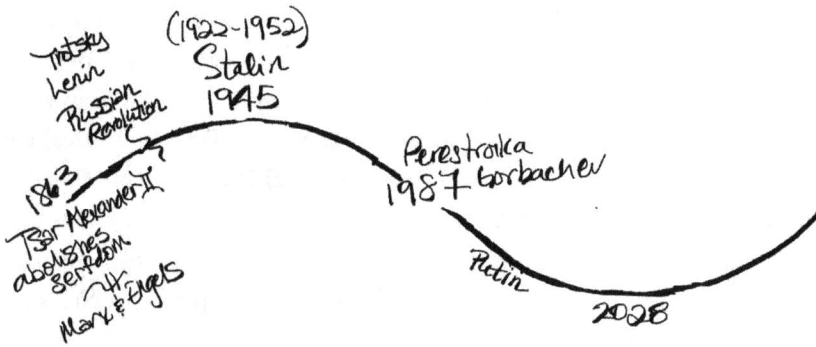

VISION   1860s

The 1860s was a time of civil unrest throughout the world, and Russia was no exception. After losing the Crimean War and valuable real estate to the Ottoman Empire, the Russian Empire was licking its wounds. In the lands along their western borders, modern day Poland and Lithuania, successful uprisings in Italy inspired demonstrators standing up for Polish independence. In 1861, gatherings of people singing Polish and Lithuanian traditional hymns drew the attention of the Russian monarchy who responded by placing a Polish autocrat in charge and instituting a draft. This backfired. In early 1863, Polish draft dodgers revolted against the Russian army in what came to be called the January Uprising. This rebellion was quashed—just like the Taiping Rebellion in China and the southern rebellion in the US—with much bloodshed and tears, towns burned to the ground, and thousands exiled. In all these circumstances, the rebellions of the agrarian workers were overturned by the industrial movement. The Russian tzar freed the serfs only to make their lives harder through taxation and punitive land reforms. Reconstruction in the US punished the Southern farmers. Industry was taking off, and those working the land were left behind.

Times of unrest often bring along great minds, and Russia in the 1860s is an excellent example of this. Leo Tolstoy wrote *War and Peace* from 1863 to 1869, and Fyodor Dostoevsky wrote *Crime and Punishment,* published in 1866. While Tolstoy and Dostoevsky are widely read to this day, the visionary that had the greatest impact at the time was the imprisoned philosopher Nikolai Chernyshevsky.

Chernyshevsky wrote a novel, *What Is to Be Done?* that outlined a vision for Russia that advocated a communal way of life, bypassing capitalism and going straight to socialism.[10] Chernyshevsky was a fan of US democracy, of President Lincoln, and of the abolishment of slavery. His work became popular in Russia as soon as it was published in 1863. The British political writer Martin Amis wrote that "Chernyshevsky's novel *What Is to Be Done?*, far more than Marx's *Das Kapital*, supplied the emotional dynamic that eventually went to make the Russian Revolution."[11] Dostoevsky brought more attention to the novel when he published his critical response in *Notes from Underground*. This war of words, a scholarly tête-à-tête, initiated Russia into this cycle as a land of new ideas and reformers. Persephone was born in books as the people of the Russian Empire struggled to survive. The tsar's reforms that abolished serfdom created a taxation system that burdened both the laborers and the landowners. In Europe and the US, the rise of industry and invention benefited the wealthy and enhanced the GDP, while in Russia, the industrial age crept in more slowly. Without the advancements in farming and manufacturing, Russia struggled to maintain the status of world power that it had gained during the time of Catherine the Great. However, the Pluto-ruled domain of petroleum was bubbling under the surface of Russia's potential. While industry evolved slower in Russia, the lubrication for future industry, oil, lay in wait in abundance under the Russian landscape. In the 1860s, as oil wells and drilling technology took off in the US, the Swedish Nobel brothers, wealthy from the invention of dynamite, began buying land in the Baku region, the land of the largest oil reserves on the planet. In 1876, the commercial production of oil began in the region of modern-day Turkmenistan.[12] The Rothschild bank joined the Nobel family in investing in this natural resource that became more and more important as cars and then planes were invented.

Between VISION and POWER, an assassinated tsar, pogroms that expelled Russian Jews, and the failure to provide a healthy heir, left the Zeus-themed monarchy in a state of weakness. In 1912, political dissidents Vladimir Lenin and Alexander Bogdanov formed the Bolshevik Party, a party intended

10. Glenn E. Curtis, ed. *Russia: A Country Study*.
11. Martin Amis, *Koba the Dread*, 27.
12. P.I. Korovkin, S.S. Cherenev. "History of Oil Industry in Russia," 808–9.

to reconstruct Russia into a Marxist socialist government. Marxist Leon Trotsky with Lenin planned the successful "October Revolution" and in 1917, the royal family was ousted, and Lenin claimed himself head of the new communist government. In fear of future coups, the tsar and his family were executed. The rise of the Bolsheviks in 1912 sent fear throughout the monarchies in Europe, many of whom were related as descendants of Queen Victoria. While World War I was triggered by the assassination of the heir apparent of Austria-Hungry, the underlying tensions between countries and the fear of uprisings within their own countries, led to a quick succession of war declarations. Russia entered on the side of Britain and France against Germany, Austria-Hungry, Bulgaria and the Ottoman Empire. The war was greatly unpopular in Russia and added fuel to the already raging fire of discontent. In 1917, with the success of the revolution, Russia pulled out of WWI. Lenin stayed in power until his death in 1924, when Josef Stalin took over. After the revolution, the new administration nationalized the oil industry, and the Nobels and Rothschilds lost much of their investment. What remained of their Russian oil assets, the Nobel brothers sold to Standard Oil of New Jersey, which later became Exxon. Vacuum and Standard Oil of New York, which later became Mobil, invested in Russian oil in 1923.[13]

POWER

As often happens, the work of the visionaries is twisted to support power-hungry dictators during the POWER time. Perhaps never has this been truer than what became of communism during the reign of Josef Stalin during the POWER time. The Union of Soviet Socialist Republics is a perfect example. While thousands fought and died to bring a new government of fairness and equality to the people of Russia during the Russian Revolutions, the ultimate result was a ruthless dictator who rose to power just prior to the POWER time and abetted a horrific genocide. During the thirty years of his reign, massive famines killed millions, purging of the intelligentsia killed hundreds of thousands, and war gave Stalin the ignominious title of having more people die on his watch than any other leader in history. Pluto's abduction is not only of the people of Russia but also of the natural resources, particularly oil, but also coal, as it was nationalized and controlled by the

---

13. Curtis.

autocratic communist party.[14] In 1953, as the POWER time came to a close, Stalin died. A succession of leaders attempted to amend the damage with varying strategies and results, while the Cold War against the US further depleted the Russian economy.[15]

JUSTICE

While the US and the USSR fought together during WWII, the pacts at the end of the war, split the world into "red" states of communism and "blue" states of democracy, leading to The Cold War. The arms race played with nuclear weapons and war technology that Russia, with half the GDP and roughly the same population of the US in 1980[16], could not win. The USSR transformed during the JUSTICE time. Mikhail Gorbachev, a leader with vision, brought in *glasnost*, a Russian term inferring transparency in government and in the judicial system. Gorbachev's work for justice in Russia led to several sweeping reforms. Declaring the Cold War over, the Berlin Wall came down in 1989, and the Soviet Union was disbanded. The government was split into fifteen different countries with the Russian Federation, a constitutional republic, being the largest. Singing revolutions in the western regions led to independence in Lithuania, Estonia and Latvia, the same regions where singing demonstrations took place in the early 1860s.

Pluto's realm of oil and gas turned a corner as well. As Gorbachev opened the doors to the West and capitalism creeped in, the oil industry, nationalized under Stalin in 1943, metamorphosized into Gazprom, a state-run corporation in 1989. By 1991, as the Soviet Union fell, Gazprom became privatized with the Russian government still holding most of its assets.[17]

While the people of Eastern Europe, the singing Persephones of the 1860s, found new freedom during JUSTICE, Demeter's role of "Mother Earth forced to bow to corporate interests" signals her continued grief as she awaits the return of her daughter.

---

14. Anthony C. Sutton, *Wall Street and the Rise of Hitler.*

15. Mark Kramer, "The Soviet Role in World War II: Realities and Myths."

16. José Luis Ricón, "The Soviet Union: GDP growth,"

17. J. Henderson, A. Ferguson, "The Turbulent History of Foreign Involvement in the Russian Oil and Gas Industry," 1–60.

REFORM: *Non-Violent Resistance and Revolution*

Not unlike in the US, the appearance of powerful, autocratic leaders can lead to a belief that the country is headed toward war and genocide, especially as the POWER time proved this to be true. Pluto begs to differ. Many fear Vladimir Putin, a man pulling the strings since he came to power in 1998. As we move into a time of revolution and reform, Russia is poised for revolution. Following the Persephone myth, Putin either becomes the benevolent ruler who bows to the will of the people or finds himself dethroned.

Massive demonstrations are already happening. Hunger strikes, thousands of people gathering in the streets and social media–organized flash mobs are increasing. People are protesting everything, from unfair elections to garbage disposal issues. In 2019, there were "hundreds of mass rallies, flash mobs and other demonstrations, a marked shift from less than a decade ago when publicly challenging authority over social concerns would have been nearly unthinkable for average people."[18]

Many alive today were alive during perestroika. They have the innate knowing of how a large body of people can transform. This awareness will support the people of Russia greatly as they move into a time of sweeping REFORMS. Look to Russia for future world leaders and as a way to move through the REFORM time with foresight, courage, and success. Look for leaders like the lawyer, Lyubov Sobol, who went on a hunger fast protesting unfair elections.[19] Or Alexey Navalny, who used Facebook and Twitter from prison to invigorate an anti-war movement, protesting Russia's invasion into Ukraine.[20] Navalny's death in 2024 in prison sparked even more demonstrations.

Reforms and a collaborative form of government are coming to Russia and the people are more than ready. The Russian visionaries—Leo Tolstoy, Peter Kropotkin, and Nikolai Chernyshevsky—were philosophers of peace and cooperation who supported a government run by the people. These are their visionaries and that is the promise of the REFORM time, especially this REFORM time, the last of the REFORM times. While there may be casualties, as no society is without violence in this time, the casualties may be minimal

---

18. Ann M. Simmons, "In a Big Shift, Russians Take to the Streets Over Everyday Complaints."
19. Andrew Higgins, "'I Am Always Asked if I Am Afraid': Activist Lawyer Takes On Putin's Russia."
20. "Navalny urges Russians to protest daily against Ukraine invasion." *Aljazeera.* 2 Mar. 2022.

as the people of Russia have in their history and in their culture, the deep connection to reform, demonstrations, and adaptability. Not to mention that Russia has nearly entirely depleted its military in its invasion of Ukraine and many citizens have already fled the nation.

Russia, in fact, may lead the world in this non-violent revolution. As Russia led the world in ousting the monarchy, look to the Russian people for a way through this next turning point.

Fear of Russia is running high in mainstream US, an irony of this cycle that will become more apparent in the next decade. In many countries throughout the world, oligarchs, supported by massive corporate powers, are in positions of authority. So much Plutonic power lies in the hands of corporate interests, banking, and oil. As Europe and other countries free themselves of Russian oil, starving Gazprom and other oil corporations, Hades' (Pluto's) power weakens, and Persephone rises. The trials of the Russian and Ukrainian people, the genocide, the wars, Chernobyl and famine are not ancient history. The people of Russia know how to rise up. They do not live in the land of superficial dreams but pride themselves on pragmatism and heartiness. They will not sit still during the REFORM time.

Middle East

Today, news reports from the Middle East reaching the West are filled with war, famine, and crisis. The great ancient Arabian and Persian civilizations appear wholly lost. Many in the US live in fear of Muslims, mistaking headwear for agents of destruction. The destruction of the World Trade Center in 2001 incited racist, anti-Islam policies and movements, with most people having little understanding of the fear and hatred that many in the Middle East hold for the west, in particular the UK and US. The rise of militant underground and above ground organizations taking an anti-American stance further fuels the righteousness of many xenophobic demonstrators in the West.

Let's go back in time to set the stage. The Islamic Renaissance (c. 800–1200 CE) brought forward many great advancements from algebra to alkalis (soap), from astrolabes to hospitals. Out of the destruction caused by the crusades and Mongol invasions (early 1000s) rose the Turkish Ottoman Empire. During the same period as the Italian Renaissance and European Reformation (late 1300s–late 1500s), the Ottoman Empire expanded to include much of the Middle East of today, with the notable exception of Persia (Iran), a rival of the Ottomans.

While colonists were landing in the New World and René Descartes was saying memorable things (early 1600s), the British Empire, under the guise of the newly formed corporation, the East India Company, began its subtle invasion into the Ottoman Empire. Tobacco first grown in Virginia made its way to Turkey and found a hospitable environment. Addicted Europeans paid top dollar for Turkish cigars. Over the course of that 248-year cycle of the Pluto (1619–1863), the Ottomans maintained their foothold in the Middle East, even defeating the Russians in the Crimean War, but went into debt to European money lenders. During the 1700s, the British Empire became a superpower hooked on tea and silk from China, cotton from India, tobacco from Turkey, and spices from Indonesia. The roads from China to Europe traversed the Ottoman Empire. Dutch, French, and British foreigners travelled back and forth with goods and ignited the fashion industry in Europe— picture Marie Antoinette gowns.

VISION

While the US was embroiled in civil war, the Ottomans spiraled into debt to the banks of Europe and other independent lenders, first to fund the Crimean War against Russia and then to build and maintain infrastructure in the form of railways and roads that Europe desired for its markets. The lenders called in the loans in the 1880s and bankrupted the Ottoman Empire. Under the leadership of Gabriel Aubaret (1825–1894), the Ottoman Public Debt Administration (OPDA) was formed to run the economy of the Ottomans in a subtle coup that rarely gets mentioned in history.[21]

Naturally, the Ottomans did not like this arrangement. The sultan, Abdul-Aziz, who came into power in 1861 mysteriously committed suicide in 1876 and Aubaret—who fought in Crimea (a lieutenant during the Siege of Sevastopol), who helped take down Peking during the Opium Wars, who was

---

21. The Turks borrowed around £3 million to finance the Crimean war. The empire had been debt free, but the advanced weaponry needed to defend the critical port area against the Russians cost them dearly. That £3 million mushroomed into almost £300 million during the VISION time, when Abdul-Aziz became sultan. He apparently had a love affair with England. By borrowing from the Bank of London and other British and French creditors, Abdul-Aziz built opulent palaces, public works projects, and a large navy. In 1867, he was the first sultan to visit England when Queen Victoria bestowed on him the Knight of the Garter.

part of the Siamese King Mungkat's adjustment to western ways (*The King and I* king) and had a very public love affair with a French actress who was the ex-lover of Napoleon III—stepped in behind the scenes to levy taxes on the people of the Middle East.[22]

This left a bitter taste in the mouths of the Ottomans who secretly sided with the Germans in WWI against the Brits. This did not go so well for them. When the Central Powers lost, a plan to divide up the Ottoman Empire was led by two diplomats, François Georges-Picot (French) and Sir Mark Sykes (British). The Sykes–Picot lines through the Middle East are like deep cuts in the skin of a living organism—still painful, still bleeding.

VISION to POWER

Meanwhile, between 1901 and 1908, oil was discovered in Persia (Iran) by British engineers, and Pluto found a new underworld to inhabit.[23] Bordering the Ottoman Empire, Persia was an independent state in transition from monarchy to a parliamentary system (1906). The joint Persian-British company, Anglo-Persian Oil Company (APOC), formed in 1909. By 1914, the British owned most of the company, and Persia had little power in the oil business. In WWI, Persia stayed neutral but was not spared the aftermath of Western and Russian post-WWI intervention. Picture Lawrence of Arabia and Gertrude Bell weaving in and out of politics providing a solid footing for European oil interests to entrench themselves. In 1921, a coup installed the military leader, Reza Khan as Shah, a position that looked more and more like a dictatorship until he was taken out by Soviet and British forces when they invaded in 1941.

Meanwhile, in 1917, sentiment for a Jewish homeland was ignited when Britain's foreign secretary, Arthur James Balfour, presented the Balfour Declaration to Walter Rothschild, the president of the Zionist federation. Supported by some of the wealthiest families in Britain, including the Rothschilds, the desire seemed little more than a fanciful wish at the time. Enter WWII, when German anti-Jewish rhetoric became genocide and the aspiration for a Jewish homeland generated increased support. As the war ended and agreements between the victors carved up countries, Israel was established as a

22 A. Johnson, "The Gabriel Aubaret Archive of Ottoman Economic and Transportation History." This PDF includes copies of Gabriel Aubaret's journals, including financial records.
23. Technically, Pluto (oil) was already living there, and the British invaded him at home.

sovereign nation (1948), a homeland for Jewish people all over the world. Between 1948 and 1950, over half a million people of Jewish descent moved to Israel, a land occupied by a largely Muslim population of around one million, many of whom were pushed into camps in border regions.[24] Seen as an aggression of the west into their lands, as soon as the British left, Jordan, Syria, Lebanon, Egypt, Iraq and Saudi Arabia invaded. Pluto was still in extreme declination and the violence started an ongoing chain reaction. Both sides increased military might, with Israel getting extra support from the US and the UK. One year later, just as Pluto left extreme declination, an armistice agreement was reached and a temporary peace established.

POWER

In the same year as the Balfour Declaration, British troops invaded Iraq, still part of the Ottoman Empire, and took control of Baghdad. By the end of WWI, Britain had laid claim to Iraq. Oil was discovered there in 1927 and by 1932, with economic alliances in place, Britain released control of the country. Enter Pluto unleashed, the Iraqis sided with the Axis Powers, and Britain invaded again, mostly to ensure their oil supply. At the end of WWII, Iraq along with Saudi Arabia, Egypt, Lebanon, Syria, and Transjordan, formed the Arab League (1945), that at the end of Pluto out-of-bounds attacked the newly formed state of Israel (May, 1948).

In 1933, a few years before WWII, oil was discovered in Saudi Arabia. A pact between the US corporation Standard Oil of California (SoCal) and the government of Saudi Arabia got oil production going by 1936. Arabia aligned with the US over Britain in an attempt to avoid European colonization. As WWII raged on, Saudi Arabia built oil wells and the infrastructure for a growing oil market, including supplying oil to the Allies. Towards the end of the war, King Abdul Aziz met with FDR on a ship in the Suez Canal that initiated a long and complicated relationship between the two countries.

While Pluto was unleashed, its very own produce, oil, became currency, and the countries that produced oil became players on the world stage in new and powerful ways. This POWER time initiated the underlying tensions, rivalries, and alliances, that continue to this day between Saudi Arabia and the US, between Iraq and Britain, between the Arab League and Israel.

24. "Survey of Palestine: Prepared in December 1945 and January 1946 for the information of the Anglo-American Committee of Inquiry. Volume 1,"

JUSTICE

Between POWER and JUSTICE, coups, assassinations, and wars plagued the Middle East. War between the Arab states and Israel continued. The Palestine Liberation Organization (PLO), formed in 1964 with the purpose of taking back Palestine, grew in membership and power.

In Iran in 1953, the Prime Minister of Iran, Mohammad Mosaddegh started making moves to get a larger piece of the oil profit pie. The UK went to the US for help. President Eisenhower declared Mosaddegh a communist and gave the CIA a reason to overthrow him, which the CIA accomplished.[25] Mohammad Reza Shah Pahlavi stepped into the role of Shah of Iran reverted the country back to a monarchy and initiated a 20-year repressive regime. Protests in 1978 lead to his exile and the installation of an Islamic theocracy under the leadership of Ayatollah Khomeini. The next year Iraq invaded Iran and an eight-year war between the two nations finally ended after the UN Security Council Resolution 598 provided an adequate, yet temporary, solution that both sides could live with. This war during the JUSTICE time is an indication of deep-seeded and complicated issues of western interference in these oil rich states.

While the Soviet Union fell along with their state-run oil company, the Middle East, lands that had been suffering under colonialization and corporate greed, began to fight back. Between Iran fighting back the Iraq invasion, and the formation of the militant organization Al-Qaeda (1988), US representative Charlie Wilson secretly funded the Afghan mujahideen (1980–1987) fighting the Soviets in the Afghan-Soviet War (1979–1989). The Mujahideen evolved into the Taliban, while Al-Qaeda evolved into a terrorist organization that began attacking the US in 1993.

In the 1980s, fighting between Israel and the Palestinian Liberation Organization flared. Resorting to violence, bombs thrown over walls, insurrections and a mounting discord in the region, the Palestinian led Intifada occurred in 1987, an escalation of the violence in the region. Israel at the time did not recognize the PLO as a legitimate organization. Hezbollah and Hamas, underground Islamic groups supporting the Palestinian cause, were formed in response to the rising tensions in the region between the US backed Israel and the Muslim population that had occupied the territory for centuries.

25. Stephen Kinzer, *Overthrow.*

By the time the JUSTICE time arrived, the Middle East had largely installed oppressive regimes of their own, supported by or created in reaction
to western organizations and fiscally dependent on oil from OPEC. The after-effects of colonization and western intervention in the Middle East is a
cauldron of unrest ready to bubble over during REFORM.

REFORM: Collapse and/or Awakening

Between JUSTICE and REFORM, the Middle East erupted in mass demonstrations and war. The Arab Spring (2011) destabilized established regimes
and invited chaos or military order. Constant conflict in Gaza and the West
Bank, civil war in Syria, famines, droughts, and the installation of new and
younger leaders, has led to a region in constant flux. Bombs and terror, a
constant reminder of unrest, are becoming a way of life for many as people
struggle just to survive.

In the REFORM stage a thousand years prior, King Solomon built a temple
and maintained a stronghold on the nation after his father, King David built
a nation during the POWER time. Similarly, Israel, in a continuous state of unrest and attack, has maintained a dominant presence through support from
its allies—US and UK. However, just as the REFORM time peaked, Solomon
died, and his sons divided the kingdom in two: Israel and Jordan. Many favor
the proposal of a two-state solution, Palestine and Israel as separate states—
not unlike the division of Judea in 931 BCE. In 2026, as the REFORM time
kicks in, if history is precedent, an uptick in the violence and intensity of the
situation may force a similar two-state solution.

The US and the UK may find themselves in situations where domestic
issues take precedence and issues of foreign interference may fall in the list
of priorities. Without adequate support and protection, both countries may
leave Israel in a difficult situation where compromise with Palestine is the
only way out.

When we use the myth of Hades and Persephone as a barometer, Hades
is the plutocrat, the oil baron, the weapons manufacturer, the profiteer in
the long war between Israel and the Islamic states. Persephone is the people
on both sides of the border—both the Palestinians who were dismissed as
insignificant when Israel became a state after WWII and the Jewish people
who fled anti-Semitic regimes throughout the world to what they hoped

was a safe haven. Zeus, who arrogantly gave his blessings on this endeavor, is both Sykes and Picot and all the bureaucrats who thought it was a good idea to carve up the Middle East in patterns that dismissed the culture and religions of the people. Demeter is weeping as war destroys farmland, food sources such as heirloom olive trees, and the environment. As the Zeuses and Hades of the world destroy the environment, dismiss the needs of the people, and carelessly accrue great wealth, the Persephones, with the help of Mother Earth, are rising.

People in Israel are demonstrating against President Netanyahu's government reforms that give less not more power to the people. Veteran-led demonstrations in Tel Aviv involving over 130,000 people, led by the grassroots organization "Brothers and Sisters in Arms," are calling out to protect Israel's democracy.

On Oct 7, 2023, Hamas attacked Israel and took hostages inciting war. This runs parallel to the Nika riots that also started a few years too soon. When revolts break out before Pluto moves out-of-bounds, they are almost always quashed with great violence. Netanyahu is acting similar to Justinian who corralled and killed everyone involved, including innocent bystanders.

The parallel dries up there. With Iran and Hezbollah inciting even more violence and the involvement of other countries including Lebanon, the situation seems to be spiraling out of control. It is unlikely that Netanyahu will reform in the way that Justinian did, nor does he have the power to control the entire region, as was the case with the Byzantine Empire. Netanyahu, like Putin, will probably be ousted as Pluto moves out-of-bounds.

Most likely, the Middle East is headed for implosion. Like in 1177 BCE, climate change, invasions, and trade agreements gone bad, led to the perfect storm. After the collapse of 1177 BCE, those with the capacity to adapt formed new societies that rose in the footprint of the Egyptian and Hittite Empires. Interestingly, that collapse was focused in the Levant in the city of Ugarit, along the Mediterranean coast of modern day Syria. This again could be the focal point of collapse and renewal.

It was the Jewish tribes and other itinerant groups that survived that collapse. In the absence of empire, these nomadic peoples moved into Judea and settled. Today, in Israel, the agreements established in kibbutzim and deep ancestral wisdom from thousands of years of diasporas, inhabiting both the land and the people can serve to support the survival of a way of life that is both honoring the land and peaceful. The people in Gaza and the West Bank, the Palestinians, who today are mostly practicing Muslims, but whose roots run through the same soil as the Jewish people living in Israel, may find refuge as well.

There is the chance for awakening in all places in the world. The destruction of violent leaders and the culling of overwhelming forces from superpowers can support a return to a more tribal and natural way of life. As the countries that are funding the unrest from afar pull resources away, the implosion could possibly lead to an enlightened way of living. Islam began as a religion during a VISION time. Its roots run deep. However, certain extremist groups have turned Islam into an oppressive, misogynistic dogma, that was not part of those roots. In the early centuries, women were educated and influential. Afterall, it was a Muslim woman who founded the first university in Baghdad. But now, patriarchy has infiltrated this religion. This will not stand when Persephone rises. She may rise with a fierceness never seen before as people rise up with unexpected success.

Europe

VISION

In Europe, in the mid-1800s nation-states were restructured through war and commerce. When Napoleon's French Empire fell towards the end of the prior cycle, European nations gathered to sign the Congress of Vienna (1815), a peace plan that quickly led to conflict. The regions of what is today Germany, Austria, and Italy were separated into smaller states. Through a series of conquests, the German Empire was founded (1871) under the leadership of the king-appointed Prussian minister-president, Otto von Bismarck. At the same time on the Italian peninsula, conflicts arising after the Congress of Vienna eventually led to the unification of Italian principalities into the Kingdom of Italy, established in 1861 and fully formed by 1871. France reorganized into the Third Republic (1870) under Napoleon III, the original Bonaparte's nephew. Spain coalesced into a new government, a parliamentary constitutional monarchy, in 1874. The Austro-Hungarian Empire was founded in 1867.

In England, Queen Victoria, a Zeus-like character in this drama, deep in mourning for her beloved Albert who had died in 1858, began to don her famous black dresses, while being crowned Empress of India (1871). The Industrial Revolution, by then in full swing, was particularly beneficial to the British economy and particularly disastrous for workers and the environment. Benjamin Disraeli, a gifted orator of the conservative party, inspired English investors to back the digging of the Suez Canal, a move that greatly enhanced trade, cut costs on goods from India and China (tea, tobacco, and textiles) and contributed to the bankruptcy and fall of the Ottoman Empire. Disraeli's rise from middle-class novelist to Prime Minister (1868), in addition to being Jewish in a country where swearing on the Christian bible was still a requirement of parliament, suggests a change in the tide in England. The East India Company dissolved into the British government in a subtle yet significant transfer of power that empowered Britain to further colonize parts of Africa, install the British Raj, and undermine the Ottoman Empire. As the saying goes, "The Sun never set on the British Empire."

POWER

After the VISION time, European countries continued to colonize and interfere in countries in Asia, the Middle East, and Africa. Through corporate investments, invasions and military coups, England, France, and Belgium used their accumulated wealth and power to undermine poorer governments. Diamond mining, coal mining, and oil, Pluto dominions, became the commodities that increased the wealth of northern nations to the vast detriment of the ransacked countries, like the Congo, South Africa, and Namibia. When revolutionaries in Russia gathered enough clout to take over the monarchy, the European monarchies, many descended from Queen Victoria, initiated WWI in fear of losing their power. To add insult to injury, in the aftermath of WWI, the vanquished were penalized and devastated by the victors. Germany and Poland suffered a depression that led to cheap available labor on mineral-rich lands. Plutocrats, in the form of corporate tycoons from Ford Motor Company, IBM, and the Harriman Brothers, invested in these lands and the political party that was friendly to Western intervention, the Nazis. Through these and other investments, including IG Farben, Germany rebuilt. Volkswagen vehicles and Luftwaffe aircraft with

Rolls Royce engines accumulated as bitterness toward England and France grew. After centuries of fighting, redrawing borders, language and religious barriers, Europe erupted into a war that drew in the entire world. Like an atomic weapon that continued a chain reaction of battles, genocides, and horror, the war ended when the new superpower on the block actually deployed an atomic weapon.

Devastated and ruined, most of Europe lay in pieces. This implosion and explosion allowed for a new way. Out of ashes rises the Phoenix. In addition to the creation of the World Bank, the IMF, and the UN, the US gifted Europe the European Recovery Act, also known as the Marshall Plan. In a move unlike any other in history, the US invested in Europe, giving money to all of the European nations—the victors, the vanquished, and the neutral. This profound political machination, while not perfect, allowed Europe to rebuild and form what eventually became the European Union. Winston Churchill, two years after the war, gave a speech suggesting the formation of just such a union. Other diplomats followed suit.

JUSTICE

Between POWER and JUSTICE, Europe rebuilt and took steps toward unity. During the JUSTICE time, the idea of a common European currency gained popularity. The Single European Act (1986) was signed by twelve European countries, establishing open borders, a unique parliament, a new form of currency and its own flag.

During JUSTICE, Germany turned a corner. The Berlin Wall came down and the burden of living on the division point of US capitalism and democracy and Soviet Union communism, came to an end. A few years later, East Germany joined West Germany in the budding European Union.

During the 1980s, Margaret Thatcher was Prime Minister of England, a conservative, monarchist, quick to declare war on the Falkland Islands, and like the US President, Ronald Reagan, was a preacher of pick-yourself-up-by-the-bootstraps thinking. Welfare suffered and unemployment rose. Meanwhile, Princess Diana and her boys captivated the attention of the nation and much of the world.

REFORM: Paradigm Shift & Awakening

The European Union is in an interesting spot going into the REFORM time. This cycle began with England and France as superpowers; Germany with an abundance of visionaries; and Spain, Italy, and Austria forming new governments. During POWER, war destroyed Europe. During JUSTICE, the individual countries of the European landscape with a history of fighting and infighting since the Roman Empire fell, formed a union. While divisions between countries and within countries persist, perhaps below the surface, the EU forming during the JUSTICE time supports the opportunity for Europe to lead the world in awakening. Laying to rest thousands of years of history of resentments, language differences, cultural differences, and beliefs, is a sign that Europe, even if just to support economic viability, is able to adapt—maybe be the most able to adapt of anywhere in the world. In addition, the lack of Pluto-ruled commodities, in particular oil, pushes Europe to forge a path forward for alternative energy and gives Persephone an easier rise.

Germans had an especially important role to play in this cycle. The ideas of communism took root in Germany during VISION. WWII started in Germanic Austria during POWER. The Berlin Wall came down without violence in the German Democratic Republic during JUSTICE. Thus Germany will likely be a focal point in the upcoming REFORM time. The change in Germany, regardless of how much power they had over the situation, is a reflection that the German people can move toward the non-violent demonstration and awakening potentials of the future.

In 2016, England chose to separate from the European Union, which makes sense in light of this cycle. The British Empire started off the current cycle as the great colonizers of the world. They managed to move through WWI and WWII with much less damage than the rest of the continent. They have aligned with the US repeatedly. During the JUSTICE time, the prime minister and the US president were so aligned in ideology that those years have come to be known as the Reagan-Thatcher years. Instead of taking down walls and crying for justice, those two built walls, engaged in more autocratic leadership than their positions warranted and entrenched their countries into policies that harmed the working and middle classes. It seems natural that England go its own way during REFORM with its unique path, more likely to suffer collapse before following redemption.

Africa

It seems unfair for me to dismiss this great continent altogether, while at the same time impossible to do it justice. By the time this cycle began, the slave trade had been terrorizing African citizens for centuries. The last ship arrived and left in 1860. As it might seem that this would be a good thing, it was the beginning of the colonization of Africa. Still a collection of small individual tribes, the British invasion began in South Africa to protect the ports for its long voyages around the cape, in 1795.

In 1867, African farmers discovered diamonds, enhancing the lure of this continent. Plutocrats from Europe poured in, notably Cecil John Rhodes. French, Dutch, and British miners followed. In 1885, a conference in Berlin included fourteen European nations who took it upon themselves to divide up Africa. Most infamously, the Belgian Congo suffered under the ruthless dictatorship of Leopold II (r. 1865–1909), who established the land as his private colony and enslaved the local population to produce ivory and rubber.

WWII extended the reach of European nations into Africa, particularly northern Africa. Ethiopia witnessed the death of over 80,000 civilians and the war plunged the Belgian-occupied colony of Ruanda-Urundi into famine. In South Africa, the government institutionalized racism with a series of regulations that formed apartheid starting in the late 1940s. At the end of the war, the process of decolonization began under pressure from the US and the USSR, who wanted to be the main bullies on the block, under pressure from nationalists within the African countries and because Europe was broke after the war and couldn't afford the maintenance. The process of decolonization took up the entire JUSTICE time, with African nations fighting for their freedom and independence against European colonizers.

During JUSTICE, Namibia fought its way to independence from apartheid South Africa in March 1990, the same year that Nelson Mandela walked out of prison. In 1994, South Africa became the last African nation to throw off its colonial shackles, with the election of Mandela, the first Black president.

European colonists laid siege to Africa for centuries in different ways under different guises. As the rest of the world began to depart after the POWER time and finally left at the JUSTICE time, Africa suffered drought, famine, pandemic, and economic depressions. However, its journey particularly mirrors Persephone's. Colonization that began precisely during the

VISION time, supported by the discovery of something particularly Plutonic (diamonds), led to massive abductions up to and through the POWER time, when a gradual intervention led to independence. As we enter the REFORM time, Africa, as witnessed during the COVID-19 pandemic[26] may be more versatile, adaptable, and able to withstand the challenges of collapse and rise to the movement of redemption. While none of my friends are thinking of Africa as a place to escape US political mayhem, I think we might be very surprised at how well many nations in this birthplace continent thrive as other governments and economies tumble. On the other hand, climate change, the twist in all plans and predictions, may hit Africa hard. Food shortages, already a huge problem, may continue until the new paradigm offers solutions for water and food that are currently unavailable.

Climate Change as Catalyst

This brings me to the final point, the game changer of all game changers, the wrench of all wrenches: climate change. This is the great unifier and the great catalyst. There is no escape from the effects of greenhouse gases out of control. Weather patterns are changing at an alarming rate. Ice caps are melting. Fires are raging. Hurricanes are becoming more intense and less predictable. Climate refugees are overwhelming states and countries. In 2019, Greece, a land known for its idyllic beaches and tourist havens, experienced an unmanageable population growth from Syrian refugees, after climate change and civil war pushed desperate people into overcrowded rafts. A wave of immigrant fear is moving through Europe and the US as a result.

While the Earth's climate has changed during several of the cycles of the past 4,000 years, none have had anything to do with human-made causes. And while some of the current changes may be due to a natural ebb and flow of climate behavior, there is clear scientifically gathered evidence that greenhouse gases are contributing greatly to the rise in temperatures and the changing weather patterns throughout the world.[27]

This is an unprecedented crisis. How like Pluto to send us such a parting gift as it moves out-of-bounds for the final time. The reformations of the

---

26. Africa had the lowest rates of infection and the lowest death rates of COVID-19. Soy, "Coronavirus in Africa."
27. NASA JPL: "Consensus: 97% of climate scientists agree."

past occurred in times when nations lived independently with clear borders, economies, and laws. Today, all economies are intertwined, borders are malleable, and international law is actually a thing. We live in a time of technology unlike any other. We are separated by nanoseconds instead of months. We can transfer funds at any time of day in a matter of seconds. We can reach millions worldwide with one post that takes a minute to write. All this is radically new.

While there may or may not be such a thing as a world order, there is world civilization. Music, thoughts, money, and germs spread between countries with ease. Between international corporations, international agreements and international communication systems, country boundaries are merely agreements from a loosely based idea of reality that could change in a heartbeat. Still operating in the old mindset of nationalism and patriotism, countries may find themselves unable to adapt and leading to collapse as the likely outcome. While the US was founded by immigrants and has prided itself on being a melting pot, anti-immigrant sentiment can potentially entrench the country in a series of useless battles, whether in the courts, the government, or on actual battlefields. This lack of understanding of the current market-state of the world—that corporate power is the underpinning of rulership throughout the world—may set the US back and send it into collapse as environmental disasters and climate change issues increase. Without the ability to adapt, US citizens' comfort-driven lives cling to destructive practices of single-use plastics, toxic chemicals to keep beneficial plants out of yards, and pharmaceuticals to mitigate symptoms of illnesses meant to help us adapt. In this world, collapse is more than likely. However, already in place are state governments with readily available power structures to pick up where a federal collapse leaves off. The power of individual states to rectify climate change will likely increase.

Each cycle begins with both the Persephones with their wise visions and the Hades with their need for power. Indigenous people throughout the world stand in solidarity protecting almost 80% of the livable land left.[28] They are the heart of the organism we call humanity. While the Hades were trampling tribal settlements on four continents, the indigenous peoples blended sacred earth practices with non-violent resistance and, in many cases, fought

---

28. Johnson and Wilkinson, 19.

back valiantly. Leaders like the Apache warrior Geronimo, the Lakota Chief Sitting Bull, the Lakota warrior and statesman Red Cloud, and the sacred hero Crazy Horse, set the stage for resistance to Manifest Destiny and the ensuing Homestead Act of 1862, an act that gave white settlers rights to native lands, a bill that managed to pass in the midst of civil war. The white man's hubris met with the deep integrity of the indigenous tribes that, throughout this cycle, protected the water and the land while their people suffered.

In my hometown, the occupied lands of the Squaxin and Nisqually Nations, the Chief of the Nisqually tribe, Chief Leschi, tried to negotiate land agreements with the appointed governor of the Washington Territory, Isaac Stevens.[29] The resulting Medicine Creek Treaty of 1854 was no treaty. It was a non-negotiable dictation of terms. Like the Underworld stolen from the Titans and given to Pluto, Governor Stevens took away the life and lands of the Nisqually, Squaxin, Chehalis, Suquamish, Duwamish, and Puyallup tribes. Forcibly removed the tribes to islands so that white men could ravage the forest, the Nisqually fought back. In retaliation, Chief Leschi was unjustly hanged in February of 1858.[30] By 1859, white settlers had exiled the native population onto small pockets of land and massacred those who remained. Today, sovereign First People's nations are standing between the corporate takeover of the Columbia River and the needs of millions of people to access natural energy and drinkable water itself. In North Dakota, tribal members are joined by environmental activists as they stand firm against the Dakota pipeline, protecting not just their land but the available drinking water of much of the state. In a few instances, native tribes are suing the government for retrieval of their lands and winning, as is the case with Maine in 1980.

During VISION, all over the world, the advent of industry—fourdriniers for paper, dynamite for mining, drills for oil, Bessemer process for steel—turned the world, especially the US, crazy for progress. The value of progress above tradition, greed above justice, capitalism above fair trade, and deceit above honest living took human habitat to war. Breathable air and drinkable water, abundant prior to 1860, had no value in Robber Baron politics.

Over the last 150 years, we have degraded our environment. Like frogs in a pot of water coming to boil, we lack awareness of how short our breath has be-

---

29. Caldbick, "Leschi (1808–1858), Part 1,"
30. Chief Leschi was exonerated in 2004 by a historical court.

come. Anti-anxiety medication masks the effects of the environmental factors creating the anxiety. Without deep and natural breaths, our immune and nervous systems go on high alert. Waiting painfully in the wings are the guardians of our livable planet. During REFORM, we are joined, and they are redeemed.

One perfect storm in one town could topple systems on the other side of the world. While the challenge of climate change for humans living on this planet is universal and unifying, it is also a possible trigger for each potential future. One unprecedented storm could destroy systems in place for food, transport, and water to millions—triggering *collapse*. One inch of rising water and centuries-old cities are wiped out for good. One earthquake in an already unstable oppressive dictatorship could trigger violent uprisings where people are both desperate and angry, both hungry and with nothing to lose. One extra storm and *revolution* erupts.

With water, food, and housing on the line, more people awaken to the needs of others, and with everything they have, join *non-violent resistors* to change environmentally destructive corporate policies and lack of government oversight.

In places where climate change is already a stark reality and where a livable environment still exists, where citizens are already involved and working towards solutions, a scientific revolution is likely to lead to a *paradigm shift*. With climate change acting as an agent of change, pushing current theories beyond their limits, with anomalies showing up in rapid and undeniable succession, millions of brilliant minds open through the portal of multiple invention, and in the time it takes to change a tire, the new paradigm presents itself.

And finally, no matter where you live or what you are doing, no matter how desperate or depressed, a wave of *awakening* begins within the soul of humanity, sweeps through its heart, and does not stop until it reaches the outermost tips of its limbs. It is the most unexpected gift of all. When indigenous peoples and seers and healers hear the calling, the beat will sound almost normal until its pervasiveness reveals a new consciousness. We might not even notice it while it is happening until everything and nothing will be different at the same time.

Chapter 16:
What Can We Do?

Celebrate

The energy of celebration, bringing in collective joy, and lightening up is essential for the coming revolution. The serious desire to fight, while seductive, is the way some revolutions will happen, but the more we open to the field of celebration as we demonstrate, share space, and create the future, the more likely we are to attain our vision.

The belief in sacrifice, joyless devotion to work, and the toil of service is part of the past paradigm. The less time we spend focused on these trains of thought, the closer we will be to the new ways.

Joyful celebration is different than the self-centered pursuit of pleasure that much celebration has come to mean, particularly in the US. Parties that celebrate substance abuse, the pursuit of sexual gratification, and music that enhances desire are not the kinds of celebrations that will support the new wave. The new wave is supported by real, honest conversations that stimulate inspiration, trigger possibilities, and open us to a collective experience of joy. Dancing, singing, and shared art collaborations provide a framework for new understandings and an awakening into the webs of support that honor all people and animals and plants and minerals.

Create

The energy of creativity automatically taps us into the new web--even if the creativity isn't "professional" or "good" or "polished"—in fact, especially if it isn't professional, good, or polished—the act of making something is about tapping into a wellspring of creation. It is about going back to Gaia, the manifestation of Earth as a planet of abundant creative presence, and recognizing within each of us the gift and joy that creativity brings. Daring to sit at an easel, a blank page, or with an instrument, poised for what wants to move through, is a radical act that connects us to a source beyond the corrupted planes of energy here now.

269

Love

Dare to share your heart with others. Dare to engage in consensual relationships that feel nurturing and supportive. A radical act is the act of stepping out of our comfort zones to allow another person into the sacred and screwed-up parts of ourselves. Let them in and let them out. Personal relationships have the chance to push us into increased awareness if we can open up to the messages they present to us.

Look Away from Fear

Wherever and however fear arises, recognize it, call it by name and remove your sight from it. Walk away. That vibration has no value. Ever. Motivation to express and transform never comes from fear. True reformation is the fearless opening to a possibility that is not yet seen—where fear has not set up shop. Information, data points on the web, can alter our direction more effectively when shared with respect, depth of knowledge and without fear. Watch your desire to use fear to make change. This will work less and less effectively as we move into the new times.

Use Doubt as a Tool for Recognizing the Future

When in doubt, notice what is doubtful and instead of being overcome and paralyzed, realize that this is the calling. Doubt is an indicator of a vision whose time is about to come. Our minds have not quite accepted the truth. Be able to recognize doubt as a mental tool of indication, rather than as an emotional blockage to manifestation.

Simplify your Life

Clear the clutter. Lighten your load. Take out the trash. Leave behind toxic relationships. Stop doing busy work for no reason. Stop accumulating stuff. Pare down. Cancel subscriptions. Cut down on technology usage and screen time. Take regular daily breaks to breathe and drink water. Cultivate simple pleasures, like cooking and poetry, knitting, and games.

Restructure your Organization.

The current organizational structures are a false pyramid scheme. Capitalism is based on the pyramids, and the pyramids were the preferred building constructions of the early phase of this precessional cycle, going back 5,000 to 10,000 years ago. The establishment of this geometry and its lack of depth, integrity, and truth arose out of consciousness of wounding, lack of vision, and nearsightedness.

Organizations that last will learn how to reorganize into more perfectly aligned geometric configurations. Throughout our homes and businesses, we will see how the pyramid has dominated the geometric structures and move this geometry into other shapes, such as octahedrons—two pyramids back-to-back, where the top and bottom mirror and keep each other in check with equal power. Why stop at the octahedron?

More complex organizational structures will be useful for some, like the icosahedron (20 faces of triangles with 12 points or 12 positions of equal power) or the dodecahedron (12 faces of pentagons making 20 points/positions of equal power). Using geometry to establish organization will enhance how we live on the planet. Using the Golden Ratio for buildings to be in alignment with how humans experience joy and beauty will be beneficial and part of the new wave.

Non-violent Resistance

During this cycle, non-violent activism has been effective for the first time in centuries. Take for instance, the Singing Revolution. It is time for us to sing, dance, and meditate in the streets. Creative, peaceful activism is the way forward. Gather in small groups or large groups. Gather for a cause that speaks to your heart. Gather because gathering builds joy and helps us release the illusion of separation.

Heightened Synchronicities

Pay attention to synchronicities. Notice the resonance and the YES! that lives within them. Follow that feeling. Each synchronicity is the world breathing YES into your life, supporting your strength to continue on your path and bring your true work alive.

Tend to Nature, Land, Air, and Water

Educate yourself and listen to those who are educated about household toxins and responsibly get rid of them. Get better at reducing your own carbon footprint. Stop accumulating garbage. Support companies that reuse. Pay attention to your purchases—the social and environmental consciousness of the company that produces, distributes and sells what you are buying. Take on 21-day practices to accumulate 0 garbage, or use less water, or drive less, or travel less. Get involved with others working to protect habitats. Write letters, make phone calls, demonstrate, sign petitions, and attend town halls. This is not a movement with leaders. This is up to us.

Conclusion

As triggers for collapse take down institutions that have been in decay for decades, and revolutions overthrow systems and leaders that have continued to oppress and violate people and nature, and benevolent rulers rise into leadership positions, as non-violent resistance instigates change, as a scientific paradigm shift brings forth new inventions and practices, the healing of thousands of years of harms, of the very nature of duality itself, of humanity's need to make others into villains, takes place. The very desire for revenge or conquering changes from within our psyches. In just recent years, men are freer to cry, and women are freer to move into power—and out beyond the duality of masculine and feminine—a wave of non-binary language and perception upsets the entire apple cart. From this place, reparations for people of color, the return of lands to native peoples, and the empowerment of women and the LBGTQIA community lead to a healing from which true awakening is possible.

Our current cycle began with two camps of visionaries: those who advocated for shared resources, communal property, and cooperation and those who advocated for survival of the fittest, competitive markets, and individual freedom. Both camps attempted to leave monarchies and dictatorships behind. The fears of Karl Marx about democracy have come to pass. Free markets are making the rich richer and the poor poorer, destroying the environment and leading to a homeless crisis in the Western world. The fears of communism and the overreach of government have also come to pass in the violent oppression of the communist government of China over its people, and laws that force sterilization, compel work, and limit free speech.

During WWII (POWER), the atrocities committed were unlike any wrongs in history. Atomic bombs, genocide, and war, all at the hands of a small group of people acting like Hades (Pluto), who extended their power through new forms of civilization—late-stage capitalism, communism, and capitalism-financed fascism. The last Pluto in extreme declination time forces us to look at what must be healed and go about the mysterious work of awakening.

There is a reason I believe this to be possible. It is not just naïve positivity. The Pluto cycle has borne witness to many just such radical transformations. No one saw the Christian movement coming. No one anticipated the Reformation or the creation of a country of refugees built on free speech. At least not most people. Not only is another time of paradigm shifting evolution about to happen, it is the last and the most condensed time of its occurrence. All kinds of things are possible at that time. It is a tipping point—a time of healing old wounds, rectifying old imbalances and rising into equality. It is a time of looking squarely at the evil and darkness in the underworld and with strength and courage accepting the challenge of compassion.

In the decades that I have been delving into Persephone's mythic and Pluto's astronomical journeys, I have had the great privilege of doing thousands of astrological readings, of hearing thousands of peoples' private dreams and struggles. I know the pain of so many who suffered during a pandemic of depression and despair, trying to hold onto a shred of hope as they tended to another year of tomato plants and seed gathering, in relationships and jobs that held no life for them any longer. Even then, the secret corner still existed in their minds. I think of all the other times in history when Pluto was just about to go out of bounds, and the despair and fear that pervaded. After centuries of crusaders sent to kill and steal, starving and tired from the Northern Isles to Jerusalem, villagers along the path grown so used to attack that the sword at the door was a touchstone as they walked out to gather eggs. Even for them, in the quiet corner of their minds was an end to the treacherous intrusions, that indeed did abruptly end in 1291. Even in our current landscape, when it seems the world has gone mad, I hear the dreams and visions of so many that I know, and I can feel awakening coming like deer before an earthquake and dolphins before a tidal wave.

From the west coast of Australia to the inlands of Costa Rica, I know of hundreds of people with available resources living on or looking for land to protect and make available for the new paradigm, a place where art and food grow together, where people live in harmony with the mess of life, where inclusiveness is woven into the landscape and into the struggle of simply living. I hear whispers of various Indigenous cultures forming new economies, of weather-changing devices, of sacred geometry dwellings that require no outsourced energy. I know lives dedicated to supporting people in transition—between homes, between relationships, between life and death and life, again. I know of gatherings created to celebrate wholeness, organizations fiercely determined to stay true to collective cooperation, yoga teachers standing on the front lines of resistance, and people with pasts filled with violence turning inward for peace. From my own place of privilege, I know that all over the world, people are secretly creating the new world—first in a quiet corner of their mind that becomes a quiet corner in their home that becomes their entire home and grows until it is visible to the next person and the next. I know that all these dreams and lives have outlived the patriarchal underpinning of plutocracy and are growing the roots of something undefinable and ineffable. Persephone's rise from the underworld and her courageous agreement to return is the very essence of the new world arising now.

APPENDICES

Appendix I:
How to Read the Sine Wave Charts

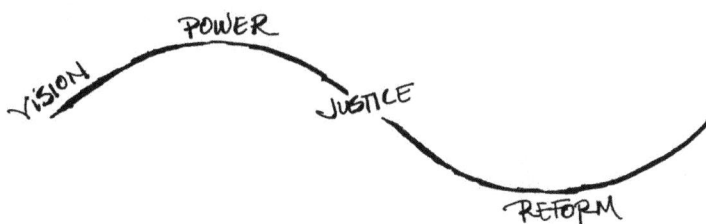

T hroughout the book, there are sine-wave graphs marked with people and events. Each sine wave represents one complete Pluto cycle. The hill crest represents the peak point of declination north, while the lowest point of the graph's valley depicts Pluto at the peak point of declination south. The date on the far left signifies the beginning of Pluto's placement at zero degrees of declination on the equatorial plane, while the middle date shows Pluto's second transit through zero degrees of declination.

Here is a chart of our current cycle. It began in 1863, peaked in extreme declination in 1945, hit the middle of the cycle in 1987, and will peak in extreme declination south in 2028.

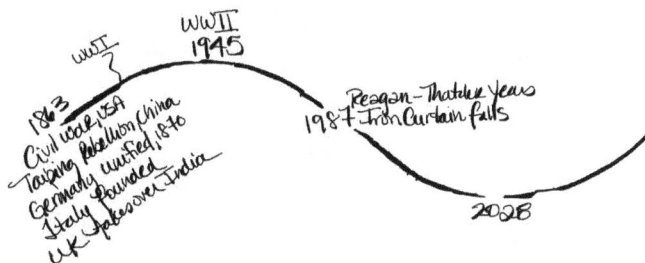

What follows are charts of all the cycles going back to 1808 BCE with the names of some of the most famous people and events, based on my own research, education in history, and contact with cultural influence about who or what has been historically labeled notable or worth recognizing years, decades, even centuries later. These charts are meant to assist with orienting time not as a linear, straightforward path, but rather as an undulating, pulsating, breathing path. If I could, I would make these charts three dimensional and show them spiraling: when we look at a spiral from the side, it appears as a sine wave. View a spiral from above, and it looks like a circle. A 3D spiral would be a more accurate representation of the Pluto cycle's existence through and effect on time, but for the purposes of this book, the 2D page will have to suffice.

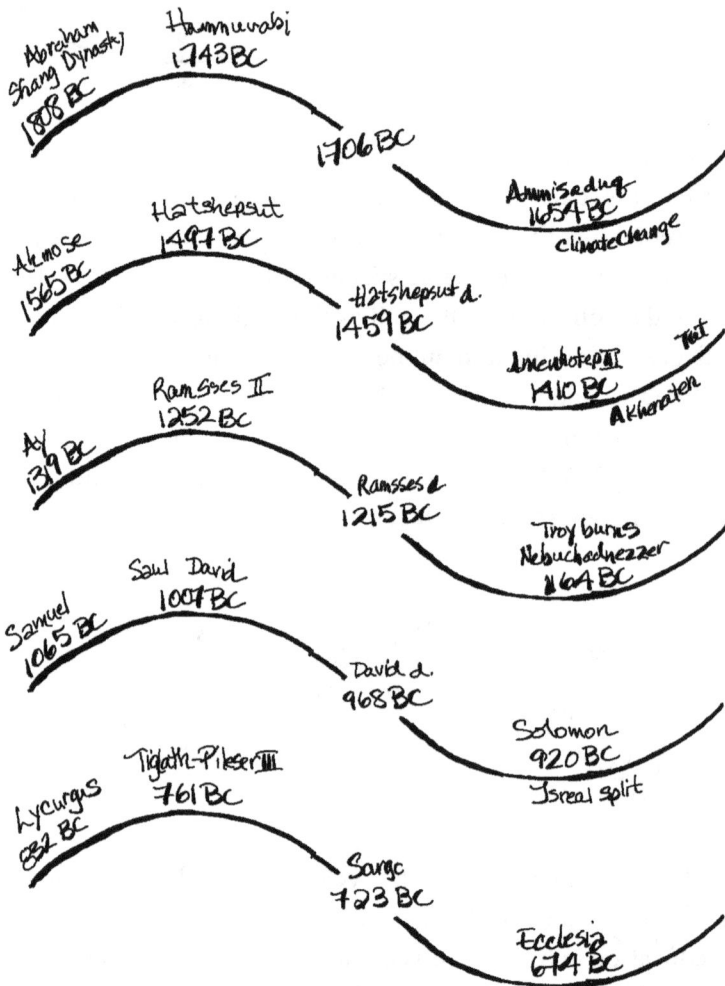

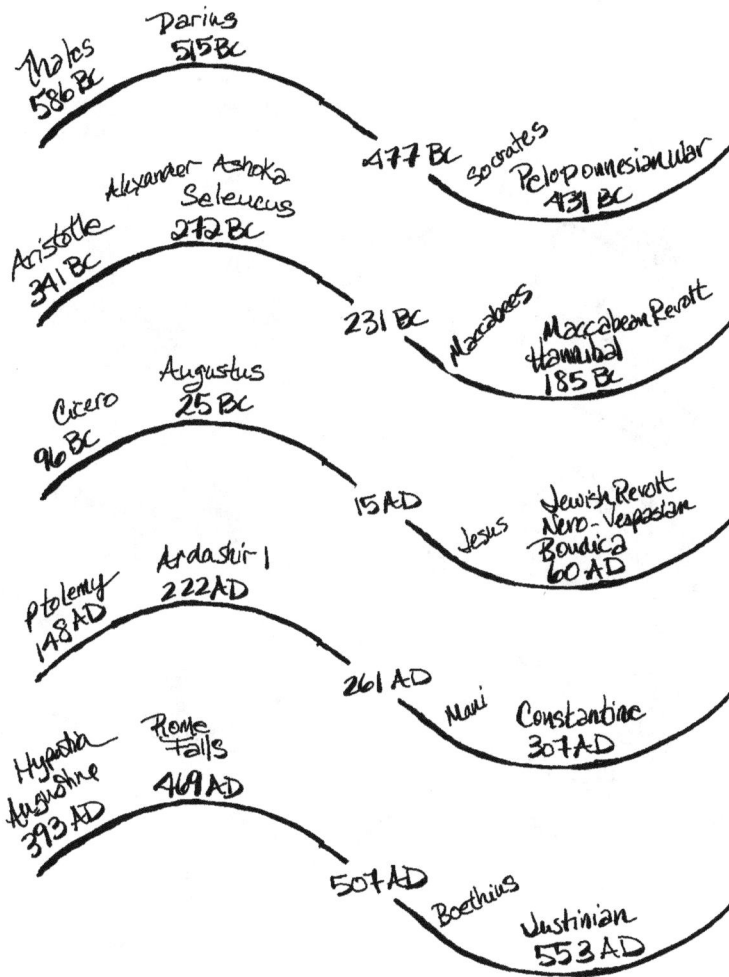

Thales
586 BC

Darius
515 BC

477 BC
Socrates
Peloponnesian War
431 BC

Aristotle
341 BC

Alexander Ashoka
Seleucus
272 BC

231 BC
Maccabees
Maccabean Revolt
Hannibal
185 BC

Cicero
96 BC

Augustus
25 BC

15 AD
Jesus
Jewish Revolt
Nero-Vespasian
Boudica
60 AD

Ptolemy
148 AD

Ardashir I
222 AD

261 AD
Mani
Constantine
307 AD

Hypatia
Augustine
393 AD

Rome
Falls
469 AD

507 AD
Boethius
Justinian
553 AD

281

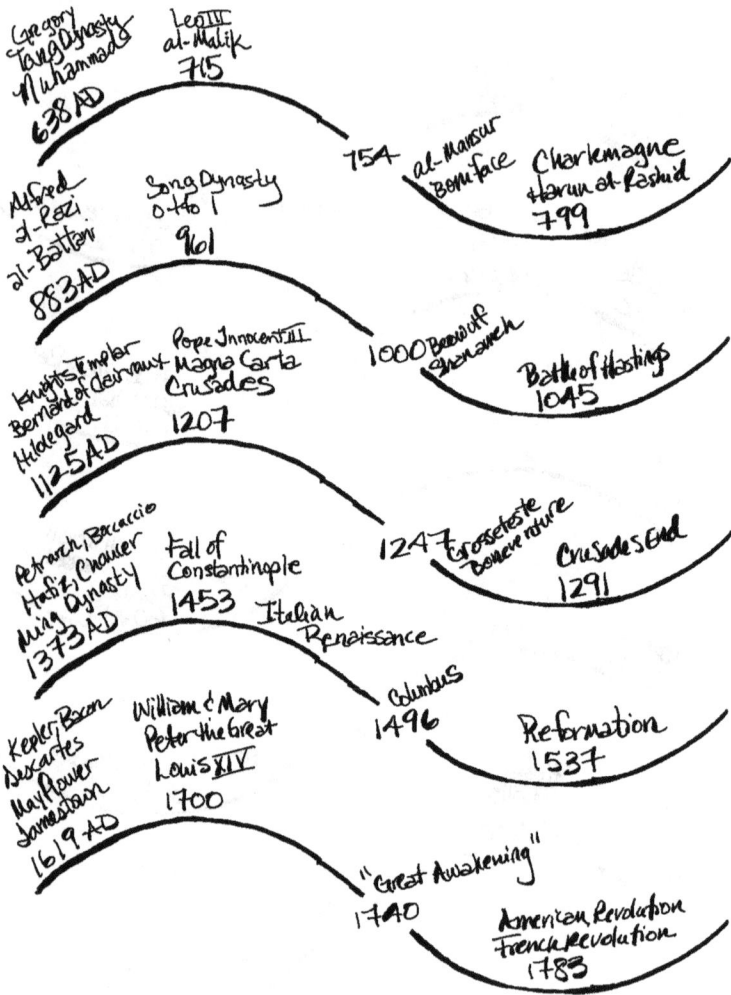

Gregory
Tang Dynasty
Muhammad
638 AD

Leo III
al-Malik
715

754 al-Mansur
Boniface

Charlemagne
Harun al-Rashid
799

Alfred
al-Rezi
al-Battani
883 AD

Song Dynasty
Otto I
961

1000 Beowulf
Grimswich

Battle of Hastings
1045

Knights Templar
Bernard of Clairvaux
Hildegard
1125 AD

Pope Innocent III
Magna Carta
Crusades
1207

1247 Grosseteste
Bonaventure

Crusades End
1291

Petrarch, Boccaccio
Hafiz, Chaucer
Ming Dynasty
1373 AD

Fall of
Constantinople
1453   Italian
Renaissance

Columbus
1496

Reformation
1537

Kepler, Bacon
Descartes
Mayflower
Jamestown
1619 AD

William & Mary
Peter the Great
Louis XIV
1700

"Great Awakening"
1740

American Revolution
French Revolution
1783

Appendix II:
Rulers & Revolutionaries

People who were declared emperor, king, queen or in some other way "ruler" of an empire while Pluto was at the peak of its journey in extreme declination north. Revolutions and independence declared when Pluto was at the peak of its journey in extreme declination south.

PEAK DATE	PLUTO OOB NORTH	PEAK DATE	PLUTO OOB SOUTH
1743–1742 BCE	(Hammurabi died c. 1750 BCE, seven years before peak.)	1654 BCE	1646 BCE. Ammisaduq, King of Babylon—made internal reforms, forgiving and freeing debt slaves
1497 BCE	1479 BCE. Hatshepsut, Queen of Egypt began her reign.	1410–1409 BCE	1391 BCE. Amenhotep III reign began. His reforms (10 years from peak)
1252 BCE	(1250 BCE traditional date of Trojan War) 1274 BCE – Battle of Kadesh (20 years off)	1165–1163 BCE	c. 1160 Nubia gains independence from Egypt.
1007–1006 BCE	1006 BCE **David** becomes King of Israel.	920-919 BCE	931 BCE. King Solomon died and Israel split in two: Israel and Judah.
761 BCE	753 Romulus founded Rome. 745 BCE. Tiglath-Pileser III becomes ruler of Assyria.	675–674 BCE	

516–514 BCE	522 BCE. Darius the Great becomes king of Persia. 510 BCE. Cleisthenes overthrows Hippias and begins the great culture of Ancient Greece. 509 BCE. Roman Republic founded.	431 BCE	431. **Pericles** deposed and then reinstated. Peloponnesian Wars. 430. Atomic theory postulated by Leucippus of Miletus.
272 BCE	268 BCE. **Ashoka Maurya** begins reign	185 BCE	171 BCE. Mithridates I crowned emperor
25–24 BCE	27 BCE. Octavian becomes **Augustus Caesar**. Rome changes from republic to empire. **Official birth of the Roman Empire.**	62–63 CE	62 CE. **Nero** has his wife killed. 64. 1st persecution of Christians 65. Gospel of Mark written.
222–223 CE	222 CE. Emperor **Severus Alexander** begins reign 223. **Ardashir I—**sole ruler of Persia	306–308 CE	306. **Constantine the Great.** Emperor of Rome.
468–469 CE	468. Vandals conquer Sicily. 476. **Fall of the Roman Empire.**	553–554 CE	527. Justinian I the Great becomes Byzantine emperor.
715 CE	715. **Charles Martel—**Frankish throne. 716. **King Ethelbad—**begins reign of Mercia (England).	799 CE	800. **Charlemagne** crowned by Pope Leo III. This marks the **beginning of the Holy Roman Empire.**

961 CE	962. **Otto I** crowned emperor of Holy Roman Empire. c. 960. **Song Dynasty** founded. Stays in power til 1279. c. 960. 1st paper money printed in China.	1045 CE	1044. **Gunpowder.** 1045. **Movable type printing.** 1042. **Edward the Confessor** becomes King of England.
1207 CE	1206. **Genghis Khan** declares himself supreme ruler. 1209. Franciscan order founded. 1209. **Otto IV** crowned Holy Roman Emperor. 1209. King John excommunicated—lays foundation for the Magna Carta (1215). 1209. University of Cambridge est.	1291 CE	1292. **Marco Polo** leaves China and travels the Silk Road. 1291. End of the Crusades. 1291. **Switzerland** founded. 1299. **Ottoman Empire founded. Osman I**—first ruler.
1453 – 1454 CE	1455. **Gutenberg prints the Bible.** 1453. Fall of Bordeaux ends 100 years War. 1453. **Fall of the Byzantine Empire.** Constantinople captured by the Ottomans. **Mehmet II**, the conquerer, takes over. 1456. Count Vlad of Transylvania begins reign.	1537 CE	1534. **King Henry VIII** breaks with Rome—declares himself Supreme Head of the English Church. 1533. **Ivan the Terrible**—assumes power at 3 years old. 1520–1566. Suleiman I—zenith of power of the Ottoman Empire. 1532. **Pizarro** conquers the Incas. 1530. Martin Luther writes the Lutheran position. 1534. Jesuit Order founded.

1700 CE	1696. **Peter the Great** becomes sole Tsar of Russia. 1688–1689. Glorious Revolution. **William III of Orange** becomes King of England. 1700–1703. Peak of King Louis XIV decadent ruler of France. 1701. Yale University est.	1783 – 1784 CE	1783. **Treaty of Paris** ends the American Revolutionary War. 1789. **The Storming of the Bastille** in France begins the French revolution.
1944 – 1945 CE	1945. US drops atomic bombs on Japan. 1945. End of WWII. 1945. **UN founded.** 1945. **World Bank and IMF founded.** 1946. Chinese Civil War-—intensification to full out war. 1943. **Chairman Mao** comes into power as Chairman of the Communist Party of China—soon to be the ruling party. 1945. Beginning of the **"Iron Curtain"** of communism. Increasing the power of Stalin.	2029--2030 CE	

Appendix III:
Definition of Terms

- f. = founded
- r. = reign
- p. = papacy/presidency

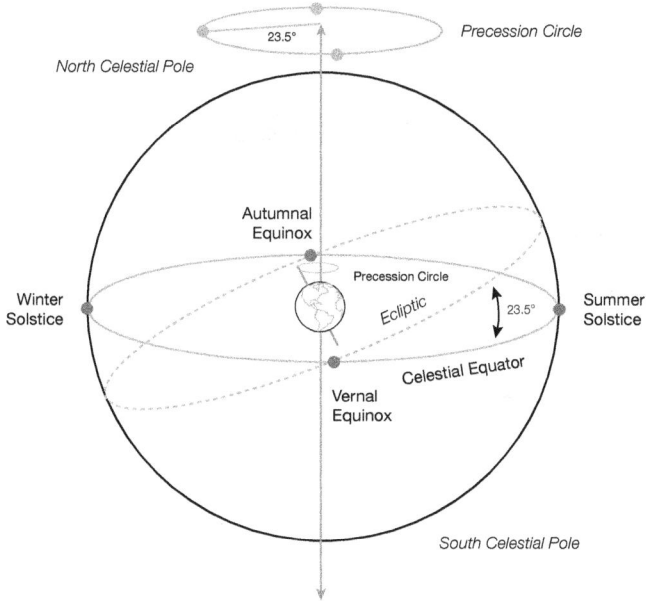

- OOB = Out-of-bounds = extreme declination
- Orbit: the path of a body around another body
- Ecliptic: the plane that the Earth revolves around the Sun in, the apparent path of the Sun around the Earth
- Equatorial plane (also called the celestial equator): formed by extending the Earth's equator into space.
- CEq = Celestial equator, the equatorial plane
- NCP = North Celestial Pole, the Earth's North Pole extended into space
- SCP = South Celestial Pole, the Earth's South Pole extended into space
- Latitude: the degree above or below the ecliptic
- Declination: the degree above or below the equatorial plane
- Inclination: the slant of a planet's orbit
- Eccentricity: the deviation of an orbit from being a perfect circle, elongation
- Ayanāṃśa: a Sanskrit term that refers to systems that account for the precession of the equinoxes.

Pluto's orbit is both eccentric, elongated (with a value of .2488), and inclined (slanted at 17.1°). Note that these 17° of inclination is related to the ecliptic.

- High Declination (Hidek): Declination between 21 and 23.44°
- Extreme Declination (Exdek or out-of-bounds, OOB): Declination over 23.44°

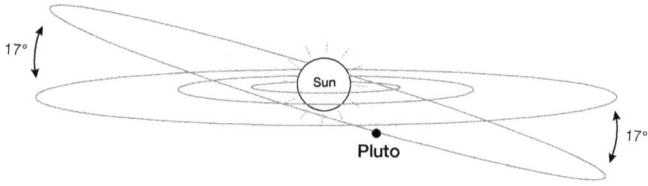

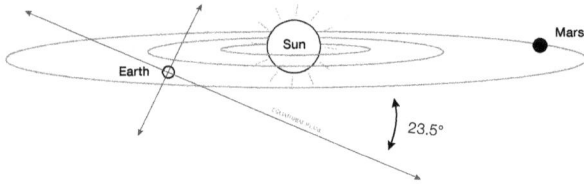

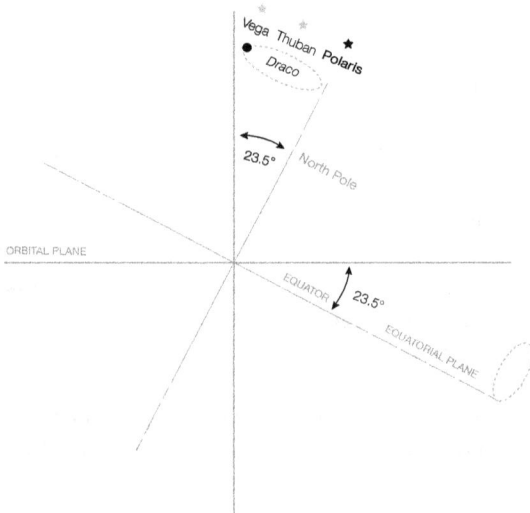

Appendix IV:
Understanding the Cycle Dynamics

T he planet we live on, Earth, travels in the orbital plane, neatly moving in a near-perfect circle, in a near-perfect plane with the other planets. The biggest planets, the gaseous ones, Jupiter, Saturn, Uranus, and Neptune, have the most circular orbits and most closely fit inside the discus.

However, Earth, like many of the planets, tilts. This tilt changes over time. Imagine a twirling toy top. A quick twist and the top both rotates and re-volves. When the top begins to slow down, it wobbles. That is like the Earth. One wobble currently takes roughly 26,000 years. Our north axis points to Polaris our pole star, but five thousand years ago, the pole star was Thuban. Currently, we tilt at 23.439°. This changing of the pole stars is due to the wob-ble and that wobble is called the Precession of the Equinoxes. Currently the Spring Equinox occurs when the Sun is at around 4° into the constellation of Pisces. As the tilt changes, the equinox point moves backwards through the constellations, so in another ~573 years, the Spring Equinox will take place at the end of the constellation Aquarius. Depending on the ayanāṃśa you use, the measurements (4° Pisces and approx. 573 years) will vary slightly.

If we extend the Earth's equator out into space, it will form an imaginary plane 23.439° off of the orbital plane.

As the Earth's tilt changes, it moves more and more into alignment with the 17° inclination of Pluto's orbit. To say it another way, Pluto's orbit and Earth's tilt are moving into alignment. Earth's equatorial plane (the Equator extended out into space) is moving into alignment by degree and direction with Pluto's inclination.

Planets as they move through space in relationship to the Earth's equato-rial plane is called declination.

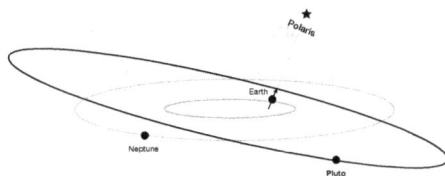

Appendix V:

The Cycle of Abraham, 1808–564 BCE

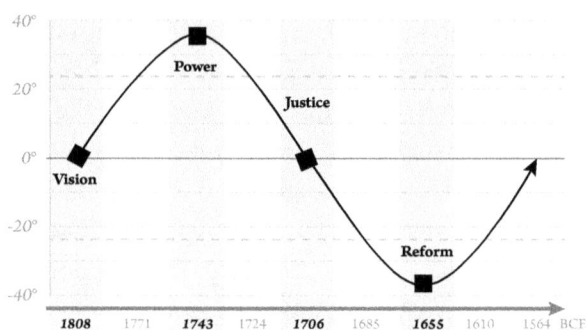

VISION   1812–1805 BCE

- Believed time of **ABRAHAM**, patriarch and founder of Judaism.

- Believed time of the scribing of the *Rig Veda* (c. 2000–1500 BCE),[1] India.[2] The Rig Veda was the first of the Vedas scribed and the Vedas were the first works of Hinduism to be written down.

- **SHANG DYNASTY** began (c. 1800), China. The Minoan temples were all constructed in the period from 1900–1450 BCE.[3]

- Around 1800 BCE in India, it is generally accepted that the Saraswati River dried up and mass migration to the banks of the Ganges ensued, with climate change being the likely culprit. Other theories include a massive earthquake or invading northerners. "In about 1750 BCE, town life on the Indus River ended. River mud then buried the remnants of the towns so deeply that historians knew nothing of the Indus people till the 1900s, when archaeologists found the ruins."[4]

POWER   1771–1723 BCE   Peak: 1743–42 BCE

- **HAMMURABI** (r. 1792–1750 BCE), King of Babylon. *Hammurabi's code* chiseled into stone c. 1772 BCE

- Babylon began to decline after Hammurabi died (1750 BCE).

- 1766 BCE is the traditional date for the founding of **SHANG DYNASTY**.[5]

- The *Hyksos*, a Semitic people from north of Palestine, invaded Egypt (c. 1730 BCE) and established their empire that extended from Greece through the Aegean and into Egypt, also known as Canaan.[6]

JUSTICE   **1707–1704 bce**

- c. 1700 beginning of Bronze Age in China

REFORM   **1685–1610 bce**   Peak: **1654 bce**

- Jacob died. (1669 bce)
- Joseph died. (1615 bce)
- Ammisaduq, King of Babylon, (r. 1646–1626 bce) instituted internal reforms, forgave debt, and freed debt-slaves.[7]
- Sumsuditana (r. 1625–1595) King of Babylon, "ruled for 30 years in relative peace."[8]
- 1627 bce. The volcano, Thera, on the island of Santorini erupted and initiated climate shifts leading to droughts and crop shortages as far away as China.[9]

The Cycle of Ahmose, 1564–1322 BCE

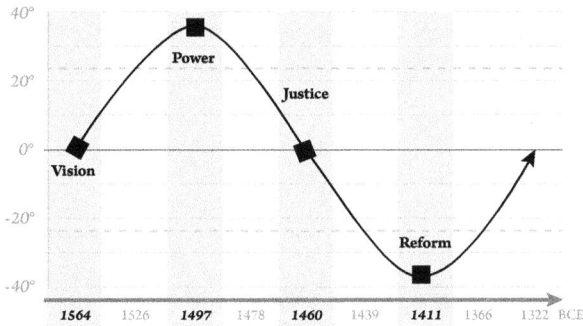

VISION   **1568–1561 bce**

- Beginning of 18th Dynasty in Egypt, the New Kingdom, (1567–1292 bce).

POWER   **1526–1478 bce**   Peak: **1497 bce**

- Thutmose I (r. 1506–1493 bce)
- Thutmose II (r. 1493–1479 bce)
- Hatshepsut (r. 1493–1479 bce) as sister and wife of Thutmose II, r. 1479–1458 bce as solo ruler)
- Egypt conquered Nubia.

JUSTICE   1460–1458 BCE

- **Hatshepsut** died 1458 BCE after being sole ruler for 21 years. **Thutmose III**, her son, took over.

REFORM   1439–1366 BCE   Peak: 1410–9 BCE

- 1430 BCE: *Assuwa* (Mycenaean, Greece) rebellion against the *Hittites*.
- **Amenhotep III**: 1391–1353 BCE.
- 1410 BCE Proposed date for the *Exodus.*
- 1406 BCE oft cited date when the *Israelites* moved into Canaan.
- c. 1400 BCE The *Lion Gate* created in Turkey.
- Archeologists have unearthed ships and cities from this time, exposing massive world trade. Objects from Egypt are found in the Agaean (Greece), in the orient and throughout the Middle East. There is a dearth of Hittite artifacts in Agaea and a dearth of Agaean artifcts in Anatolia, suggesting that Agaea had a trade agreement with Egypt. There is evidence of a global society during this time with trade embargoes, agreements, wars, espionage, market fluctuations, oligarchs, mercenaries, and wealthy businessman controlling international politics, all through the Middle East, Africa, Europe and Asia.[10]
- **Amenhotep IV, Akhetaten,**(r. 1353–1336 BCE), a powerful religious reformer, started a religion that worshipped one God, Aten. Introduced monotheism in Egypt, shifting from a pantheon of gods to the worship of Aten, a single god.

The Cycle of Ay, 1322–1076 BCE

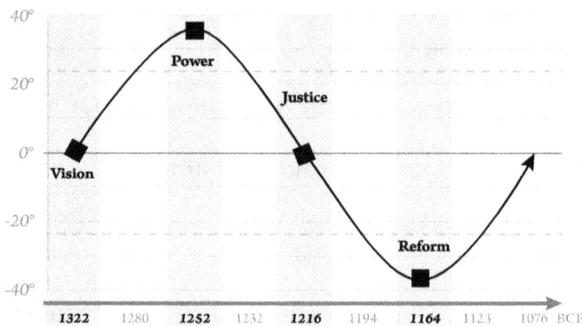

VISION   1322–1316 BCE

- **Ay** (r. 1323–1319 BCE), Pharoah of Egypt. Took down the religion of Ahkenatan and began building Egypt as a military might.

- Šuppiluliuma I (r. c. 1370–1330 bce) ruled the *Hittites*.

POWER   1280–1233 bce   Peak: 1252 bce

- Ramses II (r. 1279–1213 bce), using military initiates that were started under Ay, created one of the greatest armies in history.
- Hattusili III, (r. 1267–1237 bce) king of the Hittite empire, his wife, Pudhepa, was a high priestess and goddess-queen and ruled alongside Hattusili and during her son's subsequent reign (Tudhaliya IV r. 1237–1209 bce).
- 1274 bce: *Battle of Qadesh*: Egypt and *The Hittites* battled over a boundary at Qadesh. It ended in a stalemate with a boundary line that continues to this day. Known as one of the greatest battles in history for its use of chariots and strategy, the battle ended with one of the first non-aggression pacts, and a new pattern of foreign relations was born. Peace through equal power.
- During the Peak of the POWER time, Wu Ding during the Shang Dynasty (c. 1800–1100 bce) in China began his reign (1250–1192 bce). Wu Ding is considered one of the greatest emperors of the Shang Dynasty. His armies conquered the *Qiangfang* to the north and the *Jingman* to the south, greatly expanding the Shang Empire.
- "Wu Ding's reign was the longest of all Shang kings. ... The reign of Wu Ding is seen as the climax of the Shang dynasty before it fell into decline."[11]
- The *Hebrews* moved into Palestine. (c. 1250 bce). The *Philistines*, a local tribe in area, claimed their right to the area.

JUSTICE   1216–14 bce

- Ramses II died (1213 bce).
- Tudhaliya IV died (1209 bce).

REFORM   1194–1124 bce   Peak: 1165–63 bce

- A plunge into the dark ages of Egypt Ramses III (r. 1186–1155 bce). Considered the last great Pharaoh of Egypt.
- Nubia regained independence. Last Hittite king, Šuppiluliuma II, son of Tudhaliya IV (r. 1207–1178 bce)
- Troy burned down (1194–1184 bce)—a possible time of the *Trojan War*.

The Cycle of Samuel, 1076–832 BCE

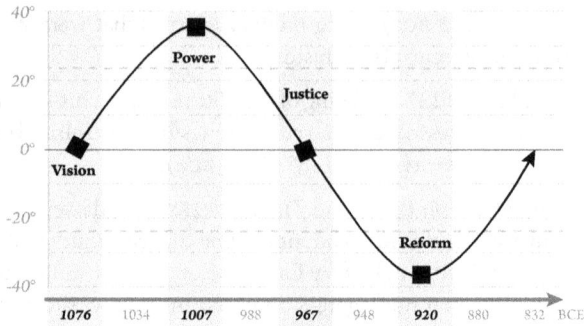

VISION   **1071–1060 BCE**

- King **CRODUS**, the last of the legendary kings of Greece, died in 1068 BCE.

- The last king of the 20th dynasty of Egypt, **RAMSES XI**, died, (1068 BCE). The 21st Dynasty (1077–943 BCE) began with **SMENDES I** (r. 1077–1051 BCE).

- **SAMUEL**, the Seer in the Hebrew Bible, shared a vision with the elder Eli. Eli heard the truth in Samuel's dream, the potential for the Hebrew people to have a homeland. He nurtured Samuel's visions and spiritual direction. If Hebrew records are correct, Samuel would have been eleven precisely during the VISION time. His awakening signaled the beginning of Israel as a unified nation.

- The Egyptian empire was in decline. Assyria collapsed (1075 BCE). The Hittite Empire had fallen. There is a dearth of power in the Middle East and an open road for new civilizations to form. In the wake of the end of these civilizations, the PHOE-NICIANS, who lived along the coast of current day Lebanon, "enjoyed full independence"[12] during this time. Known for developing the alphabet, these merchants, traders, and sailors, thrived as they spread out along the coasts of Africa around the Mediterranean.

- The ZHOU DYNASTY (1046–256 BCE) under the leadership of KING WEN (r. 1100–1050 BCE) began the takeover of the SHANG DYNASTY. Similar to the Kingdom of Judea, it was a faith-based regime. The Zhou believed in a "mandate from heaven"[13] in order to rule. They are credited with being the first feudal society.[14] In 1045 BCE, between VISION and POWER, King Wen of the Zhou Dynasty led his army to conquer the Shang army and beheaded the ruler of the Shang. When King Wen died in the battle, his son, Wu, took over. King Wen is credited with being the founder of the Zhou Dynasty during the VISION time. The Zhou Dynasty became the longest ruling dynasty in Chinese history. It was founded during the VISION time and then when on to conquer the Shang Dynasty in the period between VISION and POWER. This flows similarly to the future time period of Alexander the Great who conquered much of Europe and the Middle East during the time between VISION and POWER.

POWER   1034–987 BCE   Peak: 1007–6 BCE

- The Hebrew elders appointed SAUL OF JUDEA, a warrior who rose to prominence during the battles against the *PHILISTINES*, to be their king (1026 BCE). Saul died in battle, fell on his sword rather than be killed by the enemy, and DAVID rose into the role of King of Judea (r. 1000–970 BCE).
- KING KANG, ZHOU DYNASTY, (r. 1020–996 BCE), expanded China to the north and east.

JUSTICE   969–966 BCE

- KING DAVID died. (970 BCE)
- KING SOLOMON began a long reign. (r. 970–930 BCE)
- KING ZHOU lost a battle in the Yangtze basin, signifying a turning point in the ZHOU DYNASTY.

REFORM   948–880 BCE   Peak: 920–919 BCE

- KING MU (r. unknown–922 BCE)
- KING GONG of ZHOU DYNASTY, China (r. 922–900 BCE)
- KING SOLOMON ruled Israel (r. 970–930 BCE).
- *Temple of Solomon* finished (940 BCE).[15]
- When SOLOMON died in 930 BCE, the country began to crumble from within. His offspring were weaker leaders, and the people were not happy with the high taxes and the lavish living of the ruling class. Israel was thriving, supposedly great buildings were being erected,[16] but internally, the people were discontent and when the peak of the REFORM came and with Solomon gone, the kingdom split in two—Israel to the North (inc. Samaria) and Judah to the south (inc. Jerusalem).[17]

The Cycle of Lycurgus, 832–587 BCE

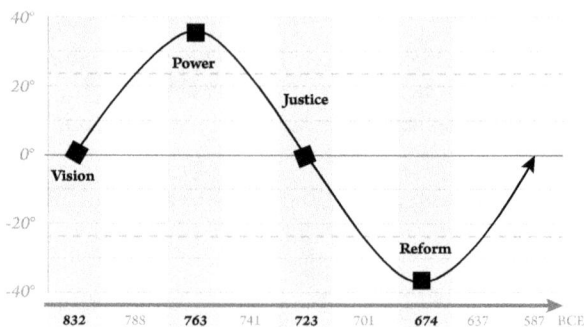

VISION   836–827 BCE

- In Sparta, c. 820 BCE, LYCURGUS visited the Oracle of Delphi in Greece and brought back the *Great Rhetra*, a new code of law. The Great Rhetra had several main components: two kings ruled side by side, land was divided into 30,000 plots to be farmed by serfs,[18] and a system of preparation for war was instituted. Boys were sent off to be trained at a young age as warriors and men continued their training, always available for war. Even girls and women trained for battle.

- The *Black Obelisk* was erected in Assyria.

- Greece emerged out of a dark age (1100–800 BCE) of drought and depopulation.[19]

POWER   788–742 BCE   Peak: 761 BCE

- In China, nomadic tribes, including the QUANRONG, overran the largest city, Haojing, and took over the ZHOU DYNASTY (c. 771 BCE). Instead of being a coalesced force and moving into a new dynasty, China fell into a collection of feudal states for the next five hundred years. (FEUDAL AGE in China 770–255 BCE)

- In 776 BCE, the first Olympic Games have come to signify the birth of the Roman Republic.[20] ROMULUS officially founded Rome in 753 BCE.

- *SPARTANS* overcame the *MESSENIANS* in the *First Messenian War* (c. 743–725 BCE).

- The ruthless conqueror, TIGLATH-PILESER III, seized the royal throne of Assyria (r. 745–727 BCE). He is known for building the first professional army and expanding the Assyrian empire.

- KING UZZIAH OF JUDAH (r. 783–742 BCE) conquered the *PHILISTINES* and the *ARABIANS*.

JUSTICE 724–722 BCE

- 727 BCE. TIGLATH-PILESER III, King of Assyria, died.
- His son, SHALMANESER V, (r. 727–722 BCE), took over Israel and deported thousands of ISRAELITES into slavery.[21]

REFORM 701–636 BCE Peak: 675–674 BCE

- 652 BCE, Babylonia revolted against Assyria.
- 650 BCE, MESSENIAN HELOTS revolted against the wealthier merchants of Sparta. Again, Sparta prevailed. The real reform took place because of the war. Unlike during the POWER time, when the SPARTANS emerged refueled by the fight in the *First Messenian War*, this time the Spartans grew tired of fighting and a transformation took place within their ranks. Non-nobles stood up and called for equal rights. The demonstrations demanded notice and the nobles reconfigured the government to include a governing body of citizens called the *Ecclesia* (f. 683 BCE),[22] an example of an early republican democracy.
- In 667 BCE, Byzantium was founded (modern day Istanbul) by KORINTHIANS.
- Possible time period of Homer and his students who scribed *The Odessey* and *The Iliad.*

End of the Cycle: 622–621 BCE

- DRACO, head of Athens, instituted a series of reforms (*Draconian Reforms*) that wrote down the laws of the people to be held accountable in a legal system, not unlike current legal systems today. Draco is considered the first legislator of Greece. His reforms led to Solon's reforms which supported the rise of the great time of Ancient Greece. While his reforms, may have supported the aristocracy in ways unintended and debt prisoners increased, these reforms were an early precursor to Greek democracy.

The Cycle of Thales, 587–343 BCE

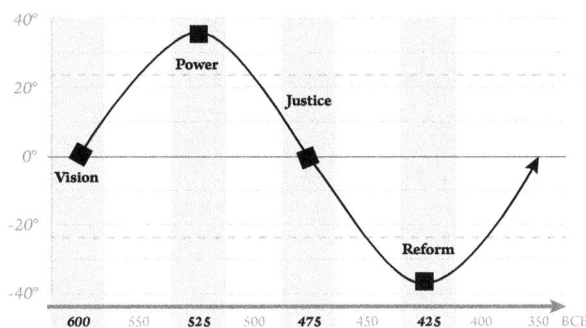

VISION   589–583 BCE

- In 585 BCE, the Ionian philosopher and "father of science," THALES, predicted a solar eclipse, the very year that Pluto crossed the ecliptic from south to north. This prediction initiated his version of the scientific method, and "signaled a major change in Greek thinking and world thinking. A new rational way of understanding reality was born, as opposed to one tied to myth or religious ritual".[23]

- SAPPHO wrote poetry (620–550 BCE).[24]

- Around 594 BCE, SOLON, King of Greece, created the laws of Athens, known as *Solon's Reforms*, and began a new age in Greece. His reforms included canceling farmers' debts, leveling out the justice system so that laws applied to all people equally and un-leveling the tax system so that the wealthy paid more. The Senate was elected by land-owning citizens and the *heliaea* (congress) was elected by all citizens. The reforms were posted in public places for all to read and then he made the government promise to obey his laws for ten years. (The government kept its promise).[25]

- From 579 BCE to 575 BCE, Neptune and Uranus joined Pluto at the Vision Point. This is the only time between 3000 BCE and 3000 CE that these three planets conjoined at the same time. The closest moment of all was in December of 577 BCE. That this alignment occurred at the beginning of a cycle gives extraordinary weight to this cycle. There is no wonder that this cycle birthed Buddhism, Confucianism, Taoism, and Zoroastrianism—the roots of the Axial Age.

POWER   542–497 BCE   Peak: 516–514 BCE

- CYRUS THE GREAT (r. 550–530 BCE), King of Persia, seized Asia Minor, including the *ASIATIC GREEKS*, for the Persian Empire (546–45 BCE).

- DARIUS I, aka Darius the Great, (r. 522–486 BCE) was a Persian dictator who expanded his empire through Thrace (the land where Thales lived) through the Middle East and into India. At the peak of the POWER time, he led his armies into the Punjab (Pakistan and Northern India), into Thrace, and built the palace city of Persepolis (Iran). At the end of his reign, just after this POWER time, his armies attempted to invade Greece in the famous *Battle of Marathon* (490 BCE) that ended in a vicious defeat for the *PERSIANS*.

- The Peisistradids: PEISISTRATUS (r. 565 BCE–528/7 BCE), and his sons HIPPARCHAS (r. 528/7–514 BCE) and HIPPIAS (r. 527–510 BCE) considered tyrants who ruled through trickery and violence, but also strengthened the economy of Athens and promoted the arts. After Hipparchas was assassinated, Hippias continued to rule for four more years, after which he was ousted and fled to Persia where he assisted Darius at the *Battle of Marathon.*

- In 508 BCE CLEISTHENES stepped into power and brought back Athenian democracy.

- Around 500 BCE, SUN TZU wrote The Art of War. Sun Tzu (c. 544–496 BCE) lived during the time of KING HELU OF WU. The Art of War inscribes codes of conduct, military strategy and overall life inspiration used even today. "In peace, prepare for; in war, prepare for peace."[26]

JUSTICE   478–476 BCE

- CONFUCIUS died.
- GAUTAMA BUDDHA died.
- 478 BCE. *Delian League* formed; an alliance between Athens and its allies, with the intention of freeing Ionia (the birthplace of Thales) from the grips of the Persian Empire.

REFORM   455–393 BCE   Peak: 431 BCE

- From 431 BCE to 404 BCE, Athens and Sparta fought each other a series of civil war called the *Peloponnesian Wars.*
- After losing an early battle in 431 BCE, PERICLES, an Athenian general and politician, gave a famous and well-documented speech, named the Funeral Oration by the Greek historian, THUCYDIDES. This speech inspired and supported Athenian democracy.[27]
- SOCRATES (c. 470–399 BCE) taught in Greece and was executed in 399 BCE. PLATO, his most famous student, began his teachings.
- Around 400 BCE, PĀNINI wrote a Sanskrit grammar book, the Ashtādhyāyī. (Date accepted among most Western scholars.)[28]

The Cycle of Aristotle, 343–97 BCE

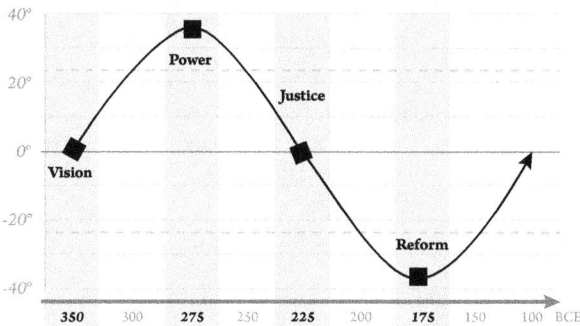

VISION 344–338 BCE

- ARISTOTLE (384–322 BCE) instructed ALEXANDER THE GREAT (356–323 BCE) in logic, strategy, and philosophy.[29]
- CHANAKYA (375–283 BCE) instructed CHANDRAGUPTA (c. 350–c. 295 BCE).[30]

Chandragupta began the MAURYAN EMPIRE in part in response to Alexander the Great's incursion into India. (322 BCE)

- In China, the Taoist philosopher ZHUANGZI (also written Chuang-tze) was writing and inspiring people.[31]

POWER 296–252 BCE Peak: 272 BCE

- CHANDRAGUPTA died just before the POWER time, in 297 BCE. His son, BINDUSARA took over and ruled the MAURYAN EMPIRE until the peak of POWER, dying in 273 BCE. During the four years of the peak of POWER (272–268 BCE), brothers fought for the throne with ASHOKA MAURYA coming out on top in 268 BCE (India). ASHOKA (r. 268–232 BCE), expanded the empire, particularly through conquering the KA-LINGAS in southern India. After witnessing the horror of war, the decimation of the KALINGA EMPIRE and the loss of 100,000 lives, Ashoka turned to Buddhism (c. 261 BCE). By the end of the POWER time, Ashoka supported the widespread conversion of Buddhism throughout the empire.[32]
- Post ALEXANDER THE GREAT, Alexandria, Egypt became an international city of trade and power.
- R. 281–261 BCE. ANTIOCH I, titled "King of the Universe", was king of the SELEUCID EMPIRE. The empire was founded in 312 BCE, by Alexander's general, SELEUCUS, in much of the footprint of Alexander's conquered lands.

JUSTICE 232–230 BCE

- ASHOKA MAURYA died (232 BCE). When Ashoka died, the MAURYAN KINGDOM moved into a slow decline. Invaders began to overrun what is today most of India. Fracturing into different kingdoms, the ending of the Mauryan empire spawned a time of religious and devotional development in many parts of India.
- QIN DYNASTY was in the process of forming (221–207 BCE). The founder and only emperor of the Qin dynasty, QIN SHI HUANG (259–210 BCE), a man in his late twenties during this window of time, led a successful revolt against the HAN (230 BCE), while the ZHOU DYNASTY moved into decline.

REFORM 208–150 BCE Peak: 185 BCE

- In 210 BCE, QIN SHE HUANGI (r. 221–210 BCE), the first and only emperor of the QIN DYNASTY died, leaving behind over 8000 life-sized ceramic soldier sculptures, named the *Terra Cotta Army*.[33] Three years later, the HAN DYNASTY (202 BCE–220 CE), known for supporting the arts, advancements in paper-making, ship building, and mathematics, stepped into power and ruled for four hundred years. Its first emperor, EMPEROR GAOZU, was not noble born but married into nobility and rose into power by freeing prisoners and leading a rebel army.

- **BIRHADRATHA**, the last Mauryan king, was assassinated and the **SHUNGA DYNASTY** (c. 185–75 BCE) known for supporting the arts, philosophy, and culture, stepped into power. The Sanskrit and Vedic scholar, **PATANJALI** wrote *The Yoga Sutras* around this time.

- Uprisings in Alexandria and other lands that **ALEXANDER** had conquered. Carthaginian general **HANNIBAL** led an army with elephants, across the Alps, to quash the revolts. Died in 181/183 BCE.[34]

- 167–160 BCE. *Maccabean Revolt*, Jewish rebels revolted against the **SELEUCID EMPIRE** and recaptured Jerusalem. Currently celebrated as *Hanukkah*.

The Cycle of Cicero, 97 BCE –147 CE

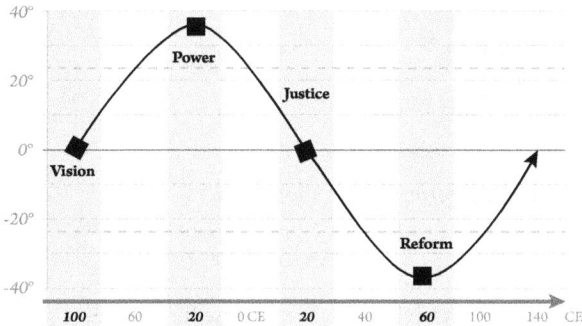

VISION   99–93 BCE

- Rome banned human sacrifices (97 BCE).

- **JOSEPH** (Jesus' father) was born c. 97 BCE.

- An insurrection broke out in the Roman Republic during an election between **GLAUCIA** and **MEMMIUS** (100 BCE). The declining popularity of Glaucia lost him the election, but his supporters rioted and beat Memmius to death. Violence erupted throughout the city of Rome and led to a period of instability in Rome.

- General **SULLA** got an education on the streets.

- Future Roman senator, **CICERO**, studied with **PHILO OF LARISSA** and was initiated into the *Eleusis mysteries*.[35] Cicero is credited with starting the "Just War" credo, validating war as necessary sometimes.

- This cycle begins with the Mayan Civilization moving into a peak time. The VISION time correlates with a beginning date of the *Mayan Calendar*, the painting of murals in the Mayan pyramids, and the founding of the city of Teotihuacan. By the REFORM time, the Mayan civilization was thriving.

301

POWER   **50–6 ʙᴄᴇ**   **Peak: 25–24 ʙᴄᴇ**

- **Jᴜʟɪᴜs Cᴀᴇsᴀʀ** crossed the Rubicon to attack his fellow general, **Pᴏᴍᴘᴇʏ**, in 49 ʙᴄᴇ.

- Five years later in 44 ʙᴄᴇ, a group of politicians assassinated **Jᴜʟɪᴜs Cᴀᴇsᴀʀ** trying to save the republic.

- In 43 ʙᴄᴇ, **Mᴀʀᴄ Aɴᴛᴏɴʏ**, **Oᴄᴛᴀᴠɪᴀɴ**, and **Mᴀʀᴄᴜs Lᴇᴘɪᴅᴜs** formed *The Second Triumvirate.*

- **Oᴄᴛᴀᴠɪᴀɴ** then forced **Mᴀʀᴄᴜs Lᴇᴘɪᴅᴜs** into exile. **Cʟᴇᴏᴘᴀᴛʀᴀ**, ruler of Egypt, (r. c. 51–30 ᴄᴇ) committed suicide.

- **Mᴀʀᴋ Aɴᴛᴏɴʏ** committed suicide and **Oᴄᴛᴀᴠɪᴀɴ** became the last man standing, changed his name and title to *Augustus Caesar* and transitioned Rome from a republic into an empire (27 ʙᴄᴇ).

JUSTICE   **14–16 ᴄᴇ**

- **Aᴜɢᴜsᴛᴜs Cᴀᴇsᴀʀ** died (14 ᴄᴇ).

- **Tɪʙᴇʀɪᴜs** (r. 14–37 ᴄᴇ) became ruler of Rome.

- **Jᴇsᴜs** was a young boy, getting lost in the temple.

REFORM   **38–93 ᴄᴇ**   **Peak: 62 ᴄᴇ**

- **Cᴀʟɪɢᴜʟᴀ** (37–41 ᴄᴇ) started this ʀᴇғᴏʀᴍ time for four crazy years and was assassinated in an attempt to return Rome to a republic, but instead **Cʟᴀᴜᴅɪᴜs** (r. 41–54 ᴄᴇ) stepped into power and focused his attention on infrastructure and the economy. After he was killed, his grandnephew, **Nᴇʀᴏ** (r. 54–68 ᴄᴇ) ruled Rome until he was killed.

- **Pᴀᴜʟ** and **Pᴇᴛᴇʀ** led the *Christian* movement and were executed in the same year, 67 ᴄᴇ.

- In 70 ᴄᴇ, Jewish revolts were quashed by General **Vᴇsᴘᴀsɪᴀɴ**, who then become emperor of Rome from 70 ᴄᴇ to 79 ᴄᴇ. Vespasian instituted reforms that benefited the people of Rome, but not the Jewish people in Rome, and oversaw the building of the Colliseum.

- **Bᴏᴜᴅɪᴄᴀ** led an unsuccessful, if inspiring, rebellion in Britain against the Roman Empire (60–61 ᴄᴇ).

The Cycle of Ptolemy, 147–393 CE

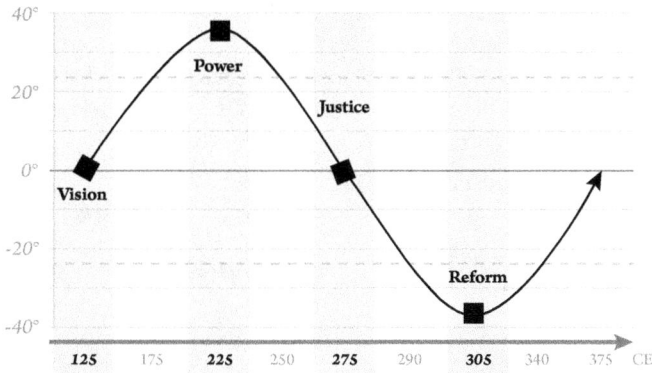

VISION   **145–150 CE**

- **CLAUDIUS PTOLEMY** (c.100–c. 170) wrote *Almagest,* an astronomy text used for centuries.

- **JUSTIN MARTYR** (100–165 CE), Christian saint who united Greek philosophy with the Christian faith.[36]

- **MARCUS AURELIUS** studying with **APOLLONIUS**. (Several years later he wrote *Meditations,* 160–170 CE). Marcus Aurelius was initiated into the *Eleusian mysteries.*[37]

- **NĀGĀRJUNA** (c. 150–250 CE), India,[38] wrote texts on Buddhism and founded *Mahayan Buddhism.*

POWER   **197–240**   **Peak: 222–223**

- **ARDASHIR I** (r. 211/212–242 CE) founded the **SASSANID EMPIRE** (Iran).

- **SEVERUS ALEXANDER** (r. 222–235 CE), ruled Rome. His death began a time of unrest, crisis, and anarchy in the Roman Empire that lasted til 284 CE.

- **HAN DYNASTY** fell (220 CE) and the **THREE KINGDOMS** period began in China.

JUSTICE   **Oct. 260–Sep. 262**

- **MANI** (c. 216–274/277 CE), founder of *Manichaeism* in Parthian Empire (Iran), started a religious movement and was executed in prison.

- **PLOTINUS** (c.204–270 CE) wrote the treatises that were included in *The Enneads* (c. 270 CE), a work that established the philosophy of Neoplatonism.

- During the **JUSTICE** time, **GALLIENUS** (r. 253–268 CE) supported a Roman Renaissance while his rule was peppered with revolts that were quashed.[39]

REFORM   285–337   Peak: 306–308

- DIOCLETIAN (r. 284–305 CE), emperor of Rome, known for the massacre of Christians and his judicial and government reforms.

- CONSTANTINE I (r. 306–337 CE), crowned at peak, known for started the Christian church and doctrine by initiating the *Council of Nicaea* (325 CE) that laid out the doctrine for the Catholic Church, instituting much of the ritual and dogma that is still in existence today. Most of the Christian gospels were scribed.

- GUPTA DYNASTY began in India in 320 CE.

The Cycle of Augustine & Hypatia, 393–683 CE

VISION   389–396 CE

- AUGUSTINE OF HIPPO wrote *Confessions*.

- HYPATIA (c. 360–415 CE), a Neoplatonist philosopher and scientist taught in the halls of Alexandria, Egypt.

- Roman Empire split in two. (395 CE)

- THEODOSIUS I (r. 347–395 CE) instituted a Christian theocracy in the Roman Empire.

- KALIDASA (GUPTA era, c. 4th–5th century), the Indian poet, considered to be the greatest Indian poet to have ever lived.[40] "Kalidasa has a deep sense of political understanding. Through *Raghuvamsa*, he conveys a message to kings and rulers that power accepted as responsibility thrives and prospers. However, power as a means to exert authority and arrogance faces doom very soon."[41]

POWER   445–486   Peak: 468–469

- ATTILA THE HUN (r. 434–453 CE) climbed the Alps and attacked the Roman Empire with an army of elephants.

- *VANDALS* and *GOTHS* take over the Roman Empire (476 CE).

JUSTICE   506–509

- *Breviary* of **ALARIC** (c. 506 CE), Roman law that restructured the empire, initiated by Roman jurists.

- **BOETHIUS,** Roman senator and philosopher, laid down a new music theory (c. 504 CE).

- **ARYABHATA** (476–550 CE) wrote *Aryabhatiya* (c. 500 CE), an astronomical and mathematical text that calculated *Pi*, described eclipses accurately and inspired the Arabic numeral system (developed three hundred years later).

REFORM   533–580   Peak: 553–554

- *Nika Riots* (532 CE), **JUSTINIAN I** (r. 527–565 CE) instituted reforms, *Justinian Code.*[42] *Hagia Sophia* completed in 537 CE.

India

India was experiencing a Golden Age (c. 320–550 CE during the Gupta Empire). During this cycle in India, there were great strides in math—trigonometry and geometry. The concept of zero was introduced. Ayurvedic medicine started during this time, along with improved surgical procedures and vaccines. The game of chess was created in India during the Gupta Empire. India had been civilized for quite some time by now, thousands of years, and even the texts that were written at this time had been around orally for hundreds if not thousands of years. Yet, the writing of them was the work of this time in India, which influenced Arabia during their upcoming Golden Age which in turn influenced Italy during the Italian Renaissance.

The Cycle of Muhammad, 638–883 CE

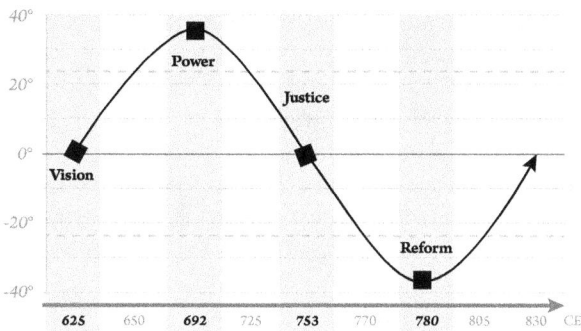

VISION 635–641 CE

- The TANG DYNASTY (China) was founded in 618 CE, but it was during the reign of T'AI-TSUNG (627–649 CE) in 638 CE, that a fourteen-year-old concubine, WU ZHAO, entered the palace of Taizong.[43] She would go on the become EMPRESS WU and rule China during the POWER time.

- The PROPHET MUHAMMAD and his followers conquered Mecca in 630 CE. Two years later, Muhammad died (632 CE). ABŪ BAKR, Muhammad's close friend, stepped into the leadership position. SUNNI MUSLIMS believe that Abū Bakr is the rightful successor to Muhammad. The next caliph, UMAR (OMAR) IBN AL-KHATTAB (r. 634–44) began a series of military campaigns to gain farmable land, a rare commodity in the deserts of Arabia.

- Population growth and the expansion/creation of a unified people led to scarcity and greater needs. The ARABS forced the ROMANS to retreat from Syria (636), defeated the Persian army (637) and conquered Egypt (641). From 636 to 637 CE, MUSLIM armies laid siege to Jerusalem, successfully taking the city from the BYZANTINES. Umar immediately issued a charter that left the Christian shrines undisturbed and cleared the rubble of the ruined Jewish Temple (destroyed in 70 CE). Upon that site, he contracted the HARAM AL-SHARIF, the "Most Noble Sanctuary,"[44] which became the third most holy site for Muslims (after Mecca and Medina). Even though he was coopting the site of the temple, he invited the Jews back into Jerusalem, a place they had been barred from since the Bar Kobha revolt.

- Irish Benedictine monk, AIDEN, under the direction of POPE GREGORY THE GREAT, established the first priory in England on Lindesfarne Island (635 CE).

- In China, the reign of EMPRESS WU (690–705 CE), one of the rare female rulers of China, guided the TANG DYNASTY through a time of expansion and growth, fending off the TIBETANS to the north and the KOREANS to the east. Her followers, in particular HSUAN-TSUNG (r. 713–755), followed suit.

POWER   692–731   Peak: 715

- In October of 680 CE, just prior to this POWER time, the Battle of Karbala, commemorated by SHIA MUSLIMS as the ten-day mourning period of Ashura, instigating greater tensions between SHIA and SUNNI Muslims and marking the beginning of the SUNNI UMAYYAD Caliphate. By the time POWER began, AL-MALIK (r. 685 –705) had been head of the Umayyad Caliphate for seven years. During his tenure, he established Arabic as the common language and the dinar as the common currency. He set up a centralized administration and the underlying structures that supported religious tolerance (Christians even held positions of leadership within government), a scientific revolution, and a creative renaissance.

- The next Umayyad caliph, AL-WALID I (r. 705–715 CE), expanded the Islamic world and moved it towards an imperial state. Successful military campaigns against the

306

Byzantines, western Europe, and Hispania entrenched Islam as an empire. In a short time, the Arabian world went from local tribal states, to being a vast kingdom with a new religion. SULAYMAN BIN ABD AL-MALIK (r. 715–717 CE) attempted to take the seat of the Byzantine empire and failed (717 CE). UMAR II (r. 717–720) successfully expanded the UMAYYAD CALIPHATE into the Iberian Peninsula.

- The Byzantine Empire was in a state of decline when LEO THE SYRIAN staged a coup and ousted THEODOSIUS. Known for being "the iconoclast," LEO III (r. 717–741 CE) ordered the destruction of statues, relics, and altars, fought off the UMAYYADS, and bolstered the economy and lands of the empire. His decision to remove icons was met with resistance and rebellion, all of which was overcome by Byzantine forces.

- At the end of the POWER time in 732 CE, CHARLES MARTEL (r. 718–741 CE), "The Hammer" of the Frankish throne (France) and his army fended off the encroaching *Muslim* army at Poitiers, an event "seen as the decisive event that saved Europe from Islamic domination; in fact, Christendom was saved by the Abbasids' total indifference to the West."[45]

JUSTICE   753–755

- Between 750 and 755 CE, a massive restructuring of power occurred in both the TANG DYNASTY and the Middle East. A revolution from 747 to 750 CE took out the Arab-centric UMAYYAD Dynasty and installed the ABBASID Dynasty, more inclusive of other ethnicities, all the while killing the *SHIA* leaders and beginning the contention between *SUNNIS* and *SHIAS* still alive today. ABU JAFAR AL-MANSUR (r. 754–775) became the second leader of the ABBASID CALIPHATE and moved the center of the Islamic world from Arabia to the small town of Baghdad, making Baghdad a hub for science, architecture, philosophy, and art. Like many historical figures, al-Mansur is a complicated character and views on him differ. To some, he set up libraries and supported the arts and infrastructure. He brought to Baghdad the teachings of Hindu numerals and translations of the *Siddhantas,* Indian astronomy texts. To others, he was a ruthless, ambitious imperialist, who entrenched the world of Islam into dangerous dogma.

- BONIFACE (675–754 CE), an English Benedictine monk, who led conversion campaigns in Germania, was martyred alongside fellow missionaries.

- Charles Murray, with all of his statistical analysis, ranks the Tang poets DU FU (712–770) in first place and LI PO (701–762) in second of the greatest writers in Chinese history.[46] Du Fu and Li Po were born during POWER and did their greatest work around the JUSTICE time.

REFORM   780–824   Peak: Sep 799

- POPE LEO III (not to be confused with LEO III, Byzantine Emperor during the POWER time), a man from a humble background was easily elected pope after a series of popes from noble birth. He aligned himself with CHARLEMAGNE, the emperor of the

BYZANTINE EMPIRE, and blessed his coronation in 800 CE, two days after his own coronation. This means that at precisely the peak of REFORM, both Pope Leo III and Charlemagne came into full power, and this began the important alliance between the BYZANTINE EMPIRE and the Roman Catholic Church that became the HOLY ROMAN EMPIRE. This alliance birthed the *Carolingian Renaissance*, a time of great art, learning, and cultural advancement.

- In 821, China and Tibet brokered a peace agreement that lasted two decades.

- HARUN AL-RASHID (r. 786–809) is the caliph of the ABBASID CALIPHATE. The compilation of tales *One Thousand and One Nights* was written around this time in Arabic. The tales were passed down and eventually translated into French by Antoine Galland during the cycle of Descartes. Galland may have taken liberties with his translations that led to movies and more movies about this time of magic carpets, wish-granting lamps, and heroic swordsmen in turbans.

- 786–830 CE. The *House of Wisdom* was founded in Baghdad. Mathematicians, philosophers, scientists, physicians, and artists gathered to share ideas, teach, learn and experiment. The Translation Movement that had its roots during the JUSTICE time is now in full swing. The ABBASID CALIPHATE paid well for translations from Greek, Sanskrit, Chinese and Latin, into Arabic, including Aristotle, Plato, Ptolemy, Hippocrates and Euclid, inspiring a field of scholars and inciting a renaissance.

- AL-MAMUN (r. 813– 833), Mamun the Great, was "receptive to the creative novelties of the outside world of unbelievers."[47] Culture flourished during this time. Teachings of the west were brought into the great libraries and schools built at this time.

- MUḤAMMAD IBN MŪSĀ AL-KHWĀRIZMĪ (780–850 CE), developed al-gebra (c. 830), Baghdad, House of Wisdom. Al-gebra is an Arabian word meaning "the reunion of broken parts". The great mathematician brought together, from his studies of Indian math, the ten-symbol decimal system with geometry, from his studies of Greek mathematics, to form a new math—algebra.

- 859 AD, FATIMA AL FIHRI (800–878 CE), a woman, founded the first university in the world, the University of Al-Karaouine, still existing and granting degrees today, in Fes, Morocco.

- The first Shia state, the IDRISID DYNASTY (c. 780–974 CE), formed in Maghreb.

- JABIR IBN HAIYAN, (c. 750–c. 816 CE), the father of chemistry, discovered al-kalis that enabled the creation of solid soap (not to reach Europe for a few more centuries). He discovered hydrochloric acid and nitric acid in his well-equipped laboratory. He wrote over 200 books, described the scientific method in detail, and was the first to distill ethanol, a fuel source. He invented waterproof cloth, glow-in-the-dark ink, a way to rust-proof iron and steel, and flame-retardant paper.

- The philosopher, AL-KINDI (801–873 CE), picked up the mantle that Jabir left behind. While al-Kindi was only a child when Jabir died, he was able to study his works and from that and his own experiments derived a theory of relativity not unlike

Einstein's. Al-Kindi, considered the father of Arab philosophy, created a foundation for pharmacology, through his methods for organizing and categorizing substances that interact with the human body.

- The largest Buddhist temple in the world, *Borobudur*, was built circa 800 CE in Indonesia during the SHAILENDRA DYNASTY (c. 750–850 CE), known for its cultural renaissance.

The Cycle of al-Battānī, 883–1128 CE

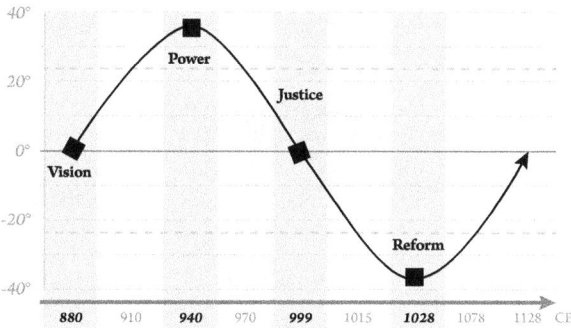

Islamic Golden Age

VISION 880–886 CE

- ABU YUSUF YA'QUB IBN 'ISHAQ AS-SABBAH AL-KINDI, AL-KINDI for short (c. 801 –873 CE), Baghdad, House of Wisdom, philosopher, polymath, musician and mathematician. Introduced Indian numerals to the Arabic world. A follower of AL-KINDI, ABU MA'SHAR, from Bahlk (787–886) Abu Ma'shar is known for his texts on astrology. After studying in India for ten years, Abu Ma'shar wrote a text that was translated into Latin in the 12th century.

- THABIT IBN QURRA (826–901) founded the field of statics, developing engineering mechanics, and understanding physical systems.[48]

- ABŪ BAKR MUHAMMAD IBN ZAKARIYA AL-RĀZĪ, AL-RĀZĪ for short (c. 854–925/935 CE), Persia (Iran) discovered sulfuric acid and derived treatments for smallpox, in particular distinguishing smallpox from measles. Sometime near the VISION time, al-Razi had a visitor from China, a brilliant physician who learned Arabic in a short time and translated Galen from Arabic to Chinese.[49] There is strong evidence for the exchange of knowledge and goods between the Abbasid Caliphate and the Tang Dynasty.[50]

- AL-BATTĀNĪ (850–929), (or Albategnius, the anglicized version of his name) was an astronomer, considered by astronomers as the Ptolemy of the Arabs, whose seminal work in trigonometry is quoted in Copernicus' work.[51] We can give thanks to

Al-Battānī for the trig tables that we had to rewrite as sophomores in high school. He is the one who invented sine and cosine—derivatives of Hipparchus' chords. While he lived a long life, it is during the VISION time that he wrote *Opus Astronomicum,* a work that extolls upon Ptolemy's *Almagest,* written at the VISION time three cycles earlier.[52]

- ABU ZAYD AL-BALKHI (850–934), one of the first cognitive psychologists, connected mental, spiritual and physical health and one of the first to talk about diseases of the soul. Al-Balkhi grew up in Bahlk, a region in Afghanistan where centuries prior Zoroaster is purportedly from, along with Rumi who was born there centuries later. al-Balkhi was a follower of al-Kindi. The threads of Indian teachings of the Vedas run strong through his work. He connected disease with emotions. He saw the world through the lens of the soul.

- During this time, AL-BATTĀNĪ (trigonometry), AL-RĀZĪ (treatment for smallpox), AL-BALKHI (cognitive psychology) were all in their 30s. AL-KINDI (brought Indian numerals to Arabia) had just died (873 CE). THABIT IBN QURRA (engineering mechanics and founder of the field of statics) was in his late 50s and Abu Ma'shar was in his 90s.

POWER   940–976   Peak: 961

- In 945 CE, the BUYID DYNASTY took over Baghdad and began their rule. An Abbasid caliph remained as a figure head, while the Buyids were the ones calling the shots from behind the scenes. During most of the POWER time, the most prominent Buyid, 'ADUD AL-DAWLA (r. 949–983), ruled in a time of relative peace and growth. Great strides in medicine, the building of a large hospital and continued support for the sciences were the power of this time. Arriving in Baghdad during a time of internal strife, al-Dawla ruled with an iron fist and suspended public demonstrations to master control. He invested in larger infrastructure projects, dams and canals, that increased food production in the farming areas.

JUSTICE   999–1002

- The Persian poet FERDOWSI wrote *Shanameh: The Persian Book of Kings* c. 977– 1010 CE.

- The Buyids stayed in power until the JUSTICE time, when they were overthrown by the *SELJUKS* (Turks) and the *GHAZNAVIDS* (Persian), who stayed in power into the next cycle, maintaining the ABBASID caliph system of rule and continuing to support the arts and sciences.

- IBN AL-HAYTHAM (c. 965–c. 1040 CE), scientist, published *Book of Optics* (c. 1011 –1021 CE). His contributions to science included understanding refraction and reflection through his studies of light, founding the field of optics. His careful experiments and calculations valued the repetition of scientific precision to arrive at theory and conclusion.

REFORM   1028–1067 Peak: 1045

- AVICENNA (980–1037), Persian polymath known for *The Book of Healing and The Canon of Medicine*, a medical encyclopedia. He settled in Rey (near Tehran), the hometown of the polymath AL-RHAZI (854–925) who lived during the VISION time.

Asia

VISION   880–886 CE

- In China, this cycle begins with ZHU WEN (r. 907–912), a young rebel and gang leader rising through the ranks of the Chinese military at the end of the TANG DYNASTY. Steeped in *Five Classics* by his father, a Confucian scholar, Zhu Wen overthrew the TANG DYNASTY and founded the Later LAING DYNASTY and starting a time when China went through five different dynasties until the POWER time.

POWER   940–976   Peak: 961

- In 960, at the peak of POWER, general ZHAO KUANGYIN staged a successful coup and became EMPEROR TAIZU of the SONG DYNASTY. The SONG DYNASTY (961–1291) brought back the *Five Classics* as both a model for government and religion, and oversaw a time of great advancement in science and the arts.

JUSTICE   999–1002

- *Tale of Genji,* the world's first novel, written by MURASAKI SHIKIBU, a noblewoman, c. 1000 CE, Japan

REFORM   1028–1067 Peak: 1045

- In 1045 CE, BI SHENG invented movable type in the SONG DYNASTY, China, beginning a time when books became more available, literacy rose, and the arts and sciences flourished.

Europe

VISION 880–886 CE

- The *Cadaver Synod*: It all began when POPE STEPHEN V (r. 885–891) selected GUY SPOLETO III to be emperor of the Holy Roman Empire, headquartered in Constantinople. The next pope, Formosus (p. 89–896), did not trust Spoleto and went out of his way to interfere in his rule. When Formosus died in 896, the next pope, Boniface VI (p. 896) was likely poisoned a few weeks after being ordained. The next pope, Stephen VI (p. 896–897), possibly insane, had the corpse of Formosus exhumed, dressed up and put on trial. With a monk sitting behind the decaying form giving him voice, the papal court declared Formosus unfit to be pope and the three blessing fingers of his dead body cut off. His bones were thrown into the river. This sounds like a likely end, but it's not. Stories vary—his bones either washed up on shore or monks fetched them. Rumors of miracles occurring in association with his bones, led Pope Theodore II to reinstate Formosus' good name in 897 CE and forbid future trials of dead people. You would think it would end there, but it does not. Sometime between 904 to 911, Pope Sergius III who had taken part in the original trial of Formosus, had his body exhumed again, put on trial again, found guilty of perjury again and this time decapitated. An interesting beginning to this cycle that endured a dark time in both Europe and in the Catholic Church.

- **ALFRED THE GREAT** (r. 871–899) became the first king of England.

POWER   940–976   Peak: 961

- From the VISION time to **POPE JOHN XII** (r. 955–964), the Catholic Church struggled with the corrupt politics of the leading aristocracy in Italy. In 960, at the peak of POWER, **KING BERENGER II** of Italy invaded the Papal States. Pope John XII reached out to **OTTO I** (r. 961–973 CE), the new king of Germany, for support in taking back the papal states. In 962, with the Germans pushing out the Italians, Otto I and Pope John came to an agreement, the *Diploma Ottonianum*. King Otto agreed to defend the lands of the papacy and Pope John made Otto the Emperor of the newly formed Holy Roman Empire, strengthening both the papacy and Germany.

- **EDGAR THE PEACEFUL** (ironic), and **ETHELRED THE UNREADY** (not-ironic) stepped into the footsteps of Alfred during the POWER time. Ruthless, barbaric, and tyrannical, the English empire took shape.

JUSTICE   999–1002

- An unknown England writer wrote the epic poem, *Beowulf*, c. 1000 CE.

REFORM   1028–1067 Peak: 1045

- With such a difficult beginning to the cycle, the Christian Church in Rome, overcome by a century of corruption, split apart in *The Great Schism of 1054*. The Easter Orthodox Churches, Greek and Russian, pulled away from the Roman Catholic Church.

- **WILLIAM THE CONQUEROR** (Duke of Normandy 1035–1087; King of England 1066–1087) came into power seven years into this POWER time. In England, **EDWARD THE CONFESSOR** (r. 1042–1066 CE), who oversaw the reconstruction of Westminster Abbey, died in 1066 without a clear heir. **HAROLD II** (r. 1066) claimed the throne, only to be ousted later that year by **WILLIAM I** at the *Battle of Hastings*.

The Cycle of Bernard of Clairvaux & Hildegard von Bingen, 1128–1373 CE

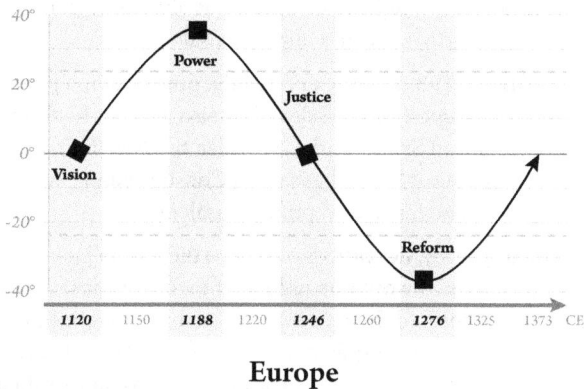

Europe

VISION   1122–1128 CE

- **ABELHARD** (1075–1160) translated Muḥammad ibn Mūsā al-Khwārizmī's mathematical work from Arabian into Latin, introducing algebra to Europe. (c. 1126)[53]

- In 1122 CE, the *Concordant of Worms* instituted celibacy among Catholic priests. In 1123 CE, the *First Council of the Lateran*, Rome, confirmed the Concordant of Worms.

- In 1126 CE **BERNARD OF CLAIRVAUX** (c. 1090–1153) wrote *On Grace and Free Choice* one of his most significant works.[54] In it, he states that *thinking* is purely the grace of God, *willing* is mixture of grace and personal responsibility, and *accomplishing* is our human responsibility to put God's grace into practice, while still recognizing our merits as a gift from God.[55]

- In 1129 CE, after meeting **HUGUES DE PAYAN**, the founder of the *KNIGHTS TEMPLAR*, Bernard initiated the *Council of Troyes*. The council established the Knights Templar as a legitimate organization within the prevue of the Catholic Church. Bernard wrote *In Praise of the New Knighthood* (1128–1141). His idealistic, faith-based ideas of knights in shining armor and chivalry, includes codes of conduct for human nobility and are the basis for our contemporary ideas of the romance of this time period. That they were written by a celibate monk who never saw battle is just another irony in history.

- **HILDEGARD VON BINGEN** (1098–1179), a mystic Benedictine nun in Germany, experienced visions that she will scribe later in her life. Her visions, her writing, her music and her understanding of health and healing inspired many including **BERNARD OF CLAIRVAUX**, **THOMAS BECKET**, **ELEANOR OF AQUITAINE** and the pope.

POWER 1188–1221 Peak: 1207

- In 1187, SALADIN, emperor of the Sassanid Empire, and his army conquered Jerusalem. The *Third Crusade* (1189—1192), "the King's Crusade", led by RICHARD I of England, PHILIP II of France, and FREDERICK I of the HOLY ROMAN EMPIRE (Germany) failed to recapture Jerusalem, but was able to negotiate a treaty for safe passage of Christian pilgrims into and out of Jerusalem.

- Pope INNOCENT III (r. 1198–1216) extended the powers of the papacy and initiated crusades not just in conquest of Jerusalem, but also against the Cathars in southern France and the Muslims in Spain. Under his order, the *Fourth Crusade* (1202–1204) left for Jerusalem, but against his wishes sacked Constantinople, weakened the Christian Byzantine Empire and failed to capture Jerusalem.

- In the last year of his papacy, INNOCENT convened the *Fourth Lateran Council* (1215). The Canons of this council would be used for horrific purposes over the following centuries. Canon 8 advocated the criminal treatment of heretics that supported the use of torture in the upcoming inquisitions. Canon 68 initiated the rule that Jews and Muslims had to wear badges, a putative measure meant to outcast them.

- At the end of this POWER time, the *Fifth Crusade* (1217–1221), initiated by POPE HONORIUS III, failed as well.

- FRANCIS ASSISI founded the Franciscan Order in 1209 CE.

- DOMINIC OF OSMA founded the Dominican Order (1206–1215 CE).

JUSTICE 1246–1249

- Between 1246 and 1249, the Franciscan monk BONAVENTURE (1221–1274), the Italian Dominican friar THOMAS AQUINAS (1225–1274), and the German Dominican friar ALBERTUS MAGNUS (c. 1200–1280), discussed Aristotle at the University of Paris. The three men were later canonized by the Catholic Church with their scholarly contributions recognized.

- In 1252, POPE INNOCENT IV (p. 1243–1254) issued the papal bull *Ad extirpanda*, that exonerated the use of torture in cases of perceived heresy, thus creating the document that would be used to torture and execute thousands of innocent people. His idea of justice, abhorrent to most of us today, was validated by the powers bestowed into the papacy during the POWER time of Innocent III.

- *The Seventh Crusade* (1248–1254 CE), launched by the French King LOUIS IX, failed to capture its intended target, Cairo.

- Around 1241 CE, merchants from the cities of Lübeck and Hamburg in the Holy Roman Empire, formed a trade agreement, a foundation for the evolving *HANSEATIC LEAGUE*.

- The league lasted for centuries and grew over time until the landscape of politics during the Reformation brought it into decline. The trade agreements, alliances and unions created an early infrastructure of trade agreements that mirrors our current state of affairs. Based in consensus decision-making, the league had its own version of justice, its own laws, and its own morality.

REFORM   1276–1310   Peak: 1291

- The crusaders loss at the Battle of Acres in 1291, sent the knights home for good. A few months later in 1291, a group of cantons in the HOLY ROMAN EMPIRE formed a confederacy of cooperation that became the OLD SWISS CONFEDERACY, the beginning of the neutral policies of Switzerland. The reforms that were instituted during the peak of REFORM are alive today in a country that has one of the few semi-direct democracies in the world.

- In 1294, Portugal and England signed the *Treaty of Windsor*, forming an alliance still active today.

- In 1307, French KING PHILIP arrested as many Knights Templar as he could find. In 1312, Pope CLEMENT V dissolved the order and two years later, many of the knights were executed.

British Isles

VISION   1122–1128 CE

- When the White Ship sank in 1120, King of England HENRY I's only son and heir went down with it.[56] When Henry died in 1135, a succession war broke out between his nephew and daughter. His nephew, STEPHEN OF BLOIS, became the next king.

POWER   1188–1221   Peak: 1207

- The sons of ELEANOR OF AQUITAINE (1122–1204) ruled England during this time, RICHARD I (r. 1189–1199) and KING JOHN (r. 1199–1216). In 1215, the aristocracy revolted and forced John to sign the *Magna Carta*, a charter that gave the barons increased power and limited the powers of the monarchy. It was annulled by POPE INNOCENT III in 1216.

JUSTICE   1246–1249

- In 1246, ROBERT GROSSETESTE translated Aristotle and developed the scientific method. In 1248, ROGER BACON published a formula for gun powder.

REFORM   1276–1310   Peak: 1291

- EDWARD I (r. 1271–1307) focused on legal reforms until rebellions in Scotland refocused him to quashing the revolts. In 1290, he issued the *Edict of Expulsion*, expelling the JEWS from England. *The First War of Scottish Independence* (1296–1328), initially led by WILLIAM WALLACE who was executed in 1305, and then ROBERT THE BRUCE (r. 1306–1329), gave Scotland independence in 1314.

Asia

VISION 1122–1128 CE

- c. 1125 **KHABUL KHAN** started the **KHAMAG MONGOL** dynasty.

POWER 1188–1221 Peak: 1207

- c. 1188, **GENGHIS KHAN** turned 18 years old. He began his warring at this age, laying siege to neighboring tribes. He quickly expanded the small tribe he inherited from his father into a vast empire. In 1206 CE, **GENGHIS KHAN** declared himself, "Khan", aka emperor. At the end of this POWER time in 1222, **GENGHIS KHAN** died, leaving an empire that stretched all through modern day China, into the Himalayas and north into modern day Russia.[57]

JUSTICE 1246–1249

- In 1246, **GUYUK KHAN** visited Arabia and brought scientific advancement to China. In 1247, **QIN JIUSHAO** published the original form of the Chinese remainder theorem.

REFORM 1276–1310 Peak: 1291

- **KUBLAI KHAN** (r. 1260–1294)
- **MARCO POLO** visited the palace of **KUBLAI KHAN**, returned to Italy, was imprisoned and wrote a book from prison. This book spread like wildfire through Europe. His descriptions of China, including paper money, eyeglasses and coal, inspired and influenced many in Europe, including, centuries later, **CHRISTOPHER COLUMBUS**.
- **TEMÜR KHAN** (r. 1294–1307)

Iberian Peninsula and Islamic States

VISION 1122–1128 CE

- **IBN TUFAYL** (1105–1185) a Sufi muslim in Granada, wrote a philosophical novel, *Hayy ibn Yaq dhan*, just after the VISION time.

POWER 1188–1221 Peak: 1207

- During this POWER time, great philosophers and scientists lived on the Iberian Peninsula including **IBN RUSHD**, also known as **AVERROES** (1126–1198), philosopher in Cordoba, Spain, **MAIMONIDES** (1138–1204), Sephardic Jewish philosopher, Torah scholar, astronomer, physician, personal physician of **SALADIN**, born in Cordoba (Spain), **NUR AD-DIN AL-BITRUJI** (d. 1204), Cordoba, Spain, Muslim astronomer, proposes physical cause for celestial motions, inspired **COPERNICUS**, **ROGER BACON** and Robert **GROSSETESTE**.

- **SALADIN**, Sultan of Egypt and Syria (r. 1174–1193), founded the **AYYUBID DYNASTY** and successfully fought off the crusaders, holding onto to Jerusalem and expanding his empire.

JUSTICE 1246–1249

- In 1249, the *ISLAMIC MOORS* lost possession of Al-Andalus on the Iberian Peninsula and traveled east into **OTTOMAN EMPIRE** territory.
- In 1247, **JALA UDDIN RUMI'S** teacher disappeared prompting him to write 30,000 verses of poetry.
- In 1247, Egypt took control of Jerusalem from the *KHAREZMIANS*.
- (In 1258, the *MONGOLS* conquered Baghdad and ended the Islamic Golden Age.)

REFORM   1276–1310   Peak: 1291

- In 1291, **KING ALFONSO III OF ARAGON** (1285–1291 CE) died and left much of the Iberian Peninsula to **JAMES II** (r. 1291–1327 CE).

The Cycle of Petrarca, 1373–1618 CE

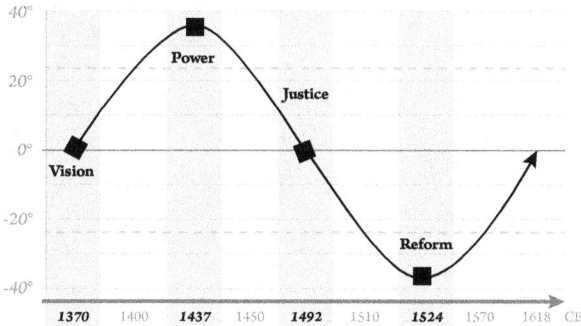

Europe

VISION   1370–1376

- **FRANCESCO PETRARCA** (1304–1374 CE) brought Plato out of obscurity, inspiring the Italian Renaissance. **GIOVANNI BOCCACCIO** (1313–1375 CE) wrote *The Decameron*, a series of stories that introduced Italian prose. The Catholic Church was in a schism, with one pope in Avignon, France and another in Rome, Italy. **CATHERINE OF SIENA** (1347–1380) had a vision that inspired her to petition the pope in Avignon to heal the schism. **GEOFFREY CHAUCER** (c. 1340–1400 CE) traveled to Italy before writing *The Canterbury Tales* that introduced English prose.

POWER   1437–1466   Peak: 1453–54

- COSIMO DE MEDICI (r. 1434–1464 CE) enhanced the banking industry in Florence. He introduced double entry bookkeeping, holding companies, and letters of credit. He gained influence and power through becoming the banker for the Catholic Church.

- In 1439, JOHANNES GUTENBURG created a moveable printing press in The HOLY ROMAN EMPIRE (Germany) and expanded literacy and education throughout Europe.

- Between 1415 and 1453, the *Lancastrian War*, the third and final part of the *Hundred Years' War* (1337–1453), ended when France defeated England, claiming all continental territory, and pushing England back to its own island. Two years later, civil war broke out in England. *The War of the Roses* (1455–1487) pitted the Lancasters against the Yorks and ended with the Tudor line victorious.

- In 1452, Pope Nicholas V issued *Dum Diversas*, a papal bull that allowed Portugal to enslave non-Christians. Initially written to support the enslavement of Muslims in an effort to deal with the threat of the expanding OTTOMAN EMPIRE. The bull was later used to legitimize the enslavement of indigenous people in both Africa and the Americas.

- In 1453, MEHMED II, Sultan of the OTTOMAN EMPIRE, captured the final holding of the BYZANTINE EMPIRE, Constantinople, thus bringing down the Byzantine Empire and making the Ottoman Empire one of the largest on the planet at the time. (During the siege of Constantinople in 1453, there was a visible Lunar Eclipse, May 22, 1453.)

- TOMÁS DE TORQUEMADA (1420–1498), the first Grand Inquisitor of the Spanish Inquisition and Catholic converted from Judaism,[58] began a friendship with Princess ISABELLA OF CASTILE (1451–1504, r. 1474–1504) after Isabella moved to Segovia in 1462. The two together are credited with starting the *Spanish Inquisition* in 1480.

JUSTICE   1492–1498

- In 1492, COLUMBUS sailed to America, LORENZO DE MEDICI died, FERDINAND AND ISABELLA expelled over 100,000 Jews from Spain, and the Dominican priest, GIROLAMO SAVONAROLA (1452–1498) inspired the citizens of Florence to demonstrate against Roman Catholic Church corruption by burning their valuables. Savonarola was excommunicated in 1496 and burned at the stake in 1498. Leonardo da Vinci painted *The Last Supper* on a wall in a church in Milan (c. 1498). MICHELANGELO carved the *Pietà* in Rome (1496–1499). SANDRO BOTTICELLI painted the *Calumny of Apelles* (c. 1495).

REFORM   1524–1553   Peak: 1537

- Most date the Reformation from the time in 1517 when MARTIN LUTHER posted his controversial document, *95 Theses*, outlining complaints against the Roman Catholic

Church. In 1520, he was excommunicated from the church and in 1522, he translated the bible into German. In 1526, **WILLIAM TYNDALE** translated the bible in England. In 1529, Luther met **HULDRYCH ZWINGLI** (1484–1531 CE), who was starting his own protest movement in Switzerland. Zwingli died in battle in 1531, while Luther and **JOHN CALVIN** (1509–1564) continued the protests and the formation of protestant religions.

- In 1534, **HENRY VIII**, King of England (r. 1509–1547), declared himself head of both church and state, separating England from the Catholic Church.

- In response to the Reformation, the Catholic Church instigated the Counter-Reformation. In 1537, Pope Paul III issued the Papal Bull, *Sublimus Deus*, forbidding the enslavement of the native peoples of the Americas, a reversal of *Dum Diversus*, with the intention of diminishing the power of the colonists, who were largely protestant. The bull extended (somewhat extemporaneously) to all Christians. In 1545, the *Council of Trent*, the Catholic Church's response to the Reformation included forced conversions, inquisitions and the formation of seminaries for priests. In 1540, **IGNATIUS OF LOYOLA** founded the *Society of Jesus*, the Jesuit Order, in Paris.

The Americas
VISION   1370–1376

- **ACAMAPICHITLI** (r. c. 1376–c. 1395 CE) was the first king of Tenochtitlan, Mayan Civilization.

POWER   1437–1466   Peak: 1453–54

- In 1427, the *TEPANECA* (a growing tribe in what is today central Mexico) killed **CHIMALPOPOCA** (ruler of the *MEXICA* people located in what is today southern Mexico), and war ensued. **ITZCOATL** (r. 1427–1440), the leader of the Mexica, triumphed and became king.

- **MONTEZUMA I** (r. 1440–1469) was the second *AZTEC* emperor. Between 1452–1454, flood and famine wreaked havoc in Tenochtitlan.

- **PANCHACUTI** (r. 1438–1472) expanded the *INCA* Empire (Peru). Between 1450–1460, *Machu Picchu* was built.

- Five tribes, including the *MOHAWK, ONEIDA, ONANDOAGA, CAYUGA*, and *SENECA* tribes, formed the *Iroquois Confederacy* in 1451 CE (current day New York state).

JUSTICE   1492–1498

- **AHITZOTL** (r. 1486–1502), expanded the *AZTEC* Empire and the city of Tenochtitlan and put down internal rebellions.

- Panchacuti's son, **TOPA INCA YUPANQUI** ruled following him from 1472 to 1493. He further expanded the empire into Ecuador. Topa's son, **HUAYNA CAPAC** took over at Topa's death in 1493 and ruled until 1527.

- In 1492, Christopher Columbus sailed the Atlantic and landed in Hispaniola.

- In 1494, Pope Alexander IV divided the Americas, giving what is today Brazil to the Portuguese and the rest to Spain in the Treaty of Todesillas.

REFORM   1524–1553   Peak: 1537

- In 1520, Hernán Cortés and his army of Spanish conquistadors invaded the Aztec Empire. The emperor of the Aztecs, Montezuma II (r. 1502–1520), handed over the keys of the kingdom to Spain and was stoned to death by his own people. In 1531, Pizarro and his army of Spanish conquistadors invaded the Inca Empire.[59] Atahualpa (r. 1532–1533) was the last ruler of the Incan Empire.

Russia

VISION   1370–1376

- Russia ruled by Khan of the Golden Hordes. Dmitry I, Prince of Moscow, was the first Russian ruler to stand up to the Mongols.

POWER   1437–1466   Peak: 1453–54

- Vasily II, ruler of Moscow, (r. 1425–1462) blinded in battle, shored up the city and further entrenched the Rurik Dynasty and the Russian Orthodox Church into Russian leadership.

JUSTICE   1492–1498

- Ivan III (r. 1462–1505). The Sudebnik of 1497 created a blueprint for Russian Law.

REFORM   1524–1553   Peak: 1537

- Ivan IV (Ivan the Terrible) reign, 1547–1584. Separated into two parts: Reform (1547–1560) and Terror (1560–1584). Ivan IV came into power during the REFORM time, surrounded by a group of reformers known as the "Chosen Council". Seven years after the REFORM time ended, Ivan's time of reform came to an end when he took over Novgorod and started the Reign of Terror.

China

In China, the Mongol dynasties collapsed, and the Ming Dynasty rose in its wake, founded in 1368. The Ming Dynasty (1386–1644) ruled for almost exactly the totality of this cycle. This was a Chinese dynasty that paralleled the Italian Renaissance with a value for the arts. It is also known as a dynasty that supported welfare and helped the poor, even if it was also known for its extreme abuse of power through torture.

India

In Southern India, this cycle corresponds with the creation and destruction of the VI-JAYANAGAR EMPIRE (1336–1614). This was an empire of peace and culture that spoke Sanskrit and supported a Hindu revival of culture and politics. It revolved around the city, Vijayanagar. There was a strong focus on music and the arts. This society managed to peacefully avoid MUSLIM conquest during this time.

Ottoman Empire

VISION   1370–1376

- The OTTOMAN EMPIRE formed the *Janissary* army of Christian soldiers in 1363.

POWER   1437–1466   Peak: 1453–54

- In 1451, Ottoman KING MURAD II died. His son, MEHMET II, became ruler and conquered Constantinople, taking down the seat of the BYZANTINE EMPIRE in 1453.

JUSTICE   1492–1498

- Spain expelled the JEWS (1492) and Portugal expelled the JEWS (1496) who were given refuge in the OTTOMAN EMPIRE.

REFORM   1524–1553   Peak: 1537

- SULEIMAN THE MAGNIFICENT (r. 1520–1566) ruled the OTTOMAN EMPIRE and instituted judicial reforms and supported the arts and sciences.

Timurid Renaissance (Persian, Central Asia)

VISION   1370–1376

- The TIMURID EMPIRE was founded in 1370 by AMIR TAMERLANE. In 1394, Tamerlane conquered Afghanistan and by 1398 conquered Dehli. By 1401, the TIMURID EMPIRE took over Baghdad and was extended from Aleppo to Dehli.
- HAFIZ (1325–1390 CE) wrote poetry in Persia.

POWER   1437–1466   Peak: 1453–54

- In the mid-1400s TIMURID EMPIRE conquered Persia.

JUSTICE   1492–1498

- TIMURID EMPIRE moved into decline.

REFORM   1524–1553   Peak: 1537

- MUGHAL EMPIRE founded in 1526 in modern-day Uzbekistan and reaching into modern-day India.

The Cycle of Kepler & Descartes, 1618–1863 CE

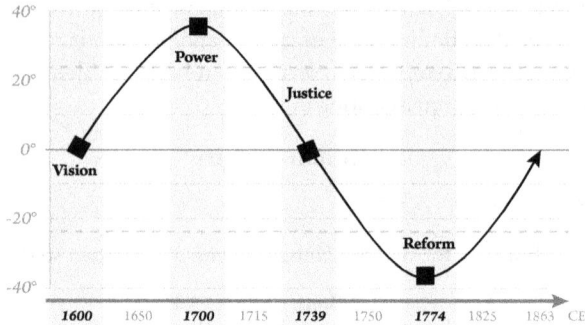

Europe

VISION   **1615–1622**

- **Francis Bacon** in England published *Novum Organum* (1620) in which he states: "Truth emerges more readily from error than from confusion".[60]

- Two significant new crops were transplanted during the VISION time—potatoes and tobacco. Potatoes were brought up from the Andes and replanted in Germany for the first time in 1621.[61]

- In 1619, *East India Trading Company* sent ambassadors to the **Ottoman Empire** to begin trade negotiations.

- **James I, King of England** (r. 1603–1625) tried to hold on to the power of the monarch by dissolving parliament for seven years from 1614 to 1621.

- **Galileo** saw the moons of Jupiter (1609), shared with Italian scholars **Copernicus'** heliocentric model of solar system (1613) and had his work banned by the Catholic Church (1616). **Johannes Kepler** wrote *Astronomia nova* (1609) and *Harmonice Mundi* (1619). **René Descartes** wrote *Musicae Compendium* (1618).

- **William Shakespeare** and **Miguel de Cervantes** both died in 1616.

POWER   **1687–1710**   **Peak: 1700**

- On June 6, 1688, **William and Mary** entered London and took over England in the *Glorious Revolution*.

- In 1687, **Isaac Newton** (1643–1727) published *Principia*, on the universal laws of motion. In 1689, **John Locke** (1632–1704) wrote *Two Treatises of Government*, a work that inspired future founders of the US.

- In 1696, **John Locke** and **Isaac Newton** designed new coinage, just after Newton became head of the Royal Mint.

Appendix V

- In 1694, CHARLES MONTAGU, THE 1ˢᵀ EARL OF HALIFAX, established the Bank of England, during a financial crisis. At the time, he was head of the Royal Society, the First Lord of the Treasury, and a personal friend and patron of NEWTON.

- KING LOUIS XIV OF FRANCE (r. 1643–1715) built *Versailles*, returned the country to Catholicism and banned Protestantism. While his reign included increased power for the monarchy, he included women in his court and encouraged the exchange of ideas and knowledge, all the while leading France into several wars, building his military, expanding the borders of France and amassing staggering personal wealth while bankrupting his country.

- From 1688–1697, the *Nine Years' War*, when France went to war with Spain, England, the Dutch Republic, the Holy Roman Empire (Hapsburgs), Portugal and Savoy. LOUIS XIV had become the most powerful monarch in Europe at the time, through the accumulation of wealth through taxes, fur trading in the Americas and spending a lot of money on infrastructure, military, and his palace at the expense of his nobles and people. France lost and won at the same time. KING LOUIS XIV maintained power and the French influence in the world grew.

- In 1700, the Spanish KING CHARLES II died childless and left a vacancy on the Spanish throne. KING LOUIS XIV was quick to install his grandson, PHILIP, whose grandmother was MARIA THERESE OF SPAIN (1638 - 1683), Infanta of Spain. Another war broke out, *The Spanish War of Succession*, over this because the Holy Roman Empire (Germany, Austria) wanted their pick for the throne. Since royalty was heavily intermarrying for alliances at this time, the right of succession was not clear. In the end, Philip became king of Spain and then king of France, too. France conceded some territory, and a truce was made in 1714, three years after Louis XIV died (1711), precisely at the end of the POWER time.

JUSTICE   1739 –1742

- GEORGE FRIDERIC HANDEL composed "The Messiah" in 18 days in 1741. J.S. BACH composed *Mass in B minor* (c. 1724–1748). Scottish philosopher DAVID HUME wrote *A Treatise of Human Nature* (1740). French philosopher, VOLTAIRE wrote *Elements of the Philosophy of Newton* in 1738, promoting and making Newton's work accessible to non-scientists. SCOTTISH JACOBITES rose up against the British monarchy, advocating for their own monarch, BONNIE PRINCE CHARLES, at the *Battle of Culloden*, 1746, where the British decisively ended the JACOBITE cause.

REFORM   1774–1795   Peak: 1783–85

- MARY WOLLSTONECRAFT wrote *A Vindication of Women's Rights*, a landmark publication speaking out for the rights and power of women. (1792)

- French inventor, NICOLAS-JOSEPH CUGNOT's first self-propelled vehicle (1769) led to enough vehicles on the road that during the VISION time of the next cycle, England created the first road laws under the *Locomotive Acts* of 1865. This initiated the process of registering vehicles, speed limits, and weight limits on trucks.

323

- Peasants' revolts in Bohemia in 1775 eventually lead to serfdom abolished in Bohemia and Hungary in 1780.

- Pitt's *India Act* put East India Company under government control in 1784.

- In 1774, **Louis XV** died, and his son **Louis XIV** became king of France. In 1789, a Paris mob stormed the bastille beginning the *French Revolution*. King Louis XIV and his wife, **Marie Antionette**, were executed in 1793. The *Reign of Terror* from 1793 to 1794 decimated France under the rulership of **Maximelien Robespierre** who was executed in 1794.

- In 1783, Britain and America end fighting and declare peace in the *Treaty of Paris*.

- Denmark abolished the slave trade in 1792, the first country to do so.

Americas

VISION   1615–1622

- Tobacco was first planted by a European, **John Rolfe**, in 1612. In 1614, Rolfe married **Pocahontas**, a Native American woman from the *Powhatan* tribe.

- In 1619, the first enslaved African were brought to the British colonies to work the tobacco farms.

- *English* settlers founded Jamestown (1606) and Plymouth (1620). The *French* settled Quebec (1608). The *Dutch* founded New Amsterdam (Manhattan, 1612) and **Henry Hudson** sailed up the river that bears his name in 1609.

POWER   1687–1710   Peak: 1700

- In 1689 in the British colony of New York, British forces quashed an armed uprising. Queen Anne placed the corrupt Lord Cornbury in charge. Ship building and barrel manufacturing made New York into a hub of trade and wealth. In 1699, the wall separating the British and Dutch colonies was dismantled to pave a street: Wall Street.

JUSTICE   1739–1742

- In 1739, Samuel Adams (1722–1803) became disillusioned with Britain when the government dissolved his father's land bank, a popular form of commerce among the colonists) and made his father liable, putting his father in debt for the rest of his life.

- In 1741, mysterious fires broke out in New York, as part of an insurrection led by the enslaved. When the plot was uncovered, 16 Blacks and 4 whites were tortured and burned at the stake.

- In 1743, Benjamin Franklin founded the *American Philosophical Society* and began his political career.

- Jonathan Edwards toured through the colonies in what has come to be called the first "Great Awakening". In 1741, he delivered his famous sermon, "Sinners in the Hands of an Angry God", in Massachusetts. His sermons inspired a fervor for freedom of religion in the colonies.

REFORM   1774–1795 Peak: 1783–85

- In North America, Oliver Evan's automatic flour mill (1785) innovated material handling leading to increased production and reduced contamination of flour and other raw materials. Eli Whitney's cotton gin (1793) significantly reduced the labor required to remove cotton seeds.

- In 1773, colonists protest against Britain's tax mandates by throwing overboard crates of tea at the *Boston Tea Party*. In 1775, the Battle of Lexington and Concord started the American Revolutionary War. By mid-June 1776, Thomas Jefferson was working on a *Declaration of Independence*, GEORGE WASHINGTON was recruiting troops for a battle in New York, and ALEXANDER HAMILTON, who had already published anti-British pamphlets in 1775, became Washington's assistant.

- In 1787, after conflict with the UK ended with the *Treaty of Paris* (1783), the Constitutional Convention in Philadelphia presents a new constitution, that was ratified by the states in 1788. In 1789, the First US Congress met in New York. GEORGE WASHINGTON was inaugurated as president. In 1792 on Wall Street, a group of financiers met under a buttonwood tree and formed the New York Stock Exchange.

- TOUSSAINT L'OUVERTURE, born an enslaved Haitian, freed sometime in the early 1770s, inspired by the *American Revolution*, was part of starting the *Haitian Revolution* (1791–1804), which ended in the abolition of slavery and an independent nation free from French rule. The *Haitian Revolution* inspired SIMÓN BOLÍVAR (1783–1830) and future revolutions that ended with independence for Venezuela (1810–1823), Ecuador (1820–1822), Peru (1809–1826), Argentina (1810–1818), Mexico (1810–1821), Chile (1810–1826), Paraguay (1811), Brazil (1822–1825), and Bolivia (1809–1825).

India

During the time when colonization was overtaking India, Samanth Ramdass, Advaita Vedantist, wrote Dasbodh, a spiritual text on the practice of Bhakti, devotion (1654). He was a teacher of Tukaram, another Indian saint and spiritual guide. Ramdass attained enlightenment at the age of 11 or 12. His birth date is contested, but if we use the commonly accepted birth date of 1608, his enlightenment falls directly into the VISION time of this cycle (1619–20). Ramdass inspired Tukaram who inspired a generations of Bhakti devotees including Gandhi in the next cycle.

China

VISION   1615–1622

- Transition from Ming dynasty to Qing Dynasty started in 1618. By 1644, the Qing (Manchu) were fully in charge.

POWER   1687–1710 Peak: 1700

- In 1683, the Qing Dynasty took over Taiwan. Emperor Kangxi (r. 1662–1722) halted invasions by Russia, coming to a peace treaty in 1689, The Treaty of Nerchinsk, that brought a large area of Siberia into Chinese rule.

JUSTICE   1739–1742

- In 1740, Chinese Indonesians revolted in Batavia (Jakarta) and the Dutch East India Company slaughtered 10,000 Chinese rebels.

REFORM   1774–1795 Peak: 1783–85

- After the Treaty of Versailles and the end of the American Revolution, the US began trade with China, particularly as Americans missed getting tea through the EIC.

Russia

VISION   1615–1622

- The dynasty of the Ivans ended in 1613 when the last Ivan died. MICHAEL ROMANOV took over and began the ROMANOV DYNASTY.

POWER   1687–1710 Peak: 1700

- PETER THE GREAT (r. 1689–1725) brought Russia into the modern age. He increased military spending, brought in technologies from Europe, and ruled the government with efficiency. He declared Russia an empire and himself an Emperor in 1721. Known for being a simple man who disguised himself to walk amongst the people, he brought the Orthodox Christian Church under state control, making Russia a theocracy, autocracy, and dictatorship.

JUSTICE   1739–1742

- PETER THE GREAT died of smallpox. Like Augustus Caesar who also died at the JUSTICE time, the leader that followed in his footsteps was a much weaker leader. ANNA IVANOVNA, daughter of IVAN V was appointed heir. She dissolved the *Supreme Privy Council*, undoing recent public policy.

REFORM   1774–1795   Peak: 1783–85

- CATHERINE THE GREAT upgraded Russia into the modern age, improved education and further expanded the empire. She was a follower of Enlightenment philosophers, especially VOLTAIRE with whom she had some correspondence. She attempted to outlaw capital punishment and pushed for all men to be treated equally, until a rebellion (1774–1775) as the REFORM time began, had her pull in the reigns. The *Pugachev Rebellion* made her realize the importance of the land-owning nobility in keeping peace within the kingdom. In response, Catherine instituted reforms that gave them more control over their lands and the people that worked them, the serfs.

The Cycle of Darwin & Dunant, 1863–2108

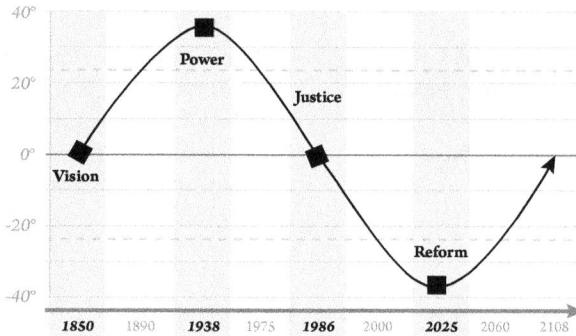

The World

VISION **1861–1865**

Politics

- In 1863, **HENRY DUNANT** inspired the formation of the *International Red Cross*. In the same year, 26 nations signed the first *Geneva Conventions*, agreeing to humanitarian rules during and after war.

- From 1863 to 1870, civil war in Germany led to the formation of the **GERMAN EMPIRE** (1871). From 1858 to 1870, civil war in Italy led to the formation of the **KINGDOM OF ITALY** (1861). From 1861 to 1867, **NAPOLEON III**, ruler of France, placed **MAXIMILIAN I**, brother of the Archduke of Austria, into the role of Emperor of Mexico. In 1867, he and his wife were executed, and Mexico declared its independence from France.

- From the 1861 to 1865, the US was embroiled in civil war that ended with the pro-industrial, anti-slavery North victorious. President **ABRAHAM LINCOLN** (r. 1861–1865) gave the *Gettysburg Address* (1863). The *13th Amendment* ended legal slavery (1865). The *14th Amendment* granted citizenship to all men, regardless of race (1868). The *15th Amendment* gave all men the right to vote (1870).

- On March 3, 1861, the *Emancipation Edict* imposed by the **TSAR ALEXANDER II** liberated the serfs in Russia. In January 1863, Polish conscripts rose up against Russian occupation in what is known as the *January Uprising*. Lithuania and Belarus followed with more uprisings. Russian forces put down the revolts.

- The **OTTOMAN EMPIRE** went into debt to European money lenders after the *Crimean War*.

- The *Taiping Rebellion* (uprising against **QING DYNASTY**), the *Second Opium War* (1856–1860) ended with British and French forces burning down the emperor's Summer Palace (1860). A year later, the Qing Emperor, **XIENFENG** (r. 1850–1861) died and his five-year-old son became ruler. **Dowager Empress Cixi** staged a successful coup, and her 47-year reign began.

Literature

- **Leo Tolstoy** published *War and Peace* (1864, Russia). **Feodor Dostoevsky** published *Crime and Punishment* (1866, Russia). **Victor Hugo** wrote *Les Misérables* (1862, France). **Karl Marx** published *Das Kapital* (1867, Germany). **Charles Dickens** published *A Tale of Two Cities* (1859, England) and *Great Expectations* (1861, UK). **John Stuart Mill** published *Utilitarianism* (1863, UK). **Lewis Carroll** wrote *Alice's Adventures in Wonderland* (1865, UK).

Business

- Bayer (f. 1863, Germany), the 2nd largest chemical company in the world BASF (1865, Germany), the dynamite/chemical company Dynamit Nobel (1865, Germany), Nestlé (1866, Switzerland), Standard Oil (original contracts in 1863, US), Travelers Insurance Company (1863, US), John Hancock Mutual Life Insurance Company (1862, Boston), Michigan Car Company (1863, US), Cargill, Inc. (1865, US), Keystone Bridge Company (1865, US), Nokia (1865, Finland) and General Mills (1866, US), to name a few.

Other Organizations

- **Florence Nightingale** founded the first *nursing school* (1865, England). **Karl Marx** founded the *First International Workingmen's Association* in London and New York (1864). **Elizabeth Cady Stanton** and **Susan B. Anthony** formed the *American Equal Rights Association* (1864, US).[62]
- Ku Klux Klan was founded in Pulaski, Tennessee in 1865 at the end of the Civil War.

Science and Technology

- The National Academy of Sciences was founded (1863).

- **James Maxwell** presented his paper, *Dynamical Theory of the Electromagnetic Field* (1864, Scotland). In 1856, **Eunice Foote's** article on the greenhouse effect came out in the American Journal of Science and Arts. Three years later, Irish scientist **John Tyndall** described the greenhouse effect to the Royal Society in London.[63] **Charles Darwin** wrote *On the Origin of Species* (1859, England). **Alfred Nobel** invented *dynamite* (1860s, Sweden). **Dmitri Mendeleyev** published his *periodic table of elements* (1869, Russia). Scottish scientist **Charles Lyell** published The Geological Evidence of the Antiquity of Man (1863).

- **Gregor Mendel** wrote *Experiments in Plant Hybridization* and founded the field of genetics (1865, Austria-Hungary/Czech Republic). **Joseph Lister** developed *anti-septic surgery* (1860s, Scotland). **Louis Pasteur** developed *germ theory of fermentation* (1861, France) and invented *pasteurization* (1864).

- The first oil well was drilled in 1859 in Titusville, Pennsylvania. JOHN D. ROCKEFELLER SR. directed the creation of the first oil pipeline (1865, Pennsylvania).

Transportation

- PIERRE MICHAUX built the first *pedal bicycle* (1860s, France). ÈTIENNE LENOIR built the first practical internal-combustion engine (1860, France). Work on the *Suez Canal* began in 1859. The *Transcontinental Railroad* track was laid down (completed in 1869, US). The *Orient Express* was first envisioned by a Belgium man in 1865.[64] Thomas Cook started the touring industry taking paying customers to Egypt and Palestine (1869, England).[65]

Religion

- RAMAKRISHNA awakened and inspired *Vedanta* (1860s, India). BAHÁ'U'LLÁH had a vision in a garden in 1863 and founded the *BA'HAI FAITH*.[66] WILLIAM MILLER started the *SEVENTH DAY ADVENTIST CHURCH* (1863, US). WILLIAM BOOTH founded *THE SALVATION ARMY* (1865, London).

POWER   1938–1949

Politics

- *The Spanish Civil War* (1938–1939) ended with FRANCISCO FRANCO as dictator of Spain.

- *WWII* (1939–1945) ravaged much of the world and destroyed millions of lives.

- HITLER rose into power in the early 1930s. Japan invaded China (1937). The German Nazi army marched into Austria unopposed (March 1938). Nazi Germany took over Czechoslovakia (September 1938). *Kristallnacht*, the "Night of Broken Glass", sparked widespread persecution of Jews. Germany and Italy signed an alliance, the *Pact of Steel* (May 1939). Germany invaded Poland, the official start of WWII (September 1939). Italy invaded British-occupied Egypt (1939). Germany invaded France (1940) and then launched attacks into Britain. Hungary, Slovakia, and Romania joined the *AXIS POWERS* (1940). Germany invaded Russia (June 1941). Japan attacked the US (Pearl Harbor, 1941) and the US declared war on Japan.

- In New Hampshire, diplomats and executives of the Allies met at the *Bretton Woods Conference* and established the infrastructure for a new world economy including the formation of the *World Bank* and the *International Monetary Fund* (1944). In February 1945, President ROOSEVELT, Prime Minister CHURCHILL, and Marshal STALIN met at the Yalta Conference to plan the final defeat. In May 1945, Germany and Italy surrendered. The US dropped two atomic bombs on Japan (August 1945) and Japan surrendered.

- In post-WWII conferences and agreements, the *United Nations* was birthed (1945), *GATT* (General Agreements on Trade and Tariffs) was formed, a precursor to the

World Trade Organization. The UN formed the *World Health Organization* (1948).

- The *Allied Powers* partitioned Vietnam, Korea, and Germany into communist and democratic states. Independence came to India, Ceylon, and Burma when Britain pulled out. The UN partitioned India into Pakistan and India (1947). Britain pulled out of Palestine and the new nation of Israel was established (1948).

- In Japan-occupied China, a rebel leader inspired by the *Russian Revolution*, Mao Zedong, gathered troops. In March 1946, civil war erupted. In 1950, Mao's forces attained victory and declared China as the People's Republic of China. Chang Kai-shek, with his nationalist army, retreated to Taiwan. China occupied Tibet (1951).

- In 1949, twelve countries in North America and Europe formed the North Atlantic Treaty Organization (NATO).

Science and Technology

- Much science and technology revolved around the war machine. Otto Hahn, Lise Meitner, and Friedrich Strassmann discover *nuclear fission* (1938, US). Walter Zinn & Herbert Anderson created the first sustained nuclear reaction (1942, US). Roy Plunkett invented Teflon™ (1938, US). Hans Ohain designed the first *jet plane* (1939, Germany). Paul Muller discovered the insecticidal properties of *DDT* (1939, Switzerland). Martin Whitaker and Eugene Wigner lead the construction of the first *operational nuclear reactor* (1943, US). Arthur Clarke conceptualized the use of the satellites for global communication (1945, UK). John Eckert, John Mauchly, Arthur Burks, and John von Neumann developed *ENIAC*, the first entirely electronic computer (1945, US). Alan Turning developed a computing device (1936, UK). David Packard and Bill Hewlett formed the *Hewlett Packard* Company (1941, US). Arthur Clarke conceptualized the use of satellites for global communication (1945, UK). John Bardeen, Walter Houser, and William Chockley invented the *transistor* (1948, US). Albert Hoffman discovered the hallucinogenic properties of *LSD* (1943, US). John Frisch and Francis Bull initiated the *fluoridation of water* (1945, US). The Manhattan Project under the direction of Robert Oppenheim developed the atomic bomb (1940s, US).

JUSTICE   1986–1989

Politics

- The *Single European Act* merged the resources of European countries and important step in the formation of the European Union (1987).

- *Palestinians* protested against Israeli policies in the first intifada (1987) that turned violent. The Islam jihadist organization, *Hamas*, was formed (1988, Palestine).

- The US intervened in the *Soviet-Afghan war* (1979–1989) by arming the Afghan rebel forces, the mujahideen. The Soviet Union retreated (1988). Osama bin Laden, who fought with the mujahideen, formed *Al-Qaeda* (1988) in the aftermath of the war.

- The *Iran-Iraq War* (1980–1988) began when Iraq invaded Iran.

- *Collapse of the Soviet Union*: **MIKHAIL GORBACHEV** became head of the Soviet Union in 1985, after the previous two heads died with less than two years in office. Gorbachev initiated perestroika, economic restructuring legislation in a time when the economy was failing, and glasnost, nudging open the doors of the closed state (1986–1988). Peaceful demonstrations of lands seeking independence from the Soviet Union were ultimately successful including the *Singing Revolution* (1988–1989, Estonia, Latvia, Lithuania), the *Velvet Revolution* (1989, Czechoslovakia), the *Christmas Revolution* (1989, Romania), and student-led protests in Kazakhstan (1986). The *Berlin Wall came down* (1989, Germany). The Soviet Union fell into 15 different states from 1990 to 1991.

- The 8888 Uprising in Burma led to the election of *Aung San Suu Kyi* of the *National League for Democracy*, but she was put under house arrest before taking office and the military took control of the country (1988, Burma/Myanmar).

- In an open election in Pakistan, **BENAZIR BHUTTO** was the first woman elected to be head of state of a Muslim country (1988). The beginning of the dismantling of apartheid (1989, South Africa), the beginning of a new democracy in Brazil (1985–1989), the *Peaceful Revolution* (Germany, 1989), the *People's Power Revolution* (1986, the Philippines), and Students in Beijing go on a hunger strike protesting the communist government. Mass demonstrations follow in Tiananmen Square. The military violently attacked protesters. Number of deaths widely varies (1989, China).

- **EMPEROR HIROHITO** (r. 1926–1989) died and his Akihito began his reign (1989, Japan).

- The Iran Contra scandal was exposed after government officials illegally sold arms to Iran and used the money to fund rebel forces in Nicaragua (1986, US).

Business

- **MICROSOFT** went public (1986, US). Two men who worked at Lehman brothers formed *THE BLACKSTONE GROUP* (1985, US). A merger between two energy companies, the Houston Gas Company and InterNorth, formed **ENRON** (1985, US). Time Inc. and Warner Communications merged to form **TIME-WARNER** (1989, US). Stock trading began in Communist China for the first time (1986, China). The stock market crashed in the US in what came to be called *Black Monday* (1987, US). With oil consumption going down, the oil market took a dive and contributed to the fall of the Soviet Union, a major oil producer. In 1987, the nationalized oil industry in the Soviet Union transitioned into the corporation, Gazprom.

Environment

- Major wake-up calls hit many parts of the world. An explosion at a nuclear power plant in *Chernobyl*, Ukraine, led to one of the largest environmental disasters (1986).

A Union Carbide pesticide plant released 42 tons of toxic gases into the environment killing over 25,000 people (1984). The Exxon Valdez oil tanker grounded and spilled 11 million gallons of oil and killed a quarter of a million birds in addition to countless fish (1989). JAMES HANSEN, a NASA scientist, went before congress warning that global warming was happening more quickly than expected (1988).

Science and Technology

- TIM BERNERS-LEE invented the *World Wide Web* while at CERN (1989, Switzerland). The World became the first commercial internet provider (1989, US) and then AOL (America Online) launched later that year. The US National Academy of Sciences launched the goals for the Human Genome Project (1988). The FDA approved *Prozac*, aka Fluoxetine (1987, US).

- The CDC first detected HIV/AIDS in 1981 and by 1986 there were over 25,000 reported cases of HIV in the US alone.[67] Rising the challenge of the AIDS epidemic, ACT UP (AIDS Coalition to Unleash Power) was founded (1987, NYC).

REFORM   2025–2035

- ???

Endnotes to Appendix V

1. Feuerstein, 105. See page 38, note 5.
2. Durant and Durant, 403. See page 38, note 6.
3. Feuerstein, 67.
4. Davis, 108. See page 38, note 7.
5. DK, *Timelines of History*.
6. David Neiman, "The History of Egypt: The Hyksos Invasion."
7. Peter Stearns and William Langer, *The Encyclopedia of World History: Ancient, Medieval, and Modern, Chronologically Arranged*.
8. *Ibid.*
9. Feuerstein, 84.
10. Cline.
11. Ulrich Theobald, "Wu Ding 武丁."
12. John P. McCay, et al. *A History of World Societies*.
13. Kate Santan and Liz McKay, *Atlas of World History*.
14. *Ibid.*
15. This famous king enjoyed the wealth gained from taxes, seven hundred wives and three hundred concubines, lavish celebrations and the building of great temples. Through David and Solomon, Israel had moved into a theocracy with the king being head of the Hebrew religion. The Divine Right of Kings and monotheism were firmly established. Hierarchy and patriarchy became the established law.
16. Amy Dockser Marcus, *The View from Nebo*. Marcus points to a lack of archeological evidence for the great buildings which are alluded to in the Hebrew bible.
17. This splitting occurred precisely at the peak of the REFORM time, a time when great kingdoms often implode if the ruler isn't high-minded enough to introduce reforms. While this may have been challenging at the time and may sound like a disaster, it actually laid the groundwork for the next cycle, when Israel moved into its great age, an age of prophets, a renaissance of sorts.
18. An early communistic ideal that in practice maintained a caste system where the poor stayed poor and the rich stayed rich
19. See page 39, note 11.
20. The first Olympic Games took place (776 BCE). These games gathered competitors from all the cities in Greece and into Spain and Turkey. Every four years, men boxed, ran, threw disci, and wrestled with men from other regions, beginning to create a coalesced society that grew into Ancient Greece.
21. See page 48, note 24.
22. The Ecclesia is the early foundation of democracy. An elected group of citizens, about 6,000 out of a population of 30,000 to 60,000, convene to vote on governing policies.
23. Herman, *The Cave and the Light*, 12.
24. https://www.poetryfoundation.org/poets/sappho
25. http://www.socialstudiesforkids.com/articles/worldhistory/lycurgussolon.htm
26. Glenn A. Parry, *Original Thinking*, 15.
27. Manly P. Hall, *The Secret Destiny of America*.
28. Panini was a great yogic scholar who Patanjali later based his yoga sutras on.
29. See page 40, Aristotle.
30. See page 40, Chanakya.
31. See page 40, note 13.
32. Armstrong, *The Great Transformation*, 358–59.

33. The sculptures included chariots, weapons, and horses as well as soldiers and were only unearthed in 1974 by farmers.

34. In northern Africa, the city of Alexandria was rising into a great multi-cultural metropolis—a place of learning, trade and technological advancement. What began as a sand pile, quickly became the center of the world during the POWER time. During the REFORM time, rebellions and uprisings were so common that a brilliant general from Carthage set out to squash them. His rebel squashing army kept going, though and over the Alps doing serious damage to the Roman forces. Using wild, yet tamed, elephants for his army (Diamond, *Guns, Germs and Steel*, 159), the Carthaginians were ultimately unsuccessful and while the Roman Empire remained until 395 CE, it was during this time that rebellions weakened the powerful empire.

35. Muraresku, 71.

36. Justin Martyr wrote letters of apology (from apologia in Greek meaning defense) to emperors talking about logos (the Universe). Justin, taught by a stoic, wanted to study Pythagorus but found the requirements too stringent. He turned to philosophy and work of Plato which served his temperament better. In his writings, he attempted to defend Christianity using philosophy and paganism as a backdrop. Ultimately, he was beheaded for his beliefs, but his works were the beginning of assimilating Christian theology with the pagan traditions of the time.

37. Muraresku, 71.

38. Nāgārjuna comes in second place (only to Sankara) in Murray's list of most significant Indian philosophers (in *Human Accomplishment*). See also: Armstrong, *History of God*.

39. "Several developments during Gallienus' reign are of particular importance. There was a sharp reduction of civilian control over the military, because Gallienus—breaking with a tradition of some seven centuries—transferred the command of the Roman armies from the senators to professional equestrian officers. At the same time, he expanded the role of the cavalry in *warfare* by creating a mobile cavalry reserve, which was to become the nucleus of the field army of the later empire. Finally, in the relatively peaceful years 262–267, Gallienus sponsored a vigorous *intellectual* renaissance at Rome. This revival is clearly discernible in the surviving art and the contemporary literature, notably that of Neoplatonist philosophers such as Plotinus." See: https://www.britannica.com/biography/Gallienus

40. Murray, *Human Accomplishment*.

41. Madhavi Narsalay. "A Poetic Genius." the week.in Dec. 27, 2015. Madhavi Narsalay, professor of Sanskrit at the University of Mumbai.

42. The year before the REFORM time began, one of the most ill-timed and devastatingly unsuccessful rebellions occurred, the Nika Rebellion. Crafty Emperor Justinian used the rivalry between factions of street gangs (Blues and Greens) to get the Greens corralled into the Hippodrome (30,000 of them) and then had his army slaughter them. If only they had waited a year (not that the revolt was planned), Pluto in extreme declination may have supported their success. However, Justinian was already trying to make reforms and the quashed rebellion gave him the power to institute the rule of law, called Justinian's code. William Weir states that Justinian "stopped a rebellion of the people and shifted western civilization from 'the changing whims of a succession of tyrants' to the rule of law--a codification of law that is the basis for much of the civil and criminal law of Europe, Africa and some of the Americas." From: William Weir, *50 Battles that Changed the World*, 18–20.

43. Accounts vary about her origin. Some say her father was a lesser general, others suggest a merchant. Regardless, he was not a significant noble or a powerful man and Wu Zhao was twenty-eighth concubine. She became consort to Taizong's son, Gaozong. When Taizong died she entered a convent with the rest of his consorts as was the tradition of the day, until Gaozong retrieved her and brought her back to his court when he became emperor.

44. Armstrong, 188

45. *Ibid.*,195.

46. Murray, 139. Murray adds the caveat that if Confucius was added into the mix, he would have won by a long shot.

47. Daniel J. Boorstin, *The Creators: A History of Heroes of the Imagination*, 65.

48. Awan, 30–33.

49. George, 579–624.

50. *Ibid.*

51. Barlow, 494.

52. Abetti.

53. J. J. O'Connor and E. F. Robertson. "Adelard of Bath."

54. Matthew S. Bracey, "Divine Grace and Human Responsibility in Bernard of Clairvaux."

55. Bernard of Clairvaux, a French Benedictine monk, brought back Augustine, the author of the "Just War" doctrine, giving the Catholic Church philosophical ammunition to send untrained citizens into foreign lands into battle. The Catholic Crusades were already in full swing with the desire of the pope to take back Jerusalem from the Muslims for Christianity. At the beginning of this cycle, Saint Bernard of Clairvaux, a French Catholic mystic, is writing his great works, that among other things instill chivalry and honor into the crusades.

56. Henry I was the fourth son of William the Conqueror. At the beginning of this cycle, Henry I scrambled to validate his daughter, Matilda, and her husband, Geoffrey of Anjou, as heirs. His only son had just died on the White Ship, that sank off the coast of Normandy. When Henry I died in 1130, England is propelled into civil war, as Matilda and Henry's nephew, Stephen of Blois fight to be ruler.

57. Often the dictator dies, like Genghis Khan, and while his son took over and continued campaigning into Europe, an unusually wet few years seems to have blocked their traversions in Austria. See: Sarah Kramer, "Scientists Finally Know What Stopped Mongol Hordes From Conquering Europe."

58. Armstrong, 15.

59. How is that Reform? Well, it's not, except if you look at it from the point of view of a conquistador. The Spanish thought they were conquering a barbarian tribe—a land of savages. They thought they were bringing modern advances: leeches and bloodletting for healing, armor and guns for fighting, crosses and holy wafers for spirituality. They thought themselves to be superior and advancing civilization. They reformed the landscape of what is today Peru with the advantage of biology (they were inoculated against certain viruses that devastated the Incan population) and steel.

60. Kuhn, 18.

61. Mohawk, 147.

62. American Bar Assocation.

63. Roland Jackson, "Eunice Foote, John Tyndall and a question of priority."

64. E.H. Cookridge, *Orient Express*.

65. Clive Pointing, *A New Green History of the World*.

66. https://www.bahai.org/bahaullah

67. "Epidemiology of HIV/AIDS–United States, 1981–2005," *MMWR* 55.21 (2 June 2006): 589–92. https://www.cdc.gov/mmwr/preview/mmwrhtml/mm5521a2.htm

Bibliography

"A Quote by Richard P. Feynman." n.d. www.goodreads.com. Accessed Dec. 21, 2023. https://www.goodreads.com/quotes/342999-from-a-long-view-of-the-history-of-mankind-seen.

Abetti, Giorgio. 1952. *The History of Astronomy*. Translated from the Italian *Storia Dell'Astronomia* by Betty Burr Abetti Henry Schuman.

Agar, Jon. 2019. "What Is Technology?" *Annals of Science* 77 (3): 377–82.

Al-Hassani, Salim T. S. 2012. *1001 Inventions: The Enduring Legacy of Muslim Civilization*. National Geographic.

Allison, Wick, Jeremy Adams, and Gavin Hambly. 1998. *Condemned to Repeat It*. Viking Press.

Amis, Martin. 2002. *Koba the Dread*. Miramax.

Anchell, Steve. 2014. "The Historical basis for the Children's Crusades, 1212 CE." *www.academia.edu*, March. https://www.academia.edu/6358217/The_Childrens_Crusade

Anderson, John E. 1943. "Outcomes of the Intersociety Constitutional Convention." *Psychological Bulletin* 40 (8): 585–88.

Armstrong, Karen. 1994. *A History of God: The 4000-Year Quest of Judaism, Christianity and Islam*. Ballantine Books.

———. 2000. *The Battle for God: A History of Fundamentalism*. Random House.

———. 2009. *The Great Transformation: The Beginning of Our Religious Traditions*. Vintage.

———. 2014. *Fields of Blood*. Anchor.

Assmann, J. 1997. *Moses the Egyptian: The Memory of Egypt in Western Monotheism*. Harvard UP.

Awan, Muzaffar K. 2014. "The Paradox of Hidden Human History." *Defence Journal* 17(8): 30–33.

Baladouni, Vahé. 1986. "Financial Reporting in the Early Years of the East India Company." *The Accounting Historians Journal* 13(1): 19–30.

Barlow, Peter, et al. 1856. "Astronomy of the Arabs." *The Encyclopaedia of Astronomy*. R. Griffin.

Beard, Mary. 2015. *SPQR: A History of Ancient Rome*. Liverlight.

Berlin, Isaiah. 2013. *Crooked Timber of Humanity: Chapters in the History of Ideas*. Princeton UP.

Bernal, M. 1987. *Black Athena: The Afroasiatic Roots of Classical Civilization Volume I: The Fabrication of Ancient Greece 1785–1985*. Rutgers UP.

Bierlein, J F. 2007. *Parallel Myths*. Ballantine Books.

Blakemore, Erin. 2019. "The Chernobyl Disaster: What Happened, and the Long-Term Impact." *National Geographic*. May 20, 2019. https://www.nationalgeographic.co.uk/environment/2019/05/chernobyl-disaster-what-happened-and-long-term-impact.

Bloom, Harold. 2002. *Genius: A Mosaic of 100 Exemplary Creative Minds*. Warner Books.

Bobbitt, Philip. 2003. *The Shield of Achilles: War, Peace, and the Course of History*. Knopf.

Bobrick, Benson. 2007. *The Fated Sky: Astrology in History*. Simon & Schuster.

Bolen, Jean S. 1994. *Crossing to Avalon: A Woman's Midlife Pilgrimage*. HarperSanFrancisco.

Bolton, Lesley. 2002. *The Everything Classical Mythology Book: Greek and Roman Gods, Goddesses, Heroes, and Monsters from Ares to Zeus*. Adams Media.

Boorstin, Daniel J. 1993. *The Creators: A History of Heroes of the Imagination*. Vintage.

Booth, Mark. 2010. *The Secret History of the World*. Abrams.

Bracey, Matthew Steven. 2012. "Divine Grace and Human Responsibility in Bernard of Clairvaux" Jan. 2, 2012. http://www.helwyssocietyforum.com/divine-grace-human-responsibility-and-bernard-of-clairvaux/

Breeze, Andrew. 2005. "Battle of Camlan and Camelford, Cornwall." *Arthuriana* 15(3): 75–90.

Bronstein, Judith. 2017. "Zionism, Medieval Culture, and National Discourse." *Memoirs of the American Academy in Rome* 62: 119–34.

Brown, Darren. 2003. *The Greatest Exploration Stories Ever Told: True Tales of Search and Discovery*. Lyons Press.

Bulfinch, Thomas. 1979. *Bulfinch's Mythology, Illustrated: The Age of Fable: The Age of Chivalry: Legends Charlemagne*. Gramercy Books.

Burckhardt, Jacob. 2020. *The Civilization of the Renaissance in Italy*. Graphic Arts Books.

Butler, Alan, and Stephen Dafoe. 2007. *The Warriors and Bankers: A History of the Knights Templar from 1307 to the Present*. Templar Books.

Butterfield, Fox. 1983. *China*. Bantam.

Caldbick, John. 2021. "Leschi (1808–1858), Part 1." www.historylink.org. March 27, 2021. https://www.historylink.org/file/21193.

Campbell, Joseph. 1962. *Oriental Mythology. The Masks of God Vol. 2*. Penguin.

———. 1990. *Transformations of Myth through Time*. Perennial Library.

———. 2013. *Goddesses: Mysteries of the Feminine Divine*. New World Library.

Cantor, Norman F. 2015. *Antiquity: From the Birth of Sumerian Civilization to the Fall*. Harper-Collins.

Caramanica, Jon. 2005. "Hip-Hop's Raiders of the Lost Archives." *The New York Times*, June 26, 2005, sec. Arts. https://www.nytimes.com/2005/06/26/arts/music/hiphops-raiders-of-the-lost-archives.html.

Carp, Benjamin L. 2012. "Did Dutch Smugglers Provoke the Boston Tea Party?" *Early American Studies* 10(2): 335–59.

Casey, Caroline. 2013. *Making the Gods Work for You*. Harmony Books.

Chang, Jung. 2013. *Empress Dowager Cixi: The Concubine Who Launched Modern China*. Anchor.

Chang, Kwang-chih. 1995. "On the Meaning of Shang in the Shang Dynasty." *Early China* 20: 69–77.

Chernyshevsky, Nikolay Gavrilovich. 1986. *What Is to Be Done?* Ardis.

Chomsky, Noam. 2004. *Middle East Illusions: Including Peace in the Middle East?: Reflections on Justice and Nationhood*. Rowman & Littlefield.

Chronicle of America. 1995. Chronicle.

Cienfuegos, Paul. 2022. *How Dare We?: Courageous Practices to Reclaim Our Power as Citizens*. 100fires Press.

Clements, Jonathan. 2005. *Coxinga and the Fall of the Ming Dynasty*. Sutton.

Cline, Eric H. 2015. *1177 BC: The Year Civilization Collapsed*. Princeton UP.

Cookridge, E. H. 1978. *Orient Express: The Life and Times of the World's Most Famous Train*. Random House.

Cosmopoulos, Michael B. 2014. "Cult, Continuity, and Social Memory: Mycenaean Eleusis and the Transition to the Early Iron Age." *American Journal of Archaeology* 118(3): 401–27.

Crosby, Alfred W. 1986. *Ecological Imperialism: The Biological Expansion of Europe, 900–1900*. Cambridge UP.

Cummins, Joseph. 2006. *History's Great Untold Stories: Larger than Life Characters & Dramatic Events That Changed the World*. National Geographic.

Cummins, Joseph, James Inglis, and Barry Stone. 2012. *The Almost Complete History of the World: 75 Incredible Events from Ancient Times to Today*. Pier 9.

Cunningham, Donna. 2023. *Healing Pluto Problems*. Weiser Books.

Curtis, Glenn E. and Library Of Congress. Federal Research Division. 1998. *Russia: A Country Study*. Federal Research Division, Library Of Congress.

Cushman, Philip. 1995. *Constructing the Self, Constructing America*. Addison Wesley.

Dalrymple, William. 2020. *The Anarchy/the Relentless Rise of the East India Company*. Bloomsbury.

Davis, Angela Yvonne. 1983. *Women, Race & Class*. Vintage Books.

Davis, James C. 2009. *The Human Story: Our History, from the Stone Age to Today*. HarperCollins.

Davis, Kenneth C. 2009. *Don't Know Much about Anything*. HarperCollins.

Dawson, Christopher. 2012. *Medieval Essays (the Works of Christopher Dawson)*. CUA Press.

de Mello, Joseph Silveira. 2000. *Declinations*. AFA.

Deacy, Susan. 2013. "From 'Flowery Tales' to 'Heroic Rapes': Virginal Subjectivity in the Mythological Meadow." *Arethusa* 46(3): 395–413.

"Definition of Redeem." n.d. www.merriam-Webster.com. https://www.merriam-webster.com/dictionary/redeem.

Dewey, Horace W. 1956. "The 1497 Sudebnik-Muscovite Russia's First National Law Code," *American Slavic and East European Review* 15(3): 325–38.

Deyle, Steven. 2009. "An 'Abominable' New Trade: The Closing of the African Slave Trade and the Changing Patterns of US Political Power, 1808–60." *The William and Mary Quarterly* 66(4): 833–50.

Diamond, Jared. 1997. *Guns, Germs, and Steel: The Fates of Human Society*. W.W. Norton.

———. 2005. *Collapse: How Societies Choose to Fail or Succeed*. Penguin Books.

———. 2020. *Upheaval: Turning Points for Nations in Crisis*. Back Bay Books.

DK. 2018. *Timelines of History*. Penguin.

Drews, R. 1988. *The Coming of the Greeks: Indo-European Conquests in the Aegean and the Near East*. Princeton UP.

Dunant, Henry. 1959. *A Memory of Solferino*. American National Red Cross.

Durant, Will. 1953. *The Renaissance: A History of Civilization in Italy from 1304–1576 AD*. Simon & Schuster.

———. 1963. *The Age of Faith*. Simon & Schuster.

Durant, Will, and Ariel Durant. 2011a. *Our Oriental Heritage: The Story of Civilization*. Simon & Schuster.

———. 2011b. *The Age of Reason Begins*. Simon & Schuster.

Eastman, Roger. 1975. *The Ways of Religion*. Canfield Press.

Eck, Diana L. 2012. *India: A Sacred Geography*. Harmony Books.

Ehrenreich, Barbara. 2007. *Dancing in the Streets*. Metropolitan Books.

Eisenstein, Charles. 2011. *Sacred Economics: Money, Gift, & Society in the Age of Transition*. Evolver Editions.

———. 2013. *The Ascent of Humanity: Civilization and the Human Sense of Self*. Evolver Editions.

Elwell, Dennis. 2008. *Cosmic Loom: The New Science of Astrology*. Wessex Astrologer.

English, Richard. 1985. "Himalayan State Formation and the Impact of British Rule in the Nineteenth Century." *Mountain Research and Development* 5(1): 61–78.

Eno, Robert. 2010/2019. *Zhuangzi: The Inner Chapters*. https://terebess.hu/english/Zhuangzi-Eno.pdf

Eric, John. 1990. *Maya History and Religion*. University of Oklahoma Press.

Ernest, William. 1970. *A History of Africa [By] W. E. F. Ward*. Aurora.

Fernández-Armesto, Felipe. 2005. *The Americas: A Hemispheric History*. Modern Library.

———. 2010. *1492: The Year the World Began*. HarperOne.

Feuerstein, Georg, Subhash Kak, and David Frawley. 1995. *In Search of the Cradle of Civilization*. Quest Books.

Feuerstein, Georg, and Jeanine Miller. 1997. *The Essence of Yoga: Essays on the Development of Yogic Philosophy from the Vedas to Modern Times.* Inner Traditions.

Figueres, Christiana, and Tom Rivett-Carnac. 2020. *The Future We Choose: Surviving the Climate Crisis.* Alfred A. Knopf.

Fox, Matthew. 2003. *Illuminations of Hildegard of Bingen.* Bear.

Frank, Andre Gunder. 1990. "A Theoretical Introduction to 5,000 Years of World System History." *Review (Fernand Braudel Center)* 13(2): 155–248.

Frankopan, Peter. 2017. *The Silk Roads: A New History of the World.* Vintage Books.

Freeland, Chrystia. 2012. *Plutocrats.* Penguin.

Freeman, Charles. 2002. *The Closing of the Western Mind: The Rise of Faith and the Fall of Reason.* Vintage.

Friedman, Thomas. 1999. *The Lexus and the Olive Tree.* Anchor Books.

Fromkin, David. 2001. *A Peace to End All Peace: The Fall of the Ottoman Empire and the Creation of the Modern Middle East.* Henry Holt.

Fry, Stephen. 2019. *Mythos: The Greek Myths Reimagined.* Chronicle Books.

Frye, Richard Nelson. 1975. *The Golden Age of Persia.* George Weidenfeld & Nicholson.

Gadon, Elinor W. 1990. *The Once and Future Goddess.* Harper San Francisco.

Garraty, John A., and Peter Gay. 1972. *The Columbia History of the World.* Harper & Row.

Garza, Alicia. 2021. *Purpose of Power: How We Come Together When We Fall Apart.* One World Ballantine.

Gendler, Everett. 1976. "Fellowship." *Fellowship of Reconciliation.*

Genet, Cheryl. 2012. *Science, Wisdom, and the Future.* Collins Foundation Press.

"George Perkins Marsh's Man and Nature (1864)." n.d. The Public Domain Review. https://publicdomainreview.org/collection/man-and-nature-1864.

George, Alain. 2015. "Direct Sea Trade between Early Islamic Iraq and Tang China: From the Exchange of Goods to the Transmission of Ideas." *Journal of the Royal Asiatic Society* 25(4): 579–624.

George, Demetra. 1992. *Mysteries of the Dark Moon: The Healing Power of the Dark Goddess.* HarperSanFrancisco.

———. 1995. *Finding Our Way through the Dark: The Astrology of the Dark Goddess Mysteries.* ACS.

Ghoshal, U. N. 1959. "On a Recent Estimate of the Social and Political System of the Maurya Empire." *Annals of the Bhandarkar Oriental Research Institute* 40(1/4): 63–69.

Given, James. 1989. "The Inquisitors of Languedoc and the Medieval Technology of Power." *American Historical Review* 94(2): 336–59.

Gladwell, Malcolm. 2000. *The Tipping Point: How Little Things Can Make a Big Difference.* Back Bay Books/Little, Brown.

———. 2008. *Outliers: The Story of Success.* Back Bay Books.

Glowacki, Kevin T. 2016. "New Insights into Bronze Age Eleusis and the Formative Stages of the Eleusinian Cults." *American Journal of Archaeology* 120(4): 673–77.

Goddard, Jolyon. 2010. *Concise History of Science & Invention: An Illustrated Time Line.* National Geographic.

Gold, Hadas. 2023. "Israeli Military Veterans, a Backbone of Protest Movement, Vow to Keep Demonstrating." CNN. April 3, 2023. https://www.cnn.com/2023/04/03/middleeast/israel-protests-military-veterans-intl-cmd.

"Graffiti: Vandalism or a Legitimate Art Form? | Castle Fine Art." n.d. www.castlefineart.com. Accessed December 21, 2023. https://www.castlefineart.com/blog/graffiti-vandalism-or-a-legitimate-art-form.

Grant, Michael. Trans 1969. *Cicero, Selected Political Speeches*. Penguin Classics.

———. 1985. *Atlas of Ancient History: 1700 BC to 565 AD*. Dorset Press.

Graves, R. 1961. *The White Goddess*. 1948. Farrar.

Green, Caitlin. 2019. "King Alfred and India: An Anglo-Saxon Embassy to Southern India in the Ninth Century AD." April 30, 2019. https://www.caitlingreen.org/2019/04/king-alfred-and-india.html?m=1.

Greenblatt, Stephen. 2012. *The Swerve: How the Renaissance Began*. Vintage Books.

Greer, John Michael. 2014. *Decline and Fall: The End of Empire and the Future of Democracy in 21st Century America*. New Society.

Grun, Bernard. 1975 (2005). *The Timetables of History: A Horizontal Linkage of People & Event*. A Touchstone Book.

Guttman, Ariel, and Kenneth Johnson. 1998. *Mythic Astrology: Archetypal Powers in the Horoscope*. Llewellyn.

Haas, Christopher. 1993. "The Arians of Alexandria." *Vigiliae Christianae* 47(3): 234–45.

Hall, Judy. 1998. *The Hades Moon: Pluto in Aspect to the Moon*. Weiser.

Hall, Manly P. 1958. *The Secret Destiny of America*. Philosophical Research Society.

———. 2005. *Lectures on Ancient Philosophy: Companion to the Secret Teachings of All Ages*. Tarcher/Penguin.

Hallgarten, George W. F. 1952. "Adolf Hitler and German Heavy Industry, 1931–1933." *The Journal of Economic History* 12(3): 222–46.

Hart-Davis, Adam. 2013. *History: The Definitive Visual Guide*. Dorling Kindersley.

Hawken, Paul. 2007. *Blessed Unrest: How the Largest Movement in the World Came into Being, and Why No One Saw It Coming*. Viking.

Hawkes, Jacquetta. 1963. *The World of the Past*. Simon & Schuster.

Hayes, Richard P. 1994. "Nāgārjuna's Appeal." *Journal of Indian Philosophy* 22(4): 299–378.

Heaton, E. W. 1975. *Solomon's New Men: The Emergence of Ancient Israel as a National State*. Pica Press.

Hedges, Chris. 2010. *Death of the Liberal Class*. Bold Type Books.

———. 2018. *America: The Farewell Tour*. Simon & Schuster.

Hedges, Chris, and Joe Sacco. 2012. *Days of Destruction, Days of Revolt*. Nation Books.

Helle Stangerup. 1987. *In the Courts of Power*. Macmillan London.

Henderson, James, and A. Ferguson. 2014. "The Turbulent History of Foreign Involvement in the Russian Oil and Gas Industry." *International Partnership in Russia*, 1–60.

Heng, Geraldine. 2015. "Reinventing Race, Colonization, and Globalisms across Deep Time: Lessons from the 'Longue Durée.'" *PMLA* 130(2): 358–66.

Henri Dunant. 2013. *A Memory of Solferino*. Ravenio Books.

Herbert George Wells. 1943. *Pocket History of the World*. Pocket Books.

Herman, Arthur. 2007. *How the Scots Invented the Modern World*. Crown.

———. 2013. *The Cave and the Light: Plato vs. Aristotle, and the Struggle for the Soul of Western Civilization*. Random House.

Herre, Bastian, et al. 2016. "War and Peace," https://ourworldindata.org/war-and-peace

Higgins, Andrew. 2019. "'I Am Always Asked If I Am Afraid': Activist Lawyer Takes on Putin's Russia." *The New York Times*, September 6, 2019, sec. World. https://www.nytimes.com/2019/09/06/world/europe/russia-lyubov-sobol-protests.html.

"History of the Royal Society | Royal Society." n.d. Royalsociety.org. Accessed December 21, 2023. https://royalsociety.org/about-us/history.

Hobson, John M. 2013. *The Eastern Origins of Western Civilization*. Cambridge UP.

Holy See Press Office, "Joint Statement of the Dicasteries for Culture and Education and for

Promoting Integral Human Development on the 'Doctrine of Discovery,'" Press.vatican. va. 30 March 2023. https://press.vatican.va/content/salastampa/en/bollettino/pubblico/2023/03/30/230330b.html.

Hourani, Albert Habib. 2013. *A History of the Arab Peoples*. Faber.

Hunt, Edwin S., and James Murray. 1999. *A History of Business in Medieval Europe, 1200–1550*. Cambridge UP.

IBM. 2012. "IBM100: IBM Is Founded." Ibm.com. IBM Corporation. March 7, 2012. https://www.ibm.com/ibm/history/ibm100/us/en/icons/founded/.

Immerwahr, Daniel. 2020. *How to Hide an Empire: A History of the Greater United States*. Picador.

Invisible Committee. 2009. *Coming Insurrection*. MIT Press.

Jackson, F. J. Foakes. 1927. "Evidence for the Martyrdom of Peter and Paul in Rome." *Journal of Biblical Literature* 46(1/2): 74–78.

Jackson Roland. 2019. "Eunice Foote, John Tyndall and a question of priority" *Notes Rec.*74105—118. http://doi.org/10.1098/rsnr.2018.0066

Jansari, Sushma. 2023. "Chandragupta and Seleucus: A Clash by the Banks of the Indus," 15–39 in *Chandragupta Maurya: The Creation of a National Hero in India*. UCL Press.

Johnson, Alexander. 2019. "The Gabriel Aubaret Archive of Ottoman Economic and Transportation History." Daša Pahor. January 29, 2019. https://www.pahor.de.

Johnson, Ayana Elizabeth, and Katharine K. Wilkinson. 2021. *All We Can Save: Truth, Courage, & Solutions for the Climate Crisis*. One World.

Johnston, S. I. 2013. "Demeter, Myths, and the Polyvalence of Festivals." *History of Religions* 52(4), 370–401.

Jones, Kimberly. 2022. *How We Can Win*. Henry Holt.

Kaelber, Lutz. 1997. "Weavers into Heretics? The Social Organization of Early-Thirteenth-Century Catharism in Comparative Perspective." *Social Science History* 21(1): 111–37.

Kaminsky, Howard. 1963. "Wyclifism as Ideology of Revolution." *Church History* 32(1): 57–74.

Keightley, Thomas. 2007. *The Knights Templar and Other Secret Societies of the Middle Ages*. Dover.

Keller, Mara Lynn. 1988. "The Eleusinian Mysteries of Demeter and Persephone: Fertility, Sexuality, and Rebirth." *Journal of Feminist Studies in Religion* 4 (1): 27–54.

Kennedy, Paul M. 1989. *The Rise and Fall of the Great Powers: Economic Change and Military Conflict from 1500 to 2000*. Vintage Books.

Kerr, Gordon. 2017. *A Short History of India: From the Earliest Civilisations and Myriad Kingdoms, to Today's Economic Powerhouse*. Pocket Essentials.

Kessler, Herbert L. 1987. "The Meeting of Peter and Paul in Rome: An Emblematic Narrative of Spiritual Brotherhood." *Dumbarton Oaks Papers* 41: 265–75.

Keys, David. 2000. *Catastrophe: An Investigation into the Origins of the Modern World*. Ballantine.

Khalidi, Rashid. 2020. *Hundred Years' War on Palestine: A History of Settler Colonialism and Resistance, 1917–2017*. Picador.

Khalili, A., Dehghan, et al. 2012. "Formation Factor for Heterogeneous Carbonate Rocks Using Multiscale Xray-CT images" Society of Petroleum Engineers. Kuwait International Petroleum Conference and Exhibition. *People and Innovative Technologies to Unleash Challenging Hydrocarbon Resources*. Vol. 2: 1054–66.

Kinzer, Stephen. 2007. *Overthrow: America's Century of Regime Change from Hawaii to Iraq*. Times Books/Henry Holt.

Kizer, Carolyn. N.d. "Persephone's Pauses" Oct 11 2024: https://www.cornellcollege.edu/classical_studies/myth/demeter/pause.html

Korovkin, P.I. and S.S. Cherenev. 2015. "History of Oil Industry in Russia," National Research Tomsk Polytechnic University, Tomsk, Russia: 808–9.

Kötke, William H. 2007. *The Final Empire*. AuthorHouse.

Krahenbuhl, Kevin. 2013. "The Albigensian Crusade: A Twist in the Story of the Crusades." *Medieval Warfare* 3(4): 6–11.

Kramer, Mark. 2020. "The Soviet Role in World War II: Realities and Myths." Davis Center. May 18, 2020. https://daviscenter.fas.harvard.edu/insights/soviet-role-world-war-ii-realities-and-myths.

Kramer, Sarah. 2016. "Scientists Finally Know What Stopped Mongol Hordes From Conquering Europe" May 28, 2016. https://www.sciencealert.com/scientists-finally-know-what-stopped-mongol-hordes-from-conquering-europe

Kuhn, Thomas S. 2012. *The Structure of Scientific Revolution*. University of Chicago Press.

Kurlansky, Mark. 2016. *Paper: Paging through History*. W. W. Norton.

Lai, Whalen. 2010. "Political Authority: The Two Wheels of the Dharma." *Buddhist-Christian Studies* 30: 171–86.

Langan, John. 1984. "The Elements of St. Augustine's Just War Theory." *The Journal of Religious Ethics* 12(1): 19–38.

Langley, Patricia. 2000. "Why A Pomegranate?" *British Medical Journal* 321(7269): 1153–54.

Lennon-McCartney. "All You Need Is Love." Capitol Records, LLC, 1967.

Levathes, Louise. 1996. *When China Ruled the Seas: The Treasure Fleet of the Dragon Throne, 1405–1433*. Oxford UP.

Lofland, John. 1993. *Polite Protesters*. Syracuse UP.

Ludden, David. 2002. *India and South Asia*. ONEWorld Publications.

Macmillan, Margaret. 2010. *Dangerous Games: The Uses and Abuses of History*. Modern Library.

Mahler, Edward. 1901. "The Exodus," *Journal of the Royal Asiatic Society of Great Britain and Ireland*: 33–67.

Mann, Charles C. 2005. *1491: New Revelations of the Americas before Columbus*. Knopf.

Mansfield, Peter. 1976. *The Arab World*. Crowell.

Marciniak, Barbara. 2010. *Path of Empowerment*. New World Library.

Marcus, Amy Dockser. 2000. *The View from Nebo*. Little Brown.

Masha Gessen. 2020. *Surviving Autocracy*. Riverhead Books.

McArthur, Neil. 2014. "Hume's Political Philosophy." Paul Russell. Ed. *The Oxford Handbook of Hume*. Oxford UP. Online edn: https://doi.org/10.1093/oxfordhb/9780199742844.013.15.

McKay, John P., Bennett D. Hill, and John Buckler. 1996. *A History of World Societies: From Antiquity through the Middle Ages*. Houghton Mifflin.

Menzies, Gavin. 2008. *1434 Intl*. HarperCollins.

Mews, Constant J. 2004. "Bernard of Clairvaux, Peter Abelard and Heloise on the Definition of Love." *Revista Portuguesa de Filosofia* 60(3): 633–60.

Meyer-Knapp, Helena. 2003. *Dangerous Peace-Making*. Peace-Maker Press.

Michael Hamilton Morgan. 2008. *Lost History: The Enduring Legacy of Muslim Scientists, Thinkers, and Artists*. National Geographic.

Miles, Margaret M. 2012. "Entering Demeter's Gateway: The Roman Propylon in the City Eleusinion." 114–51, in *Architecture of the Sacred: Space, Ritual, and Experience from Classical Greece to Byzantium*. Cambridge UP.

Mill, John Stuart. 1961. *The Philosophy of John Stuart Mill. Ethical, Political and Religious*. Edited and with an Introduction by Marshall Cohen. Modern Library.

Milner, Ian. 1941. "National Socialism: A 'Non-Economic' Revolution?" *The Australian Quarterly* 13(3): 49–59.

Mintz, Sidney W. 1986. *Sweetness and Power: The Place of Sugar in Modern History.* Penguin.

Mohawk, John. 2000. *Utopian Legacies.* Clear Light.

Mor, Menachem. 1986. "Two Legions: The Same Fate? (The Disappearance of the Legions IX Hispana and XXII Deiotariana)." *Zeitschrift Für Papyrologie Und Epigraphik* 62: 267–78.

Morison, Samuel Eliot. 1978. *The Great Explorers: The European Discovery of America.* Oxford UP.

Muldoon, James. 1978. "Papal Responsibility for the Infidel: Another Look at Alexander VI's 'Inter Caetera.'" *The Catholic Historical Review* 64(2); 168–84.

Muraresku, Brian. 2020. *The Immortality Key: The Secret History of the Religion with No Name.* St. Martin's Press.

Murray, Charles A. 2003. *Human Accomplishment: The Pursuit of Excellence in the Arts and Sciences, 800 BC to 1950.* HarperCollins.

Narsalay, Madhavi. "A poetic genius." the week.in Dec. 27, 2015.

NASA JPL: "Consensus: 97% of climate scientists agree." Global Climate Change. A website at NASA's Jet Propulsion Laboratory (climate.nasa.gov/scientific-consensus). (Accessed July 2024.)

"Navalny Urges Russians to Protest Daily against Ukraine Invasion." 2022. www.aljazeera. com. March 2, 2022. https://www.aljazeera.com/news/2022/3/2/alexei-navalny-urges-russians-to-protest-daily-against-ukraine.

Neiman, David. 2017. "The History of Egypt - The Hyksos Invasion." *World History Encyclopedia.* Last modified April 11, 2017. https://www.worldhistory.org/video/1142/the-history-of-egypt---the-hyksos-invasion/

Netanyahu, Benzion. 2001. *The Origins of the Inquisition in Fifteenth Century Spain.* New York Review Books.

Newman, Paul F. 2006. *Declination in Astrology.* Wessex Astrologer.

North, J. A. 1979. "Religious Toleration in Republican Rome." *Proceedings of the Cambridge Philological Society* New Series 25(205): 85–103.

Nothiger, Andreas. 1991. *World History Chart.* Viking Penguin.

O'Boyle, Lenore. 1966. "The Middle Class in Western Europe, 1815–1848." *American Historical Review* 71(3): 826–45.

O'Connor, J. J., and E. F. Robertson. 1999. "Adelard of Bath." School of Mathematics and Statistics, University of St Andrews, Scotland, Nov. 1999. https://mathshistory.st-andrews.ac.uk/Biographies/Adelard/

O'Toole, Dan. 2013. *1000 Events That Shaped the World.* National Geographic.

"Our Story | Mallinckrodt Pharmaceuticals." 2013. Mallinckrodt. 2013. https://www.mallinckrodt.com/about/our-story/.

Ovason, David. 2002. *The Secret Architecture of Our Nation's Capital: The Masons and the Building of Washington, DC.* Perennial.

Parry. Glenn Aparicio. 2015. *Original Thinking: A Radical Revisioning of Time, Humanity, and Nature.* North Atlantic.

Pettigrew, Richard Franklin. 2019. *Triumphant Plutocracy.* The Academy Press.

Petersen, John L. 2008. *A Vision for 2012.* Fulcrum Group.

Phillips, Leigh, and Michal Rozworski. 2019. *The People's Republic of Walmart: How the World's Biggest Corporations Are Laying the Foundation for Socialism.* Verso.

Platt, Steve R. 2019. *Imperial Twilight: The Opium War and the End of China's Last Golden Age.* Vintage Books.

Ponting, Clive. 2007. *A New Green History of the World.* Penguin Group.

Prince, J. Dyneley 1904. "Review of The Code of Hammurabi, et al.," *The American Journal of Theology* 8(3): 601–9.

Ramakrishna. 1958. *The Gospel of Sri Ramakrishna*. Ramakrishna-Vedanta Center.

Ravitch, Diane, and Abigail M. Thernstrom. 1992. *The Democracy Reader*. HarperResource.

Reid, T. R. 2005. *The United States of Europe: The New Superpower and the End of American Supremacy*. Penguin Books.

Reston, James. 2007. *Warriors of God*. Anchor.

Richardson, Heather Cox. 2020. *How the South Won the Civil War: Oligarchy, Democracy, and the Continuing Fight for the Soul of America*. Oxford UP.

Ricón, José Luis. 2016. "The Soviet Union: GDP Growth." Nintil. March 26, 2016. https://nintil.com/the-soviet-union-gdp-growth.

Risi, Armin. 2004. *TranscEnding the Global Power Game*. Light Technology.

River, Lindsay, and Sally Gillespie. 1987. *The Knot of Time*. Womens Press.

Robert Lloyd Kelley. 1978. *The Shaping of the American Past*. Prentice Hall.

Robertson, Arlene, and Margaret Wilson. 1979. *The Complete Book on the Power of Pluto*. Seek It.

Rolleston, T. W. 2012. *Celtic Myths and Legends*. Courier.

Roser, Max, Joe Hasell, Bastian Herre, and Bobbie Macdonald. 2016. "War and Peace." Our World in Data. 2016. https://ourworldindata.org/war-and-peace.

Roy, Arundhati. 2006. *An Ordinary Person's Guide to Empire*. Penguin.

Roy, Tirthankar. 2016. *The East India Company*. Penguin UK.

Rubenstein, Richard E. 2003. *Aristotle's Children*. Houghton Mifflin.

Ruppert, Michael C. 2009. *Confronting Collapse*. Chelsea Green.

St. Armand, Barton Levi. 1972. "Usher Unveiled: Poe and the Metaphysic of Gnosticism." *Poe Studies (1971–1985)* 5(1): 1–8.

Saad, Lydia. "What Percentage of Americans Own Guns?" *Gallup.com*, Gallup, 13 Nov. 2020, news.gallup.com/poll/264932/percentage-americans-own-guns.aspx.

Santon, Kate, and Liz McKay. 2006. *Atlas of World History*. Parragon.

Sassoon, Donald. 2019. *The Anxious Triumph*. Penguin UK.

Scahill, Jeremy. 2008. *Blackwater: The Rise of the World's Most Powerful Mercenary Army*. Basic Books.

Schultze, Carol, and Charles Stanish. 2023. "Copper Metallurgy in the Andes," in E. Ben-Yosef, et al. (eds.), *"And in Length of Days Understanding" (Job 12:12)*. Springer.

Schlesinger, Arthur Meier. 1917. "The Uprising Against the East India Company." *Political Science Quarterly* 32(1): 60–79.

Schwoerer, Lois G. 1990. "Locke, Lockean Ideas, and the Glorious Revolution." *Journal of the History of Ideas* 51(4): 531–48.

Scott, Karen. 1992. "St. Catherine of Siena, 'Apostola.'" *Church History* 61(1): 34–46.

Seaman, Gerald R. 2003. "Catherine the Great and Musical Enlightenment." *New Zealand Slavonic Journal* 37: 129–36.

Segev, Tom. 2001. *One Palestine, Complete: Jews and Arabs under the British Mandate*. Henry Holt.

Sexton, Jared Yates. 2021. *American Rule: How a Nation Conquered the World but Failed Its People*. Dutton.

Shapiro, Svi. 1999. "Introduction: A Life on the Fringes/My Road to Critical Pedagogy." *Counterpoints* (46): 1–29.

Shcharansky, Anatoly, and Ron Dermer. 2004. *The Case for Democracy*. Public Affairs.

Shorto, Russell. 2009. *Descartes' Bones: A Skeletal History of the Conflict between Faith and Reason*. Vintage Books.

Silva, Freddy. 2017. *First Templar Nation*. Simon & Schuster.

Simmons, Ann M. 2019. "In a Big Shift, Russians Take to the Streets over Everyday Complaints." *The Wall Street Journal*, September.

Solomon, Robert C., and Mark C Murphy. 2000. *What Is Justice?: Classic and Contemporary Readings*. Oxford UP.

Soy, Anne. "Coronavirus in Africa: Five Reasons Why COVID-19 Has Been Less Deadly than Elsewhere." *BBC News*, 7 Oct. 2020, www.bbc.com/news/world-africa-54418613.

Spade, Dean. 2020. *Mutual Aid: Building Solidarity during This Crisis (and the Next)*. Verso.

Starhawk. 2002. *Webs of Power*. New Society.

Stearns, Peter N., and William L. Langer. 2001. *The Encyclopedia of World History: Ancient, Medieval, and Modern, Chronologically Arranged*. Houghton Mifflin.

Stone, Merlin. 1978. *When God Was a Woman*. Houghton Mifflin Harcourt.

———. 1993. *When God Was a Woman*. Barnes & Noble.

Strauss, William, and Neil Howe. 1997. *The Fourth Turning: An American Prophecy*. Broadway Books.

Subhash Kak, and David Frawley. 2001. *In Search of the Cradle of Civilization*. Quest Books.

"Survey of Palestine." 1946. https://www.bjpa.org/content/upload/bjpa/a_su/A%20SURVEY%20OF%20PALESTINE%20DEC%201945-JAN%201946%20VOL%20I.pdf.

Susan Wise Bauer. 2007. *The History of the Ancient World: From the Earliest Accounts to the Fall of Rome*. W.W. Norton.

Sutton, Anthony C. 1976. *Wall Street and the Rise of Hitler*. Clairview Books.

Tarnas, Richard. 2006. *Cosmos and Psyche: Intimations of a New World View*. Viking.

———. 2011. *The Passion of the Western Mind: Understanding the Ideas That Have Shaped Our World View*. Ballantine Books.

Taylor, Joan E. 2009. "On Pliny, the Essene Location and Kh. Qumran." *Dead Sea Discoveries* 16(1): 1–21.

Teeple, John B. 2006. *Timelines of World History*. Dk Pub.

Thacker, Alan. 2020. "The Cult of Peter and the Development of Martyr Cult in Rome. The Origins of the Presentation of Peter and Paul as Martyrs," 250–76. In Roald Dijkstra, ed., *The Early Reception and Appropriation of the Apostle Peter (60-800 CE): The Anchors of the Fisherman*. Brill.

Thapar, Romila. 1996. "The Theory of Aryan Race and India: History and Politics." *Social Scientist* 24(⅓): 3–29.

The Kingfisher History Encyclopedia. 2004. Kingfisher.

Theobald, Ulrich. 2011. "Wu Ding 武丁" http://www.chinaknowledge.de/ Dec. 29, 2011. http://www.chinaknowledge.de/History/Myth/personswuding.html

Thompson, Glen. 2017. *Deconstructing the Enigma of American Plutocracy: A Primer*. Panem Et Circenses.

Thucydides, and Paul Woodruff. 1993. *On Justice, Power, and Human Nature*. Hackett.

Tillich, Paul. 1976. *Love, Power, and Justice: Ontological Analyses and Ethical Applications*. Oxford UP.

Tinniswood, Adrian. 2019. *The Royal Society*. Hachette UK.

"Top 5 Quotes by J. Christopher Stevens." n.d. A-Z Quotes. Accessed December 21, 2023. https://www.azquotes.com/author/36158-J_Christopher_Stevens.

Trexler, Richard C. 1983. "Neighbours and Comrades: The Revolutionaries of Florence, 1378." *Social Analysis: The International Journal of Social and Cultural Practice* 14: 53–106.

Tuchman, Barbara W. 1978. *A Distant Mirror: The Calamitous 14th Century*. Vol. 1. Knopf

———. 2011. *The March of Folly*. Random House.

Tyl, Noel, and Ashley Wendy. 1995. *Communicating the Horoscope*. Llewellyn.

UN General Assembly Security Council. 1987. https://main.un.org/securitycouncil/en/content/resolutions-adopted-security-council-1987

Van Doren, Charles. 1993. *A History of Knowledge: Past, Present, and Future.* Ballantine Books.

Vandana Shiva, and Kartikey Shiva. 2020. *Oneness vs. the 1%: Shattering Illusions, Seeding Freedom.* Chelsea Green.

Walker, Barbara G. 2013. *The Woman's Dictionary of Symbols and Sacred Objects.* Harper Collins.

Watson, Peter. 2006. *Ideas.* HarperCollins.

———. 2009. *Ideas.* HarperCollins.

———. 2013. *Ideas.* Weidenfeld & Nicolson.

Weatherford, Jack. (2004) 2012. *Genghis Khan and the Making of the Modern World.* Three Rivers Press.

———. 2015. *The Secret History of the Mongol Queens: How the Daughters of Genghis Khan Rescued His Empire.* Broadway Paperbacks.

Weikart, Richard. 2004. *From Darwin to Hitler: Evolutionary Ethics, Eugenics, and Racism in Germany.* Palgrave Macmillan.

William Weir. 2001. *50 Battles that Changed the World: The Conflicts that Most Influenced the Course of History.* The Career Press.

Weis, Rene. 2000. *The Yellow Cross.* Penguin Books.

Welton, Neva, and Linda Wolf. 2001. *Global Uprising.* New Society.

Wescoat, B. D., and Ousterhout, R. G. Eds. 2014. *Architecture of the Sacred: Space, Ritual, and Experience from Classical Greece to Byzantium.* Cambridge UP.

Westerhoff, J. 2006. "Nāgārjuna's 'Catuṣkoṭi.'" *Journal of Indian Philosophy* 34(4): 367–95.

Westin, Leigh. 1999. *Beyond the Solstice by Declination.* Gheminee.

Wilber, Ken. 2007. *A Brief History of Everything.* Shambhala.

Williams, Chancellor, and Murry N. Depillars. 2012. *The Destruction of Black Civilization: Great Issues of a Race from 4500 BC to 2000 AD.* Bn.

Winik, Jay. 2002. *April 1865.* HarperCollins.

Wright, Edmund. 2006. *The Desk Encyclopedia of World History.* Oxford UP.

Wright, Robert. 2001. *Nonzero.* Vintage.

Zakaria, Fareed. 2020. *Ten Lessons for a Post-Pandemic World.* W. W. Norton.

Zinn, Howard. 2015. *A People's History of the United States: 1492–Present.* Routledge.

Zupan, Mark A. 2017. *Inside Job: How Government Insiders Subvert the Public Interest.* Cambridge UP.

Index